THEORIES OF SOCIAL PSYCHOLOGY

MARVIN E. SHAW
University of Florida

PHILIP R. COSTANZO
Duke University

THEORIES OF

SOCIAL

PSYCHOLOGY

McGraw-Hill Book Company

New York   St. Louis   San Francisco   London   Sydney   Toronto   Mexico   Panama

THEORIES OF SOCIAL PSYCHOLOGY

Library of Congress Catalog Card Number 71–88890
ISBN 07-056495-7

11 12 13 14   K P K P   7 9 8 7

PREFACE

The field of experimental social psychology has developed explosively during the past twenty-five years. Following the pioneering work of Kurt Lewin and his associates, almost every aspect of social behavior has been brought into the laboratory and subjected to experimental study. This research provided a mass of data concerning social relations that demanded integration into more-comprehensive theories of social behavior. Social psychologists have not been remiss in attempting to respond to this demand; numerous theories have been proposed to explain observed phenomena, varying from specific hypotheses to more general theoretical formulations. Unfortunately, presentations of the various theories are widely dispersed in journals, monographs, and books. The purpose of the present undertaking is to present in condensed form the more promising theories in social psychology. We hope that the availability of the theories in a single volume will encourage the student to become more familiar with them, stimulate the researcher to test the implications of the theories more extensively, and inspire the theorists to modify and extend their theories in response to new evidence and ideas.

In reviewing social psychological theories it became evident that some systems are best conceptualized as orientations and others as theories. For example, reinforcement "theory," cognitive "theory," field "theory," and the like are really general approaches to the analysis and conceptualization of behavior, whereas consistency theories, theories of leadership, and the like are formulations regarding specific social phenomena. These latter theories often represent specific applications of the more general orientations and their derivative theories. The plan of the book takes cognizance of this distinction. Following an introduction to the field of social psychology and the nature of theories, sections dealing with the reinforcement orientation, the field-theoretical orientation, the cognitive orientation, and the psychoanalytic orientation are included. Each section begins with a chapter describing the basic concepts of the general orientation, followed by one or more chapters presenting more-limited theories adopting the general approach. Specific theories vary greatly in the rigidity with which the theorist has adhered to the general orientation. Therefore, the classification of a given theory as representing a given orientation means only that it adheres more closely to that orientation than to any other. Finally, a section dealing with theories that do not appear to be based upon any one of the major orientations is included, followed by a section comparing the various theories on several characteristics.

We are indebted to many people who have contributed to this book in one form or another—so many that it would be impossible to name them all. First of all, we are indebted to the many theorists whose "brainchildren" are summarized in this text. Needless to say, without them there would have been little to write about. We are aware that our abbreviated presentations can scarcely do justice to their theories, and we apologize for this inadequacy, as well as for any errors that we may have inadvertently made in our presentation. We are grateful to Franz Epting, Stephen Margulis, Edward E. Jones, Darwyn E. Linder, and William C. Schutz, each of whom read one or more chapters and made significant criticisms and suggestions. We are especially grateful to O. J. Harvey for his insightful review of the entire manuscript. Although we profited greatly from the comments of each of these readers, they are in no way responsible for any shortcomings of this book. We are also indebted to the following publishers and organizations for permission to quote from their copyrighted works: Academic Press; Addison-Wesley Publishing Company; American Psychological Association; Appleton-Century-Crofts; American Sociological Association; Basic Books, Inc.; Chandler Publishing Co.; Columbia University Press; Harcourt, Brace, & World, Inc.; Harper & Row, Publishers; Holt, Rinehart & Winston, Inc.; J. B. Lippincott Co.; McGraw-Hill Book Co.; The Macmillan Co.; Oxford University Press; Pergamon Press; Plenum Publishing Co.; University of Chicago Press; John Wiley & Son, Inc.; and Yale University Press.

MARVIN E. SHAW

PHILIP R. COSTANZO

CONTENTS

THEORIES OF SOCIAL PSYCHOLOGY

INTRODUCTION
PART 1

Throughout recorded history man has been deeply interested in social behavior. Even the most casual observer notes that individuals behave differently when in the presence of others than when alone and that behavior varies depending upon which others are present. The patterns of responses to others becomes highly complicated with the formation of social units, such as families, clans, institutions, and nations. Although interest in social behavior is rooted in antiquity, the delineation of social psychology as a specific area of study is a comparatively recent development. For example, the first textbooks in social psychology appeared less than a century ago (McDougall, 1908; Ross, 1908).

Modern social psychology has been largely empirical in nature, basing its propositions and conclusions upon observations in controlled situations. Areas of concern include attitudes, conformity, leadership, social perception, social motivation, power relations, social exchange, small-group interaction, and similar problems. As a result of the empirical approach, a considerable amount of data about social behavior has accumulated. To be useful, such data must be organized in a systematic way so that the meaning and implications of these data can be understood. Such systematic organization is the function of theory. This book is an attempt to present theories of social processes that have been proposed by modern social psychologists.

It is necessary at this point to define two critical terms in the title of this book which are used extensively in the following pages: *social psychology* and *theory*. Each term has been defined in a variety of ways, but we have adopted minimal definitions. *Social psychology is the scientific study of individual behavior as a function of social stimuli.* By "scientific" we mean to imply only that observations are made under controlled conditions; armchair speculations are not acceptable data of social psychology. The specification of behavior as "individual" is an attempt to emphasize the social psychologist's concern for the individual as the unit of analysis, as opposed to larger units such as groups and institutions which are the concern of anthropologists and sociologists. Finally, "social stimuli" refers to man and his products. Thus, another person is a social stimulus, and the things which he creates, such as social groups, norms, and other social products, also serve as social stimuli. It should be clear that "social stimuli" includes the effects of past social experience to the extent that those effects (the things the individual brings with him to the present) are unambiguously derivable from social factors.

That is, social psychology may study the effects of social stimuli that are mediated by enduring processes such as attitudes and norm internalization. On the other hand, personality characteristics such as manifest anxiety, self-confidence, and conceptual systems are excluded because the historical antecedents of such characteristics are not clearly social in nature.

A theory is a set of interrelated hypotheses or propositions concerning a phenomenon or set of phenomena. This is indeed a minimal definition of theory. Nevertheless, we believe that it encompasses the essential elements of the concept as delineated by the philosophy of science. In the following sections, the meaning of both social psychology and theory is explored more fully.

THE FIELD OF SOCIAL PSYCHOLOGY

The definition of social psychology given in the preceding section does not adequately reflect the wide range of issues and problems encompassed by this field of study. A consideration of the area and scope of social psychology and of its relation to other social sciences may provide a better understanding of this field.

Area and Scope of Social Psychology

The definition of social psychology presented above is only one of many definitions that have been suggested. A review of other formulations may contribute to the understanding of the domain of social psychology.

"Social psychology is the scientific study of the experience and behavior of individuals in relation to social stimulus situations" (Sherif & Sherif, 1956, p. 4).

"Social psychology can be defined as the science of interpersonal behavior events" (Krech, Crutchfield, & Ballachey, 1962, p. 5).

"Social psychology is the scientific study of human interaction" (Watson, 1966, p. 1).

"Social psychology is the study of the individual human being as he interacts, largely symbolically, with his environment" (Dewey & Humber, 1966, p. 3).

"Social psychology is a subdiscipline of psychology that especially involves the scientific study of the behavior of individuals as a function of social stimuli" (Jones & Gerard, 1967, p. 1).

"Social psychology is the scientific study of the experience and behavior of individuals in relation to other individuals, groups, and culture" (McDavid & Harari, 1968, p. 13).

Social psychology is all of these things; however, it is easy to get the impression that all of human behavior falls within the domain of social psychology. The Dewey and Humber definition is especially broad, since it is difficult to imagine a situation in which an individual fails to interact with his environment. In practice, the field of social psychology is more limited than implied by the various definitions. The areas included in the field may be classified under three major headings: (1) the study of social influences on individual processes, (2) the study of shared individual processes, and (3) the study of group interaction.

The category labeled "social influences on individual processes" includes those phenomena which (1) may be influenced by social stimuli, (2) may also occur in the absence of any social stimulus, and (3) usually are not shared by persons who are not exposed to the immediate stimulus situation. Perception, motivation, learning, and attribution are examples of such phenomena. The major variables influencing these processes probably are not social in nature; hence they have been studied primarily by non-social psychologists. However, to the extent that social variables are determinants of these processes, or that these processes are determinants of social behavior, the social psychologist must (and does) study them. On the other hand, most of the theories formulated to account for such individual processes have been developed by others and are not social psychological in nature. The theorist merely incorporates the effects of social variables into a more-comprehensive theory. For this reason there are relatively few social theories concerning these individual behaviors.

"Shared individual processes" refers to those phenomena which (1) are basically individual in that their manifestation does not depend upon the immediate presence of social stimuli, (2) derive directly from social stimuli, and (3) are usually shared by others in the same social group. Language and social attitudes are examples of such phenomena. The development of language and social attitudes depends upon interaction with others in the social group, but once they have developed they function more or less independently of the social group. For example, a person who "knows the English language" may make use of this skill to help organize his thoughts when he is alone; he is able to speak and write whether others are present or not. Imitation and modeling behavior are also examples of this category, although the degree to which these processes are shared by others in the group is probably less than in the case of language and social attitudes.

The category labeled "group interaction" includes all those processes which (1) depend upon interaction with others and (2) are manifested only when others are present, at least in spirit. Leadership, communication, power relations, authority, conformity, cooperation and competition, and social roles fall into this category. The behavior that occurs is, of course, behavior of individuals, but it is behavior in response to immediate social stimuli. Perhaps because this category is uniquely social in nature, more social theories have been formulated about these phenomena than those of either of the other two categories.

The Place of Social Psychology in the Behavioral Sciences

Among the behavioral sciences, social psychology is most closely related to anthropology and sociology. Anthropology is usually defined as the science of man. It is concerned primarily, but not exclusively, with primitive man.

More specifically, anthropology is the study of man in relation to distribution, origin, classification of races, environmental and social relations, physical characteristics, and culture. Thus the province of anthropology is that of entire cultures and their analyses, both singly and in relation to each other. Anthropology is an extremely important field for the social psychologist. We are socialized in a specific culture; and the motives, values, and aspirations of that culture tend to bias our view of the behavior of people in other cultures. The findings of anthropologists can help overcome this bias and can identify the tremendous diversity in human behavior from culture to culture. The social psychologist cannot hope to understand fully the individual's behavior in social situations without an awareness of the culture's influences upon his behavior.

Sociology is, of course, closely related to both social psychology and anthropology. It is the science of society, social institutions, and social relationships. More specifically, sociology is the systematic study of the development, structure, and functions of human groups conceived as organized patterns of collective behavior. The sociologist is interested primarily, but not exclusively, in group behavior, institutions, and intergroup relations. His major problems concern the ways in which the behavior of people is similar or different because of group-membership influences. Since man almost inevitably spends much of his waking life as a member of various social groups, the findings of sociologists are of great value to the social psychologist in his attempt to understand social behavior.

Anthropology, sociology, and social psychology thus represent three levels of analysis in the study of social man. Anthropology considers the entire culture; sociology deals with smaller collectivities within the larger culture; and social psychology is concerned with the behavior of the individual in response to social influences. Whereas both sociology and social psychology are interested in behavior within groups, sociology is interested in the fact that all members of the group are subject to the same influences, and social psychology is concerned primarily with the influences which play upon the individuals as members of the group. The social psychologist finds the principles established by anthropologists and sociologists indispensable, but the focus of his interest is basically different from that of either the anthropologist or the sociologist. This difference is reflected not only in the unit of analysis but also in the method of study. Sociology and anthropology rely largely on descriptive analysis with relatively little effort toward generalization; social psychology, on the other hand, relies primarily on experimental investigations for the purpose of formulating general laws which can be incorporated into social theory.

THEORY IN SOCIAL PSYCHOLOGY

Social psychology, like other sciences, seeks to *understand* the phenomena being studied. If one understands a phenomenon, he can *predict* it to the extent that the relevant variables are known, and he can *control* it to the extent that he has power over the relevant variables. The converse, however, is not true; a person may be able to predict and/or control a phenomenon without understanding it. For example, it is not difficult to imagine a primitive man who could accurately predict that the sun would rise in the east and set in the west without any understanding of the system producing these events. Similarly, it is quite possible for an automobile driver to control his vehicle without any understanding of the causal relationships between his actions and the behavior of the automobile. Although understanding is the major goal of science, prediction is nevertheless important because it is the process which permits verification of empirical and theoretical generalizations. Control is, of course, highly important in the application of scientific discovery, but its significance for science is limited to situations in which control is necessary for further investigation.

In attempting to understand social behavior, the social psychologist uses both experience and theory. Experience provides the raw data upon which understanding is based; theory organizes experience so that its implications for more-general social behavior are recognized. Not all experience provides acceptable data, however. Only that experience which meets the criteria for admission to the body of scientific knowledge is acceptable. In general, experience that meets these criteria derives from experimentation, or at least from observations under controlled conditions. Thus only propositions that are based upon objective observations that are public and repeatable are admitted to the body of scientific knowledge.

Empirical data are essential for understanding social behavior, but empiricism alone does not lead to major advances in any science. Empirical data must be organized and interrelated so that they can be interpreted and unified. This is the function of theory. The role of theory in advancing science was emphasized by both Campbell (1921) and Conant (1953). Campbell noted that it is unusual for new laws to be suggested merely from experimentation; Conant asserted that all really revolutionary and significant advances that have occurred during the history of science have been the result of new theories. Although the above statements are undoubtedly true for the physical sciences, it is not so clear that they also apply to social psychology. Perhaps this is because no "really revolutionary and significant advances" have been made by social psychologists. Regardless of the truth of these extreme statements, however, it cannot be doubted that theory plays a most significant role in social psychology.

The Nature of Theory

In the introduction to this chapter we defined theory as a set of interrelated hypotheses or propositions concerning a phenomenon or set of phenomena. Although this definition is adequate for the purposes of this book, it is by no means the only definition that might be proposed. The following examples are representative:

"Theories are sets of statements, understandable to others, which make predictions about empirical events" (Mandler & Kessen, 1959, p. 142).

"It will be convenient for our purposes to define a theory simply as a set of statements or sentences" (Simon & Newell, 1956, p. 67).

"Basically, a theory consists of one or more functional statements or propositions that treat the relationship of variables so as to account for a phenomenon or set of phenomena" (Hollander, 1967, p. 55).

"The term *theory* is normally applied to the higher order integration of hypotheses into systematic networks that attempt to describe and predict broader ranges of events by allowing one hypothesis to qualify another or to specify the conditions under which another will be appropriate" (McDavid & Harari, 1968, p. 21).

"A theory is a symbolic construction" (Kaplan, 1964, p. 296).

Despite the variations in wording, these definitions are not inconsistent with our definition in any essential characteristic, with the possible exception of the one proposed by Kaplan. The bare statement that a theory is a symbolic construction, however, does not do justice to Kaplan's detailed and insightful treatment of the nature of theory. He suggested that a theory is a way of making sense out of a confused set of data; it allows us to use, modify, or discard habits as the situation demands. A theory is thus a device for interpreting, criticizing, and unifying established laws. Theorizing does not mean that a person learns by experience, but rather that he learns from experience. The *from* learning is the process that requires symbolic constructions; these constructions can provide vicarious experience which the person never actually undergoes. The process of symbolic construction makes use of empirical data, but it goes beyond the data and points to new insights. This view of "mental work" in the formulation of scientific propositions is similar to that propounded by Polanyi (1968), although Kaplan apparently did not interpret this process as reflecting indeterminacy in the real world as Polanyi did.

Theory is thus in part a summary of known "facts" and in part conjecture about the implications of facts and the probable relationships among them. In a sense, it may be regarded as an attempt to map the real world, although theories differ in the degree to which this is true. That is, some theories employ concepts (constructs) that are not assumed to represent any specific thing in the real world. Nevertheless, all theories purport to say something about actual events and phenomena and are not merely fictitious representations of imaginary situations.

For purposes of this book, we shall distinguish between "theory" and "orientation." In contrast to theory as a set of interrelated hypotheses, *orientation* refers to a general approach to the analysis and interpretation of behavior. In psychology, these general orientations are often called *systems,* although they are sometimes referred to as theories. Such systematic orientations provide the general framework within which theories are formulated. General orientations that have been most influential in social psychology are the stimulus-response reinforcement approach, the field-theoretical orientation, the cognitive orientation, and the psychoanalytic orientation. As we shall see, most of the theories in social psychology derive from these general approaches, either singly or in combination.

Functions of Theory

We have already indicated that theory plays a very important role in social psychology, and we have pointed to some of the functions performed by theory. It is probably not feasible or even desirable to list all the functions of theories in social psychology; however, it may be useful to point to some of the major purposes served by theory. In the first place, theory is a convenient way of organizing experience; it permits us to handle large amounts of empirical data with relatively few propositions. This fact means that theory enables the social psychologist to deal in a meaningful way with information that would otherwise be chaotic and largely useless.

But a theory does much more than this. A second function of theory is that it enables us to go beyond the empirical data and to see implications and relationships that are not evident from any datum taken alone. It has been asserted that propositions contain within themselves certain consequences, and no conclusion can be drawn that is not inherent in the propositions under consideration. On the other hand, some philosophers have maintained that by proper juxtaposition of two or more propositions it may be possible to discover truths that are not contained in these propositions. The story is told of the priest who told guests at a party that the first person who confessed to him was a murderer. Later a young man entered the room and introduced himself as the first person to confess to the priest. No one would have difficulty in drawing the immediate inference that the young man was a murderer, yet this conclusion is not inherent in either statement. Regardless of the merits of the two positions, it is clear that interrelated hypotheses can reveal conclusions that are not evident from data considered in isolation.

This function of providing insights beyond the empirical data provides the basis for a third function of theory: it is a stimulus and a guide for further empirical investigation. Theory leads to predictions about events not yet observed and encourages the researcher to examine the consequences of these predictions. This leads to further empirical data, which may either support the theory or suggest needed modifications or even rejection of the theory.

Mandler and Kessen (1959) suggested that theory also performs an anticipatory function. It indicates the kinds of events that the individual may expect to occur under specified conditions, even if those conditions have not been encountered before. This function can be valuable not only for everyday behavior, but also in guiding the experimentation of the researcher. In a sense, we may say that theory provides a bridge to something "out there" and thus makes our world seem more logical, reasonable, and organized.

Undoubtedly other functions of theory could be mentioned, but those outlined above are the ones of major importance for social psychology.

Kinds of Theories

As Marx and Hillix (1963) have pointed out, theories may differ in a variety of ways. Obviously, they differ in regard to subject matter (some deal with leadership, others with attitude change, etc.), generality, precision, rigor of prediction, and origins of postulates (empirical versus rational). But theories also differ in other respects that are perhaps more basic than these. Einstein (1934) distinguished between *constructive* and *principle theories*. Constructive theories attempt to build up a map of more-complex phenomena from the materials of a relatively simple scheme which constitutes the starting point. Principle theories, on the other hand, use the analytic method. The starting point of such theories is a set of empirical data, rather than hypothetically constructed elements as in the constructive method. The advantages of the constructive method were said to be clarity, completeness, and adaptability; those of principle theories were held to be logical perfection and a secure foundation. Heider's (1946) p-o-x theory (see Chapter 8) is an example of a constructive theory in social psychology; whereas Bandura's (1966) theory of imitation is an example of a principle theory (see Chapter 3).

A somewhat similar classification, reductive versus constructive, was referred to by Marx (1951). *Reductive theories* attempt to explain phenomena by appealing to lower levels of analysis. For example, the theorist may attempt to explain social motivations in terms of physiological needs. *Constructive theories* take the reverse approach; they attempt to explain phenomena by appealing to higher levels of abstraction. This distinction is not very useful for the explication of social theories.

Kaplan (1964) considered several classifications; however, he appeared to prefer the classification which distinguishes between *concatenated theories* and *hierarchical theories*. This classification is similar to Einstein's distinction between constructive and principle theories. A concatenated theory is one whose component propositions (laws) form a network of relations which constitutes an identifiable pattern. Each proposition typically converges on some central point, each proposition specifying one of the factors which plays a part in the phenomenon that the theory is supposed to explain. In the usual case, a concatenated theory consists of tendency statements that are meaningful only in their joint application. Fiedler's (1964) contingency model of leadership effectiveness (see Chapter 12) is an example of a concatenated theory in social psychology. A hierarchical theory is one whose component propositions are deduced from a set of basic principles. A proposition is explained by showing that it is a logical consequence of the set of principles. Similarly, a phenomenon is explained if it can be shown to follow from the principles, given a set of specified initial conditions. In its ideal form a hierarchical theory consists of (1) a calculus whose sentences contain names and meanings for the theoretical entities being considered, (2) a set of definitions couched in observational terms, and (3) an interpretative model that specifies the conditions under which the postulates of the calculus are true. There is probably no theory in social psychology that meets the requirements of an ideal hierarchical model, but French's (1956) theory of social power (see Chapter 6) fits the general class.

The types of theories that we have considered so far are based upon the form of the theory. It is also possible to classify theories on the basis of content. Kaplan (1964) noted that every theory demarcates an explanatory shell for the phenomena with which it deals. This shell contains all that is necessary and sufficient to explain the phenomena, according to the theory. The classification of theories as *molar* or *molecular* is based on the radius of the explanatory shell. In psychology, a molar theory might refer to the person as a whole, whereas a molecular theory might consider neural connections within the organism. In social psychology, theories referring to group phenomena, such as those described in Chapter 12, might be considered molar theories; consistency theories (described in Chapter 8) are molecular theories.

The molar-molecular classification is sometimes confused with the *field theory* versus *monadic theory* dichotomy (Kaplan, 1964). A field theory explains the phenomena under consideration in terms of relations among certain elements, whereas a monadic theory explains by reference to the elements (or attributes of the elements) which are related. Either type of theory may be either molar or molecular, since the distinction depends upon what propositions say about phenomena rather than upon the range of the theory, that is, upon what the propositions are about.

For purposes of this book, we will consider the constructive-versus-principle theories distinction with regard to form, and the molar-versus-molecular distinction with respect to content. Not all the theories that are considered in the following chapters fit neatly into these classes, but in Chapter 14 we indicate the class which best describes each theory.

Levels of Analysis

The question of kind of theory is often confused with the notion of level of analysis, which in turn is used with a variety of meanings. In social psychology, level of analysis often refers to the unit of analysis. For example, Krech and Crutchfield (1948) identified three levels of analysis: the individual level, the level of individual behavior in groups, and the level of group and institutional behavior.

When the level concept is applied to theories, it may also refer to a variety of characteristics. Kaplan (1964) noted at least five different meanings of the term:

1. Level may refer to the *range* of the theory; that is, the degree to which it applies to a specific class of subjects or to persons in general.

2. It may refer to the *scope* of the theory; that is, to the number of different kinds of behaviors that the theory attempts to explain.

3. The level of a theory may refer to its *abstractness*. This aspect involves the length of the reduction chain connecting theoretical terms with observable ones. In psychology this would probably refer to the number of intervening variables in the system.

4. A fourth use of the levels concept refers to the *length of the deductions* in the theory; that is, the steps between its first principles and the laws in which it finds application. Kaplan cited the difference between miniature theories of psychology and the usual sociological theory as an example. (There appears to be a close connection between abstractness and length of the deductions of a theory, although the two aspects are conceptually independent.)

5. Level of a theory may refer to the *radius of its explanatory shell;* the smaller the radius, the higher the level of the theory. Thus molecular theories are said to be of a higher level than molar theories.

When a theory is referred to as being of a higher or lower level, there is often the implication of value. A higher-level theory is somehow regarded as "better" than a lower-level theory. It should be clear from our brief consideration of the various meanings of level that this implication of value is not justified. The level of the theory, by any definition, has nothing to do with its scientific standing. In the next section we consider some of the characteristics of a theory which *are* relevant to its standing.

Characteristics of a Good Theory

The question of what constitutes a "good" theory quickly resolves to the problem of validation. On what bases is a theory acceptable to members of the scientific community? Frank (1957) asserted that a system of propositions is acceptable as a theory if the system is logically correct and its conclusions agree with observable facts. In his view, these two criteria are generally acceptable to scientists. Kaplan (1964), however, suggested that more-extensive criteria should be considered. His criteria for the validation of theories included (1) norms of correspondence, (2) norms of coherence, and (3) pragmatic norms. Norms of correspondence refer to the degree to which a theory fits the facts. A theory is acceptable to the extent that its predictions agree with what is already known and/or can be verified by future observations. Norms of coherence involve several aspects of the theory. First, the theory should fit in with the body of theory that is already established. That is, theories that are wholly self-contained cannot be validated. A second aspect of coherence is that of simplicity, which is internal to the theory itself. Kaplan distinguished between descriptive simplicity and inductive simplicity. Descriptive simplicity refers to the description itself, whereas inductive simplicity refers to the thing being described. Although descriptive simplicity may be an important criterion of acceptability, inductive simplicity is of greater significance since it deals with the manageability of the theory. Finally, norms of coherence may include the esthetic aspect of the theory; some theories provide more intrinsic pleasure from contemplation than others. Kaplan suggested that this norm has little bearing on behavioral science today. The pragmatic norm deals with the question of what the theory can do for science. A theory is acceptable to the extent that it serves our scientific purposes.

For our purposes, it is helpful to classify characteristics of a "good" theory into two broad classes: (1) characteristics that are *necessary* if the theory is to be accepted and (2) characteristics that are *desirable* but not essential to acceptance. The first category consists of three criteria, including the two criteria suggested by Frank: (1) logical consistency and (2) agreement with known data. The first criterion merely points to the fact that a theory must be internally consistent. The various propositions in the theory must not be inconsistent or contradictory. Incompatible predictions from the same theory are untenable. The second characteristic means that the predictions of the theory agree with known facts and future observations; that is, observations made subsequent to the formulation of the theory. A theory that is supported only by data that were available at the time the theory was promulgated may be said to have low antecedent probability of being true. This conclusion is based upon the fact that the theory itself is designed to fit the data; the fact that the theorist has been successful in this endeavor says little about its predictive power. In addition to Frank's criteria, we would add a third characteristic necessary to an acceptable theory: testability. It may seem that this property is inherent in the "agreement with data" requirement; however, it is possible for a theory to fit all the known data and yet be untestable. For example, the psychoanalytic notion of repression, in its crudest form at least, is not testable although it agrees with observations: if a person does not recall a traumatic experience, he is repressing it; if he does recall it, he obviously was not repressing it. Therefore, both recall and failure to recall agree with the theory; there is no behavior that is *not* in agreement with the theory. For a theory to be testable it must be capable of being refuted. A theory can never be "proved," since this would require observation of all possible instances of the phenomenon, an obviously impossible requirement. Instead, the validity of a theory is more or less probable depending upon the amount of evidence supporting it. On the other hand, a theory can be disproved. One unequivocal negative instance is sufficient to refute a theory, although in practice such an instance seldom occurs. Most commonly, data that do not fit the theory lead the researcher to review his procedures to determine whether the instance is in fact a negative one. Rarely, if ever, does the review indicate clearly that the theory is invalid; instead, it may suggest revision of research procedures or revision of the theory. However, several equivocal negative instances may call for rejection of the theory.

In addition to these characteristics necessary to an acceptable theory, there are several other characteristics that are desirable. Each of the following should be qualified by the "other things being equal" caveat.

First, a good theory should be as simple as possible, both in terms of description and deduction. Its propositions, corollaries, and hypotheses should be stated in clearly understandable terms so that it is easily communicable to others in the field. The derivation of predictions should be straightforward and unequivocal.

Second, a theory should be economical in that it explains the phenomena in question with as few principles as possible. While Occam's razor and Morgan's canon may be passé, it is still true that a theory that accounts for a given phenomenon with a few propositions is preferable to a theory that requires a greater number.

Third, a good theory should be consistent with related theories that have high probability of being true. The fact that a theory is inconsistent with related acceptable theories does not necessarily mean that it is invalid, but it does reduce the antecedent probability that it is true. Conversely, integration into the body of established theory increases the probability that the theory is a valid explanation of the phenomena under consideration.

Fourth, an acceptable theory should be readily interpretable in the sense that it provides a bridge to something in the real world. A theory that is difficult to relate to observable phenomena is not likely to contribute much to either science or everyday living.

Finally, a good theory should serve a useful purpose, not only in the sense that it explains what it is supposed to explain, but also in relation to the advancement of science. In other words, a good theory provides the basis for research. It stimulates and guides the scientist in his effort to understand his world.

PROBLEMS OF THEORY CONSTRUCTION IN SOCIAL PSYCHOLOGY

If social psychologists have been late comers in the business of theory development, it has been because, at least in part, of problems related to the criteria for acceptance of a theory. The major problems faced by the theorist in social psychology are those related to definitions, reliability of data, scope of the theory, and kind of theory.

Definitions

It is obvious that the terms used in theory construction must be precisely defined; unfortunately, the terms used in social psychological theories often do not meet this requirement. Basically, a definition provides a set of terms which is synonymous with the term defined so that they can be used interchangeably (Kaplan, 1964). The set of terms in the definition must be precise enough so that the meaning of the term is clear; that is, different persons will interpret it in the same way. Some definitions are merely nominal in that one term is substituted for another, as in a notation system; for example, "Let X stand for the individual group member's report of personal satisfaction with the group process." Theory, for the most part, requires "real" definitions (Hempel, 1952). These definitions state the essential nature or attributes of some entity or theoretical construct. Precisely this type of definition is least adequate in social psychology.

The social psychologist, at some point in his theorizing, formulates concepts concerning the phenomenon under consideration. He needs some term for labeling each concept so that it can be conveniently referred to. In selecting this term, he has the choice of a term taken from everyday language or of a new term coined for this specific purpose. In either case, there are problems of definition and usage. If a term is chosen from the common language, the definition must not only specify the entities to which the term refers as a scientific term but also must eliminate some surplus meaning that derives from the common language. If he chooses to coin a new term, it gives the impression of being esoteric, requires special definition, and cannot be as easily remembered and communicated as a more-familiar term. An example of this type of term is Cattell's (1948) "syntality" (see Chapter 12). In either case, the meaning of the term is likely to remain vague to many persons in the field.

Although this kind of definitional problem may be more common in social psychology than in some other disciplines, it is by no means unique to social psychological theories. One attempt to overcome the vagueness of theoretical terms is the use of operational definitions (Bridgman, 1927). The basic notion is that a concept is synonymous with the operations that are necessary for its measurement and manipulation. For example, an operational definition of "leadership" might be number of votes cast in an election of a leader. The main difficulty of the operational definition, as applied in social psychology, is that the operations are usually not coextensive with the conceptual definition of the term. That is, the theorist usually has a concept in mind that has a certain meaning for him. He then devises operations that he believes will measure the concept and calls these operations a definition of the concept. Unfortunately, he may also devise other operations that he believes will also measure the concept. Thus, the same concept may have two or more operational definitions and, presumably, two or more meanings. Obviously this can lead to confusion. It may be properly objected that this use of the operational definition is at variance with Bridgman's thesis, but this fact does not improve definitions in theories of social psychology.

To the extent that terms are not unambiguously defined, it is difficult to evaluate a theory in terms of internal consistency, agreement with data, and testability. For example, the theory may be internally consistent if a given term is defined in one way but inconsistent if it has another meaning. Adequate definitions would do much to improve theories in social psychology.

Reliability of Data

The problem of the reliability of data is a critical one for the construction of theory in social psychology. The degree to which the theorist relies upon empirical data in the initial formulation of the theory varies from relative independence to complete dependence. It is obvious that the quality of the theory is directly related to the reliability of the data upon which it is based. Data reliability also enters into the process of theory evaluation. The success achieved in determining the degree to which the theory "fits the facts" and in subsequent testing of the theory is very much dependent upon the reliability of data.

Problems of reliability of data arise in social psychology in several instances. In the first place, there is the problem of measurement. To obtain data at all, it is necessary to measure the stimulus and response variables in the social situation. Unfortunately, measurement in social psychology is not as reliable as physical measurement; the researcher and theorist must rely upon less than completely reliable measuring instruments, at least in many instances. For example, formal techniques for the measurement of attitudes have existed for more than forty years, but the average reliability of attitude scales is on the order of .75 (Shaw & Wright, 1967). Other measuring instruments in social psychology suffer a similar deficiency in reliability.

Most data relative to social theories derive from experimentation, and there are numerous problems of reliability associated with this source of data. The quality of the data obtained from experimentation is a direct function of the adequacy of the experimental design. The ingenuity of the investigator in designing a study that tests the implications of a theory is thus an important determinant of the reliability of the data. The inexactness of experimental procedures is revealed by the low probability that a given experimental finding can be replicated and by the fact that negative results seldom lead to hypothesis rejection. As we indicated earlier, negative results usually lead first to a reconsideration of experimental procedures; it is generally easy to identify sufficient inadequacies in the experimental design to permit retention of the theory.

Another aspect of experimentation is the problem of experimental control. The control and manipulation of variables is of course basic to experimentation. Social behavior is so complex and influenced by so many variables that the problem of control becomes acute. At best, the experimenter is able to control the major known variables influencing the phenomenon in question; control of other variables hinges upon the adequacy of randomization. Effects of unwanted variables almost inevitably contaminate experimental results from social psychological studies.

One kind of unwanted variable is that of the experimenter himself. Orne (1962) and Rosenthal (1966) have demonstrated bias that is often introduced into the experiment by the investigator. The experimenter apparently communicates some of his expectations to the subject, often in subtle, difficult-to-identify ways. Such biases reportedly enter into experimental results even when data are collected by an assistant who is unaware of the purpose of the experiment. Although there is still some question regarding the extent of such effects, it is nevertheless true that experimenter biases sometimes do influence results. This source of error in data certainly creates a problem in the development and testing of theories.

Scope of the Theory

The social psychologist who aspires to theoretical greatness is faced with still another set of problems, those related to the scope of the theory: *comprehensiveness, restrictiveness,* and *generality.* Comprehensiveness refers to the range of phenomena which the theory will account for and/or the range of persons to which it applies. Restrictiveness refers to the qualifications that must be appended to the propositions or hypotheses included in the theory; that is, the limitations of the theoretical principles. Generality refers to the degree to which the theory can be extended to include situations and events not specifically included in the phenomena that the theory is supposed to explain. These aspects of a theory are of course interrelated. In general, the more comprehensive, the less restrictive, and the more general the theory, the more useful the theory is likely to be. However, the theorist must take care that his attempts in this direction do not lead to overgenerality. The danger is that the theory will become so all-inclusive that it explains everything and nothing. That is, a theory that is so general that it can explain anything that happens cannot be very predictive and contributes little to our understanding of the phenomena of interest. The theorist's task is to construct the theory in such a way so that it includes as much as can be adequately handled by the set of theoretical principles, but restrictive enough so that it does not suffer from overgenerality. The theory of cognitive dissonance

(Festinger, 1957) is an example of a theory that was overgeneralized in its initial form; one of the major contributions of research and theory over the past ten years has been the restriction of this theory to more-limited situations (see Chapter 8).

The Problem of Kind of Theory

The theorist must make a number of initial decisions about the theory before he can begin construction. In fact, he must at some point make the decision that he will try to explain a set of phenomena and that the form of this explanation will be a theory rather than a model. It will be recalled that a theory purports to say something about the real world. A model, on the other hand, postulates a system that represents the kind of situation that might exist, but it does not necessarily reflect what is "out there." A model describes the phenomena in "as if" terms; therefore, it demonstrates how a particular phenomenon or set of phenomena *could* occur but not necessarily how it *does* occur.

Once the decision has been made to construct a theory, the theorist still must decide what kind of theory: concatenated or hierarchical? molar or molecular? constructive or reductive? constructive or principle? Unfortunately, there is no set of rules or principles to guide this choice. For example, if the constructive type is chosen, the theory can be expected to be clear, complete, and adaptable; if the principle type is chosen, the theory can be expected to have a secure empirical basis and should be logically sound. Of course, it is possible to achieve all these advantages with either type, but the probabilities are different. Similarly, there is no logical basis for preferring either a molar or a molecular type of theory, despite the prevalent tendency to believe that a molecular explanation is somehow more basic than a molar one. In the final analysis, it is largely a matter of personal preference which kind of theory is chosen; however, it is well to keep in mind the different consequences of this choice.

Despite the various problems associated with theory construction in social psychology, a number of useful theories have been formulated. A consideration of some of the more-prominent theories in social psychology is the purpose of this book. Most of the theories selected satisfy at least the minimal criteria for a good theory.

PLAN OF THE BOOK: AN OVERVIEW

The general purpose of this work is to present the major theories of social psychological behavior. The intent is to familiarize the student with general principles and propositions of these theories and with some of the related experimental data relevant to them. Our goal is primarily that of exposition rather than that of evaluation. We have tried to present and clarify the essential characteristics of each theory so that the student will be able to understand the theoretical framework, the interrelations among hypotheses, and the predictions inherent in each theory. Although evaluation is not a primary goal of the book, we have commented on some of the more-obvious strengths and weaknesses of each theory. The reader will undoubtedly be able to identify other evaluative aspects that we have neglected to mention.

We have approached the task of theory exposition by first presenting a description of the general orientation that provides the basis for the various theories being considered. The presentation of each general orientation is followed by an exposition of the several theories that have been developed within that orientation. In deciding whether a given theory derives from a given general orientation we recognized that theories vary in the degree to which they are firmly based on the more-general system. Our classification suggests only that the particular theory is more nearly representative of the orientation to which it is assigned than to any other orientation. In addition, there are some theories that are clearly eclectic in the sense that they do not rely upon any one of the more-general orientations or that they make use of principles drawn from one or more of the general approaches. These "transorientational" theories are presented separately.

Following this general design, Part 2 deals with reinforcement theories. Chapter 2 describes the stimulus-response reinforcement approach, followed by a presentation of theories based on this orientation in Chapters 3 and 4. Chapter 3 deals with Miller and Dollard's (1941) theory of social learning and imitation and Bandura's (1966) vicarious process theory of imitation. The Miller and Dollard theory is historically interesting and relates directly to the more-recent theory proposed by Bandura. Chapter 4 considers theories dealing with group interaction processes, including Homans' (1961) theory of elementary social behavior, Thibaut and Kelley's (1959) theory of interaction outcomes, and Adams and Romney's (1959) behavior theory of authority relations.

Part 3 is devoted to field theories. The basic concepts and constructs of the field-theoretical approach are described in Chapter 5, based largely upon the views of Kurt Lewin. Chapter 6 is concerned with theories of social psychology which take this general orientation, including Heider's (1958) theory of interpersonal relations, Cartwright's (1959) formal theory of social power, and Deutsch's (1949) theory of cooperation and competition.

The cognitive orientation is dealt with in Part 4. The basic concepts of cognitive theory are expounded in Chapter 7 and related theories are described in Chapter 8. The major cognitive theories in social psychology are the consistency theories. We present Heider's (1946) p-o-x theory, Osgood and Tannenbaum's (1955) principle of congruity, Newcomb's (1953) theory of communicative acts, and Festinger's (1957) theory of cognitive dissonance.

Part 5 is devoted to the psychoanalytic orientation. The general principles of the psychoanalytic approach are outlined in Chapter 9, and psychoanalytically based theories are presented in Chapter 10. The psychoanalytic theories in social psychology that we consider include Sarnoff's (1960) theory of attitude organization and change, Bennis and Shepard's (1956) theory of group development, Schutz's (1958) three-dimensional theory of interpersonal behavior, and Bion's (1949a, b; 1959) theory of group function.

Transorientational approaches that draw upon one or more of the traditional orientations or represent unique orientations are considered in Part 4. Chapter 11 deals with social judgment and attribution theories, including Festinger's (1950, 1954) social comparison theory, Jones and Davis' (1956) theory of correspondent inferences, Kelley's (1967) theory of external attribution, and Sherif and Hovland's (1961) social judgment theory. Chapter 12 presents several theories dealing with group processes, including Cattell's (1948) group syntality theory, Stogdill's (1959) theory of group achievement, Fiedler's (1964) contingency model of leadership effectiveness, and Willis' (1964) descriptive model of social response. Chapter 13 considers role theory. In some respects role theory may be considered a general orientation; in others a theory of social behavior. For lack of definitive criteria regarding its appropriate classification, we elected to include it under the transorientational heading. Its major characteristics and some of its specific applications are described, primarily as depicted by Biddle and Thomas (1966).

Finally, Part 7 is devoted to a consideration of similarities and differences among the several theories discussed in the preceding chapters. An attempt is made to indicate what is unique to each theory and what it has in common with other theories with respect to orientation, conceptualization, and kind of social phenomena it attempts to explain.

THE REINFORCEMENT ORIENTATION
PART 2

2 | THE REINFORCEMENT-THEORY ORIENTATION

The study of human and animal learning constitutes a large portion of contemporary psychology—such a large portion, in fact, that any single chapter aimed at presenting a comprehensive view of the principles of learning would be a pretentious one indeed. Therefore, in the present chapter our intent is not to present all there is to present in the area of reinforcement and learning. Many other texts specifically directed at the exposition of learning theory and research have better approached this goal of comprehensiveness (Hilgard, 1956; Kimble, 1961; Hall, 1966; Kimble, 1967). This chapter is directed toward the exposition of the basic principles and constructs of reinforcement theory so that they may be understood in the subsequent two chapters dealing with reinforcement theory in social psychology. The chapter does not take a unitary approach to the discussion of reinforcement theory, but rather it attempts to present several interpretations of selected reinforcement phenomena. It would be faulty to refer to the language of B. F. Skinner, Clark Hull, Kenneth Spence, or of any other single person as *the* language of reinforcement psychology. Many theorists have contributed to the conceptual framework of the reinforcement orientation.

The chapter consists of three sections. The first section is aimed at presenting a *brief* historical foundation for contemporary conceptions of learning and reinforcement. The second portion identifies and defines some important constructs considered in this section, such as *stimulus* and *response, drive, response strength, generalization, discrimination, reinforcement,* and *extinction.* Where relevant, several orientations, particularly those of Hull and Skinner, are brought to bear upon the identification of these constructs. The third and last section explicates two applications of reinforcement theory to a social psychological phenomenon—attitudes.

BRIEF HISTORICAL INTRODUCTION

Observations of the efficacy of reward and punishment in the learning process were probably made quite early in human history. However, the formal beginnings of reinforcement theory occurred at the turn of this century. At that time Edward L. Thorndike (1898) and Ivan P. Pavlov (1902) made independent and similar discoveries concerning the role of reinforcement. Thorndike posited that the basis of learning was the formation of a bond between sensory input and impulses to action. He referred to the organism's propensity to emit a given response to a designated stimulus as a habit or "bond." In his early thinking, Thorndike (1913) saw S-R connections as being strengthened by practice and positive consequences and weakened by disuse and negative consequences. The effect of practice on S-R connections was referred to by Thorndike as the *law of exercise*. This law is probably the earliest formal predecessor of contemporary conceptions of the probability of response occurrence. The law of exercise stated that the more frequently a given sensory input is followed by a given response, the greater the probability that the connection will be repeated.

Although Thorndike initially considered the law of exercise to be central to any S-R association, he later revised his thinking to account for the predominant role of reinforcement. His *law of effect* slightly predated Pavlov's *law of reinforcement* and held that any S-R connection gains its major strength from the consequences that follow it. If positive consequences or a satisfying state of affairs occurs as a function of the organism's response to a stimulus configuration, the organism will probably repeat that response in order to gain reward. On the other hand, if a response is followed by negative consequences or an annoying state of affairs, the organism will avoid reestablishing this same S-R bond.

Although Thorndike's system was revised by him on several occasions (1932, 1935, 1949), the substance and saliance of his major propositions remained basically intact. Despite the continuing controversy that persists in learning theory concerning the nature and role of reinforcement, contemporary conceptions of reinforcement can readily be traced to Thorndike's law of effect.

While Thorndike was formulating his early principles of association, Pavlov was quite independently arriving at similar propositions. Thorndike's goals differed greatly from those of Pavlov. Thorndike was aiming at the practical application of learning principles to the educational process. Both his research and theorizing were done with this goal in mind. Pavlov, on the other hand, did not initially foresee the implications of his data and theory. He was a physiologist seeking neurological explanations for the digestive process. He was seeking a viable method for the measurement of digestive secretions. To this end, he labored to discover a technique whereby the internal process of digestive secretion might be made directly observable. His early investigations led him to the discovery of the "Pavlov pouch," which isolated digestive secretion from particles of food. Through the use of this pouch (see Kimble, 1967) and the insertion of gastric fistula in the stomach wall, Pavlov was able to measure the extent and quality of the gastric secretions of dogs. This research won him the Nobel Prize in 1904. More significantly for the fate of psychological science, his research on digestion led him to the study of salivation as an interrelated form of digestive secretion. He found that a dog would salivate at the mere sight and anticipation of food. Pavlov considered this salivary reflex to be a "psychic reflex" because of its anticipatory components.

In his 1910 book, *The Work of the Digestive Glands,* Pavlov substituted the term "conditioned reflex" for "psychic reflex" (Kimble, 1967). In this same book he stated his initial principles of conditioned reaction. Kimble (1967, p. 30) summarized these principles in the following manner:

1. The conditioned reflex based on food can be elicited only when the dog is hungry [drive, deprivation].[1] It is not the animal's desire which is essential, however, but the availability of a strong unconditioned reflex to *reinforce* the conditioned reaction [reinforcement].

2. Repeated elicitation of the conditioned reaction by the presentation of food led to the disappearance of the conditioned response, especially if the presentations occurred in rapid succession [extinction].

3. This disappearance was not caused by fatigue, because allowing the animal to eat restored the reflex [spontaneous recovery].

4. Moreover, the inhibition of one conditioned reflex did not necessarily arrest all conditioned reflexes. The inhibition of a reflex conditioned to food has little or no effect on the strength of a reflex conditioned to acid [specificity of reinforcement, discrimination].

5. In addition to these "natural" reflexes in which the conditioned stimulus was the sight of the unconditioned stimulus, it was possible to form conditioned responses to neutral stimuli such as a tone presented simultaneously with food ["true" conditioning, secondary reinforcement, stimulus substitution].

6. Sometimes the elicitation of a strong reflex led to the inhibition of a relatively weak one. For example, a response conditioned to the sight of bread might be completely obliterated by the presence of another dog in the laboratory room [interference].

As one can see quite lucidly, Pavlov sowed the initial seeds that later germinated into some of the major constructs of reinforcement theory. Pavlov, like Thorndike, revised and supplemented his theory in many of his later works, but his early thinking and research still stand up as a revered ancestor of current reinforcement theory.

Although Pavlov's classical conditioning model was the most pervasive influence in American learning psychology in the early 1900s, the work and thought of his younger Russian contemporary, Bechterev, were more specifically psychological (Kimble, 1961). Bechterev (1908) was concerned with the establishment of an "objective" as opposed to an "introspectionist" psychology, and to this end, the subject matter of his research was the overt, observable behavior of men and animals. Bechterev, like Thorndike, was interested in the practical application of his findings to a wide variety of fields extending from psychiatry to social psychology. Bechterev's most-unique contributions to reinforcement theory were his experiments on the *instrumentality* of behavior. These included his ingenious paradigms of avoidance and escape learning, in which the organism's reinforcement was his escape from or avoidance of punishment (Bechterev, 1932). To assign Bechterev a "first" in the establishment of instrumental conditioning would indeed be a mistake.

[1] Bracketed comments are the authors'.

Thorndike's early work with cats in puzzle boxes definitely predates that of his Russian contemporary. However, Bechterev's clear and systematic statements on the methods of measuring the associative (conditioned) reflex make his early instrumentalism singularly important in the history of reinforcement theory.

With the establishment of Thorndike's connectionism, Pavlov's physiological orientation, and Bechterev's objectivism, the groundwork was laid for the birth of American behaviorism. At the time of the foundation of behaviorism in American psychology, it was literally a science in search of a method. The analysis of consciousness by introspectionist techniques had become stale and unproductive. John B. Watson (1913), virtually reiterating the statements of Bechterev, wrote that the time was ripe for the establishment of an objective psychology. He vehemently criticized subjective methods as nongeneralizable and thus unscientific. In his search for a scientific methodology Watson went as far as to attempt a refutation of Thorndike's effect principle and to attribute learning phenomena to the mere habitual occurrence of S-R connections (Watson, 1914). Watson later saw reinforcement as that which serves to maintain behavior *learned* by a mere contiguous relationship between stimulus and response and continued exercise of that relationship by the organism.

According to Hilgard (1956), Watson was concerned with eliminating the residual subjectivity of such concepts as "satisfiers" and "annoyers." In addition to capitalizing upon Thorndike's law of exercise, Watson also emulated both the physiological approach of Pavlov and the concern with objectivity that Bechterev voiced. Thus, American behaviorism was born through the coalescence of the three aforementioned basic approaches to conditioning and reinforcement. Watson (1919) seized upon the conditioned reflex as *the* paradigm and prototype of all learning. Since his concern for objectivity was paramount, his units of measurement were generally muscular movements, glandular secretions, and the responses which ensue from them (Hilgard, 1956). Although he did maintain that there was organismic intervention between stimulus and response, he saw these intervening events as miniature, covert, stimulus-response connections. Furthermore, Watson maintained that eventually as more-refined measurement procedures were devised, these internal intervening states would be directly observable and measureable (for example, movement of tongue during thinking) (Hilgard, 1956).

Although Watson's brand of behaviorism was not earthshaking in its originality, it echoed the tenor of the times in American psychology after its unsuccessful introspectionist era. As such, it provided the impetus for the development of various approaches to the study of the functional aspects of behavior, especially learning and reinforcement.

Four major theoretical positions grew out of Watson's "behavioristic revolution." These four positions are represented by the theories of Tolman, Guthrie, Hull, and Skinner. Both Tolman's (1932) and Guthrie's (1935) theories were essentially nonreinforcement approaches to learning. Tolman saw reinforcement as facilitating performance and not learning. He demonstrated this point in his latent learning experiments (Tolman & Honzik, 1930). The mere exposure of a rat to a stimulus configuration led to its learning the elements of that configuration; the introduction of reinforcement activated this learning into the performance of a specified task. Tolman's theory has been referred to as an S-S theory because he conceived of learning as occurring with the organism's integration of environmentally contiguous stimuli (signs). In addition to serving as a devil's advocate to conventional reinforcement theories, Tolman's theory has served as a precedent for the formulation of current cognitive theory.

Guthrie viewed reinforcement similarly to Watson. He saw it as maintaining behaviors learned under the contiguous association of stimulus and response. Furthermore, Guthrie's position was that learning fully occurs on the basis of one-trial contiguous association. In complex behavior, such as social behavior, Guthrie postulated that each simple contiguous association within the complex net is learned in a single trial, and thus the illusion of incremental learning is created by considering only the beginning and final elements (S-R) of complex sequences.

Although the theories of both Guthrie and Tolman yielded much research and controversy in the area of learning theory during the thirties, forties, and fifties, they exist today only in their amalgamation into two general reinforcement approaches. Most contemporary approaches to the problems of learning and reinforcement may be classified as belonging to one or the other of these two general approaches. The first of these is the operant orientation articulated by B. F. Skinner. The second, the mediational orientation, was first extensively outlined by Clark Hull and subsequently revised by Spence, Miller, Mowrer, and their students.

Skinner's orientation is fundamentally based on the direct observation of the frequency of a designated behavior as a function of the reinforcement which is a consequence of that behavior. He deemphasized the teleological basis for increases and decreases in a given behavior by deemphasizing the role of unobservable, "internal" processes. Hull and the mediationists, on the other hand, constructed an elaborate system of postulates and theorems to explain the organism's internal states that lead to variations in the quality or quantity of respondent or operant behavior.

These two current viewpoints will not be elaborated upon here. Instead, they will be linked to our discussions of constructs and reinforcement applications to social phenomena to be presented in the subsequent sections of this chapter.

TERMS AND CONSTRUCTS

The following discussion of reinforcement constructs is directed at providing the reader with an understanding of contemporary conceptions of some basic principles of learning. We do not pretend to cover all the terms that are in any way relevant to reinforcement theory. Rather, we hope to acquaint the uninitiated reader with those terms that provide an adequate basis for our discussion of the social reinforcement theories presented in Chapters 3 and 4.

Stimulus and Response

Kimble (1961) defines a *stimulus* as an external or internal event that occasions an alteration in the behavior of the organism. The alteration in the behavior of the organism is termed a *response*. The stimulus and response taken together constitute the basic bond of all learning, the reflex.

Advocates of a Skinnerian approach to learning would essentially agree with Kimble's definition of a stimulus with one qualification. This qualification is that whether the event referred to as a stimulus be internal or external, it must in all cases be physical or material. Furthermore, they would maintain that for a stimulus to be relevant to the scientist it must be observable and manipulable. Thus, although Skinnerians might concede that "internal" stimuli exist, they usually do not view them as appropriate to the analysis of behavior.

Keller and Schoenfeld (1950), representing the Skinnerian point of view, see stimuli as serving three functions:

1. *Elicitation:* an eliciting stimulus is a part or change in a part of the environment which elicits a specified (almost built-in) response, generally referred to as an unconditioned response. An example of an eliciting stimulus might be the sight of food; an example of the response it elicits might be salivation.

2. *Discrimination:* a discriminative stimulus is one that does not elicit the conditioned response directly but sets the occasion for its occurrence. When present, a discriminative stimulus signals the organism to respond to the eliciting stimulus.

3. *Reinforcement:* reinforcing stimuli are those stimuli that occur as a positive or negative consequence of a response. Thus, food might serve as a reinforcing stimulus when it is administered to a deprived animal after it performs a designated response.

For the Skinnerian, a response cannot be logically separated from its eliciting stimulus and can simply be defined as an alteration in the behavior of the organism that occurs as a function of the eliciting stimulus being presented.

The mediationist would concur with Keller and Schoenfeld's aforementioned three functions of stimuli; however, because their definition of stimuli is a much broader one, they would tend to attribute additional functions to stimuli. For them, stimuli can be external or internal, environmental, physiological or conceptual. In this context mediationists tend to bifurcate stimuli and responses into external (S, R) and internal (s, r). The internal (physiological and conceptual) stimuli and responses are the essense of mediation. Whereas a Skinnerian might abide by a strict S-R paradigm, the mediationist would probably subscribe to an S-r-s-R paradigm. The first paradigm goes no further than stating that an external environmental object or change results in a given response. The second (mediational) paradigm would hold that an external environmental object or change results in an implicit response (r) to that change, and this r then gives off implicit cues (s) that mediate the resulting external response or environmental alteration. These internal r's may be manifold. They can be drives, concepts, physiological secretions, and the like. All these r's, however, in some way alter the internal state of the organism and as such produce new but internal stimuli (s) which then lead to external responding.

In the discussion above of mediational and nonmediational views of stimuli and responses, the differences in orientation between these two reinforcement approaches become apparent. These differences as well as some relevant similarities will be emphasized in our discussion of other relevant behavioral concepts.

Drive

The first postulate in Hull's (1952) system proposes an underlying biological source for the activation of behavior sequences. Hull maintained that the need of organisms for certain specified goals (for example, food, water, sexual contact) is unlearned and based upon metabolic processes within the organism. Experimentally, one may elicit goal-oriented movement by manipulating the external conditions which serve to activate the underlying need structure. Depending upon the strength of the underlying drive energy, the experimenter may condition the organism to perform various simple and complex tasks to reach its desired goal. The speed, strength, and frequency of the performance of the specified task are utilized as indicators of the strength of drive. Correspondingly, the strength of drive can be manipulated by varying the time and/or amount of deprivation or stimulation. In the Hullian or mediational system, then, drive is a force within the organism that, when it reaches an optimum strength, activates behavior in the direction of reinforcement and hence reduction in the drive. According to the mediationists, drive is a variable which intervenes between various antecedent and consequent conditions. It differs from *need* in that need is the underlying *biological state* of the organism (and thus one of the antecedent conditions), and drive is an energizing principle which directs the organism to the alteration of that need state. Although the strength of drive often corresponds to the underlying need state, this is not always hypothesized to be the case. For example, with extreme amounts of water deprivation the animal approaches death; hence his level of available energy drops and this drop leads to a decrement in drive, but physiological *need* for water remains maximal.

Dollard and Miller (1950) have a view of drive very similar to Hull's. They define drives as strong stimuli that impel action. In their analysis, the strong stimulus is the antecedent condition, the impulse to action (drive) is the intervening condition and the action and ensuing reinforcement (reduction in drive) the consequent conditions. Dollard and Miller maintain that *any* stimulus, when increased in strength, may result in a drive. However, they divide drive into two basic kinds: (1) primary, or innate, drives and (2) secondary, or learned, drives. They note that although any stimulus may become strong enough to act as a drive, *primary, or innate, drives* are special classes of stimuli that are the primary basis for motivation. Examples of these primary drives are hunger, pain, thirst, and sex. The strength of these drives varies with the intensity of deprivation or exposure (in the case of drives to avoid a given noxious stimulus). According to Dollard and Miller, *secondary drives* are derived from socially inhibited primary drives. Examples of secondary drives are drives toward monetary rewards, verbal rewards, specific food objects, etc. These socially learned secondary drives do not directly result from concomitant biological needs but nevertheless play the same role as primary drives in impelling the organism to act in a way to reduce the strength of the drive. Furthermore, secondary drives often become socially acceptable alternatives to tabooed primary drives, and as such they serve to reduce the strength of the inhibited primary drive by mere association.

Mowrer, Spence, Osgood, and other noted mediational theorists have views of drives that do not differ essentially in orientation from Hull's and Dollard and Miller's. In summary, then, the mediationists see drive as having energizing and directive functions. It is biologically based and, depending on its strength, impels the organism to move toward drive-reducing reinforcement. Drive is something within the organism that is experimentally manipulated from without by deprivation or noxious exposure. Furthermore, secondary, or learned, drives can become impulses toward action through their association with primary biologically based drives. Almost all social motivation is attributed to secondary drives.

Keller and Schoenfeld (1950), as spokesmen for the Skinnerian approach, consistently note that drive is a term (not a state) that can be used to describe the animal's strength of response after certain experimental operations (deprivation or stimulation). The most-meaningful differences between the Skinnerian and mediational definitions of drives can be extracted from Keller and Schoenfeld's statements of what a drive is not. They note the following points:

1. A drive is not a stimulus. They feel that drives have neither the status nor functions of stimuli. "It is not a part or change in a part of the environment; it is not, in itself either eliciting, reinforcing or discriminative; and it is not correlated with a single response to give us our behavioral unit, a reflex" (p. 276). They maintain that equating a drive with a stimulus is confusing the effect of the stimulus with the stimulus itself.

2. A drive is not a response. Although a drive is established by the operations of deprivation and stimulation, it is not in any sense a response to these operations, for it does not follow the same course of strengthening or weakening that a response like bar pressing might.

3. A drive is not a physiological concept. Keller and Schoenfeld maintain that drive-directed behavior can be observed and defined without referring to underlying physiological states which impel the organism to act. For them, the operations used to establish drive define it, and the response which ensues defines its strength. They feel that the most-glaring disadvantage of treating drive as a physiological state is the tendency it fosters of assuming that something physiological intervenes between the establishing operation and the reflex changes (response).

4. A drive is not pleasure directed:

Hedonic philosophies do not stick close to the facts of behavior in ascribing an objective existence to pleasure, and stressing the procurement of pleasure *per se* as a motive or the purpose of all motives. We do not deprive an organism of pleasure, but of food; we do not reduce hunger with pleasure, but with food, and the purpose of the organism is irrelevant to either deprivation or satiation (p. 278).

In the statement above, Keller and Schoenfeld indicate that the result of food reward is not food reward itself. Furthermore, since one cannot specify what changes go on within the animal because it has been food-rewarded for a given response, then theorizing about these results is both a blind and unscientific practice.

In summary, the Skinnerians conceive of drive merely as a term to express the relationship between some antecedent operations of the experimenter (deprivation or overstimulation) and the strength of the organism's resulting response. On the basis of this conception of drive, Skinnerians have uniformly held that a separate category for secondary or social drives is irrelevant. They feel that some "drives" which have been labeled as social are not specifiable as drives at all (for example, mastery) because the establishing operations cannot be specified. Those "secondary" or "social" drives for which establishing operations can be specified are in no way different from "primary" drives to the Skinnerian.

Response Strength

Measures of the strength or vigor of responses are as plentiful as the universe of possible responses. General categories of measures that have been frequently used as indicators of strength of response include (1) rate or latency measures, (2) measures of magnitude, and (3) probability measures (Hall, 1966). These measures are generally found to vary as a function of (1) the antecedent conditions (amount of deprivation or stimulation, stimulus-presentation variables, etc.) and (2) former practice with the response under conditions of reinforcement. As with drive, there is overall agreement between mediational and nonmediational theorists on the operations necessary to increase the strength of response and on appropriate measures of response strength. Furthermore, there is general agreement that the antecedent operations and the ensuing strength of response when evaluated conjointly serve as indicators of drive. For example, if twenty-four hours of water deprivation leads an animal to respond more vigorously to a stimulus configuration than two hours of deprivation, the interpretation would be made that increased deprivation established heightened drive. The strength of the ensuing response indicates the success of this establishing operation. This is a first-order interpretation from the data and, as such, would be accepted by mediationists and nonmediationists alike.

Mediationists, however, would tend to go beyond the observable data and make second- and third-order interpretations. Thus, a complete discussion of response strength would necessitate a discussion of concepts such as "habit strength," "reaction potential," and "incentive motivation." One of Hull's (1952) basic postulates stated that an organism's tendency to react to a stimulus is a function of the multiplicative relationship between strength of habit and strength of drive (Hull, 1952). Operationally, habit strength (associative strength) increases through the continued pairing of a stimulus with a reinforced response. Nevertheless, habit strength, like drive, is postulated to be a phenomenon internal to the organism. In Hull's theory, then, the probability that a response will occur is dependent upon the interaction of two inferred states of the organism (habit and drive).

Although specific explanatory concepts such as "habit strength" are not as crucial to the mediationist approach now as they were in the mid-1950s, the mediational orientation remains basically the same. That is, to explain constructs and measures such as drive and response strength, reference must be made to the internal processes (physiologic or "psychic") of the organism. The organism is at all times seen as a participant in his own learning, and if, for example, its response is significantly stronger on trial 2 than on trial 1, the assumption is made that as a function of experiencing trial 1, the organism has undergone some qualitative or quantitative internal change prior to trial 2.

Nonmediationists resist this teleological orientation and stick close to their operations in defining measures such as response strength and response probability. For them, the probability that a response will occur is a function of the number of times it has occurred in the past under conditions of reinforcement. The strength of a response in terms of rate, latency, or magnitude measures is considered by Skinnerians to vary as a function of the antecedent establishing operations and not the underlying propensities of the organism.

Generalization

The discovery of the principle of stimulus generalization has generally been attributed to Pavlov (Keller & Schoenfeld, 1950; Hilgard, 1956; Hall, 1966). In brief, generalization is that process whereby a novel stimulus evokes a response which had been previously learned to a separate but similar stimulus. Generalization is an important explanatory concept in learning theory because it makes plausible the proposition that all behavior can be defined and modified on the basis of learning principles. If each S-R bond were to be learned discretely, then it would be illogical to attribute the acquisition of complex repertoires to learning. The rapidity with which a child acquires linguistic responses is a case in point. If each word and each structure in language were learned through single S-R connections, it would take an infinite amount of time to learn language and its usage. The child accomplishes the bulk of language learning in three years (age three to five years). Thus, if the learning theorist is to propose an explanation for the child's rapid language growth, he needs an economizing construct such as generalization as an explanatory base.

There have been many experimental demonstrations of stimulus generalization with many species (Watson & Rayner, 1920; Anrep, 1923; Bass & Hull,

1934; Hovland, 1937; Guttman & Kalish, 1956; Perkins & Weyant, 1958; Thomas & Lopez, 1962; McAllister & McAllister, 1963). These studies have shown that generalization is a replicable phenomena with human and animal subjects using verbal, visual, or tactile stimuli and either classical or instrumental paradigms.

According to Hall (1966), a number of points of view have been taken in interpreting stimulus generalization. He notes that the least-controversial point of view is the one taken by Brown, Bilodeau, and Baron (1951). They discuss generalization simply as an empirical phenomenon that is manifested by a transfer of training situation. Thus, a learned response to stimulus A will transfer to a previously neutral stimulus B under certain conditions (for example, similarity of the stimuli, instructional set).

Lashley and Wade (1946) proposed that generalization results from the organism's failure to discriminate between stimuli. Thus, they see generalization not as a process but as the failure of a process (discrimination). Hull, on the other hand, took the position that generalization is an organismic *process* in which the learning of a given response takes place to a "zone" of stimuli. Those stimuli closest to the one (S_1) to which the response (R_1) was conditioned have the strongest tendency to also evoke R_1. Those stimuli outside of the zone cannot evoke R_1. This concept of "stimulus zone" has been more frequently referred to as a *generalization gradient*. Simply stated, a gradient of generalization is based on the similarities in the cue properties of stimuli; the less similar the cue pattern, the less the generalization (Miller & Dollard, 1941). Both Hull (1943) and Miller and Dollard (1941), proceeding from a Darwinian framework, imply that stimulus generalization is functional to the survival of the organism and thus is dependent on *innate* organismic processes. Furthermore, Hullians dispute Lashley and Wade's proposition that generalization is merely the failure to make discriminations. The studies of Hovland (1937), Bass and Hull (1934), and Brown, Bilodeau, and Baron (1951) indicate that subjects can discriminate accurately between stimuli toward which they have shown a generalized response. Razran (1949) amalgamated the positions of the Hullians and Lashley and Wade by proposing a two-process theory of generalization. The first of these processes was referred to as a pseudogeneralization, or, simply, apparent generalization, due to the failure to discriminate. The second process Razran termed "true generalization" or the organism's capacity to engage in the active process of generalizing stimuli.

The Skinnerian view of stimulus generalization is much like that of the Hullians, namely, that generalization is a functional and adaptive process that can be defined by the response characteristics of the organism. The Skinnerians construe generalization as the basis for consistency in human behavior and, in doing so, come close to agreeing with the Hullian conception of generalization as the organism's innate capacity to economize and organize his perceptions. Keller and Schoenfeld (1950, p. 116) defined generalization as "an increase or decrease in the strength of one reflex, through reinforcement or extinction, is accompanied by a similar but smaller increase or decrease in the strength of other reflexes that have stimulus properties in common with the first." They, like the mediationists, define "common stimulus properties" in terms of the similarity and contiguity of the cue components of two or more stimuli.

The question arises whether stimulus generalization can occur with two or more stimuli that do not have common stimulus properties. This question is particularly relevant to verbal and social stimuli where the *physical* cue properties of objects similar on other than physical dimensions are very dissimilar. For example, the words *love* and *affection* have few common physical elements (for example, length of word, constellation of letters, common letters); nevertheless both verbally and socially, they often elicit similar responses. Words such as *love* and *affection* are similar predominantly with regard to meaning, and as such, a generalized response to both presupposes that "internal reference" is made to their meaning components. This concept of *mediated generalization* is a very important one with regard to verbal or social learning. Mediated generalization occurs to stimuli for which external physical properties differ, but which have meaning equivalence.

Discrimination

Keller and Schoenfeld (1950) have referred to generalization and discrimination as a "natural pair." Just as organisms learn to economize their behaviors by generalizing stimuli, they also learn to respond specifically to separate stimuli. Both processes are highly functional and adaptive for the organism. For both mediationist (Miller & Dollard, 1941) and nonmediationist (Keller & Schoenfeld, 1950) discrimination is established when a previously generalized response is rewarded in the presence of one cue (stimulus) and not rewarded in the presence of a second cue (previously generalized). In this case, the formerly generalized response will become specific to the cue situation that leads to reward and drops out to the cue situation that does not. Thus, if finger withdrawal is conditioned to a tone of 1,000 cycles per second and generalizes under conditions of reinforcement to a zone of stimuli ranging from 750 to 1,250 cycles per second, then discrimination between the 750- and 1,250-cycles-per-second tones can be established by reinforcing finger withdrawal to the 1,250-cycles-per-second tone. In this example, the 1,250-cycles-per-second tone would be referred to as the *discriminative stimulus,* or the stimulus which sets the occasion for reinforcement. Discrimination becomes increasingly difficult as stimuli become increasingly similar.

In the arena of everyday living, stimuli can seldom be specified as altogether discriminative or altogether generalized. In this sense the dual learning processes of discrimination and generalization occur in complex nets as a function of social context variables. For example, a child may generalize the "stimuli" mother and aunt as females, or perhaps as look-alikes. His response to both of them as females might be generalized; however, the commands of his aunt and mother will probably be discriminated and his response to each specific in its nature, latency, magnitude, and other attributes.

Varieties of Reinforcement

As noted earlier in this chapter, contemporary conceptions of reinforcement can be readily traced to Thorndike's law of effect. Theorists subsequent to Thorndike became concerned with the surplus meaning of concepts such as "satisfiers" and "annoyers," and thus the literature is replete with definitions and redefinitions of reinforcement. Nevertheless, with the exception of the nonreinforcement explanations of learning, Thorndike's description of the manner in which reinforcement functions to maintain behavior has not been substantially contested. The centrality of reinforcement to learning theory is exemplified by the inability of the present authors to discuss the principles of drive, response strength, generalization, and discrimination without making reference to the reinforcement process.

Skinnerians provide the simplest definition of reinforcement, so simple in fact that it has often been referred to as a tautology. They define *positive* reinforcers as those stimuli that serve to strengthen responses when presented (for example, food strengthens bar pressing) and *negative* reinforcers, as those stimuli which strengthen responses when removed (for example, the withdrawal of shock strengthens avoidance responses) (Keller & Schoenfeld, 1950). The mediationists concur with this definition of reinforcers, but they go on to explain the whys and wherefores of the response strengthening process and thus embellish reinforcement with additional meaning. Hull (1952) theorized that reinforcement serves to strengthen responses *because* it reduces drive, satisfies need, and builds up habit tendencies. Thus, according to the mediationist, at the same time that reinforcement is resulting in observable changes in the external responses of the organism, it also functions to enforce unobservable changes in the internal states and expectations of that organism. These internal alterations function to strengthen, weaken, or eliminate the observable occurrence of the specified response on subsequent learning trials. Despite orientation or explanation, reinforcement is seen as that consequence of a response that serves to strengthen and maintain its bond to the eliciting stimulus and to increase the probability of future response occurrence.

Reinforcement may take many forms varying from objects necessary for physiological survival (for example, food and water) to elements of social interaction (for example, approving nod or word). The efficacy of physical reinforcements, such as food and water, can be controlled for and predicted from the antecedent manipulations of the experimenter, such as deprivation or overexposure. In most cases, the efficacy of social reinforcements is not under the direct control of the "manipulator" but is said to be dependent upon some vague concept such as the past social reinforcement history of the organism. Thus, a distinction can be made between reinforcement that is effective because of *controlled* antecedent conditions and reinforcement for which effectiveness is the result of *uncontrolled* antecedent conditions. It might be said that the more social a reinforcer, the less prone it is to antecedent experimental control. Dollard and Miller would probably state (1) that all uncontrolled reinforcement antecedents were established through their former association with controlled antecedents and (2) that most uncontrolled reinforcement antecedents result from secondary rather than primary drive states.

The effectiveness of reinforcement also varies as a function of the schedule of its administration. A frequently replicated finding has been that *partial reinforcement* (reinforcement which does not occur on every trial) leads to slower learning but stronger retention of a response than *total reinforcement* (Jenkins & Stanley, 1950; Grant & Schipper, 1952; Goss, Morgan, & Golin, 1959). Since very few responses receive 100 percent reinforcement in the socioenvironmental situation, most social learning occurs on a partial reinforcement schedule. This factor is extremely relevant to the observed strong resistance to change of attitudes, values, norms, and the like.

Ferster and Skinner (1957) have articulated four kinds of partial reinforcement schedules for experimental free-response learning situations:

1. *Fixed interval:* reinforcement is administered at some fixed period of time after a previous reinforcement. Thus, an organism on a 60-second fixed-interval schedule will receive reinforcement for the first response that occurs 60 seconds or more after the previously reinforced response.

2. *Variable interval:* reinforcement is administered at some variable period of time after a previous reinforcement. Thus, an organism on a 60-second variable interval schedule will receive reinforcement for the first response which follows a randomly selected time interval—the average time of the intervals being 60 seconds.

3. *Fixed ratio:* reinforcement is provided after every n^{th} response. Thus, an organism might receive reinforcement on every tenth response, every twentieth response, etc. . . . in a fixed fashion.

4. *Variable ratio:* reinforcement is provided on an *average* of every n^{th} response. Thus, an organism on a 15:1 variable-interval schedule might receive reinforcement after ten responses, then five responses, then twenty responses, then ten responses, etc., to an average of one reinforcement per fifteen responses.

All the above schedules have been used and comparatively tested in experimental situations. For the purposes of this presentation, however, it is sufficient to say that the effectiveness of any one of these schedules is situationally dependent. They are merely presented here as a display of variable methods of inducing partial reinforcement effects.

Before we leave this brief discussion of reinforcement, it should be noted that reinforcement has been divided on the basis of its *primary* versus its *secondary* nature. *Primary reinforcement* is reinforcement that has been specified by the experimenter as the organism's reward for performing a designated response. Its effectiveness may be and often is controlled by the antecedent operations of the experimenter (for example, deprivation). *Secondary reinforcement* can be defined as a stimulus that has not been previously rewarding but becomes so through its association with a primary reinforcer. Secondary reinforcement has been consistently found to maintain a learned behavior after the cessation of primary reinforcement. For example, if a rat is trained to pass through a runway to reach a white goal box where he is rewarded with a food pellet, then after the removal of food he will continue to run to a white goal box for a longer period of time and at a faster rate than he will to a black goal box. In this case, the color of the goal box becomes secondarily reinforcing through its association with the primary reinforcer and thus becomes able to elicit and maintain the designated response.

In summary then, reinforcement varies as to (1) its makeup (for example, physical versus social), (2) the schedule of its administration (for example, partial versus total), and (3) its primacy (primary versus secondary). Despite which variety or combination of varieties of reinforcement is used in any specific case, the range of functions and roles of reinforcement remain the same. Although there is controversy among theorists as to where in this range reinforcement rightfully belongs, at minimum reinforcement serves to maintain and strengthen the performance of an S-R connection, and at maximum it is the moving principle of all behavior.

Extinction

Extinction can be defined most simply as the progressive decrement in response tendency under conditions of nonreinforcement. Under continued conditions of extinction, a formerly learned response can drop out entirely. Complete extinction is generally not immediate but, depending upon the prior conditions of learning, will take several trials. The organism's *resistance to extinction* is often utilized as a measure of the strength of response (Miller & Dollard, 1941; Keller & Schoenfeld, 1950; Hall, 1966).

The extent of this resistance has been found to be a function of several factors:

1. The amount of prior reinforcement: "Most investigators have found that resistance to extinction is an increasing function of the amount of reward obtained during the acquisition of trials" (Hall, 1966, p. 263).

2. The strength of drive during extinction: where drive level is high during extinction (for example, an animal that has been deprived of food for a long period of time) and previous performance of the task led to the relevant reward, resistance to extinction will be stronger (Perin, 1942).

3. The amount of work (effort) involved in performing the conditioned response: responses requiring much effort to perform will show less resistance to extinction than those requiring less effort (Hall, 1966).

4. The schedule with which reinforcement was administered during the learning period: as has already been stated, partial reinforcement has generally been found to be more efficacious than total reinforcement in maintaining a learned response under conditions of nonreinforcement.

The resistance of humans to the extinction of previously learned responses is an important factor in social behavior. It has important implications for the individual's resistance to attitude change, the extinction of first impressions in person perception, and similar social phenomena. According to learning theorists (Miller & Dollard, 1941; Keller & Schoenfeld, 1950), resistance to extinction in the social situation should follow the same "laws" as resistance to extinction in the experimental-learning situation.

Several theoretical explanations have been invoked to explain the occurrence of extinction. The Skinnerians, as they customarily do, choose to define and explain the extinction process only in terms of their operations. Therefore, they propose that extinction occurs because positive reinforcement is removed and the organism's response becomes ineffective in the attainment of reward. Guthrie (1935) deviated somewhat further from the observable data in proposing an *interference* interpretation of extinction. He proposed that extinction occurs because when reward no longer follows the conditioned response, it leads to the organism's performance of extraneous responses that interfere with the recurrence of the conditioned response.

An *inhibition* interpretation of extinction was first proposed by Pavlov (1927) and later expanded by Hull (1943). The concept of inhibition deviates even further from the data base than interference and delves within the organism for an explanation of extinction. Pavlov saw extinction occurring because the singular presentation of the conditioned stimulus without reward leads to a central inhibitory state that prevents the conditioned response from occurring. Thus, he proposed a cortical basis for extinction. Hull, on the other hand, postulated a two-process theory of inhibition. He referred to the first process as *reactive inhibition* and the second as *conditioned inhibition*. Simply stated, reactive inhibition occurs as a negative reaction to having made a response (reinforced or not). A frequently cited reason for this negative reaction (negative drive state) has been fatigue. Conditioned inhibition occurs when enough reactive inhibition accumulates to produce a "drive to rest." When rest (cessation of responding) does occur, it serves as a reinforcer and drive reducer because reactive inhibition dissipates. Therefore, resting (nonresponding) becomes a conditioned response in its own right. In Hull's system, reactive inhibition and conditioned inhibition summate to produce the organism's total inhibitory potential. This total inhibitory potential will preclude the occurrence of the conditioned response when it exceeds the organism's reaction potential. Therefore, with the continued nonreinforcement of a previously acquired response, extinction occurs because inhibitory potential is bound to eventually exceed reaction potential.

Although there have been many studies attempting to test the relative viability of these different interpretations of extinction, the issue is still quite unresolved (Hall, 1966).

REINFORCEMENT THEORY AND SOCIAL PHENOMENA

Our foregoing discussion of the central constructs of reinforcement theory would have little relevance to the purpose of this text if it were left to stand alone. For that reason, this section will present two systematic and direct applications of reinforcement theory to a social psychological phenomenon— attitude formation and change. Two approaches are presented not because they are mutually exclusive and oppositional, but because of the unique orientation each provides in interpreting social behavior. As can be extracted from our previous discussion of reinforcement constructs, these two approaches are the operant, nonmediational approach and the mediational, intervening-variable approach. The proponents of both of these approaches believe that social behavior is merely a special case of general behavior and as such is definable in terms of the general laws of reinforcement theory.

The first reinforcement application that we will consider here is the operant approach to attitudes proposed by Daryl Bem (1964); the second, the mediational approach proposed by Leonard Doob (1947).

An Experimental Analysis of Beliefs and Attitudes

Bem begins the discussion of his operant approach to attitudes by paraphrasing a statement of Skinner (1957). He states that social interaction is made up of "that subset of human behaviors developed and maintained by members of the social community who are, in turn, specifically conditioned to mediate the consequences of those behaviors" (Bem, 1964, p. 1). Thus, Bem views social behavior as arising from the power of the social community to reinforce individual members and groups for emitting desired behaviors. He believes that there is no need to invoke novel concepts to explain and define the development of social behaviors. Thus, throughout his theory Bem uses the terminology and approach of B. F. Skinner. Before we proceed with an exposition of Bem's theory, it seems necessary to first consider four assumptions upon which it is based:

Assumption 1. Behavior, whether verbal, social, or otherwise, is assumed by Bem to be a datum in its own right. He does not see the need to invoke the explanation that overt behavior is merely a reflection of one's underlying attitude, belief, or internal state. What is necessary to identify concepts such as attitude and belief is a functional analysis of the relationship between the controlling environment and observable behavior. Thus, an attitude is evaluated in terms of the reinforcement contingencies that led to its formation and the environment that elicits its behavioral expression.

Assumption 2. Stimulus and response are the basic conceptual units to be used in the description of all behavioral phenomena, and these two concepts need be defined and measured only in physical terms. The stimulus or response unit that is chosen for analysis is up to the discretion of the investigator. In the analysis, the physical properties of stimuli are the independent variables (for example, presentation variations), and the responses and measures of their strength are the dependent variables.

Assumption 3. The principles of behavior (the functional relationship between stimuli and responses) are few in number. Complexity such as that apparent in social behavior arises only as a function of the variety of environmental conditions within which these principles are operative. Thus, the analysis is inductive, and complex behaviors are induced from simpler functional relationships.

Assumption 4. The analysis must shy away from any allusion to the internal physiological or conceptual states of the organism at the time behavior is occurring.

Proceeding from these assumptions, Bem presents his social applications of the Skinnerian approach in three sections: (1) the functional relationships between stimuli and responses in the classification of social behaviors, (2) sources of control of attitudes and beliefs in "others" in the social community, and (3) the controlling variables in attitudes and beliefs in oneself. Wherever possible, we will attempt to link Bem's discussion to our previous discussion of basic reinforcement principles.

FUNCTIONAL RELATIONSHIPS   For Bem, social interactions are a subset of a larger class of behaviors which Skinner has called *operants.* Skinner has defined an operant as a response that operates upon the environment to produce satisfaction of basic needs and thereby reinforce the organism. More simply, an operant is a voluntary response of the organism that is directed toward reinforcement. Bem conceives of an operant as a member of a three-term relation involving discriminative stimulus, operant response, and reinforcing stimulus. On the basis of these considerations, Bem arrived at two functional relationships that social operants bear to stimuli.

The first of these relationships is that of *reinforcement control.* Reinforcement control occurs when a stimulus that is presented as a consequence to an operant response is rewarding to the responder. Under this condition, the reinforcing stimulus gains the capacity to *control* or govern the recurrence and strength of the operant response. In the case of reinforcement control, the reinforcing stimulus is always *specifically* indicated by the response itself. For example, the verbal operant, "I want a piece of cake," demands the presentation of a particular reinforcing stimulus—cake. This type of verbal operant is referred to as a *mand,* for it is a de*mand* or com*mand* for a specific reinforcing stimulus (Bem, 1964). In social interaction, mands are enforced as part of an individual's repertoire by the social community's continued reinforcement of that mand with a specific stimulus.

The second functional relationship that Bem cites is that of *discriminative control.* When an operant response is nearly always reinforced in the presence of a given stimulus and almost never in its absence, that stimulus functions to enforce discriminative control over operants and is referred to as a discriminative stimulus. For example, if a rat receives food for pressing a Skinner box bar only when a light is on, his bar-pressing responsiveness will drop to zero when the light is off. In this case, the light (discriminative stimulus) sets the occasion for the emission of the operant response (bar pressing) and in this way *controls* the occurrence of that response. Bem, following Skinner, refers to a social operant that is under discriminative control and only generalized (nonspecific) reinforcement control as a *tact.* A unique property of tacts is that they come under sharper discriminative control as a function of their continued pairing with any number of reinforcing stimuli. Bem offers the example of the child's learning of the concept "daddy" through increasing discriminative control. At first, the child will emit the response "daddy" in the presence of many adult males, but eventually he will learn to emit "daddy" only in the presence of his father. This learning is accomplished through the continued pairing of his father with the many reinforcers that only he can administer to his child. Thus, a tact is an operant that has been reinforced with several reinforcers but only in the presence of a specific discriminative stimulus. Not all operants are clearly distinguishable into mand and tact categories, but as we will see later, the individual's capacity to discriminate between mands and tacts is the essence of social behavior for the Skinnerian.

With the functional relationships of reinforcement and discriminative control and the processes of manding and tacting clearly in mind, let us move on to definitions of beliefs and attitudes. According to Bem, operants that can be referred to as tacts will in time lead an observer to express his "belief" about the discriminative stimuli. For example, if person X puts on his coat and hat, it can serve as a discriminative stimulus for X's departure. The observer might then state, "I believe X is going outside." The strength of the observer's belief is a function of the number and definiteness of tacts under the same discriminative control. Therefore, if X puts on his hat and coat, shakes hands with the host, thanks the host for a pleasant evening, waves good-by to the other guests, and says, "I am going now," the strength of the observer's belief that X is leaving will be great.

Thus, Bem defines *belief* as ". . . a set of operants which an observer (possibly the individual himself) discriminates as under the control of a common class of discriminative stimuli" (Bem, 1964, p. 13). From this perspective, then, one need not posit an underlying and "internal" controlling factor in a belief, for beliefs are under the control of directly observable discriminative stimuli.

Attitudes are a subset of beliefs that acts as tacts of the *reinforcing effects* of a discriminative stimulus upon an individual. Thus the statement, "I hate spinach," is a tact in that spinach in word, presence, or thought serves as a discriminative stimulus for the response. However, this discriminative stimulus has negatively reinforcing effects and will be avoided. An attitude is therefore defined as ". . . a set of operants which an observer (possibly the individual himself) discriminates as under the control of the reinforcing effects of a particular class of stimuli on the individual's behavior" (Bem, 1964, p. 13).

Beliefs and Attitudes: Sources of Control in the Behavior of Others

For Bem, the most essential skill in social interaction is the individual's ability to make mand-tact discriminations in the behavior of others. His central thesis is that the amount of control that others exercise over an observer's beliefs is a function of the extent to which the behavior of these others has tact properties. If the behavior of others is seen as being under the control of specific reinforcement consequences, it becomes less credible and less objective. In other words, if change in one's beliefs becomes the specific reinforcing stimulus for another's manding behavior, that manding behavior should be theoretically ineffective. On the other hand, if another's message to an observer is itself a tact and is additionally accompanied by other tacts (for example, a doctor wearing a white coat and stethoscope and speaking about personal hygiene), that message will probably be effective in molding or changing the belief of the observer.

Bem notes that there are three sources of stimuli upon which mand-tact discrimination in the speaker-hearer relationship are based. These are (1) the mand-tact characteristics of the past behavior of the speaker or similar speakers, (2) the behavior of others who are discriminated as being capable of making mand-tact discriminations of the speaker, (3) the discrepancies and consistencies between the speaker's verbal behavior and the individual's own tacts of the environment.

Before proceeding to elaborate upon these three sources of stimuli, it should be emphasized that Bem does *not* see mand-tact discriminations as intervening processes that mediate between the speaker's verbal response and its resultant effect upon the hearer. Instead, Bem is quite explicit in defining mand-tact discriminations as overt behavior: "to discriminate one stimulus from another is to respond differentially to them" (p. 15).

Mand-tact characteristics in the past behavior of a speaker. The utilization of the past behavior of the speaker as a source of stimuli for making mand-tact discriminations of his present communication is defined by Bem in terms of "communicator credibility." Several studies (Hovland & Weiss, 1951; Hovland, Janis & Kelley, 1953; Kelman & Hovland, 1953) have shown that a persuasive message is more efficacious in changing attitude when the communicator is a very credible one than when his credibility is questionable. A speaker who has a reputation for tacting should be seen as credible, whereas a speaker who has a reputation for manding should be seen as less credible. In the Hovland and Weiss study, identical belief statements about atomic submarines were said to be made by J. Robert Oppenheimer (a communicator who tacts) and *Pravda* (a communicator who mands). As expected, the audience altered their own beliefs in the direction of the persuasive message to a greater extent with the tacting communicator than with the manding communicator. Thus, from a Skinnerian framework, the interpretation would be made that Oppenheimer's statements were under discriminative control (science, past experience with atomic subs, reasoned opinion), but *Pravda's* statements were under reinforcement control (they were made strictly to propagandize the hearer, and the hearer's belief change serves as the reinforcement for the "overt" written response of *Pravda*). In summary, then, the credibility of any communicator attempting to change the beliefs of an audience is a positive function of his past history of tacting.

Sources of stimuli for mand-tact discrimination in the behavior of others. When a hearer is not capable of discriminating the mand from the tact properties of a speaker's verbal behavior, he relies on the social group to help him make this discrimination. The ability of the group to guide (control) an individual's behavior and belief system is established through reinforcement and punishment contingencies. In this sense, the group which is serving as a reference point for any single mand-tact discrimination should be a relevant one; that is, one that has a prior history of reinforcing the individual for holding norms related to the mand-tact discriminative task at hand. For example, a drug company in presenting a given medication as a remedy for a particular malady might state that "three out of four doctors have found drug X to be effective in treating illness Y." In this example, the relevant group, doctors, has a past history of setting norms about medication that are based upon tacts and that have reinforcement value for the individual patient. According to Bem, the same holds true for other specialized social communities such as clubs and churches. When the social group selected as a reference point for the making of a difficult mand-tact discrimination is not relevant to that discrimination, it can still affect the beliefs of the individual. In this case the group's role is normative. An example of this might be the effect of the political beliefs of a nonpolitical local woman's club on one of its members.

Mand-tact sources of stimuli in the discrepancies and consistencies between the speaker's verbal behavior and the hearer's own tacts of the environment. The essence of the consistency between the speaker's and hearer's tacts that Bem postulates as necessary for successful persuasive communication is contained in the following statement:

> The techniques of persuasive communication may be usefully viewed as a set of techniques designed to confer tact properties upon belief statements emitted by the speaker. The individual, it is hoped, will then emit the same statements as tacts, and engage in other behaviors which would characteristically be under the same discriminative control as the tacts. To attain these ends, the speaker must build up the tact properties of the desired terminal beliefs by beginning with tacts already in the individual's repertoire (Bem, 1964, p. 24).

Bem attributes the so-called boomerang effect (eliciting attitude change in the opposite direction of the speaker's appeal) of persuasive messages to the speaker's presentation of tacts that are totally inconsistent with the already existing tact properties in the individual's repertoire. In this case, the tacts emitted by the speaker serve as mands to the listener in that they appear to him to be under specific reinforcement control (the reinforcement being the hearer's radical belief change) rather than under discriminative control. Bem's consistency principle may be extended to apply to the findings on one-sided versus two-sided communications as well. In brief, it was found (Hovland, Lumsdaine, & Sheffield, 1949) that one-sided arguments were more effective than two-sided arguments in bringing about strong speaker-hearer agreement when the hearer's initial position agreed with the speaker's message. On the other hand, two-sided communications were more effective with individuals initially opposed to the speaker's position. Bem argued that in the first case the speaker's tacts were consistent with those of the agreed listeners and inconsistent with those of the opposed listeners. In the second case, the speaker verbalized the tacts already in the repertoire of the listener, and even though he advocates a position contrary to the listener's previous tacts, his arguments nevertheless appear to be under discriminative control.

The Skinnerian interpretation of consistency has been proposed by Bem as an alternative to cognitive dissonance interpretations of attitude formation and change (see Chapter 8).

Beliefs and Attitudes: Sources of Control in an Individual's Own Behavior

In this portion of his theory, Bem deals with the case in which the individual is both the speaker and the hearer, the observer and the observed. He states that the way in which the individual discriminates the sources of control in his own behavior is not functionally different from the way in which he discriminates the sources of control in the behavior of others. "The individual will be viewed, in other words, as a self-persuasive communicator of whom the listener, the individual himself, makes mand-tact discriminations" (p. 33). Bem views this self-persuasive process in two steps: self-awareness and self-persuasion.

SELF-AWARENESS   To the Skinnerian, self-awareness involves the individual's ability to discriminate the tact properties of his own behavior that serve as sources of control for himself and social others. This ability is acquired in three ways:

1.   The social community's *selective reinforcement* of the overt responses that accompany private (self-known "internal") events. For example, the child's emission of the overt responses of rubbing his eyes and yawning might be met with the mother's response, "I know you feel tired, but soon you will go to sleep." This sequence of events will establish the response, "I'm tired," in the child, and this response might then *generalize* to a whole host of private events (for example, legs feeling weak, drowsiness, crankiness, and similar responses). Thus the child becomes able both to discriminate those stimuli that occasion his tiredness and to make his "internal" state publicly known.

2.   Through the process of *stimulus generalization* private events may come to control overt responses that tact public events without explicit discrimination training. This event will occur because of the common properties in the private and public events. Here, Bem gives the example of perceiving oneself as having "butterflies in the stomach." The tacts of many emotional states originate in this process (for example, "I feel like I'm going to blow up" for anger). In short, this second process of self-awareness involves equating one's internal state with a known external event through metaphorical generalization of common properties.

3.   Many private discriminative stimuli come to serve as tacts through their association with parallel overt stimuli (contiguity) or through their formerly serving as overt discriminative stimuli. For example, thinking (private stimuli) is often associated with saying (overt stimuli) something to oneself.

Although Bem concedes that these three sources of self-awareness are somewhat inadequate, he attributes this inadequacy not to the behavioral analysis but to the fact the individual is often left unaware of the self-variables which do serve to control his response. Furthermore, Bem argues that several studies (for example, Schachter & Singer, 1962; Schachter & Wheeler, 1962) have demonstrated that the discriminative stimuli for one's attitude lie in his overt behavior, not in his internal state.

SELF-PERSUASION   Self-persuasion is seen as arising from self-awareness, or, in other words, from the discrimination between the mand-tact properties of one's own behavior. Therefore, Bem sees self-persuasion as being in no way a different process from persuasion by others. The only difference between self-persuasion and persuasion by others is the source of the emitted tacts. If an individual discriminates his own behavior as mand-controlled, he will be less likely to alter his attitudes or beliefs to fit that behavior than if he perceived it as being tact-controlled. Examples of this proposition are numerous. Studies have shown (1) that if one improvises an argument which goes against his initial opinion, he will alter his initial opinion in the direction of the argument more so than one who merely reads aloud arguments constructed by others (King & Janis, 1956); (2) that "winners" of a debate in which each participant advocated arguments contrary to their initial opinions were more prone than "losers" to change their beliefs in the direction of the arguments they pursued (Scott, 1959); (3) that subjects who performed a task contrary to their opinion for $20 changed their opinion less than subjects performing the same task for $1 (Festinger & Carlsmith, 1959).

In all the studies above, Bem concluded that subjects who merely read arguments, lost debates, and were paid exorbitantly to perform a "deception" task were under the control of the mand characteristics of the experiment and the experimenter's behavior. Thus, their own behavior was discriminated as a response to those mands. On the other hand, subjects who improvised, won debates, and performed a "deception" task for small rewards were under the control of the tacts in the experimental situation and hence saw themselves as emitting tacts. Therefore, attitude change as a response to one's own overt persuasive behavior, like attitude change in response to another's overt persuasive behavior, is a positive function of the number and strength of tact properties in the specified behavior.

The Behavior of Attitudes:
A Mediational Approach to the Study of Attitudes

Doob (1947), like Bem, maintains that social behavior is merely a complex form of behavior, and therefore those terms that are relevant to the description of general behavioral processes are also relevant to the description of social processes. Doob's application of a Hullian behavior theory to the study of attitudes is nowhere near as comprehensive as the Skinnerian approach of Bem. Nevertheless, its importance is underlined by the attempt it makes to rigorously define attitudes in terms of standard behavioral principles. Essentially, Doob's behavioral description of attitudes is little more than a microscopic analysis of a behavioral *definition* of an attitude.

He begins his analysis with the following rather lengthy definition of an attitude:

> An attitude is an implicit response which is both anticipatory and mediating in reference to patterns of overt responses, which is evoked by a variety of stimulus patterns as a result of previous learning or of gradients of generalization and discrimination, which is itself cue- and drive-producing, and which is considered socially significant in the individual's society (p. 136).

He then analyzes this definition into seven component parts, and with this analysis one can see clearly the mediational-learning approach to attitudes.

"An attitude is an implicit response." An attitude is one's implicit response to a stimulus pattern, which is recurrent with each presentation of that stimulus pattern. It must be an immediate response, and it may be conscious or "unconscious" and verbal or proprioceptive. The overt response that is an expression of the underlying (implicit) attitude is the result both of the attitude state and other tendencies within the individual (drive, habit).

It is *"anticipatory . . . in reference to patterns of overt responses."* An anticipatory response (antedating response) as defined by Hull is one that originally preceded a rewarded response. As a function of its temporal association with the rewarded response it occurs before its time in the sequence of responses in anticipation of the performance of the rewarded response. In the case where an attitude is the implicit response in question a sample paradigm is described by Doob as follows:

> If an individual, for example, dislikes a fruit or a person, he tends to avoid eating the fruit or meeting the person. Originally, the avoidance occurred only after actual contact has been established and after that contact had proven to be punishing and the withdrawal to be rewarding. When a thorough investigation reveals no actual prior contact, some process of *generalization* or *discrimination* must have occurred, since all behavior has antecedents . . . (p. 141).

In this example, the contact with either a person or a fruit is the final or "punished" response in the sequence. Through continued contact, the individual builds up a set to avoid making a response that will be punished. This "set" in time will move up in the behavior sequence and will tend to occur with the initial presentation of the actual or a similar stimulus pattern. Thus, the anticipatory set to approach or avoid an object is characteristic of an attitude. Like final responses in a behavior sequence, these anticipatory sets tend to generalize to a whole host of objects. Thus, if an individual forms a set to avoid apples, he may also form a set to avoid applesauce, apple pie, etc. Doob points out that responses that most closely precede the goal response are most likely to be learned and to antedate other responses not directly leading to the goal response. In the social sphere, one of these anticipatory responses is referred to as an attitude.

It is *"mediating in reference to patterns of overt responses."* Doob notes that although the anticipatory nature of attitudes reflects its temporal relation to a goal, its mediating attribute refers to its functional relationships to goals. Mediating responses serve the function of increasing the probability that positive reinforcement will follow a goal response. The mediating response is an implicit one that occurs after the presentation of the stimulus pattern and prior to the performance of an overt goal response. Attitudes can be easily evoked because they are "internal" or mediating responses and as such need not conflict with overt behavior. Thus, an individual can see his boss (stimulus pattern), experience feelings of dislike (mediating-attitude response), and then give him a pleasant "hello" (overt response). In this case, the attitude becomes a substitute for the appropriate goal response, for it would not be functional for the individual to make overt negative responses to his boss. This mediating response in its substitutive function also increases the probability that positive consequences will follow the overt goal response.

In those instances where the implicitly mediating response can be consonant with the subsequent goal response, it becomes facilitating to the attainment of positive reinforcement. Mediational reference, whether substitutive or facilitative, is often made to a pattern of overt responses rather than discrete overt responses. Thus, the positive attitudes that are involved in liking other people might result in different overt expressions of liking depending upon the object. Thus, one mediating response might be the same for a generic category of objects (for example, fruit in general). Once again, the basic difference between the anticipatory implicit response and the mediating implicit response is that the former prepares the organism for his interaction with a goal object, and the latter mediates the consequences of interaction with that object.

It is *"evoked by a variety of stimulus patterns."* The stimuli which elicit attitudes are various, they may be internal or external, cue produced or drive produced. According to Doob, the arousal or evocation of an attitude results from two broad psychological processes: perception and learning. Perception promotes responses of paying attention to a given stimulus pattern because of some previous familiarity with that pattern. Learning, on the other hand, defines the factors in the past history of the individual that led to this familiarity (for example, a bond between the stimuli and attitude). Thus, the individual perceives a given object (or state within himself), and this perceptual event leads to the evocation of one's habitual orientation toward that object. Once this orientation is determined, the overt response to the object can occur. Thus, an individual might perceive the object spinach (stimulus) that leads to anticipatory or mediating internal responses (attitude and orientation), and these internal responses then define the occurrence and mediate the consequences of the overt responses. Simply, then, perception of a stimulus pattern depends upon drive or set (which orients the individual's response) as well as upon the external stimulus configuration. The set to respond to an object or a class of objects often provokes or activates the implicit attitudinal response. Thus, two people holding similar attitudes toward a given object or class of objects might overtly respond differently because of differences in internal stimuli, such as drive level, at the moment of response. Thus, the effect of many stimuli (internal and external) upon the individual must be assessed before predictions can be made about the manner in which attitudes will anticipate or mediate overt responses.

It is "evoked . . . *as a result of previous learning or gradients of generalization and discrimination."* We have already noted that attitudes may be evoked by various stimuli; the question of why they are evoked at all is the subject of the fifth component of Doob's definition of an attitude. He states that there are at least three reasons why attitudes are evoked. The first of these is the previous learning of the individual. Thus, some stimuli might have become elicitors of attitudes through the simple process of conditioning. For example, if the taste of a given food object is negatively reinforcing to the individual, the type of package which contains that food may in time come to serve as a negative reinforcer. Thus, the individual might have a negative attitude toward cellophane wrappings or square boxes.

The second reason why attitudes are evoked is the process of generalization. As noted in our discussion of terms and constructs, Hull asserted that responses are conditioned to a "zone" of stimuli that consists of stimuli in varying degrees of similarity to the conditioned stimulus. Thus, attitudes toward a given object may be formed on the basis of this object's similarity to another object for which an attitude already exists. The less striking the similarity, the less probable it is that attitudinal generalization will occur. Similarity may occur on many dimensions. Where the similarity is physical, we can conceptualize it in terms of color, size, shape, intensity, or other physical attributes. Where similarity is based upon meaning, we have the process of mediated generalization. Here we can speak of a semantic gradient as differentiated from a physical gradient, but in either case generalization is a process that can fix one's attitudes toward a whole class of objects.

Lastly, attitudes may be evoked through the process of discrimination. This process is operative when one's attitude is directed toward a specific object rather than a class of objects (for example, a specific Republican rather than the general class of Republicans). Discrimination and generalization often go hand in hand in attitude formation. For example, both generalization and discrimination are involved if one holds a particular attitude toward certain "types" of Republicans but not other "types."

The strength of an attitude is partially attributable to the position of the attitude object on a particular generalization or discrimination gradient.

It is *"itself cue- and drive-producing."* An attitude is cue producing in that its evocation serves as a stimulus for another response (the overt one). Thus the evocation of a given attitude leads to the emission of cues that guide the ensuing response in an appropriate direction. As noted earlier in our discussion, the cues that an attitude gives off help the individual to anticipate the occurrence and consequences of his response. Attitudes are drive producing in that they set the occasion for and mediate rewards. In this role, an attitude once evoked can occasion the buildup of a drive to act in a particular way toward a particular object in order to gain reinforcement. Thus, if John sees Mike, his implicit response might be one of dislike. This "attitude" of not-liking may occasion an increment of drive energy to act on that dislike. If this drive energy directs John to strike out aggressively against Mike, John's behavior might then be self-reinforcing in that its occurrence reduces the intensity of the drive state. In a Hullian behavior system John's behavior could not be considered a function of drive alone, but it would also be seen as dependent upon his "habit strength" for aggression.

In this context it seems timely to note that an attitude can be altered or extinguished in several ways:

1.   By weakening its drive strength by making its consequent responses nondrive reducing. In other words, if one removes the reward associated with a goal response, the preceding implicit attitudinal response will also be weakened.

2.   By setting up stronger competing drives. For example, if nation A holds an attitude of dislike for nation B, but both nations later come to more strongly dislike nation C, nations A and B could probably band together against the more intensely disliked nation C, and thus the stronger competing drive will supersede the weaker one and perhaps lead to a diminution in the strength of the attitude which produced the initial drive.

3.   By diminishing the number of stimuli that can evoke the attitude through a process of continual discrimination.

4.   By punishing the overt behavior that an attitude mediates.

It is *considered socially significant in the individual's society."* Doob notes that the first six components of his definition of attitude could be well applied to many other psychological phenomena. "Psychologically, therefore, attitude is not and—it is deliberately maintained—should not be distinguished from the larger subclass of responses to which it appears to belong." Its only distinguishing characteristic should be its significance to functional properties of the individual's society. An attitude object and the many individual attitudes toward it become significant only within a social context. Thus, in an ancient sun-worshiping society one's attitude (both its direction and strength) toward the sun would be highly significant and relevant. In modern Western civilization one's view of the sun would infrequently be referred to as an attitude, except in specific instances, and would more likely be referred to as an opinion (for example, "the sun is hot today").

3 ‖ THEORIES OF SOCIAL LEARNING AND IMITATION

Two basic contexts within which learning occurs are the *physical* and the *social* context. The physical context simply refers to the material dimensions of the "field" of behavior. The social context moderating the learning process refers to the actual or implied presence and/or participation of "others" while learning is occurring. Social context variables have been shown to be operative with animals as well as with humans (Miller & Dollard, 1941). However, for the purposes of this presentation, we will predominantly concern ourselves with social context variables in human learning.

Social context factors in human learning are manifold, but most often they can be defined in terms of the roles of the social "others" in the learning situation and the relationship which these others bear to the learner. These social "others" vary in the degree to which they participate in the learning process of the learner. The most direct participation of another in an individual's acquisition of responses occurs in the didactic student-teacher relationship. The least-direct participation occurs in the situation in which the mere presence or implied presence of a nonparticipating other results in increments in learning and performance. Allport (1924) has referred to this latter process as *social facilitation*. Between these two extremes there are many degrees of social participation that define social context. In the following two chapters, we will concern ourselves predominantly with two broad cases of social context variation in human learning. These are (1) learning through the *observation* of the behavior and consequences of the behavior of others and (2) learning through the interdependent nature of rewards for the participants. This second contextual variation will be dealt with in the next chapter.

A sizable proportion of human learning occurs through the observation of the behavior of other humans. Despite the hackneyed admonition, "Do as I say, not as I do," individuals and particularly children tend to use the behavior of others as paradigms for their own behavior. This proposition has been demonstrated repeatedly in experimental situations. The classic experimental prototype of the observational learning situation involves two classes of people—the observer and the "behaver," or *model*. Generally, the model will behave in certain specified ways that do or do not lead to reward; the observer will then be placed in the same field of behavior as the model had been performing in, and measures of the degree of his *imitation* of the model will be taken. Two important variables in the observational learning process have been (1) the relationship that exists between the model and the observer and (2) the occurrence, amount, and quality of reinforcement that is contingent on the model's behavior. The former is generally dealt with in terms of *identification*. As this factor becomes more relevant, there is less need for direct reinforcing contingencies for imitation to occur.

Although there have been many hypotheses and paradigms of imitative behavior, only two appear to fit our criteria for theories. These two are the approaches of Miller and Dollard (1941) and of Bandura and Walters (1963). Although the major sections of this chapter will be devoted to these two theories, the less-extensive hypotheses of Mowrer (1960) and Skinner (1953, 1957) will also be dealt with in their relationship to these theories.

A THEORY OF SOCIAL LEARNING AND IMITATION

Miller and Dollard (1941) have articulated a Hullian-based theory of social learning and imitation. Their principal and basic assumption is that human behavior is learned; to comprehend its complexity "one must know the psychological principles involved in its learning and the social conditions under which this learning took place" (p. 1). Although they maintained that social learning could be explained by general-learning principles, particularly those principles stated by Hull, they nevertheless considerably modified the principles of Hullian-learning theory to arrive at their own theory of social learning.

Fundamentals of Learning

The four principles that Miller and Dollard saw as being fundamental to all learning, whether individually or socially based, are *drive, cue, response,* and *reward*. These principles were seen as interrelated by Miller and Dollard. Furthermore, in reading their description of these four factors, one is struck with their interchangeability. Thus, a drive may be a cue, and a cue may become a drive or a reward; a reward may become a cue, and a drive may itself be a response. This interchangeability should be kept in mind as the reader grapples with the definitions and operations of these constructs.

DRIVE   In Chapter 2, we briefly discussed Miller and Dollard's conception of drive. Here we will deal with it somewhat more extensively.

Drive is defined as any strong stimulus that impels the organism to act. Miller and Dollard viewed some stimuli when aroused as being consistently strong enough to be regarded as drives. These stimuli are those that are essential to the maintenance of the organism. They are *primary* and usually innately biological, and they constitute the primary basis for motivation. Primary drive stimuli include hunger pangs, fatigue, thirst, pain, and sexual needs. With humans in a civilized society, primary drives seldom reach the heights necessary to impel responding incontrovertibly. Miller and Dollard maintained that social organization tends to obscure the primacy of primary drives. They held that in Western society, only extreme and purportedly atypical cases of war, famine, and poverty tend to activate biologically based drives. Therefore, proceeding from their Hullian-based assumption that drives are a necessary precedent to responding and are the moving principle of behavior, they conceptualized a *secondary* category of drives that assumes the directive functions of socially obscured primary drives.

Although Miller and Dollard propose that secondary drives gain their strength through a contiguous association with primary drives, they implied that socially based acquisitions of drives are more dynamically predicated. They located the source of the evolvement of secondary drives in society's facilitation of the "sublimation" of primary needs in socially acceptable directions. When social conditions inhibit the expression of primary drives, secondary drives assume their function; and according to Miller and Dollard they become a façade behind which primary drives are hidden. Thus hunger (primary drive) may be channeled toward a specific food object (secondary drive stimulus) and sex (primary drive) toward a particular sexual object (secondary drive stimulus).

Acquired drives are identified as synonymous to social needs and thereby are rewarded and extinguished by the aspects of the social context within which they are operative. There is no one-to-one relationship between primary and social needs, but more often a social need has several underlying primary drives. For example, money and approval as objects of social needs can stem from several primary drives, such as hunger, pain, and sex.

Miller and Dollard maintained that without either primary or secondary drives there would be no occasion for overt behavior to occur. Therefore, since they observed imitation to be an empirical fact, they found it necessary to conceptualize a *drive to imitate* as its base. Here the assumption is made that as an aspect of socialization, matching the responses of others becomes a rewarded response in its own right. The more regular the reward, the more firmly established the drive to imitate becomes. Thus, in the case of imitation, (1) the behavior of another serves as a cue; (2) this cue leads to an internal response; (3) this internal response produces a drive to imitate whose strength is based upon previously rewarded imitation trials; (4) this drive to imitate activates imitative responding; (5) imitative responding leads to a reward that in turn leads to the reduction of drive and an increment in the probability that imitation will occur on succeeding trials. From this paradigm it becomes apparent that internal responses are cue produced, external responses are drive produced, increased probability of response is reward produced, and acquired drives are *response produced* (usually by internal responses). For Miller and Dollard, this holds not only for the operation of the drive to imitate but for the operation of all acquired drives.

Therefore, while the complex chain of relationships that transpire between drive, cue, response, and reward culminate in the occurrence of a given behavior, the direct precedent for the establishment of a secondary drive is the internal response (r). This conception of acquired drives presents a dilemma with regard to imitation. Since imitation is known to occur, and if its occurrence presupposes a drive to imitate and this drive to imitate is based upon an internal response, then for the *initial* occurrence of imitation to be explained it must be assumed that the internal response leading to the drive to imitate is in the repertoire of the subject before imitation ever takes place. Does this elevate the drive to imitate to a primary drive? Miller and Dollard never fully dealt with this problem. This same observation can be made concerning most acquired drives.

CUES   Cues determine when and where a response will occur and what response will be made. In Miller and Dollard's vocabulary, a cue is somewhat synonymous with the definition of discriminative stimulus presented in Chapter 2. The difference between cue stimuli and drive stimuli is a matter of strength and distinctiveness. Any stimulus may acquire drive value when it is made strong enough to impel the organism to act. Any stimulus may acquire cue value in terms of its distinctiveness from other stimuli. A cue is distinctive from another different cue in that it leads to a specific class of responses that occur in a specific locale and at a specific time. Thus, a low-intensity tone may be made to signal the occurrence of a response that is different from that signaled by a high-intensity tone. An extremely high-intensity tone may become a drive stimulus in that it impels the organism to respond in a way to discontinue its noxious effect. Miller and Dollard, then, see cues and drives as two aspects of the same phenomena, stimuli.

One of the most important classes of cues in the social learning situation is the behavior of others, whether that behavior be directed at the subject or merely occurs in his presence. Thus, the extended hand of another in a social situation serves as a cue for the extension of the individual's hand, and the response of shaking hands ensues. In this case the cue given off by the social other is a distinctive one and dictates the nature, occurrence, and timing of the respondent's behavior. In the case of imitative learning, the behavior of a model serves to introduce several cues to the observer. These cues become relevant if they are connected with a subsequently rewarded response. Upon observing the overt behavioral responses of a model to certain cues that lead to reward and those cues that do not, the observer acquires a hierarchy of cue values operative in the behavioral field. Extrapolating from Miller and Dollard's analysis, two types of cues seem to operate in the observational-learning situation. The first type is the *response* of the model; the second, the cue properties of the behavioral field itself. It seems that it would be rather difficult to distinguish the functions of these two categories of cues in the modeling situation.

Cues, like drives, can acquire value. A relatively nondistinctive cue can acquire distinctive cue value if it evokes a response that leads to reward. It can also acquire value if it is generalized to a strong and already distinctive cue. In cases where the relevance of the relationship between observer and model is minimal, the model's behavior must acquire distinctive cue value before it occasions the imitative response of the observer.

RESPONSE   Miller and Dollard made the curious but apparently logical statement that before any response to a specific cue can be learned and rewarded, it must first occur. Thus they made the assumption that individuals possess an "innate" repertoire of responses that are not initially linked to cues. Learning occurs when a given response is rewarded in the presence of a distinctive cue. However, what is learned? If the response is already part of the subjects repertoire, it is certainly not the response that is learned but rather the bond between a specific cue and a specific response. Nevertheless, reward can increase the probability of the occurrence of a given response already in the *innate hierarchy,* and a new hierarchy of responses is produced. Miller and Dollard referred to this new hierarchy as a *resultant hierarchy.*

In this functional conception of response, Miller and Dollard attached great importance to the mechanism of trial-and-error learning. In the social context, a participating or observed social other can serve to reduce the frequency of trials and errors in the learning of cue-response connections. Thus, these theorists state that if an observer has learned to attach appropriate responses to the cues of a model's performance (that is, if he has learned to copy), imitation can limit the occurrence of trial and error, and "correct" performance can occur after simple observation of another. Miller and Dollard ascribed a similar role to direct-teaching methods. That is, the role of a "teacher" is to limit the range of trial-and-error responding in the learner. They cite Ford (1939), who proposed that one important function of culture (society, social groups) is that it provides a storehouse of solutions to recurrent problems. Therefore, the role of society's older members is to induce its younger members to perform responses that will result in reward and to avoid extraneous and unrewarding responses.

The proposition that any response emitted by the individual is innately available to him before it is learned to a specific cue pattern seems to limit Miller and Dollard's conception of novel responses. They asserted that novel behaviors result from new combinations of "old" responses. As we shall see later in this chapter, Bandura and Walters found this conception to be unsatisfactory.

Finally, it should be noted that Miller and Dollard viewed responses as being both overt and covert. In all paradigmatic cases of mediational learning, covert responding precedes overt responding, and the following paradigm is generated:

$$\text{Cue} \longrightarrow (\text{Internal response} \longrightarrow \text{Drive}) \longrightarrow \substack{\text{External} \\ \text{response}} \longrightarrow \text{Reward}$$

This paradigm is generally applicable to all learning situations, including social-learning and imitation situations.

REWARD   The mechanism of reward or reinforcement has already been discussed in Chapter 2 and also in relation to the above concepts. Since Miller and Dollard's conception of reward is not essentially different from the general mediational approach to reinforcement previously discussed, we will be brief in our discussion of this concept.

Reward is that mechanism which determines whether or not a response is repeated on successive trials. If a response is unrewarded, the tendency to repeat it to the same constellation of cues is weakened. Individuals will seek to make the cue-response connection that results in reward. When reward occurs, its chief function is to reduce the strength of drive. In fact, Miller and Dollard use the term "reward" synonymously with drive reduction. Rewards, like drives and cues, can acquire value. Since reward is functionally defined as drive reduction, then the nature of the drive dictates the nature of the reward. Primary drives are reduced in their intensity by primary rewards, and secondary or acquired drives are reduced in their intensity by secondary or acquired rewards. Food is a primary reward that serves to reduce the primary drive of hunger; an approving nod is a secondary reward that reduces the acquired drive for social approval. Acquired rewards initially gain their potency as drive reducers through their association with primary rewards. In the social-learning situation most rewards are acquired and secondary and therefore reduce the intensity of social drives, which are also acquired and secondary.

Mechanisms of Imitation

Miller and Dollard proposed that three processes or mechanisms of imitation could account for most or all imitative behavior. These three mechanisms were referred to as *same behavior, matched-dependent behavior,* and *copying.*

SAME BEHAVIOR   This first mechanism of imitation was not discussed in detail by the theorists because, in fact, it does not warrant such coverage. Simply, same behavior occurs when two individuals respond to independent stimulation by the same cue, after each has learned to make the appropriate response himself. Examples of this process are plentiful. Some common ones might be (1) two people taking the same bus because they are going to the same destination and (2) two people waiting in line to purchase tickets at the box office of a theater. Same behavior may result from imitation, but it need not.

MATCHED-DEPENDENT BEHAVIOR   This second process of imitation tends to occur in two-party interactions in which one of the parties is older, smarter, or more skilled than the other. Thus, for example, young children will *match* the behavior of, and be *dependent* upon, older people. Extrapolating to the imitation situation, the observer who is in some manner in a lower relative position than the model will match his behavior and be dependent upon him for appropriate cues as to when to do so. The theorists offered the following pattern case of matched-dependent behavior.

Two brothers were playing while awaiting the return home of their father. Father usually returned home with candy for each of the children. While playing, the older child heard a footfall on the entry stairway. For him, it served as a cue for the father's return, and he responded to it by running in the direction of the stairway. For the younger child, the father's footfall did not yet serve as a distinctive cue and thus did not rouse him to running. On many occasions, the older brother's running did not lead to running in the younger boy; he might have continued playing or just continued sitting. However, on this occasion the younger boy ran behind his older brother. When both had reached the father, they each received candy. On subsequent similar occasions the younger child would more frequently run at the mere sight of his brother's running. Under continued candy reward the younger boy's behavior stabilized, and he would run at the sight of his brother's running in all situations, even though the time and place stimuli were variable. Thus, he had learned to *imitate* his older brother, but his father's footfall had still not acquired distinctiveness as a cue. This pattern case can be represented by the following set of paradigms:[1]

1. *Behavior of imitation* (younger brother)

Drive ------------------------- Appetite for candy
Cue ------------------------- Leg twinkle of older brother
Response --------------------- Running
Reward ----------------------- Eating candy

2. *Behavior of leader* (older brother)

Drive ------------------------- Appetite for candy
Cue ------------------------- Father's footfall
Response --------------------- Running
Reward ----------------------- Eating candy

3. *Complete paradigm of matched-dependent behavior*

	LEADER		IMITATOR
Drive	Appetite for candy		Appetite for candy
Cue	Father's footfall	➤Dependent➤	Leg twinkle of leader
Response	Running	➤Matched➤	Running
Reward	Eating candy		Eating candy

This case and these paradigms simply illustrate Miller and Dollard's concept of matched-dependent behavior. Throughout the above analysis of matched-dependent behavior, it is quite apparent that the theorists see imitation as an object of instrumental learning and solely explainable by the "laws of instrumental learning." Thus, learning *to* imitate is akin to learning *to* peck, *to* press, *to* run, *to* push, and so forth. By implication, then Miller and Dollard do not see imitation as a unique type of learning. That is, individuals do not necessarily learn *through* imitation, but rather they learn to imitate. In matched-dependent behavior, the crucial characteristics are the cues exhibited to the imitator by the leader. These cues are utilized by the imitator because they are more stable and distinctive than other environmental cues. However, the cues from the leader's behavior are in no way different in

[1] All three paradigms and the ones to follow taken from Miller and Dollard, 1941.

function from any other cues within the broad class of acquired cues. With some modification, other social-influence processes such as conformity and attitude change can be conceived of in a matched-dependent learning model.

In addition to the foregoing pattern case of matched-dependent learning, Miller and Dollard discussed four other illustrative cases. In doing so, they asserted that their purpose in using illustrative cases was not to anecdotally prove their hypotheses but rather to exhibit varying circumstances under which matched dependent behavior will occur. In this respect, the theorists have attempted to define matched-dependent behavior as a function of varying social contexts. Although we will not extensively detail these cases here, we will briefly specify each general contextual variation.

1.   *Common goal but differing responses.* In this case both imitator and leader seek the same general goal; however, the goal for one involves a different set of responses than the goal for the other. In an illustration of the theorists, the common goal was the reduction in the hunger drives of two children. The younger of the two was parentally permitted to reduce hunger drive with a familiar food object (cornflakes) and in a familiar context (late afternoon before the parents dined). The older child was recently placed on an adult menu and thus being trained to a new secondary goal (for example, meat and potatoes). She now was to eat adult food at adult dinner times. Therefore, although the drive toward the old secondary goal (cornflakes) was in a period of extinction training, it was still aroused when the conditions constituting the formerly relevant context were recreated. Thus the leader's behavior in this case served as a cue for the imitator's anticipation of goal-directed behaviors to eat also. However, since the older child was in extinction training with regard to the eating of cornflakes at a time separate from the adult's eating time, she is punished rather than rewarded for requesting "equal treatment." This common-goal–differing-responses prototype yields the following paradigm:

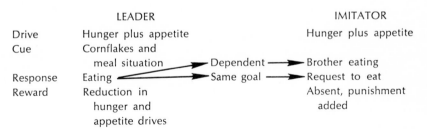

	LEADER		IMITATOR
Drive	Hunger plus appetite		Hunger plus appetite
Cue	Cornflakes and meal situation	→ Dependent →	Brother eating
Response	Eating	→ Same goal →	Request to eat
Reward	Reduction in hunger and appetite drives		Absent, punishment added

In this case, the conditions of learning the initial set of responses (eating cornflakes together) set up the bases for imitation of the leader by the imitator. The leader's behavior served as a cue and had also acquired secondary drive value. Thus, the imitator was *dependent* upon the eating of the leader in making her response which, while *not matched* (eating versus request for food), nevertheless was directed at a common goal. Under continued conditions of absence of reward the imitative behavior of the older child would be bound to drop out.

The conclusions drawn from the above case can be summarized in the following hypothesis: *the drive to imitate will be aroused in an individual when he is confronted with another's response to a familiar and formerly pleasant cue situation to which his own response is blocked.*

It is difficult to view this prototypic case as an instance of imitation since imitative behavior does not in fact occur, except perhaps through simile (eating is like requesting to eat) or through some construct like matching another's overt response with a similar internal response.

2. *Secondary reward.* In this case, the imitator gains secondary reward from hearing or seeing the response of another and he therefore matches that response. Once successfully matching the response, he also gains secondary reward from his own behavior, especially if it meets with the approval of the leader. The imitator is also dependent upon the cues of the leader for the specification of when and what responses will occur. Consider the following paradigm, cited by Miller and Dollard, of a child playing "peek" with his mother.

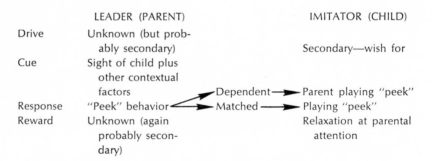

	LEADER (PARENT)	IMITATOR (CHILD)
Drive	Unknown (but probably secondary)	Secondary—wish for
Cue	Sight of child plus other contextual factors	Dependent ⟶ Parent playing "peek"
Response	"Peek" behavior ⟵ Matched ⟶	Playing "peek"
Reward	Unknown (again probably secondary)	Relaxation at parental attention

A confusing factor here is that the leader's response serves both as a cue for the imitator's response and a secondary drive-reducer. Furthermore, the response of the imitator serves as a response as well as a secondary reward. Thus, taking a closer look, the behavior of the leader serves as a cue upon which the imitator is dependent; a response, which the imitator matches; and the reward object, which leads to drive reduction in the imitator.

The hypothesis suggested by this case is that an *individual will match and be dependent upon that behavior of another which has secondary reward value for him.* Furthermore, through generalization, his own behavior will also become secondarily rewarding.

3. *Testing.* In this case the leader serves to test the viability of a given response for the imitator. If the leader's response is successful, the imitator will match it. The leader's "test" response serves as a cue for the imitator's

matched response. *Thus, the successful responses of another acquire cue distinctiveness and occasion imitation.*

4. *Secondary drives of imitation and rivalry.* Here, imitation derives from the observation of the rewarded responses of another. Miller and Dollard hypothesized that observing the rewarded responses of a leader occasions a drive to imitate. In this respect, this case of matched-dependent behavior is much like that of testing. However, these theorists proposed that a drive to imitate transmutes into a drive to compete when the imitator has already learned the appropriate response and the conditions of reward are such that only one person at a time can make the response. Here the imitator and the leader will compete to receive the earliest administration of reward. Thus, although the follower is dependent on the cues set up by the leader for the initiation of a response sequence, having already learned the response sequence, he may seek to complete it with greater speed than the leader in order to be the first to be rewarded. Thus, *imitation once established will lead to rivalry between leader and imitator when the availability of rewards is limited.*

Copying

Miller and Dollard described copying as a more complex form of imitation than matched-dependent behavior. In both copying and matched-dependent behavior, the imitator connects his responses to cues derived from the responses of a model. Furthermore, in both, the punishment of non-matched responses and the reward of matched responses eventually establishes the observer's imitation of the model. The most-important distinction between these two processes of imitation is that in matched-dependent behavior, the imitator responds only to the cues of the model, although in copying he also responds to cues of *sameness* and *difference* produced by his own and the model's response.

In the copying situation, the model performs behaviors that have cue value to the observer. As the observer approximates the behavior of a model, he responds to the sameness or difference between his and the model's responses as well as the sameness or difference between his responses on the current approximation and on previous approximations. Thus, if an observer is attempting to imitate the voice of a model, he will evaluate the similarity between his voice production and the model's voice production on the basis of similarity of vocal cues, such as loudness or pitch. He will also evaluate the cue relationship between his current approximation and a past approximation. If the past approximation was a closer match, for example, he will tend to find the differences in his response (amount of air expended, width of vocal chords) and use these as cues for future matching responses.

When he matches the model's behavior, he is rewarded and attends to the cues inherent in the match so that he might recreate that match on future trials. The response to cues of sameness and difference is greatly facilitated by the presence of a "critic" who rewards the imitator for matches and punishes him for nonmatches. Once the individual becomes an accomplished "copier" of a given response, the cues in his attempted match that signal difference will acquire anxiety value and the cues that signal sameness will acquire reward value, and the copier may therefore act as his own critic.

In line with their entire analysis of social behavior, Miller and Dollard asserted that if copying occurs, that is, if individuals "make" their responses the *same* as other individuals' responses, then there must exist a *drive to copy*. They indicated that this copying drive may have components of anxiety, over loss of social approval, and reward in the form of learning new experiences or skills from others. The theorists attribute social conformity to the drive to copy and equate this drive with such concepts as the "herd instinct" (Trotter, 1917) and "compulsions of a moral order" (Sumner & Keller, 1927). Copying is viewed as the source of uniformity in social behavior.

Comment and Evaluation

Miller and Dollard's theory of social learning and imitation served a valuable historical role. Despite some prior treatises on the nature of imitation (Tarde, 1903; McDougall, 1908) and some early learning-theory approaches to imitation (Humphrey, 1921; Allport, 1924), it was the first extensive and systematic attempt to apply "the laws of learning" to the pervasive social behavior called imitation. Furthermore, the theory advanced by Miller and Dollard still has relevance to the interpretation of imitation.

The theory itself had for many years received wide acceptance. However, the empirical evidence in its support is mainly based upon the investigations of the theorists, and there have been few instances of independent replication of their findings.

Several difficulties do arise with the interpretation of some of Miller and Dollard's conceptual definitions, as well as with their articulation of imitative processes. These difficulties have often been noted in the text of the chapter, but for the sake of convenience, we will list some recurrent ones here:

1. It is often difficult to distinguish the functions of drives, cues, responses, and rewards because in Miller and Dollard's terminology these constructs are interchangeable when certain conditions prevail.

2. A dilemma is created by the proposition that a drive is both produced by and produces a response. In the case of single responses, a response must occur before one can be driven to perform it again, and a drive must exist before the response occurs at all. To circumvent this problem, Miller and Dollard proposed the concept of an innate hierarchy of responses; however, it is rather difficult to conceive of "innate social responses."

3. One of Miller and Dollard's cases of matched-dependent learning seems to deal with nonimitative but contingent responses as opposed to imitative, contingent responses (see case 1 in the text of this chapter).

4. Miller and Dollard do not explain, except in passing, the acquisition of novel social responses. However, as we shall see later on, none of the social-learning theories discussed deal adequately with the acquisition of novel responses.

A VICARIOUS PROCESS THEORY OF IMITATION

Albert Bandura and his associate (Bandura, 1962; Bandura & Walters, 1963; Bandura, 1966) have articulated a data-based theory of imitation. Their major proposition is that imitation is a form of *associative* learning and can be explained by an S–S contiguity paradigm. Their approach, therefore, limits the role of the reinforcing consequences of both a model's and observer's behavior. Reinforcement is viewed as a facilitator of *performance* but is hypothesized not to affect *acquisition* or *learning*. The vehicle of imitative learning in Bandura's theory is the contiguous relationship between the stimuli in the model's environment and his response to them. The object of the observer's learning is this contiguous relationship regardless of whether or not reinforcement results from it. Thus, the observer can learn merely by observation of a model and need not perform the response under conditions of reinforcement.

Bandura has referred to learning by observation as *vicarious* learning and has distinguished this view of imitation from several other popular views, including those of Skinner (1953, 1957), Mowrer (1960), and Miller and Dollard (1941). Before proceeding to a discussion of Bandura's theoretical conceptions, we will briefly consider his criticisms of the above traditional approaches.

Bandura's Evaluation of Other Theories of Imitation

Bandura viewed Miller and Dollard's conception of matched-dependent learning as a special case of instrumental discrimination-place learning. That is, the model's behavior provides discriminative stimuli for the timing and placement of responses that already exist in the observer's repertoire. Matched-dependent behavior has been demonstrated only in the circumstance where the observer is deprived of necessary environmental cues, and thus it is almost exclusively dependent upon the behavior of the model. Bandura asserted that imitation cannot generally be described as place learning but rather involves *response* learning. That is, observers will combine diverse behavioral elements into *novel* responses simply through the observation of the responses of a model. Furthermore, contrary to Miller and Dollard's position, neither the model nor the observer has to receive reinforcement for observational learning to occur. Bandura (1965a) demonstrated this latter point in a study that clearly indicated that observers learn novel repertoires through observation both without making immediate matching responses and without reinforcement. A central proposition of Miller and Dollard's approach is that a response must be present in the repertoire of the subject before he can imitate that same response when emitted by a model under conditions of reinforcement. Bandura maintained that this position runs into difficulty in accounting for the *acquisition* of novel responses and places a severe restriction on what can be learned from models.

Skinner's (1953, 1957) approach is defined as being quite similar to that of Miller and Dollard. In this approach, the model's behavior is seen by the observer as discriminative stimuli for reinforcement. This discriminative-stimulus function is endowed on a model's behavior through the differential reinforcement of his various responses to cues in the behavioral field. An observer is initially shaped to emit a matched response through the process of *successive approximation.* That is, he is rewarded for each approximation of the model's response. With each response of the observer the requirements for reward become more stringent. Thus, the observer must make closer and closer matches with each response in order to consistently attain rewarding consequences. According to Bandura, Skinner's model, like that of Miller and Dollard, can account for the discriminative and reinforcement control of previously learned matching responses, but it does not in any way deal with the acquisition of novel responses through observation (Bandura, 1966).

Bandura maintained that a distinction must be made between acquisition and performance for the process of imitation to be clearly articulated. Thus, reinforcement is seen as facilitating performance but *not* inducing learning through observation. This position is not new with Bandura. The reader will recall our brief discussion of Tolman's concept of latent learning in Chapter 2.

There have been numerous studies that have shown that reinforcing consequences serve only to activate behavior learned under conditions of nonreinforced observation (Kanareff & Lanzetta, 1960; Walters & Parke, 1964; Bandura, 1965; Kanfer, 1965). Bandura cited these findings as providing support for his position that the contiguity between the stimuli in the field and the model's response to them is sufficient to lead to the acquisition of responses by the observer. Reinforcement serves only to activate this learning into performed acts. Thus, the proposition that modeling occurs because imitative responding is *instrumental* in the attainment of reward has been strongly questioned by Bandura.

Mowrer (1960) has articulated a two-process theory of imitation based upon the concept of proprioceptive feedback. Unlike Miller and Dollard (1941) and Skinner (1957), Mowrer's theory "emphasizes the classical conditioning of positive and negative emotions to matching, response-correlated stimuli" (p. 8). Thus modeling is viewed as being dependent upon the contiguous association of the model's behavior with its reinforcing consequences. Through continued observation of these contiguous events, the observer eventually attaches positive affect to responses that lead to reward and negative affect to responses that lead to punishment.

Simply, Mowrer's two processes differ in terms of the directness of the reinforcing consequences for the observer. The first process involves the direct reinforcement of an observer by a model. This reinforcing consequence is contiguous to the model's performance of a given response. With the continued enforcement of the contiguous association between the model's behavior and the observer's reinforcement, the model's responses take on positive value. Through the process of stimulus generalization the observer can in time closely reproduce the model's responses and thus receive self-rewarded feedback. Mowrer referred to his second process of imitative learning as "empathetic" learning. In this case a model performs responses for which he himself is reinforced. It is assumed that the observer vicariously experiences the rewarding consequences of the model's behavior and "intuits his discomforts and satisfactions." When placed in the behavioral field, the observer will be capable of reproducing the model's responses because they have gained positively reinforcing value. This latter process is a higher-order form of classical conditioning in which the observer experiences sensory feedback empathically while the model is being rewarded.

Bandura noted that while Mowrer's conception of "empathetic" learning overcomes his criticism of the position which holds that a response must be performed before it can be learned, it still fails to explain the occurrence of imitative learning when neither model nor observer is rewarded. Furthermore, although Mowrer viewed the feedback from a model's responses that an observer experiences as sensory and peripheral, Bandura hypothesized that this feedback is centrally mediated. Thus, for Mowrer the aggressive responses of a model occasion the same sensory feedback whether expressed toward a peer or toward an authority figure. On the other hand, Bandura saw aggressive responding varying as a function of the target, and the nature of differing expressions of aggression being mediated by central processes of target and context discrimination. This latter proposition has received strong empirical support (Bandura & Walters, 1959; Bandura, 1960).

An Overview of Bandura's Theory

Bandura refers to his theory of imitation as a mediational-stimulus contiguity theory. According to this approach, "during the period of exposure modeling stimuli elicit in observing subjects configurations and sequences of sensory experiences which, on the basis of past associations, become centrally integrated and structured into perceptual responses" (p. 10). Thus, through contiguous stimulation, an antecedent stimulus can eventually elicit imaginal or symbolic representations of associated stimulus events even though they are no longer present (Bandura, 1966). Bandura proposes that a model's response to cues in a stimulus field leads to "internal" imaginal responses in the observer that can be retrieved when the observer is placed in the behavioral field. Therefore, without either responding or being rewarded, the observer integrates cue connections in the model's responses and the behavioral field and thereby becomes able to imitate the model's response.

The observer's ability to attach verbal labels to the model's behavior greatly facilitates this process of symbolization. The representational responses that occur in the observer, whether they be verbal associates or imaginal responses, come to serve as internal cues that mediate the observer's matched external responses in the behavioral field. Thus, the internal representational cues become discriminative stimuli for overt matching patterns of behavior.

The foregoing paragraphs provide the reader with an overview of Bandura's theoretical orientation toward modeling. The remainder of this presentation will be devoted to Bandura's articulation of the behavioral effects of an observer's exposure to modeling stimuli and his conception of the relevance of vicarious classical conditioning to the modeling process. It should be noted that throughout these analyses his propositions are related to a data base and derive directly from it.

Behavioral Effects of Exposure to Models

Bandura noted that the exposure to models leads to three general effects in the observer. These are (1) modeling effects whereby the observer acquires novel responses through the cognitive integration of contiguous cues, (2) inhibitory and disinhibitory effects through which an existing class of the observer's behavior is *modified* by his observation of the responses of a model, and (3) facilitation effects whereby the observations of another's behavior may facilitate the occurrence of previously learned but noninhibited responses in the observer.

MODELING EFFECTS   Modeling effects occur in that situation in which an observer acquires new response patterns through observing a model perform highly novel responses. Most novel responses contain elements or segments of behavior that are already established in the observer's learned repertoire. Bandura maintains that the observational-learning situation introduces the observer to novel combinations of contiguous cues which he integrates on a central level and through which he arrives at a new integrative behavior pattern. Thus, it is the patterning of the components of the model's response and those of the ensuing response of the observer that defines novelty. In addition, novel responses are also identified as occurring when already established behavior patterns come under *new* stimulus control. In this case the learned responses occur to a set of cues to which they had not occurred previous to the specific observational experience involved.

Bandura noted that studies have indicated that modeling effects occur with a whole host of responses, including physically expressive aggression (Bandura, 1965b), self-reinforcement (Bandura & Whalen, 1966), self-imposed delay of reward (Bandura & Mischel, 1965), linguistic structuring (Bierman, 1965), and many others. In all these cases an observer watched a model utilize a unique pattern of response and subsequently displayed that pattern of response when placed in the same behavioral field. Hence, we speak of a modeling effect. Since none of the subjects in any of the experiments above had an opportunity to practice an observed response pattern before criterion performance was judged, Bandura reiterates that the combining and chaining of matching responses must have occurred through central symbolic and mediating processes, and thus the behavior was learned in "no-trials." One important aspect of no-trial or observational learning is the subject's ability to engage in *covert rehearsal* of the response to be performed.

Bandura noted that although empirical data provide support for his stimulus-contiguity explanation of modeling effects, the finding that a majority of observers fail to reproduce the *complete* pattern of the model's response indicates that the contiguity of sensory stimulation is a necessary but not a sufficient condition for imitative learning. In addition to this major associative process, Bandura proposed the following factors as being *facilitative* in the production of modeling effects:

1. Strength of motivation to attend to the stimuli
2. Sensory and receptive capacities of the observer based upon prior training in discriminative observation
3. The presence of incentive-oriented sets that focus observing responses
4. The observer's prior utilization of all necessary component responses of the total behavioral sequence

INHIBITORY AND DISINHIBITORY EFFECTS   "The occurrence of inhibitory effects of exposure to models is indicated when, as a function of observing aversive response consequences to a model, observers exhibit either decrements in the same class of behavior or a general reduction of responsivity" (Bandura, 1966, p. 20). Bandura posits that an opposite or disinhibitory effect might also occur as a function of observation. In this latter case, the observation of a model performing either rewarded or unpunished socially unacceptable responses leads to increments in the same class of behavior or a general increase in socially disapproved behavior. In both these cases, the direct reinforcement or punishment of the observer is not a prerequisite. Rather, the positive, negative, or lack of reinforcement of the model is vicariously experienced by the observer while he is observing. Thus, like modeling effects, inhibitory and disinhibitory effects are said to be learned in no-trials.

Bandura's proposition that there are both inhibitory and disinhibitory effects that occur as a function of observation has received impressive experimental support. Walters, Leat, and Mezei (1963) and Walters and Parke (1964) have shown that when an observer witnesses a peer model undergo punishment for engaging in prohibited play activities, his propensity to engage in the same deviant acts is decreased. On the other hand, Bandura, Ross, and Ross (1961, 1963) and many others (Siegel, 1956; Lövaas, 1961; Larder, 1962) have shown that when a peer model engages in aggressive behavior without negative consequence, it increases the probability that an observer will also engage in similar tabooed aggressive behaviors when placed in the same behavioral field.

Bandura viewed the source of inhibitory and disinhibitory effects to be the occurrence of *vicarious reinforcement*. That is, if the negative behavior of an observer is inhibited or enhanced by observing a model performing that same behavior followed by rewarding or punishing consequences and this observer is not himself reinforced for these acts, then the assumption is made that he experienced the reinforcements of the model, and when placed in the behavioral field, he will display or inhibit the model's reinforced responses on the first trial. Research has revealed that vicarious reinforcement is as efficacious (Kanfer & Martson, 1963) as direct reinforcement at producing behavioral increments. Vicarious reinforcement processes have also been shown to be moderated by the same variables (magnitude, percentage, schedule) as direct reinforcement (Bandura, 1966).

Bandura offers four reasons for the efficacy of vicarious reinforcement in inhibiting or disinhibiting the responses of a model:

1. It provides the observer with information about the probability of attaining reinforcement through the emission of certain specified responses.
2. It provides the observer with knowledge about the stimuli in the field and helps to direct his *attention* to these stimuli.
3. It provides the observer with a display of the incentives which he might receive for performing a given act.
4. It provides the observer the opportunity to view the affective reactions of the model to receiving a given reinforcement (that is, it provides pleasure and pain cues to the observer).

This final reason is probably further mediated by correlated feelings of pleasure or pain in the observer as he witnesses the model being reinforced. It should be noted that with regard to the socially prohibitive aggressive and deviant responses displayed by a model, lack of negative reinforcement is equally as powerful as positive reinforcement in promoting imitative responses in an observer (Walters & Parke, 1964). Bandura has attributed this finding to a contrast-of-reinforcement effect. The contrast spoken of here is the contrast between society's usual negative reinforcements for deviant behavior and the lack of negative reinforcement in the contrived modeling situation.

RESPONSE-FACILITATING EFFECTS   Response-facilitating effects of exposure to models occur in that situation in which the model's responses serve as discriminative stimuli for the observer. This discriminative-stimulus function of a model's responses facilitates the occurrence of similar responses in the observer. These effects differ from both modeling and inhibition-disinhibition effects in that the responses facilitated are not novel but are already firmly ensconced in the repertoire of the subject, and they are not generally socially prohibited responses. Examples of behaviors that might be susceptible to the facilitating effects of a model's response might be (1) making contributions to a charitable cause, (2) volunteering for a chore, (3) looking at the ceiling, and innumerable others.

Bandura notes that the instrumental theories of imitation (Miller & Dollard, 1941; Skinner, 1957) have been almost exclusively concerned with the discrimination function of social cues. That is, the behavior of a model has a facilitative effect on like behaviors of the observer in that it occasions consequent reinforcement and hence becomes distinctive as a cue.

Vicarious Classical Conditioning

The classification above of the effects of exposure to models was predominantly based upon investigations of the social transmission of instrumental classes of response (Bandura, 1966). In this section we will deal with Bandura's conception of the processes of vicarious classical conditioning that function in imitative behavior.

VICARIOUS EMOTIONAL AROUSAL   Bandura asserted that social cues that signal the emotional arousal of a model can lead to emotion-provoking properties in the observer through the same classical conditioning process that established the positive or negative value of non-social environmental stimuli. Thus, the affective responses of a model to a cue situation may elicit similar affective responses in an observer. With the continued pairing of the model's emotional response with the eliciting social cues, the cues themselves gradually acquire the power to elicit emotional responses from the observer. This process involves much more than just parallel reactions to a naturally emotion-provoking cue (for example, shock, fear object). Rather, the concept of vicarious emotional arousal involves an actual "imitation" of the emotional response of a witnessed model by an observer, whether or not that observer is directly confronted with the arousing cue. As an example, Bandura refers to a study in which Lazarus, Speisman, Merdkoff, and Davison (1962) found that college students exposed to films of primitive subincision puberty rites showed increased autonomic responsivity (said to reflect emotional arousal). It is Bandura's proposal that gradually the cues that occasioned an expression of pain in the subincised other acquired the power to independently elicit emotional pain reactions in the observer. Thus, the observer does not have to be actually placed in the behavioral field containing the emotionally arousing cues in order to experience emotional arousal. Therefore, Bandura maintained that vicarious emotional arousal might occur merely from the simple observation of another's emotional experience.

VICARIOUS CLASSICAL CONDITIONING   When vicarious emotional arousal is induced in an observer, vicarious classical conditioning can occur if those stimuli that aroused emotional reactions in the model (and hence vicariously in the observer) are associated with previously neutral stimuli. In this case, the neutral stimuli gain the power to elicit the emotional response in both the model or performer and the observer. This phenomena has been empirically demonstrated (Barnett & Benedetti, 1960; Berger, 1962). Furthermore, Bandura and Rosenthal (1966) have found that the initial arousal level of the observer prior to vicarious conditioning procedures moderates the intensity of the vicariously conditioned response. Specifically, these investigators found that an inverted U-shaped relationship obtains between the observer's initial level of arousal and the magnitude of his conditioned vicarious response. Therefore, increased levels of initial emotional arousal lead to increased magnitude of the conditioned response up to an asymptotic point above which increasing the level of arousal decreases the intensity of the vicariously conditioned emotional response.

Bandura (1966) has explained this finding by proposing that observers under high levels of preconditioning arousal will more frequently invoke "stimulus neutralization stratagems," or, more simply, competing responses, to combat the effect of additional arousal. This proposal derives from Bandura and Rosenthal's (1966) postexperimental questionnaire data.

Finally, it should be noted that Bandura proposed that just as an observer's responses may be vicariously conditioned either instrumentally or classically through exposure to a model, they also may be vicariously extinguished through simple observation. Thus, for example, an observer witnessing a model approaching a stimulus which he (the observer) had always avoided would gradually undergo vicarious extinction of the avoidance response if he observed the model experiencing no adverse consequences. Bandura postulated that this latter process should be highly relevant to psychotherapy and behavior change.

Comments

As we mentioned at the outset of our discussion of Bandura's theory of imitation, it is in all respects a data-based system of interrelated hypotheses. It constitutes the most-comprehensive theory of imitative learning extant in social psychology since the classic theory of Miller and Dollard. One need only refer to the presentation of Bandura's theory in this chapter to evaluate its testability. The empirical support which he offers for his concept of vicarious no-trial learning through modeling is indeed impressive.

At present this theory is in a state of flux. As such, it may be subject to subtle or even gross changes. This state of flux is occasioned by the ongoing research program in which Bandura and his associates and students are presently engaged. In the short space of time between Bandura and Walters' (1963) book and Bandura's (1966) chapter in *Advances in Experimental Social Psychology,* there have indeed been some research-based additions to and changes in the theoretical framework. Although Bandura's theory eminently fulfills the criterion of generating research, and although its reliance on data predisposes it to desirable flexibility, there is one conceptual flaw that might be noted. That is, although one of Bandura's primary criticisms of both Miller and Dollard and Skinner is that neither theory can adequately explain the emergence of truly novel responses, his propositions do little to better this condition. Miller and Dollard assume that for a response to be imitated it must already exist in the imitator's repertoire. Bandura stated that for a response to be imitated its components must exist in the imitator's repertoire. Neither concept, however, specifically defines how either the "whole" response or its *components* initially appeared in the imitator's repertoire. Perhaps the concept of an "absolutely" novel response is an unrealistic one, and instead theorists in the area might be better able to deal with the different degrees of novelty of various responses.

A t the outset of Chapter 3, we indicated that we would consider two broad cases of social context variation in human learning. That chapter presented theories dealing with the first of those cases, learning through the observation of the behavior and consequences of the behavior of others. In this chapter we exposit three theories that are examples of our second case of social context variation. All three of these theories deal with the reciprocal exchange of rewards and punishments in an interactive context. The three theories are (1) Homans' (1961) theory of elementary social behavior, (2) Thibaut and Kelley's (1959) theory of interaction outcomes, and (3) Adams and Romney's (1959) functional theory of authority interactions.

The first two of these theories bear a superficial similarity to each other. They both conceptualize the formation, maintenance, and outcomes of dyadic relationships in terms of a behavioristic-economic model. Thus, the basic proposal of both of these theories is that dyadic interaction will most probably be continued and positively evaluated if the participants in that interaction "profit" from it; that is, if the participants view the interaction as being more rewarding than it is costly. As these theories proceed from this basic proposal to a description of determining and limiting conditions of interaction exchange, basic differences between the two theories become apparent.

The third theory presented in this chapter is a functional analysis of authority- "underling" relationships. It is based on the premise that dyadic authority relationships, like all dyadic relationships, are based upon the reciprocal exchange of rewards between the one in authority and the person over whom he wields it. This conception of authority is quite different from the more-customary conception of authority based upon the passing on of unidirectional commands and rewards from one person to another.

A THEORY OF ELEMENTARY SOCIAL BEHAVIOR

George C. Homans (1961) proposed this theory with the intent of explaining the *elementary* face-to-face social interchange that occurs between two persons. The theory is based upon the disciplines of behavioristic psychology and elementary economics. Through an admixture of these two fields Homans has articulated an explanation of social behavior predicated upon the "psychological" exchange of rewards (positive reinforcements) and costs (negative reinforcements) that he conceptualized as occurring during the direct interpersonal interaction between individuals. Homans limited the behavior that he considered explicable through his analysis by the following criteria:

1. It must be social; thus when a person acts, he must be directly reacted to positively or negatively by another.

2. When a person acts, he must be rewarded or punished by the person toward whom his action is directed and not by a third party.

3. The behavior examined must be actual and not merely a norm or societal expectation of appropriate behavior.

Thus, Homans defined *elementary social behavior* as occurring in two-party interactions involving the direct and immediate exchange of rewards and punishments between the participants in the interaction. He sees as his theoretical goal the explanation of this two-party exchange as an inherent part of all social interaction. His method of explanation is deductive. Thus, he proceeded from the empirical propositions that he derived from behavioral psychology and economics, and from them he deduced more-specific propositions about the social behavior under scrutiny.

Homans began his analysis with a consideration of some of the empirical generalizations that have been formulated through the study of animal behavior. From these, he deduced terms and propositions relevant to the human exchange process. He then offered several pattern cases illustrating his deduced propositions. In our presentation we follow the same sequence; however, we exposit only one of his pattern cases of human exchange—that of distributive justice.

Propositions Derived from Studies of Animal Behavior

Homans began his theoretical analysis of human social exchange with a discussion of several propositions derived from the study of animal behavior. He justified this beginning on two counts: (1) some of the propositions relevant to a description of human social behavior have been best established through investigations with animal subjects and (2) the unity of science dictates that, when possible, scientists ought to demonstrate that the propositions within their field are more generally applicable. Nevertheless, he acknowledged the considerable gap that exists between the behavior of men and the behavior of animals.

The class of behavior which Homans chose to examine in detail is *operant* or *voluntary* behavior. He was not concerned with the study of muscle twitches, salivary responses, and the like. In selecting the operant behavior of animals as the starting point of his theoretical analysis, Homans rightfully credited the theory and research of B. F. Skinner. Since we have already defined the class of behaviors referred to as operants (see Chapter 2), we will proceed to state and describe Homans' primary propositional derivatives from animal behavior. Before we encounter Homans' first proposition it is important to note that Homans, like Skinner, was not concerned with the teleology of learned responses, but rather he was concerned with how learned responses serve to alter the external environment.

PROPOSITION 1: DEPRIVATION AND SATIATION   This proposition is based upon the Skinnerian conception of drive. Simply stated, it holds that *"the more fully an animal has been deprived of a positive reinforcer, the more often it emits an activity so reinforced; the more fully it has been satiated the less often it does"* (Homans, 1961, p. 28. Italics ours).

In this proposition and in those that follow, Homans substituted the term *activity* for the term *operant*. As we shall see later, *activity* is one of Homans' major descriptive terms in the theory of human social exchange. With regard to animals, it was Homans' contention that the two variables that determine the rate of emission of an activity are the state of the animal and the rate at which it is reinforced. This first proposition deals with the *state* variable and implies that as one deprives an animal, he increases that animal's drive to emit a response for the sake of attaining the appropriate positive reinforcement. From this proposition, Homans derived the concept of *value* as it applies to human behavior. That is, as the individual is increasingly deprived of a given positive reinforcer, that reinforcer gains increasing *value* for the individual. This concept and its implications for human social behavior are discussed in a later section of this chapter.

PROPOSITION 2: REINFORCEMENT RATE   We noted above that the two variables governing the rate of emission of an activity are *state* of the animal and *rate* of reinforcement. The rate variable is expressed in the following proposition: *"the more often an activity is reinforced, the more often the animal emits it; the more often an activity is punished, the less often an animal emits it"* (Homans, 1961, p. 28. Italics ours). Homans stated that when he speaks of "more often," he is not speaking of total and continuous reinforcement, but rather he acknowledged that this proposition must be qualified by the schedule of reinforcement utilized. Thus, intermittent, variable-ratio reinforcement that is often administered is most efficacious in increasing the rate of activity of the animal. However, since it is rather difficult to establish the reinforcement schedule operative in certain human social exchanges, it is more realistic for the sake of generalizability to state this rate proposition in terms of "more often"—"less often." Lastly, this proposition must be qualified by the *state* of the animal. If it is satiated, increasing the frequency of reinforcement will be of little consequence in increasing the rate of emitted activity.

PROPOSITION 3: STIMULUS CONTROL   This proposition deals with environmental stimuli other than reinforcing stimuli. It was stated that *"any feature of the environment that appears in some conjuncture with the emission of a reinforced activity, tends on its subsequent reappearance to elicit that activity"* providing that these later reappearances are also accompanied by reinforcement (Homans, 1961, p. 22. Italics ours). This proposition emphasizes the "three-term" relationship between *stimulus, activity,* and *reinforcement.* In this relationship a stimulus acquires its control over activity when it consistently precedes the occurrence and reinforcement of that activity. Homans views this three-term relationship as the source of environmental-, physical-, or social-stimulus control over the organism. Thus, if one can specify the discriminable features of the environment which lead an organism to emit a given activity resulting in reinforcement, one can control that organism's behavior.

PROPOSITION 4: PUNISHMENT AND COST   Punishment or negative reinforcement serves to decrease the probability of subsequent occurrence of an activity. However, Homans noted that for both men and animals some activities get both rewarded and punished. In fact, in many instances, the attainment of reinforcement involves enduring some prior degree of punishment. Thus, animals might have to perform fatiguing responses to attain reward. Many similar examples may be conceived of with humans. Therefore, Homans stated the proposition that *punishment (in the form of the presence of aversive conditions or in the withdrawal of reinforcing ones) that the organism cannot avoid if it is to emit positively reinforced activities are called the costs of these activities. Furthermore, high cost tends to depress the rate of emission of an activity and by virtue of this decrease makes more frequent the emission of some alternate activity.* An alternative activity in the instance where making a reinforced response is extremely costly would be the organism's escape from the environmental conditions eliciting that response. This escape in and of itself is an alternatively rewarded response.

Although Homans acknowledged that it is difficult to imagine an animal evaluating and weighing the relative costs of separate activities, he nevertheless added the following corollary to proposition 4: *"the costs, or unavoidable punishment, of any one activity include the withdrawn or foregone rewards of an alternative activity"* (Homans, 1961, p. 26). This corollary presupposes that the emission of one reinforced activity precludes the possibility of simultaneous emission of alternative rewarded activities. The absolute costs of an activity vary with the permanence of the costly components of that activity. Thus, extinction renders an activity permanently costly and eventually precludes its occurrence; satiation renders an activity costly only until the organism once again becomes deprived; and occasional punishment renders an activity costly until it is withdrawn, at which time the activity will recur. As we shall see later in this chapter, the concept of cost is a cornerstone of Homans' theory of human exchange.

PROPOSITION 5: EMOTIONAL BEHAVIOR   *"The withdrawal of a positive reinforcer releases the emotional behavior we call aggression, and the presentation of a positive reinforcer may release, besides the reinforced activity, some degree of positive emotional behavior"* (Homans, 1961, p. 29. Italics ours). Homans noted that it is particularly difficult to interpret the emotional components of a pigeon's response. However, he based this proposition on

the observation made by many behaviorists that if you abruptly stop reinforcing an animal, it will behave in a way that indicates a rage response.
Nevertheless, Homans conceded that this proposition is more applicable to
men than to subhuman animals.

Now that we have stated and described the five basic propositions that
Homans derived from studies of animal behavior, we are ready to define the
major terms and propositions of his theory of human exchange. The similarity
between the above five propositions and the five presented in a subsequent
section of this chapter should be quite apparent to the reader.

Human Exchange: Terms

Homans, like Bem, Doob, Miller and Dollard, Skinner, and Bandura,
asserted that the "laws" of individual animal behavior are sufficient to account
for human social behavior when the complications of mutual reinforcement
are taken into account. Nevertheless, Homans began his analysis of human
social exchange by defining several "novel" terms that are extrapolations of
the terms that are used in the study of animal behavior. Apparently, Homans
went through this extrapolation in order to render the terms of human
exchange uniquely human. The two classes of terms which Homans defined
are *descriptive terms* and *variables.*

DESCRIPTIVE TERMS   These are the terms used to describe the *kind* of
behavior which the individual is engaged in. In this category there are three
basic terms: (1) activity, (2) sentiment, and (3) interaction. As we have noted
earlier, *activity* is Homans' translation of Skinner's *operant.* Thus, activities are
any voluntary behaviors emitted by the organism. This definition makes the
class of behaviors referred to as activities infinite in scope. Therefore, since
Homans was predominantly concerned with those classes of activities that are
appropriate to human social behavior, he chose to single out an inherently
social activity that he referred to as *sentiments.*

Sentiments are "the activities that the members of a particular verbal or
symbolic community say are signs of the attitudes and feelings a man takes
toward another man or other men" (Homans, 1961, p. 33). They may or may
not be verbally expressed symbols, but in all cases they are overtly discriminable symbols (for example, a kiss, a handshake, or a nod). In Homans'
system, sentiments are not defined by the internal states of the individual but
by his overt behavior or *activities.* They resemble other kinds of human social
activities in that they may be *exchanged,* and in this process of exchange they
reward and punish the behavior of a social other. Thus, like all behavior,
sentiments have an effect on the external environment and the organisms
within it. For example, a face-to-face human social exchange might involve
person A emitting an activity, that directly or indirectly affects person B.
Person B might then respond to person A's activity by emitting a discriminable
sign of a positive or negative sentiment. Person B's sentiment serves as a reinforcer or punisher of person A's behavior. Sentiments may also be the subject

of a transitive exchange. That is, the positive sentiment of one party to an interaction might occasion the return of positive sentiment by the second party to that interaction.

The two situations depicted above would both be classed as *interactions* in Homans' system. *Interactions* are defined as occurring when "an activity (or sentiment) emitted by one man is rewarded (or punished) by an activity (or sentiment emitted by another man" (Homans, 1961, p. 35). It is apparent from Homans' definitions of his descriptive terms that these terms are hardly independent of one another. As noted, *sentiments* are a special class of emitted *activities;* the exchange of nonsentiment activities, sentiment activities, or both constitutes an *interaction.*

TERMS DEFINING VARIABLES   The two major variables in Homans' system are *quantity* and *value.* These two variables constitute the quantitative variations of activities, sentiments, and interactions.

Quantity is a frequency variable. With regard to activity, it is "the number of units of activity that the organism in question emits within a given period of time" (Homans, 1961, p. 36). As we noted in our discussion of animal-behavior propositions, the quantity or frequency of an activity is a function of the *state* (deprivation or satiation) of the organism and the *rate* at which it has been reinforced or punished. Quantity, being a frequency dimension, is usually measured by a simple counting procedure. However, the units of activity in human exchange are often difficult to count, because in fact they are difficult to specify. For example, we can quite accurately count the number of times a pigeon pecks at a target or the number of times a rat presses a bar in a Skinner box; however, it is more difficult to count the number of positive sentiment activities that are exchanged in a two-party interaction. In the latter situation, criteria are less clearly specified and observations are accordingly less reliable. Homans acknowledged this difficulty, but he indicated that the quantity of human-exchange activity can be assessed by specialized experimental-observational techniques. In these cases, the unit of activity in question would have to be defined by the experimenter, and its definition would in turn determine the behaviors to be counted. In this context he cited the interaction analyses of Bales (1950) and Chapple (1940), as well as sociometric analyses. One quantity measure that Homans depicted as being easily countable is the absolute amount of time a person spends with another person over total time observed. On this basis one can evaluate the relative time, for example, person A is engaged in interactions with persons B and C. Measures of the quantity of behavior emitted by one person toward another are measures of *frequency of elementary social behavior.*

Value was defined in terms of the degree of positive or negative reinforcement an individual receives from another's unit of activity. The greater the degree of positive reinforcement provided by a unit of activity, the higher the value of that unit; the greater the degree of negative reinforcement from a unit, the lower its value. It should be emphasized that the assessment of value in human exchange must be made on a unit-by-unit basis. For just as the efficacy of reinforcement might change for an animal on each trial in a sequence, so the value of a given activity (as reinforcer) can change from one unit emission to another. For example, person A may become *satiated* with the positive units of activity directed at him by person B, and as a result, the value of these units of activity will be reduced. According to Homans, the measurement of value presents even greater difficulties than the measurement of quantity. The primary problem in measuring value is the specification of "degree" of reinforcement per unit activity.

Homans suggested that the measurement of value per unit activity can be deduced from the methods of measuring the effects of deprivation states in animals. That is, the longer an animal has been deprived of food, the more "valuable" food becomes for him. The assessment of how "valuable" a reinforcement will be to an animal necessitates the examination of that animal's immediate past history with that reinforcement. If we assume that a given object (food) is inherently valuable to the animal, then an immediate past history of deprivation from that object enhances its value. In the human-interaction situation, the same principles hold. That is, if we assume that social approval is desirable and valuable to person A, then the longer he has been deprived of social approval in the past, the more valuable it becomes in the present. Furthermore, person A will emit unit activities that have the greatest probability of being approved of by person B. As person B emits various sentiment activities indicating approval, person A may become satiated and, as such, the value of approval will decline for him. Homans granted that the assessment of the past history of reinforcement of an animal is more exacting (counting hours of deprivation, weighing it, etc.) than the assessment of the past social-reinforcement history of a person. However, he believed that *value* need not be measured any more precisely than on a "more-or-less" basis in order for human interaction to be explained and its products predicted.

Homans noted that there are two components of value. They are (1) the component that specifies the constant value of an activity regardless of the state of the organism and (2) the component that specifies the value of an activity at a particular point in time and that varies as a function of state of the organism. Thus, each individual has a built-in hierarchy of values with regard to social activities. Therefore, the social approval of another may be more important than the physical help of another for an individual. The second component dictates the value of an object at some point in time. Therefore, although approval might be absolutely more valuable than physical help, the individual at a given point in time might attach a greater value to the physical help of another if he has been deprived of the help of another for a much longer period of time than he has been deprived of another's approval.

Considering both value and quantity of the activity of a social other in an interaction, Homans proposed that an individual should expend a greater *quantity* of time interacting with a social other who emits reciprocal activities that are highly valued than he would with an individual who emits activities which are less highly valued. Propositions of this sort are considered in the next section.

Human Exchange: Propositions

Homans articulated five propositions regarding human behavior that were derived from the propositions about animal behavior and that utilized the terms discussed in the preceding section. However, in the course of presenting these propositions he introduced two heretofore undefined terms: *cost* and *profit*. Although these terms are not formally linked to propositional statements, they appear in corollaries that Homans derived from the five major propositions.

PROPOSITION 1: STIMULUS CONTROL AND ITS GENERALIZATION   This proposition states that *"if in the past the occurrence of a particular stimulus-situation has been the occasion on which a man's activity has been rewarded, then the more similar the present stimulus-situation is to the past one, the more likely he is to emit the activity, or some similar activity, now"* (Homans, 1961, p. 53. Italics ours). Proposition 1 is clearly a deduction from proposition 3 about the stimulus control of animal behavior. Additionally, Homans has here invoked the principle of stimulus generalization to explain how like social situations and similar activities emitted by social others might become generalized and thereby elicit like responses. Consider the following example, person A has at some time in the past emitted a help-requesting activity directed at person B and this activity occasioned person B's emission of positive-helping activity toward person A. Person A responded to person B's help-giving activity by emitting positive-sentiment activities toward B. At present, person C is emitting help-requesting activities directed at person B and resembling the help-requesting activities of person A in the past. Since in that past interaction, person B's help-giving activity had been reinforced by person A, he is, according to proposition 1, likely to perform help-giving activities toward person C, in order to experience C's rewarding positive sentiment activity toward him.

PROPOSITION 2: REINFORCEMENT FREQUENCY   Homans deduced this proposition from animal proposition 2 about the effect of rate of reinforcement on the emission of a response by animal subjects. It stated that *"the more often within a given period of time a man's activity rewards the activity of another, the more often the other will emit the activity"* (Homans, 1961, p. 54. Italics ours). Homans put it very succinctly when he stated that the more often one man thanks another man for his help, the more often the other man will give help to the first man. This proposition refers to the variable of quantity of activity and furthermore indicates that the quantity or frequency of one person's activity is *proportional* to the frequency of another person's reciprocal positive sentiment activity toward the first person.

PROPOSITION 3: MAGNITUDE OF REINFORCEMENT   This proposition deals with the value variable as it affects human exchange. *"The more valuable to a man a unit of the activity another gives him, the more often he will emit activity rewarded by the activity of the other"* (Homans, 1961, p. 55. Italics ours). Thus, the greater the person's need for help, the more valuable help becomes and the more thanks he will give when he receives it. The following corollary has been deduced from the last two propositions: *"the frequency of interaction between Person and Other depends upon the frequency with which each rewards the activity of the other and on the value to each of the activity he receives"* (Homans, 1961, p. 55. Italics ours).

PROPOSITION 4: REACTIVE INHIBITION AND SATIATION   This proposition, which states that *"the more often a man has in the recent past received a rewarding activity from another, the less valuable any further unit of that activity becomes to him"* (Homans, 1961, p. 55. Italics ours), serves to qualify proposition 2. It proposes that in human exchange, men become satiated by the positive sentiment activities of other men. Because of this satiation, their "drive" for further units of activity from these same others decreases. As a result, the probability that interaction between these two parties will presently continue is also decreased. When the value of a given activity from another is once again increased through the person's being deprived of that activity, proposition 2 will once again apply.

The above four propositions all deal with the consequences of rewarding activities for the initiation and maintenance of social interaction. However, human interaction, as well as involving the exchange of rewards, at times also involves the exchange of punishments. Homans did not view the exchange of punishments per se as a relevant component of social interaction, for when punishments are in fact exchanged, the interaction in question will generally close. Thus, rather than hypothesizing about the broad class of punishments that can be *directly* administered by one party to another, he chose to analyze an *indirect,* but nevertheless potent, class of punishments. It is here that the concept of *cost* arises in Homans' system. For the purposes of his theory, he defines cost as a value forgone. Thus "for an activity to incur cost, an alternative and rewarding activity must be forgone" (Homans, 1961, p. 59). For example, the cost of person B's giving help to person A might be the rewards that he forgoes by not using the time spent helping person A in pursuing his own work. The performance of nearly every rewarded unit of activity in a social interaction involves some amount of cost. That is, the performance of any given unit of activity precludes the performance of another unit of activity (which may be more or less rewarding than the first).

These considerations concerning cost led Homans to formulate two corollaries, one to proposition 3 and the other to proposition 4. Respectively, they are (1) *"the more cost Person incurs in emitting an activity, the less often he will emit it"* and (2) *"the more often Person has emitted a costly activity, the more costly he finds any further unit of that activity"* (Homans, 1961, p. 60. Italics ours). Both these corollaries must be qualified because in order for either to apply, the reward value and reward quantity of the unit of activity in question must remain constant, decrease, or increase less than the cost of that activity. This qualification is directly relevant to Homans' formulation of the *profit* derived from a social exchange.

In any two-party social interaction, the *profit* which accrues to either party in that interaction is equal to the rewards he receives minus the costs he incurs from engaging in that interaction. Profit can be evaluated only on single units of activity exchange; thus when we speak of the discontinuance of an interaction, we are speaking of a specific component unit of that interaction. Hence, person A might have several different kinds of exchanges with person B, and some may be profitable and others unprofitable. If one or more of these component interactions are in fact unprofitable, these will be discontinued; however, the total relationship between A and B might still exist with regard to other units of activity that they exchange. Although Homans extracted his concept of profit from elementary economics, he was not in any sense speaking of actual monetarylike profits, but rather psychological profits. Therefore a man who patronizes a fine but expensive restaurant and thereby spends $30 for a meal is incurring a sizable cost. However, this cost might be outweighed by the rewarding components of such a palatable feast. In this instance he is extracting a profit, for his psychological and appetitive rewards are greater than the monetary costs he expends to obtain them.

Returning to the two-party social interaction, an activity may be profitable for one or both parties in that interaction. Thus, if person A emits a help-requesting activity toward person B, he incurs a cost by forgoing the value of asking someone else or, more appropriately, by forgoing the self-satisfaction from solving a problem without help. Person B, if he responds to person A's request with help-giving activity, incurs the cost of forgoing the value of using his own time for his own purposes. If person A's rewards gained through and from the contribution of B's help and time exceed the costs he incurred by forgoing the solving of his own problem, the interaction will be profitable to him. If person B's rewards in the form of person A's approval and gratitude exceed the costs of the time he sacrificed, then he too made a profit. The fact that both parties profited from their exchange of activities increases the probability that the interaction will be continued. However, if the interaction becomes one in which person A frequently emits similar help-requesting units of activity and person B frequently reciprocates by emitting similar help-giving units of activity, it will in time result in a loss. That is, person A will eventually become satiated in his need for help from B, and person B will become satiated in his need for approval from A. In this case the cost will come to exceed the rewards and the interaction (at least with regard to these same activities) will be discontinued. This interaction outcome is predicted by proposition 4 stated above. Too great a *quantity* of exchange of the same rewards leads to a decrease in the *value* of those rewards and hence an increase in the cost incurred in emitting them.

When the costs of engaging in a specific interaction come to exceed the rewards consequent upon that interaction, the parties in that interaction will discontinue it and, furthermore, will seek out alternative activities either with one another or with alternative social others.

The Rule of Distributive Justice

Distributive justice as well as being an illustrative rule of exchange in Homans' theory also was used by Homans to generate the fifth and last proposition. In social relationships, the rule of distributive justice holds that *"a man in an exchange relation with another will expect that the rewards of each man be proportional to his costs—the greater the rewards, the greater the costs—and that the net rewards, or profits, of each man be proportional to his investments—the greater the investments, the greater the profit"* (Homans, 1961, p. 75. Italics ours). When the desired proportionality between rewards and costs, and investments and profits, does not accrue from social exchange, the rule of distributive justice is violated. The probable results of this rule violation are expressed in Homans' fifth and last proposition, which states: *"the more to a man's disadvantage the rule of distributive justice fails of realization, the more likely he is to display the emotional behavior we call anger"* (Homans, 1961, p. 75. Italics ours). A corollary to this proposition holds that if the failure of distributive justice in a social exchange is to the man's advantage rather than to his disadvantage, he will be likely to experience a level of *guilt* proportional to the extent of his undeserved advantage.

Distributive justice, then, is more than an applied case of social exchange; it is also a rule that is operative in all areas of social behavior.

In any social exchange, distributive justice can be characterized as the process of *fair exchange* of rewards and costs. If we assume, as Homans does, that participation in one activity precludes participation in an alternate activity, and further that the more valuable the alternate activity the greater the cost the person incurs in engaging in the first activity, then engaging in the first activity when the alternate activity is highly rewarding *should,* if fair exchange applies, lead to proportionately high rewards.

Let us conceptualize a situation where fair exchange does not exist. Person A emits help-requesting activity toward person B. Person A does not forgo a great deal of value in not performing the behaviors himself because they require specialized talents which he does not have. Therefore, his cost in emitting the help-requesting activity is low. Person B responds to person A's request by emitting help-giving activity toward person A. If person B is a rabid baseball fan and in order to help person A, he forgoes attending a world series game for which he has tickets, he is incurring considerable cost in helping person A. If person A through the help of person B's specialized knowledge solves an important and relevant problem, he gains a sizable reward. Further, if person A does not emit rewarding activities toward person B proportionate to person B's investment of time and energy, person B gains little reward. In this case, the exchange of activity and rewards is disproportionate to the initial degree of cost and investment of the participants. Person A, whose cost and investment were low, reaps greater profits than person B, whose total costs and investment were high. According to proposition 5, this should lead person B to become angry and person A to become guilty. If this relationship between person A and person B exists in all unit exchanges that they engage in, that is, if the rule of distributive justice is frequently violated then person B should discontinue engaging in exchanges with person A.

Homans stated that one's evaluation of whether or not he is receiving a just return on his investments in a social exchange is based upon his past experience in other social exchanges. These past experiences set up expectations of "exchange rate" in individuals. In our above example, person A would not experience guilt if he did not experience the exchange of rewards as disproportionate to the original investment. That is, if his past experience was such as to lead him to expect large rewards for small investments, the situation depicted above would be considered "just" by him. On the other hand, if person B had been accustomed to small rewards for large costs (if he were a "martyr type," for example), then he might not experience anger at the depicted exchange. When there are conflicting and noncomplementary standards between two interacting individuals of what a fair rate of exchange is, it will probably be impossible for the rule of distributive justice to determine the course of interaction. In this case the most likely eventuality would be a discontinuance of the exchange. This concept of individually differing expectations of reciprocal or just rewards is very much like Thibaut and Kelley's (1959) concept of *comparison level,* discussed in a later section of this chapter.

Research on the applications of the rule of distributive justice has usually been done in industrial settings where the rewards and costs of employees can be evaluated through the measurement of worker satisfaction. If one wishes to pursue the analysis of the construct of distributive justice further, the studies of Homans (1953), Sayles (1958), Benoit-Smullyan (1944), Zaleznik, Christensen, and Roethlisberger (1958), Zaleznik (1956), and Adams (1953) are recommended.

Comment

Homans has articulated an interesting explanatory approach to dyadic social interaction. This approach, like the ones that follow it in this chapter, is based upon a modified law of effect. That is, if an interaction yields satisfying outcomes, it will be recreated; if it yields unsatisfying outcomes, it will be discontinued. Homans used an economic interpretation of satisfying and unsatisfying situations by asserting that an interaction will be satisfying if it yields a psychological profit to the interactor and will be unsatisfying if it results in a psychological loss. The theory is logically consistent, testable, and generally satisfies the minimal criteria for acceptance.

In sections of his theoretical exposition not presented here, Homans applied his theory to several areas in social psychology. Specifically, he cited studies in conformity, competition, authority, and social influence and reinterpreted their findings within an exchange-theory framework. His reinterpretations are incisive and interesting, and the interested reader may wish to refer to Homans book for further details. Nevertheless, while Homans has reinterpreted existing findings in a lucid manner, his theory has not generated independent research and thus has not been subjected to test. On the surface, the lack of relevant research is surprising. Homans has made a clear statement of his propositions and hypotheses and has apparently defined his terms in an operational fashion. However, upon closer examination, it becomes obvious that the manner in which Homans exposited his basic terms, especially "value," is not very conducive to experimental operationalism. The determination of how valuable an activity is to a specific interaction participant would be very difficult. Although this determination might be made in specific situations where the experimenter has control over the antecedent reward conditions of the subjects, antecedent control can be established for only relatively few instances of social behavior.

Gewirtz and Baer (1958) demonstrated that the efficacy of social reinforcers in children is a function of the experimentally *established* or aroused drive for those reinforcers. Thus, they have shown that the value of a social reinforcer increases with increasing deprivation, and as the value increases, the efficacy of the reinforcer in increasing the frequency of the specified response also increases. Nevertheless, experimental findings such as this are few. The varied activities involved in social relationships would be difficult to classify on a simple scale of value. The assessment of an individual's past social reinforcement history is virtually impossible.

In order that Homans' well-stated and concise hypotheses be subject to empirical test, the terms and concepts upon which these hypotheses are based need to be more precisely defined and linked to experimental operations. Removing the vagueness and indefiniteness from Homans' terms would undoubtedly decrease their conceptual generalizability, but it would at the same time increase their functional utility as experimental variables.

A THEORY OF INTERACTION OUTCOMES

Thibaut and Kelley (1959) proposed a theory to explain the manner in which two or more persons in an interactive relationship are dependent on one another for the attainment of positive outcomes. They note that their approach "takes as its independent variables the possibilities of reciprocal control possessed by the members of a collectivity. Only that control mediated by the ability to affect another person's outcomes (such as rewards, payoffs, reinforcements, and utilities) is considered" (Thibaut & Kelley, 1959, p. 4). The dependent variables in their analysis are the products of interdependent relationships, such as norms, roles, and power. Thus, Thibaut and Kelley were concerned with the various forms of interdependent social interactions and the outcomes of each of these forms. Once the dimensions of objectively interdependent relationships were established, Thibaut and Kelley posited certain predictions about what the participants in an interdependent relationship do to maintain a relationship that is viable, stable, and reciprocally rewarding.

A basic premise of Thibaut and Kelley's theory is that a socially significant interaction will be repeated only if the participants in that interaction are reinforced as a function of having participated. That is, a social act must yield positive outcomes to the individual if it is to be continued. In a dyad, both participants must experience positive outcomes for the target interaction to continue. The rewards that accrue to each individual in a collectivity are often varied and frequently difficult to specify. Positive payoffs from social interaction may be material (object gain) or psychological (gain in status, power, affection, etc.).

A corollary premise of this theoretical system is that one of the goals in an interdependent social interaction is the *maximization* of positive outcomes for each of the participants. Although the maximization of outcomes is functional to the individual, it is also functional to the group because it increases the probability that the group will maintain its integrity as a unit.

An Overview of the Theory

Thibaut and Kelley stated that the essence of any interpersonal relationship is *interaction*. In their theorizing they were predominantly concerned with *dyadic* interaction. They defined dyadic interaction as occurring when two people emit behavior in one another's presence. The behavior emitted by each person must at the very least have the possibility of affecting the other person. Every individual has an extensive repertoire of behaviors that may be emitted in an interaction. One might analyze the behavior occurring in an interaction in many different ways. A microscopic analysis would involve considering in its intricacy every single unit of behavior that a person emits. A macroscopic analysis, on the other hand, would involve viewing only the general end products of a total sequence of interactive behavior. Thibaut and Kelley claimed to have taken a middle course between these two extremes. They designated the *behavior sequence,* or *set,* as their unit of analysis. Each specified interactive unit (behavior sequence) consists of a number of verbal and motor acts that are sequentially organized and directed toward a goal. Some of the responses within this sequence are *instrumental* in that they move the individual toward the goal, and others are *consummatory* in that they engender the individual's enjoyment of the goal state. In all cases the individual responses within the sequence are serially dependent. That is, each single response is dependent upon the one preceding it in the sequence. This sequential organization apparent in behavior sequences indicates that the individual maintains a consistent orientation in reference to the goal throughout the sequence. For this reason, behavior sequences are alternately referred to as *sets*.

In a two-party interaction, each party may produce any given set, or behavior sequence, that is initially within his repertoire. The production of a given sequence can depend upon his own internal need state or the instigation of the other person. The "stream of interaction" between two individuals can be described in terms of the items in their repertoire which each produces in the presence of the other, in response to the other, or as stimuli to the other.

Although the outcomes of interactions may be described in many ways, Thibaut and Kelley chose to consider the *rewards* and *costs* that accrue to the individual as a consequence of his having participated in an interaction. Rewards are the satisfactions and gratifications that a person receives from having participated in a given interaction with another. Costs are those factors that serve to inhibit the performance of a given behavior sequence. They are the negative consequences of emitting a sequence of behavior in an inter-active context. Thus, the outcome of any interaction is considered to be a resultant of the rewards received and the costs incurred.

In an interaction, the rewards that one gains and the costs that he incurs may be determined by factors external to that interaction or by factors inherent in that interaction. The first category of *exogenous determinants* includes the individual's own needs, values, and abilities or the situational context of the interaction. Exogenously determined rewards and costs may be alternatively gained or incurred by the individual. That is, one particular interaction is not essential to their attainment. The second category of reward-cost determinants is referred to as *endogenous determinants*. These are inher-ent in the interaction. Therefore, "the specific values associated with A's repertoire depend upon the particular item in B's repertoire with which, in the course of interaction, it is paired" (Thibaut & Kelley, 1959, p. 16). The items in B's repertoire, then, might either interfere with or facilitate A's attain-ment of positive outcomes. Endogenously determined rewards or costs could not accrue to an individual except through interaction with at least one other individual.

The major analytic technique used by Thibaut and Kelley is the *outcome matrix*. The outcome matrix is formed by noting all the behaviors that two individuals might jointly perform. Each cell of this matrix contains one item of *each* individual's repertoire. Hypothetically, at least, all items of A's behav-ior repertoire are represented on the horizontal axis of the matrix, and all items of B's repertoire on the vertical axis. Figure 4–1 below illustrates a hypothetical outcome matrix. The rewards gained and the costs incurred by each person are entered in each cell of the outcome matrix. Therefore, in Figure 4–1 the pairing of behavior sequence a_1 with behavior sequence b_2 will yield a quantity of reward to both A and B (r_A, r_B) and a certain cost to both A and B (C_A, C_B). If rewards and costs are combined into a single measure of goodness of outcome, a simplified matrix such as that presented in Figure 4–2 is generated.

The interpretation of Figure 4–2 is relatively clear. If person A enacts behavior a_1, and person B enacts behavior b_1, person A receives six units of positive outcome and person B receives two units of positive outcome. On the other hand, if person A enacts behavior a_2 while person B enacts behavior b_2, then person A receives two units of positive outcome and person B receives five units of positive outcome. Thus, the paired enactment of behav-ioral units by two parties in an interaction yields positive outcomes to both parties. In a cooperative relationship, both parties are likely to attempt to maximize their own positive outcomes by enacting those behaviors that yield the greatest positive outcomes for their partner. In the situation in which the paired sequences of behavior do not yield maximal outcomes to both parties, it is likely that the cooperating parties will alternate the paired behavior

A's repertoire

B's repertoire	a_1	a_2	...	a_n	a_1a_2	a_1a_3	...	$a_1a_2...a_n$
b_1	r_A, c_A / r_B, c_B	etc.	...					
b_2	etc.							
⋮	⋮							
b_n								
b_1b_2								
b_1b_3								
⋮								
$b_1b_2...b_n$								

FIGURE 4–1. Matrix of possible interaction outcomes. (Reprinted with permission from J. W. Thibaut and H. H. Kelley. *The social psychology of groups*. New York: Wiley, 1959.)

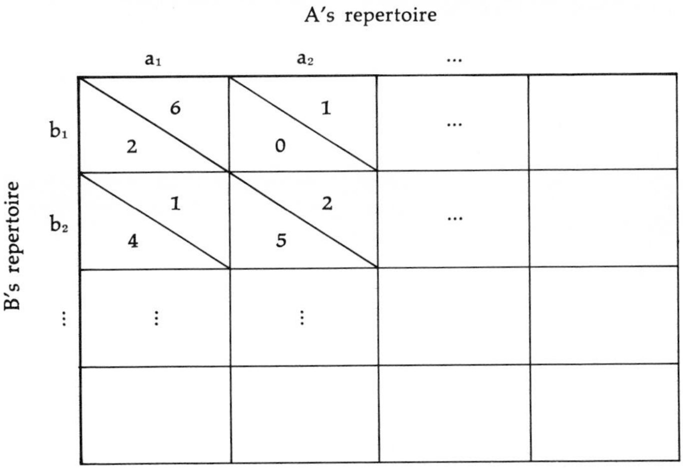

A's repertoire

	a_1	a_2	...	
b_1	6 2	1 0	...	
b_2	1 4	2 5	...	
⋮	⋮	⋮		

B's repertoire

FIGURE 4–2. Matrix of possible outcomes, scaled according to overall goodness of outcomes. (Reprinted with permission from J. W. Thibaut and H. H. Kelley. *The social psychology of groups.* New York: Wiley, 1959.)

sequences that they enact in order that both parties attain maximal positive outcome some of the time.

In a competitive relationship, each member of the dyad is likely to enact those behavioral sequences that have the greatest probability of maximal self-reward. However, in interdependent competitive relationships, persons A and B might cooperate for the attainment of maximally positive outcomes.

The outcome matrix, in addition to representing the joint outcomes accruing to the members of a dyad, also aids in "assessing the viability of a group (dyad), the satisfactions, and patterns of interdependence of its members, and the processes through which the members influence and control one another" (Thibaut & Kelley, 1959, p. 24). Thibaut and Kelley made several assumptions about the nature of the outcome matrix:

1. All relevant possibilities of rewards and costs for a given interaction are represented in the cells of the matrix.

2. All the possible behaviors of A and B peculiar to the target interaction are represented in the margins of the matrix.

3. The values for rewards, costs, and goodness of outcome vary across time. Thus, interaction does not merely involve the repetition of the most rewarding joint behaviors, but rather it consists of successive movements from one cell to another in search of the most-optimal outcome on a given trial. The variation in the reward-cost values of a given cell may be because of many factors. Two prominent ones are satiation and fatigue, both of which tend to increase the cost and lower the reward of emitting a behavior.

4. The matrix is not known to the participants prior to interaction. Instead, the participants continually discover the possible outcomes as well as their partner's (opponent's) repertoire as the interaction progresses.

Although the matrix of outcomes is a descriptive and analytic tool, Thibaut and Kelley asserted that it might also be used predictively. When individuals have searched out the contingencies within a matrix, their behavior should stabilize and they should enact those behaviors with the greatest probability of positive outcome. The nature of the matrix in terms of the objectively available outcomes accruing from the joint enactment of two individuals will then determine their most-adaptive behavior sequence. As the matrix changes, the predictions of which behavior sequences of the participants will predominate also change. Furthermore, the pattern of objectively available outcomes can be used to predict the form of interdependent relationship that will develop with interaction. Thus, power and dependence relations may be predicted on the basis of the control one party has over the positive outcomes of the second party.

As noted above, neither participant in a dyad is initially aware of the outcomes he might attain by interacting with the other. Thus, at the outset of interaction, each member samples the outcomes available to him in the target interaction. They will sustain the interaction after this sampling period only if the experienced or inferred outcomes are sufficient to warrant continued interaction. The adequacy of experienced or inferred outcomes is evaluated on two criteria: (1) the comparison level (CL) and (2) the comparison level for alternatives (CLalt). The first of these is the standard by which an individual evaluates the attractiveness of a relationship; the second is the standard by which an individual decides whether or not he will remain in a relationship. These two criteria are separate ones because, for example, an individual may continue a relationship regarded as unattractive if it is the best available to him at the time. The CL is the minimum level of positive outcome which an individual feels he deserves from any relationship. If a given relationship yields outcomes which fall above the CL it should be relatively attractive to the member; if the outcomes fall below the CL it should be relatively unattractive. There are several determinants of comparison level, and they are discussed in a later section of this chapter.

Thibaut and Kelley defined CLalt as "the lowest level of outcomes a member will accept in the light of available alternative opportunities" (Thibaut & Kelley, 1959, p. 21). The alternative relationship used as a standard to compare a perspective relationship to is generally the member's best available alternative. For a dyad to be formed the jointly experienced outcomes must exceed each member's CLalt. The CLalt is discussed more fully in a subsequent section of this chapter.

The overview above of Thibaut and Kelley's theory should provide the reader with the necessary understanding of their orientation as well as a sufficient command of their vocabulary to consider the more-specific details of the system. The subsequent sections detail the following considerations: (1) the determinants of reward and cost, (2) the formation and evaluation of relationships, and (3) the products of interaction.

The Determinants of Rewards and Costs

The rewards and costs in interactive relationships may be determined by several factors. As we have noted previously, some of these factors are external to the stream of interaction (exogenous factors) and others are dependent upon the stream of interaction (endogenous factors).

EXOGENOUS DETERMINANTS   Rewards and costs that do not directly ensue from social interaction and that are in fact determined by factors outside the interaction are termed *exogenous*. Exogenous determinants of rewards and costs may include the individual needs and abilities of the participants, the preinteraction similarities or differences in their attitudes or values, and the situational context of their interpersonal contact with one another. In many cases, the exogenous determinants of rewards and costs cited by Thibaut and Kelley are factors which have been found to correlate with sociometric choice (Jennings, 1950; Winch, 1952; Newcomb, 1956). Some of the more-important exogenous determinants discussed by Thibaut and Kelley are ability, similarity, proximity, and complementarity. Let us briefly consider each of these.

Abilities. Persons who are preferred or chosen by others as dyadic partners often have abilities that the nonchosen do not possess. Thus, they possess a greater potentiality for rewarding the other in an interaction. However, depending upon factors such as the person's willingness to participate jointly with the other, his own needs that require specific behaviors from the other, etc., the interaction may also involve more or less cost. Nevertheless, a generally positive outcome is more likely in relationships with more-able than in those with less-able individuals. Thus, outcomes are at least partially determined by the abilities of the participants. This is particularly true in interactions in which the goal is problem solution or task completion. Ability has intentionally not been specifically defined here. Depending upon the nature of the interaction engaged in, reward-cost determining abilities may be general (intelligence, for example) or may consist of specific skills.

Similarity. There has been much research showing that individuals with similar attitudes and orientations are more prone to select one another as friends, mates, or partners. Thibaut and Kelley have asserted that these findings may be interpreted in a reward-cost framework:

> If we assume that in many value areas an individual is in need of social support for his opinions and attitudes then another person's agreeing with him will constitute a reward for him. . . . Thus two people with similar values may provide rewards for each other simply by expressing their values. This may also be a low-cost operation, since it is easy for a person to express the values he really feels (Thibaut & Kelley, 1959, p. 43).

Thus, preinteraction similarities between participants in a dyad should facilitate the attainment of positive outcomes by both members during the interaction.

Proximity. Citing experimental evidence from several sources (Festinger, Schacter, & Back, 1950; Gullahorn, 1952; Powell, 1952; Newcomb, 1956; and

Williams, 1956), Thibaut and Kelley designated physical proximity as an exogenous determinant of rewards and costs in social relationships. It takes greater effort and therefore involves greater costs to form and maintain physically distant relationships than to form and maintain physically close relationships. Proximity, particularly in natural social settings, might be confounded with similarity, and to this extent these two variables might very well coact in the formation of a relationship. Nevertheless, if one controls for the similarity of the two members of a dyad, those dyads in which the members are in physically close proximity to each other should be more long lasting and should yield a greater opportunity for positive outcomes than the dyads in which the members are spatially separated.

Complementarity. Thibaut and Kelley stated that the formation of a dyad is facilitated by the members being able to reward one another at low cost to themselves. Therefore, complementarity should also be a determinant of outcomes. That is, in a complementary relationship each person can perform activities for the other that the other cannot perform for himself. Thus each can provide something that the other *needs* and cannot procure himself. A dominant person will have the opportunity to exercise his dominance in relationship with a dependent person; in this same relationship, the dependent person could receive his dependency gratifications from the dominant one (Winch, 1955). In a complementary relationship, such as the one just cited, the rewards for both participants are high (need gratification), and the costs are low (the emission of behaviors consonant with one's orientation), and thus outcomes are positive for both.

According to Thibaut and Kelley, the exogenous determinants of rewards and costs function as "boundary conditions" or givens for any interactive relationship. However, the maximum rewards and minimum costs that are potentially available to individuals in an interactive relationship can be achieved only when certain factors endogenous to the relationship are operative. Thus, the exogenous determinants set the limits of achievement of positive outcomes in an interaction setting, and the endogenous factors determine whether or not these outcomes will actually be attained.

ENDOGENOUS DETERMINANTS   The endogenous factors that determine reward-cost contingencies are those factors that arise during and as a consequence of the interaction process. Thus, they are factors internal to a specific dyad or group. Endogenous factors, when optimal, facilitate the maximization of positive outcomes for the participants in an interaction; when they are less than optimal, they attenuate potential positive outcomes.

The endogenous interference with or facilitation of optimal reward-cost possibilities results from the combinations of behavior sequences enacted by the members of a dyad. In a dyad, person A may enact a behavior sequence (a_1) that is incompatible with B's enactment of a behavior sequence (b_1). Insofar as sequence a_1 is incompatible with sequence b_1, it serves as an interference to the performance of b_1 when they occur in combination. Furthermore, if sequence b_1 is incompatible with A's performance of a_1, then these particular sets of the two participants are mutually incompatible and symmetrically interfering.

Consider the following example of a dyadic relationship in which person A and person B are brothers. Person A enacts behavior sequence a_1 involving the playing of some popular records on a phonograph located in the study. Person B, however, is attempting to enact behavior sequence b_1 involving study. It is apparent in this example that behavior sequence a_1 is incompatible with b_1 and thus reduces B's reward probabilities. On the other hand, b_1 is also incompatible with a_1 in that it attenuates A's enjoyment of the records (for example, having to turn down the volume). Thus behavior sequences a_1 and b_1 are symmetrically interfering and thus mutually incompatible. The enactment of the combined a_1b_1 behavior sequences interferes with A and B maximizing their rewards at minimal costs.

To maximize rewards at minimum costs, either person A or person B in the example above might change his behavior sequence. Thus person A might enact behavior sequence a_2, which might involve polishing his shoes in preparation for the next day, and thus allowing B to study for a longer period of time. Person B, on the other hand, might switch to behavior sequence b_2 and delay studying in order to listen to some of his favorite records along with person A. Thus, the enactment of either the joint behavior sequence a_2b_1 or a_1b_2 would be mutually facilitating to persons A and B and thus maximize the rewards and minimize the costs of participating in this particular relationship.

Thibaut and Kelley noted that response interference in a dyad may exist at two levels: (1) person A may enact a behavior sequence that interferes with person B's *production* of a given set and (2) person A might enact a behavior sequence that interferes with B's appreciation of the products of his behavior, or his *consummation* of rewards contingent upon his behavior. In the first case, B's costs are likely to go up although his rewards will be only secondarily affected. In the second case, B's rewards will decrease in value and, additionally, his costs will also increase as a function of A's production of an interfering sequence.

With regard to A's enactment of a behavior sequence (a_1) which interferes with B's production of behavior sequence b_1, Thibaut and Kelley stated that *"inhibiting or incompatible response tendencies accompanying the production of behavior increase the optimal cost of the behavior, whether in the form of annoyance, embarrassment, anxiety, or the increased effort required to make the appropriate responses"* (Thibaut & Kelley, 1959, p. 53. Italics ours). As we have implied above, interference is often *mutually* produced by the behavior sequence enactments of both parties in a dyad. Thibaut and Kelley invoked a conflict hypothesis to explain the *amount* of cost increase under conditions of set incompatibility. They suggested that the costs induced by interference are proportional to the conflict aroused by the incompatible situation. That is, if a_1 arouses only weak competing tendencies to sequence b_1, then the cost incurred by B will be relatively small. On the other hand, if a_1 arouses strong competing tendencies to b_1, then the cost of B's enactment of b_1 will be high. For example, if a_1 arouses in person B a tendency to enact a behavior sequence with potentially attractive outcomes that at the same time conflicts with sequence b_1, then the cost incurred by B in performing b_1 will increase greatly.

When B's *appreciation* of the rewards of performing a given behavior sequence is interfered with by A's enactment of a_1, Thibaut and Kelley postulated that there should be a drop in the value of the reward. That is, insofar as a_1 interferes with B's attentive, interpretive, or consummatory responses at the point of reward, then reward value drops, merely because the reward cannot be fully "appreciated."

The formation and maintenance of a relationship is, in part, contingent upon the compatibility of the sets produced by the participants. Thus, for a relationship to survive, the participants must either *synchronize* incompatible sets or, if they cannot, eliminate them. Thibaut and Kelley stated that "behaviors may be synchronized so that only compatible responses are simultaneously performed. Such synchronization may be produced by cues that simultaneously arouse reciprocal or compatible behavior or by the existence of normative prescriptions which co-activate reciprocal role behavior" (Thibaut & Kelley, 1959, p. 63). Thus, if sets a_1 and b_1 are incompatible, they would not be produced simultaneously, but instead the participants would seek out appropriate joint-behavior sequences. Although a_1 is incompatible with b_1, it may be compatible with b_3 and hence paired with b_3 instead of b_1 in future interactions. However, "persistently interfering behaviors may be eliminated from the relationship" (Thibaut & Kelley, 1959, p. 63). Thus, the behavior sequences of one or both of the participants that consistently instigate low-reward–high-cost outcomes regardless of the sets with which they are paired will be eliminated from the relationship. If these sets are not eliminated, the flow of interaction will be inhibited and the relationship will be jeopardized.

The Formation of the Relationship

Once the initial contact is made between two individuals, the formation and survival of the relationship depend upon the levels of outcomes the individuals experience or expect to experience. Our earlier discussion of the CLalt led to the conclusion that individuals will form and remain in those relationships that promise to yield the best-possible outcomes. In the initial formative phase of a relationship, the participants explore the matrix of possible outcomes in an attempt to evaluate the objective outcome values potentially available in that relationship. Thibaut and Kelley noted that this process of exploring the matrix is accomplished by (1) *experiencing samples of the outcomes* in segments of the matrix and making inferences about the positivity of these outcomes and by (2) *forecasting trends* in the outcomes, particularly with regard to their stability.

If the initial contact between two persons results in sample outcomes that fall well below the CLalt, then the relationship will generally proceed no further. That is, if the projected outcomes of forming a particular relationship are not competitive with the outcomes possibly available in other alternative relationships, the individual would gain little and lose much by entering into the interaction on a more permanent basis. If, however, the outcomes sampled on initial contact fall well above the CLalt, the individual will then attempt to forecast trends to determine whether or not these positive outcomes will remain stable across time. If it is likely that the outcome matrix will remain stable, the individual will probably engage in repeated interaction with the target person in order to establish the relationship. When the level of the initially sampled outcomes is only marginally above the CLalt, the individual will attempt to determine if the outcomes will tend to get better or worse in the context of a more permanent relationship.

This process of exploring the matrix of possible outcomes serves to reduce the uncertainty involved in entering into social relationships. This exploration becomes very crucial when permanent relationships, such as marriage, are in their formative stage. Certain broad factors influence the exploration process. These factors were considered from the points of view of the *"production of behavior"* (the stimulus side) and of the *"perception of behavior"* (the response side).

THE PRODUCTION OF BEHAVIOR   The factors considered under this rubric are those that affect the behaviors that each person selects from his repertoire to produce in the formative stages of a relationship. The four factors dealt with by Thibaut and Kelley are strangeness, accessibility and cultural norms, autistic hostility, and autistic friendliness.

Strangeness. The early stages of most relationships are characterized by stereotypic politeness and other stereotyped forms of behavior. Thus, in general, individuals usually restrict the range of behaviors which they are willing to display to new acquaintances. This situation is particularly relevant when the two persons making initial contact are somewhat "strange" or unfamiliar to one another. A pattern case might be the initial meeting between a Negro who has had his predominant social contacts with other Negroes and a Caucasian who has had his predominant social contacts with other Caucasians.

The stranger any two people making initial contact are to each other, the greater difficulty they will have in exploring the matrix of possible outcomes because each individual will display very little of his behavioral repertoire. Thus, the perspective participants in the relationship remain relatively uncertain as to whether the interaction in question exceeds their CLalt. In this case, the individuals will have to expend more effort in exploring the matrix before arriving at a decision to form the relationship.

Accessibility and cultural norms. As we have already mentioned, in the initial contact between two persons there is generally an air of stereotypic politeness, serving as a "low-cost protection" against the premature formation of intimate relationships. On the other hand, it renders individuals relatively inaccessible on initial contact. Thus, the matrix of possible outcomes can only be minimally sampled. Thibaut and Kelley attributed this situation to cultural norms that proscribe the acceptable degree of intimacy between two individuals in a casual social contact.

Autistic hostility. Newcomb (1947) proposed that if an initial state of hostility exists between any two individuals, it will tend to preclude the initiation of further communication, rendering a resolution of the hostility virtually impossible. It is quite apparent that this state of affairs will severely limit the production of behaviors from one's repertoire and thus restrict the items of behavior sampled on first contact.

Autistic friendliness. In many ways, autistic friendliness is the converse of autistic hostility. If two individuals initially "hit it off," perhaps because they are very similar to each other in needs, values, and attitudes, they will most likely maximize their production of behavior in each other's presence. That is, they will tend to communicate more frequently with each other. The outcomes sampled in this process, however, will be biased because unfavorable outcomes will be underrepresented and favorable outcomes overrepresented. Nevertheless, under conditions of autistic friendliness the individual has a firm basis for forecasting positive trends and will thus probably enter into the relationship on a more permanent basis.

THE PERCEPTION OF BEHAVIOR   This step in the formation of a relationship involves the factors which influence one's evaluation and appraisal of another's responses with an eye toward the forecasts he might make of future outcomes. Four factors which are relevant to this process are the availability of cues, the effect of primacy of cues, the organization of perceptions, and the states of the observer. We will consider each of these briefly.

The availability of cues. Thibaut and Kelley noted that the cues available as a basis for the evaluation of another's behavior are at least partially determined by the behaviors that the other emits. At the outset of a relationship the cues available are usually those of external appearances. From these, certain inferences are made about the likely behavior repertoires of the subject. As the interaction progresses, however, but depending upon the other's strangeness and accessibility, more-concrete behavioral cues become available to the person. With this development the individual will have to engage in much less extrapolation to forecast outcomes. Thus, the certainty with which one forecasts outcome trends should be directly proportional to the cues available in the other's behavior productions.

The primacy effect. The perceptions of another's behavior and the outcomes that might spring from it are likely to become more differentiated and accurate with increasing interaction. However, data concerning the so-called primacy effect indicate that early information is more influential in molding one's perception of another and his behavior than subsequent information. However, Thibaut and Kelley did not note that the primacy effect has been shown to be situationally dependent, and in certain cases recency of information seems to be a more-potent determinant of one's perceptions.

The organization of perception. Simply, this factor deals with the manner in which the various behaviors of another unfold before the eyes of the person. That is, the manner (order of presentation of salient elements, the consistency of information, etc.) in which another presents himself to us will determine the way in which we organize our perceptions of him. The primacy effect is a special case of this latter factor.

States of the observer. The state of the observer (his needs, emotions, and anxieties) at the point of initial contact with another will in part color one's perception of that other and hence affect one's interpretation of the outcomes that might be available in a continued interaction with that other.

The Evaluation of the Relationship

Earlier in this chapter, we noted that Thibaut and Kelley posited two standards by which dyadic relationships are evaluated. They are the comparison level (CL) and the comparison level for alternatives (CLalt). In this section we deal with the determinants of the attractiveness of relationships; hence, we are predominantly concerned with the comparison level.

The CL can be represented as the neutral point on a continuum ranging from dissatisfaction to satisfaction. If the outcomes of a given relationship exceed this hypothetical neutral point, the relationship will probably be regarded as attractive and satisfactory. If these outcomes fall below this neutral point, the relationship will probably be considered to be unsatisfactory and unattractive. The CL is defined "as being some modal or average value of all the outcomes known to the person (by virtue of personal or vicarious experience), each outcome weighted by its salience (or the degree to which it is instigated for the person at the moment)" (Thibaut & Kelley, 1959, p. 81). It is apparent then that the CL is subject to situational as well as moment-to-moment changes. That is, it should vary as the individual experiences or observes new outcomes which change the hypothetical average or modal value of outcomes. The CL should also change as situational factors alter the salience of certain outcomes. Thus, the major determinants of CL are one's past experience with outcomes in social relationships and the momentary and general salience of certain outcomes. In the following discussion, both of these determinants are considered, as well as individual variation in comparison level.

EXPERIENCED OUTCOMES   According to Thibaut and Kelley, one's CL is highly dependent upon the level of outcomes that he has experienced in past relationships and that he is experiencing in present relationships. The more superior the outcomes an individual is accustomed to experiencing, the higher his CL will be for future relationships. This follows from the assumption that an individual's comparison level is the average of the positivity of outcomes he has experienced in past relationships. This formulation makes the implicit assumption that individuals will be attracted only to relationships that exceed this average level, and, therefore, other things being equal, each relationship entered should raise the individual's CL. This proposition should be qualified, however, in that individuals are sometimes forced by circumstance to enter high-cost–low-reward relationships, and these relationships will serve to reduce the CL for the evaluation of future relationships. Thibaut and Kelley compared their conception of CL to Helson's (1948) concept of adaptation level for psychophysical phenomena. For example, an individual who in his occupation is accustomed to lifting 200-pound packages will consider a 50-pound weight rather light, but an individual who customarily lifts nothing over 5 pounds in the course of a day will consider a 50-pound weight heavy. The relevance of this concept to CL seems rather apparent.

SALIENT OUTCOMES   Regardless of their positivity, not all outcomes that have been experienced, personally or vicariously, are equally salient. Hence, in the determination of one's CL, more-salient outcomes that have arisen from past relationships will be more heavily weighted than less-salient ones. "Certain outcomes will be highly salient because of the particular circumstances in which the person is asked to make an evaluation of his situation. Others are likely to be salient under almost all circumstances" (Thibaut & Kelley, 1959, p. 84). An example of outcomes that vary in salience as a function of circumstance might be the stereotypic case of an American tourist overseas forming a relationship with another American tourist with whom he would not ordinarily form a relationship if at home. In this case, the salience of the outcomes available in the relationship is heightened by several factors, such as language problems, loneliness, unfamiliarity with surroundings, and many others.

Those outcomes that are likely always to be heavily weighted are prone to be highly salient, regardless of whether or not there exist momentary instigations to them. That is, these outcomes are salient across situational variations. With regard to this order of outcome, Thibaut & Kelley proposed the following hypothesis: *"the generally and persistently salient outcomes are those perceived by the individual as instances of variations in rewards and costs for which he himself is primarily responsible—variations over which he has some degree of control"* (Thibaut & Kelley, 1959, p. 85. Italics ours).

As we have noted, the positivity of a person's outcomes is likely to fluctuate with changes in interaction or in the situations in which interaction takes place. The individual, in order to maintain positive outcomes and avoid negative ones, will be prone to alter his behavior sequences to fit the interactive situation at hand. He can be only partially successful in making these adjustments because only part of the variability between relationships and relationship settings is under the control of the individual. The remaining variability is because of external controls. Attempts to adjust the variability due to external forces is postulated to be nonadaptive and costly. Therefore, the outcomes that are most salient to the individual are those over which he can initiate adjustive control. The outcomes that are susceptible to the individual's control maintain their salience across interactive situations and constitute a stable factor in the determination of CL. These are the outcomes that the individual will seek to attain in nearly all interactions, and they are therefore heavily weighted in the person's CL. Thibaut and Kelley stated that "the outcomes under his (the person's) control will tend to be highly salient under most circumstances; those under the control of others are salient only if they are currently being experienced or if obtrusive cues are present in the immediate situation" (Thibaut & Kelley, 1959, p. 86). Thus, outcomes are weighted in terms of the individual's responsibility over them. This responsibility factor is so determinate that Thibaut and Kelley posited that the CL is roughly approximate to the modal value of those outcomes over which the individual has control.

Certain predictions stem from this proposition concerning the relationship between salience and control. For example, an individual should undergo greater changes in his comparison level if he *achieves* his outcomes than if these outcomes are *ascribed* to him. This prediction has been partially supported from a different framework in a study by Linton (1945). Based on some propositions of Festinger (1954), Thibaut and Kelley also posited that an individual will use the amount of control his social peers have over their outcomes as comparison points to evaluate their own control. Thus, the control that relevant social others enact over their outcomes also enters into the person's computation of his CL.

INDIVIDUAL DIFFERENCES AND COMPARISON LEVEL   The individual difference parameters in CL that Thibaut and Kelley considered are rather broad. That is, they did not generate lists of traits, personality components, or specific social orientations and relate these factors to CL. Instead, they concerned themselves with the differences between individuals in their perception of their own power and effectiveness to attain and control outcomes in future relationships. That is, individuals who are optimistic, and therefore see themselves as capable of attaining and controlling presently unattainable outcomes, will of course have a higher CL than individuals who are rather pessimistic about their power to attain attractive but presently unattainable outcomes. The former individuals will tend to emphasize the reward components of unattainable outcomes, and the latter will tend to emphasize the cost involved in attaining presently unattainable outcomes.

Thibaut and Kelley cited experimental evidence (Dickinson & Beam, 1931; Gouldner, 1954; Scott, Banks, Halsey, & Lupton, 1956) which indicates that individuals who perceive themselves as having the power to control outcomes will generally tend to *idealize* unattainable states. They posited that individuals who possess this tendency toward idealization will possess higher CL's than individuals with an opposite "debunking" tendency. Higher CL's in idealizers stem from their tendency to expect more from relationships than debunkers. In brief, then, an individual's CL will be much affected by his perception of his own power to attain favorable outcomes. Furthermore, Thibaut and Kelley asserted that the CL is generalizable and that persons who have high CL's have a constantly high expectation for the satisfaction he is able to gain in social relationships. Thus, the individual through his experi ences with outcomes in past relationships maintains a "general conceptior of his worth in interpersonal relationships" (Thibaut & Kelley, 1959, p. 97)

Power and Dependence in Dyadic Relationships

The matrix of outcomes indicates that each person in a dyadic inter- action has at least the possibility of exercising power over the other. This power is usually manifested by one individual's capability of controlling the reward-cost positions of the other individual. Assuming that the relationship in question yields outcomes that exceed the CLalt for both parties, these outcomes are attractive and desirable. Thus, if person A is *dependent* upon a particular unit of person B's behavior to attain a given positive outcome, then person B yields an amount of power over A which is proportional to the positivity and dispensability of that outcome. The CLalt is all important in the stability of power and dependence relationships in a given dyad. If the average outcomes from a given relationship fall below the average outcomes available in one's best alternative relationship, the bases of power and dependence in that particular dyadic relationship will be weak, and, in time, the dyad will be dissolved. Thus, the CLalt is the crucial evaluative dimension in determining the individual's dependency upon or power within a dyad.

In this section we deal with the types, consequences, and strategies of power that Thibaut and Kelley postulated as arising in dyadic relationship. Throughout this discussion, we make the assumption that the persons in the dyad understand the facts of the outcome matrix; that is, they are aware of the outcomes available to them as a function of various joint behavioral productions.

TYPES OF POWER   Thibaut and Kelley defined power in a dyad as a func- tion of "A's ability to affect the quality of outcomes attained by B" (Thibaut & Kelley, 1959, p. 101). The theorists focused on two types of power: (1) A's ability to control B's fate and (2) A's ability to control B's behavior.

Fate control. If A can alter B's outcomes by varying his own behavior, he has fate control over B. The matrix presented in Figure 4–3 is an illustration of fate control. The outcome values in the cells of the matrix represent the units of positive outcome above B's CLalt. Since all values are positive and above zero, it is apparent that the portion of the relationship exhibited in Figure 4–3 is above the CLalt for B.

In the situation depicted in Figure 4–3, A can control the magnitude of B's reward by enacting either behavior sequence a_1 or a_2. From the outcome values presented, it is obvious that B has no control over the level of outcome he will receive. If A enacts a_1, B receives one unit of positive outcome, and if A enacts a_2, B receives four units of positive outcome, regardless of what behavior sequence B selects to enact. Thus, B is completely *dependent* upon A for the level of outcome he will receive, and A wields *power* over B in terms of the level of outcome he produces for him. The greater the range of out-

A's repertoire

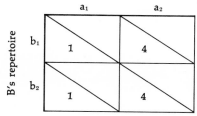

FIGURE 4–3. Illustration of A's fate control over B. (Reprinted with permission from J. W. Thibaut and H. H. Kelley. *The social psychology of groups.* New York: Wiley, 1959.)

come values that A can produce for B, the greater A's fate control over B and the greater B's dependence on A. Thus, if the value 9 were substituted for the outcome value 4 in Figure 4–3, A would have even greater fate control over B, and B would be even more dependent upon A for outcomes.

Behavior control. If A can make it desirable for B to vary his behavior by varying his own behavior, he has behavior control over B. Figure 4–4 represents an illustrative case of A's behavior control over B. In this example, if A varies his behavior sequence from a_1 to a_2, then in order for B to maximize his outcomes, he must vary his behavior sequence from b_2 to b_1. The amount of behavior control that A exercises over B is a function of the amount of gain in outcome units that B will experience by adjusting his behaviors. Thibaut and Kelley noted that in the behavior control situation, B's outcomes do not vary as a function of either A's behavior or B's behavior, but rather they are contingent upon the joint enactment of a given a, b sequence. Thus,

FIGURE 4–4. Illustration of A's behavior control over B. (Reprinted with permission from J. W. Thibaut and H. H. Kelley. *The social psychology of groups.* New York: Wiley, 1959.)

A's repertoire

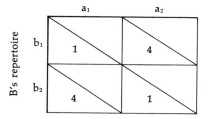

unlike fate control, in behavior control B plays a role in the attainment of outcomes. A's power in this situation stems from his ability to "force" B to emit a specific behavioral sequence to the exclusion of any other behavior sequence in order to gain maximal outcomes. Once again, then, A wields power over B, and B is dependent upon A.

THE CONVERSION OF FATE CONTROL TO BEHAVIOR CONTROL   Thibaut and Kelley noted that fate control may be used to control behavior. Referring again to Figure 4–3, we see that A can control B's behavior by always enacting a_2 when B enacts b_1 and always enacting a_1 when B enacts b_2. Thus, in effect, through fate control A has also initiated behavior control over B. To accomplish this conversion, A must have adequate information about B's choices and, furthermore, must follow a set rule when matching his choices to B's. Thus, the information A gleans from the interactive situation might be that B has two behavioral sequences available to him and that he tends to enact these sequences alternately. The rule that might then emerge for person A is that: *on each trial in which I expect B to enact b_1, I will enact a_2; and on each trial on which I expect B to enact b_2, I will enact a_1.* This is only one of several matching rules that A might apply. He can just as easily alter the rule and have the a_2b_2 sequence as the maximally rewarding one.

In order for converted fate control to operate, A must communicate the matching rule to B either directly or implicitly by repeated application of the rule. The converted fate-control situation can be an uncomfortable and unpredictable one for B if A does not adequately communicate the rules or if he misapplies the rules. Thus, the converted fate-control matrix can cause considerable uncertainty and conflict in B.

Mutual fate control may occur if both A and B have fate control over each other. This situation is illustrated in Figure 4–5. This mutual fate-control situation can implicitly be converted to mutual behavior control through the joint application of rules by A and B, once they have sufficient information about each other's repertoire. Through an exploration of the outcome

FIGURE 4–5. An illustration of mutual fate control that gives rise to implicit conversion. (Reprinted with permission from J. W. Thibaut and H. H. Kelley. *The social psychology of groups.* New York: Wiley, 1959.)

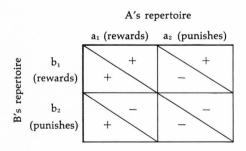

matrix the most mutually satisfactory cell (a_1b_1) will emerge as the one in which interaction will stabilize, according to the theory. Since the joint occurrence of a_1b_1 maximizes rewards for both, each dyad member is both dependent upon and in behavior control of the other member. Hence, just as fate control may be converted to behavior control, mutual fate control can be converted to mutual behavior control.

PATTERNS OF INTERDEPENDENCE   When A has fate control over B, but to exercise this control would affect his own outcomes in a negative way, then A's power over B is minimally usable. For example, Figure 4–6 presents a situation in which A will affect his own outcomes if he chooses to exercise fate control over B. In this situation (in contrast to the partial outcome matrix shown in Figure 4–3) A would be rather reluctant to use his power over B, because in doing so he would reduce his own outcomes.

A might also be reluctant to use his power over B if B possesses counterpower over him. This situation is depicted in Figure 4–7. In this case, although A has fate control over B, B has an equal amount of fate control over A.

FIGURE 4–6. A affects himself if he exercises his fate control over B. (Reprinted with permission from J. W. Thibaut and H. H. Kelley. *The social psychology of groups.* New York: Wiley, 1959.)

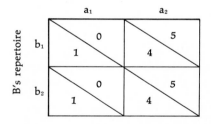

FIGURE 4–7. B and C have power counter to A's fate control over them. (Reprinted with permission from J. W. Thibaut and H. H. Kelley. *The social psychology of groups.* New York: Wiley, 1959.)

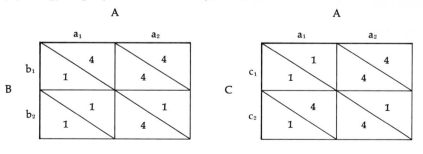

B might also hold counterpower to A's fate control through having behavior control over A as exhibited in Figure 4–7. Thus, although A has fate control over B, if he wishes to maximize his outcomes, he must enact a_2 jointly with B's b_1 or a_1 jointly with b_2 in order to achieve maximal rewards. Thibaut and Kelley noted that this act does not guarantee that B can reduce A's outcomes, but it does give him the opportunity to keep his own outcomes high by providing incentives for A's enactment of a_2. One might also conceptualize a matrix in which both dyad members hold behavior control over each other. In the latter three cases, the usable power of each member is limited by the counterpower held by the other member. Thus, the members are *interdependent* upon each other for the maximization of their positive outcomes.

THE CONSEQUENCES OF POWER   The consequences of power are considered from the standpoint of both the dyad and the individual.

For the dyad. A dyad in which both parties hold equal and high amounts of power over each other (an ideal but seldom real situation) will consist of members who are more highly interdependent and hence will be a more-cohesive dyad. A general proposition might be that the greater the correspondence and extent of power held by both members of a dyad, the greater the cohesiveness of that dyad. Thibaut and Kelley further noted that the greater power the members have over each other, the greater the convergence and hence similarity in values and attitudes. Thus, interdependence begets further interdependence.

For the individual. The possession of power or control in the dyadic situation yields the following benefits to the high-power person: (1) He gains better reward-cost positions. (2) He controls the interaction by dictating the pattern of changes in behavior sequences. This stems from his greater certainty in predicting what the outcomes will be under various joint-behavioral enactments. The person with power can *motivate* the other to change behavior at will by manipulating that power. (3) The value and attitude changes occurring in a dyad will generally converge on the attitudes and values of the high-power person. Thus, the high-power person not only has great influence over the other's values and attitudes but also can retain his own values and attitudes with little change.

STRATEGIES OF POWER   Thibaut and Kelley listed seven possible strategies for increasing power in the dyad:

1.   Raising one's CLalt so that the dyadic partner can merely keep above it. This has been referred to as "one-upmanship."

2.   Reducing the dyadic partner's alternatives, thus preventing him from using strategy 1.

3.   Improving one's ability to deliver rewards through a host of techniques, such as better tools and ingratiation. This strategy can also involve increasing the dyadic partner's susceptibility to rewards.

4.   Reducing the dyadic partner's skill through interference or some similar technique.

5. Creating a need in the dyadic partner for one's behavioral product.
6. Devaluing the dyadic partner's product.
7. Reducing one's time perspective; that is, one can increase his power by deferring his attainment of favorable outcomes to some future time. This strategy will serve both to limit the dyadic partner's power and to devalue his rewards.

Comment and Evaluation

Thibaut and Kelley's theory of interaction outcomes has been very influential in social psychology. They appropriately stated that their approach is more a point of view or frame of reference than a theory. The frame of reference they proposed has been applied to many aspects of social interaction processes, the most notable of which are power relations, interdependency, and interpersonal accommodation. The interrelated hypotheses concerning these processes are logically consistent and testable and are not inconsistent with other acceptable theories. The empirical evidence relevant to the theory is generally supportive, although some hypotheses agree with the data only under special conditions.

Many of the hypotheses proposed by Thibaut and Kelley have been experimentally tested in varying contexts. Their hypotheses are stated in a fashion that renders them both provable and refutable by empirical findings, indeed a positive attribute of their theoretical system. Furthermore, because of the flexibility of the outcome matrix as a conceptual tool, the system and its hypotheses can be altered by empirical refutations without a complete renovation of the conceptual framework.

Characteristically, the research that the theory has generated has concentrated upon *dyadic* interaction. This is entirely reasonable, for the theory itself is more amenable to the dyad than it is to more-complex relationships. Despite some of the predictions that Thibaut and Kelley (1959) made about complex relationships, it is difficult to initiate research using the concept of a three- or four-dimensional outcome matrix. For example, a four-person group consisting of members who can each initiate three possible behaviors yields a matrix with so many combinations of four person's responses that it becomes too complex to deal with in a time-limited empirical study. Perhaps some future developments in Thibaut and Kelley's analytic method will render it more applicable to complex groups.

The research based upon Thibaut and Kelley's theoretical hypotheses about dyadic interaction has yielded findings that provide moderately strong support for the theory. It is not feasible to offer a complete review of these studies in all their complexity in this text. However, certain general findings should be noted. Although several models have been used to investigate the concepts of outcome maximization, outcome control, interdependent relationships, and cooperation in a dyadic situation, two popular ones have been the "minimal social situation" and the two-person bargaining process.

THE MINIMAL SOCIAL SITUATION   The minimal social situation was first used as an experimental framework to investigate learning within the simplest possible social situation (Sidowski, Wycoff, & Tabory, 1956). It consisted of a situation in which two subjects, totally unaware of one another's presence, were placed in two separate cubicles. Each cubicle contained a control panel with two push buttons. The subjects were told simply that they could push either button as often as they liked and that the object was to garner as many points as they could. In actuality, neither subject had control over his own outcomes (shock or points), and instead his outcomes were totally dependent upon the responses of the other subject (of whose presence he was unaware). In this general situation Sidowski, Wycoff, and Tabory (1956) and Sidowski (1957) found that subjects, even though unaware of the presence of another, learned by trial and error to reward rather than to shock or penalize each other.

In a Thibaut and Kelley framework, Sidowski's minimal social situation can be viewed as an example of mutual fate control. The trial-and-error learning of "cooperation" that occurred in that situation can be interpreted as the implicit conversion of fate control to behavior control. Taking this point of view, Kelley, Thibaut, Radloff, and Mundy (1962) did a partial replication of the Sidowski et al. (1956) and Sidowski (1957) studies. Their findings indicated that in the minimal social situation individuals reward each other more than they punish each other only when they respond simultaneously and/or are informed about the nature of their relationship. Fewer than half of the dyads achieved solution (that is, converted fate control to behavior control by enacting mutually rewarding responses) under all conditions except the informed condition. These findings are consistent with those reported by others (Scodel, Minas, Ratoosh, & Lipetz, 1959; Willis & Joseph, 1959; Shaw, 1962). For example, Shaw found that dyads stabilized their responses in the mutually rewarding cell only when they were told that they were in a cooperative situation. Thus, it appears that the hypothesis that individuals will adopt behavior exchanges resulting in maximum rewards for both persons is consistent with experimental data only under certain conditions.

Rabinowitz, Kelley, and Rosenblatt (1966) replicated some of the findings above and, in addition, showed that the same results emerge in dyads where member A is under the fate control of B, and B under the behavior control of A. Although there are many aspects of the studies above that we have not discussed, it can be generally concluded that these studies as presented provide qualified support for several of Thibaut and Kelley's hypotheses about outcome control and the conversion of fate control to behavior control in interdependent relationships.

TWO-PERSON BARGAINING PROCESS   Siegel and Fouraker (1960), Schenitzki (1962), and Kelley, Beckman, and Fischer (1967), using interpersonal bargaining situations, have all generally found that subjects will make concessions to the person with whom they are negotiating that result in maximally rewarding outcomes for both negotiators. That is, when each of two subjects is instructed to bargain to obtain his own best outcome, both will engage in a series of bids and counterbids until they arrive at a bargaining solution that yields an acceptable level of profit (defined by the experimenter) to each subject. The process of bidding is equivalent to the exploration of the available outcomes by the members of the dyad. These findings are in line with Thibaut and Kelley's propositions about the nature of dyadic relationships.

Related research that has investigated factors such as interpersonal accommodation, cooperation, and competition in various forms of experimentally constructed games has also supported the utility of the outcome matrix as an analytic and predictive tool (Luce & Raiffa, 1957; Schelling, 1960; Wilson & Bixenstine, 1962). An excellent review of the findings of these studies and related ones appears in Jones and Gerard (1967).

In summary, the empirical research generated by Thibaut and Kelley's theory has been moderately supportive. This is particularly true with regard to their propositions concerning the general utility of the outcome matrix as an analytic tool and the general propensity of participants in dyads to accommodate one another in order to mutually maximize their rewards beyond some preestablished level of comparison. The evidence concerning the conversion of fate control to behavior control is less supportive, suggesting that this process occurs only under special conditions.

A FUNCTIONAL THEORY OF AUTHORITY INTERACTIONS

Adams and Romney (1959, 1962) analyzed authority interactions in terms of operant-conditioning principles. They noted that authority can be characterized as the behavioral control that one person has over another. Their analysis presents the basic paradigms representing the authority interaction sequence and specifies the determinants of this sequence.

Adams and Romney viewed authority as a bilateral phenomenon based upon reciprocal reinforcement. Thus, in any authority sequence both the subordinate and superordinate persons have the power to reinforce one another. This factor will become increasingly clear in the following section. The discussion begins with a statement of Adams and Romney's assumptions about authority, followed by an analysis of the definition of authority, a basic paradigm of an authority sequence, the determinants of authority interactions, and the functional interrelation of authority sequences.

Assumptions

Proceeding from the central notion that authority "is a relation between persons in which A commands or otherwise specifies some behavior of B and B complies with or carries out the commands of A" (Adams & Romney, 1962, p. 227), Adams and Romney noted three assumptions on which their analysis is based.

1. Authority relationships are *asymmetrical*. That is, one person in the relationship has greater power over the other person than that other person has over him.

2. Authority relationships as well as being asymmetrical are also *stable*. That is, the same person is in the superordinate position, across most of the interactions in which the two people engage. This does not preclude the possibility that there can be reversals in the superordinate-subordinate relationship in certain situations.

3. Although it is customarily assumed that authority is institutionalized by society and society's definition of roles, Adams and Romney assumed that functional authority relations can arise in any social interaction regardless of society's legitimization of the relationship. Thus, authority relationships are defined operationally.

Definition of Authority

Adams and Romney's definition of authority states that *"A person, A, has authority over Person B, in a given situation, when a response of A, under the control of deprivation or aversive stimulation and specifying its own reinforcement, is reinforced by B"* (Adams & Romney, 1962, p. 229. Italics ours). This definition contains six basic statements and implications which necessitate explanation.

1. Authority is a social relationship that is under the dual reciprocal control of both A and B. Thus, each person's behavior serves as a stimulus for the other person.

2. To maintain the relationship, each person's behavior must be reinforcing to the other.

3. Nevertheless, the relationship is asymmetrical because although A's initial response specifies its own reinforcement, B's does not. Thus, reinforcement is administered by B's response if it serves to reduce A's deprivation or remove an aversive stimulus. B's reinforcement from A is not specified or inherent in his response.

4. Authority relations are only relevant in given situations and contexts, and although single authority relationships are generally consistent with A and B's overall relationship, this pattern is reversible in specific situations.

5. The specification that A's behavior is under the control of deprivation or aversive stimulation indicates that for an authority sequence to be understood, the antecedent factors leading to A's initial response must also be comprehended and specified.

6. In order for the entire authority sequence described in this definition to be meaningful, it should be noted that persons A and B must communicate with one another. The presence of B not only helps to set the occasion for A's initial response, but A's reinforcement is contingent upon B's response.

The Basic Paradigm of an Authority Sequence

As can be noted by the characteristics of the definition above, authority is a reciprocal phenomenon in which both parties in an interaction emit responses that serve as stimuli to the other and one in which both parties reinforce the other. The authority sequence may be described as follows: A, who is under the control of some depriving or aversive condition, emits a response that serves as a stimulus for B and that specifies its own reinforcement; in turn B emits a response that provides A with the reinforcement requested or commanded; B's response as well as serving as a reinforcement for A also serves as a stimulus for A's verbal reinforcement of B; A's verbal response is then B's reinforcement. This entire sequence takes place in a general context in which person B's presence serves as a discriminative stimulus for person A's initial requesting or commanding response. The authority sequence is illustrated in the Figure 4–8.

The figure is divided into two parts, with the top part representing the stimuli and responses related to A and the bottom part the stimuli and responses related to B. The deprivation state here is A's water deprivation, and this summates with the discriminative stimulus of B's presence ($S_d + S_B^D$) to set the occasion for A's initial response (R_{A1}). A emits the response, "give me water," and this response serves as a discriminative stimulus for B (S_{A1}^D). In response to this stimulus, B responds (R_{B1}) by giving water to A. The water that A receives from B serves both as a reinforcing stimulus (S_{B1}^R), reducing the deprivation state, and a discriminative stimulus (S_{B1}^D) for his verbally expressed reinforcing response, "thank you" (R_{A2}). The verbally rewarding response of A is a reinforcing stimulus to B (S_{A2}^R).

The interaction above is one in which person A is in authority over person B because his response specifies the nature of B's response, and B in fact carries out the specified response. Nevertheless, it is also apparent that this authority relation is characterized by reciprocal reinforcement in that as a consequence to B's response, he receives the generalized verbal reinforcer, "thank you," from A. A's authority might be weakened either by himself or by B. If B did not respond to R_{A1} by emitting R_{B1}, then R_{A1} would be an unreinforced authority response and would undergo some extinction, at least

FIGURE 4–8. Authority sequence with initial response under control of deprivation. (Reprinted with permission from J. S. Adams and A. K. Romney. The determinants of authority interactions. In N. F. Washburne (Ed.), *Decisions, values and groups.* Volume 2. New York: Pergamon Press, 1962.)

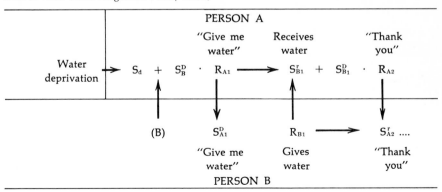

within the A-B relationship. On the other hand, if A did not respond to R_{B1} with the generalized verbal reinforcer R_{A2}, then R_{B1} would undergo extinction and A's authority over B would be weakened.

Adams and Romney made two assumptions specifically related to their basic paradigm of an authority sequence. The first is that prior to the sequence in question, there existed some temporal contiguity between R_{A1} and S^r_{B1} in the presence of person B. That is, person B gained discriminative stimulus value in setting the occasion for R_{A1} prior to the specific authority sequence. A second assumption is that the sequence analyzed is a finite one. That is, although reciprocal reinforcing sequences are *theoretically* infinite, they are in practice finite. Extending the behavior sequence beyond the limits indicated in Figure 4–8 (except perhaps for a reinforcing, "you're welcome," on the part of person B) would be socially inappropriate. Thus, reciprocal reinforcement within a given behavior sequence usually terminates at the point at which each individual exchanges a reinforcement with the other and infrequently extends beyond that point. According to Adams and Romney, authority sequences are fairly short in length, compared with other forms of interpersonal interaction.

The Determinants of Authority Interactions

According to the theory, the factors or variables that control the interactive behavior in authority sequences include reinforcing-stimulus variables, deprivation- and aversive-stimulus variables, and discriminative-stimulus variables.

REINFORCING-STIMULUS VARIABLES   Reinforcing stimuli increase the probability of occurrence of a preceding response. In the authority sequence depicted in Figure 4–8, B's giving water to A and A's thanking B in return are both reinforcing stimuli. As such, they increase the probability that on some future occasion A will emit the same response and initiate the same behavior sequence, and that B will follow through by continuing the sequence culminating in his own reinforcement. Thus, A's control or authority over B in this particular sequence of behavior is partially a function of previous reinforcing contingencies in similar situations.

Reinforcing stimuli, as well as increasing the probability of occurrence of a specific response within a sequence, also are necessary to establish the discriminative function of other stimuli within the sequence. For any stimulus to become discriminative it must be paired with a reinforcing stimulus. That is, reinforcement must occur in its presence and not occur in its absence. Thus, returning to the sequence in Figure 4–8, B's presence would not be a discriminative stimulus for A's request for water unless, in the past, it has been temporally contiguous with the reinforcement of this request. Furthermore, the past absence of B in the situation should have accompanied the nonreinforcement of A's request.

When the nonreinforcement of A's request on the part of B occurs, it tends to weaken A's authority over B. The continuation of this nonreinforcing contingency will eventually lead to the extinction of the authority sequence in question. Adams and Romney additionally proposed that nonreinforcement in authority relations may be *punishing* under certain circumstances. Thus, nonreinforcement in the authority sequence is said to have, at times, consequences beyond those of extinction. They reasoned that since many forms of noncompliance in social situations are accompanied by aversive stimulation ("go fly a kite!"), it may acquire conditioned negative-reinforcing consequences. Thus, insofar as B's noncompliance to A implies the punishment of A_b response, A on future occasions will attempt to avoid punishment by avoiding person B. By the same token, if B's compliance is not followed by A's generalized reinforcement, then B will avoid A. Editorializing for the moment, it seems that this hypothesis is a departure from Adams and Romney's basic assumption that an authority sequence is discrete and finite. That is, if authority sequences are discrete, noncompliance in one sequence would not seem to justify the generalization of noncompliance to other sequences involving the same two individuals. As such, it is difficult to conceptualize the avoidance situation depicted unless noncompliance characterized the relationship across many of the behavior sequences internal to it. Although noncompliance in a single sequence might tend to weaken the authority relation in related sequences, it seems unlikely that interpersonal avoidance would be a by-product. For example, although a father's authority may be tested by the noncompliance of his child in a single behavior sequence, it is unlikely that either the father would lose all controls over the child or that he would avoid him.

It has been noted that the authority relationship is one which is characterized by reciprocal reinforcement. Therefore, both persons A and B serve as the agents of reinforcing stimuli. Adams and Romney considered each of these separately.

A as reinforcer. Person A can act as a direct mediator of B's reinforcement and an indirect mediator over his own reinforcement by B. Thus, A can reinforce B's compliance with his request, and he might do this in several ways. He may thank him verbally, shake his hand, give him material rewards, withdraw threat, and so forth. Thus, it is apparent that A can wield considerable control over B through his "power" to directly mediate B's rewards. The greater the range of reinforcers that A can administer to B, the greater his authority and control over B. Furthermore, A's reinforcement of B indirectly controls his own behavior. The efficacy of his reinforcements to B consequent upon his verbal request or command will in part determine the probability of recurrence of that request.

B as reinforcer. The nature of B's role as a reinforcer is quite different from that of A. B's reinforcing response has no "degrees of freedom," for its content is dictated or "manded" by A's verbal response. The question here is not what reinforcer or how much of a reinforcer B should administer, but whether or not he will administer the reinforcement specified by A. His control over A then is much more limited than A's control over him, and although reinforcement is reciprocal in an authority relation, the relation is nevertheless asymmetrical.

A and B as conditioned reinforcers. Both A and B may act as conditioned reinforcers to one another. That is, insofar as A has directly mediated reinforcement for B in past situations or insofar as others resembling A have mediated direct reinforcement for B, then the mere presence of A can reinforce some of B's responses, and no direct reinforcement need be given. Where B has served as direct reinforcer to A in past situations, he too may become a conditioned reinforcer. In this case, the mere presence of B will act to maintain and strengthen the authority relationship. Furthermore, the conditioned-reinforcer characteristics of A or B may be generalized to individuals similar to them. For example, all policemen may act as conditioned reinforcers for an individual, providing that at least one policeman engaged in a previous authority relation with that individual. In many cases, the generalization of conditioned reinforcement can serve to induce institutionalized authority.

DEPRIVATION- AND AVERSIVE-STIMULUS VARIABLES AFFECTING A   It has been noted that the existence of a deprivation state in A or an aversive stimulus to A, coupled with the presence of B, are conditions for the emission of A's initial response (command, request, etc.). Thus, the response, "give me water," is more likely to occur under conditions of A's water deprivation than under conditions of satiation.

In an authority relation, there is an inverse correspondence between A's initial state of deprivation and A's response and B's reinforcement. That is, A's response must specify the conditions that are the *inverse* of his deprivation state, and B must present these conditions in order for A to be reinforced. In this sense, the deprivation of A controls the response which he makes in the presence of B. The same holds true for situations of aversive stimulation.

Adams and Romney noted that their analysis of authority sequences is an ideal model and as such might deviate from actual circumstances. (Nevertheless, they assumed that their model is generally applicable.) Thus, they acknowledged the situation in which A might emit the response, "give me water," when he is not thirsty. A might in this instance be merely asserting his dominance over B. In this case, the expressed verbal response of A does not inversely correspond to his deprivation state, nor does B's reinforcement. However, Adams and Romney noted that other behavioral cues emitted by A may reflect his deprivation state and specify the true nature of the reinforcement requested. For example, in the case where A requests water out of a need for sheer dominance over B, the "imperative mood" of the response may be conveyed to B and responded to by the act of submission (giving of water).

DISCRIMINATIVE-STIMULUS VARIABLES   Adams and Romney distinguished two types of discriminative-stimulus variables controlling A's initial response in an authority sequence: (1) the stimulus characteristics of B and (2) the situational stimuli, excluding B. It is obvious that without the presence of another person, A could not exercise any authority, and hence his initial response could not be reinforced. However, there are some more-specific aspects of B that serve as discriminative stimuli for A's response. B is a particular individual. That is, the stimulus characteristics of a B who has reinforced A in the past are different from the characteristics of a B who has not. B might also be an "incumbent" in a particular role (son, employee, student), and his presence may serve as a discriminative stimulus for only a narrow range of A's responses. B might also set the occasion for only one class of responses from A (elevator operator, ticket seller, etc.). Therefore, B may vary in his range of discriminative-stimulus functions.

Situational variables that constitute discriminative stimuli for A's initial response can be conceptualized in terms of the physical or social context within which a given authority sequence is initiated. Thus, A would probably not issue the command, "turn on the radio," if there were no radio in the immediate environment; nor would A customarily request his wife to "iron his shirt" in the midst of a cocktail party. Thus, the context provides A with discriminative-stimulus cues that control his response and dictate its appropriateness.

Discriminative-stimulus control, whether its source is another person or the situational surround, can occur only after differential-reinforcement training. That is, the individual is trained to emit certain responses and not to emit others in the presence of certain stimuli. Where the controlling discriminative-stimulus variables are highly complex, extensive discrimination training will be necessary. For example, if a response will only be reinforced in the presence of stimuli A to L, but not in the presence of stimuli M to Z, there are many discriminations that the individual will have to learn. It is possible, then, that the initial stages of learning the role of various discriminative stimuli may result in response error. This response error might even be reinforced if certain conditions prevail. Thus a person might initially come under the control of some "irrelevant" variables. With increasing training, however, these irrelevant variables should lose their controlling effect over the individual.

The Functional Interrelation of Authority Sequences

Authority sequences in groups larger than the dyad may be functionally related to one another in three ways. First, one authority sequence or some element of it might control another authority sequence or some element of it. Another condition of interrelationship exists when two sequences, or parts of them, are controlled by common or similar variables. Lastly, two sequences may be related in the situation in which two simultaneous initial responses specify incompatible reinforcement responses to B and thus result in authority conflict. Each of these is considered separately.

ONE SEQUENCE EXERCISES FUNCTIONAL CONTROL OVER ANOTHER Adams and Romney designated two situations in which one sequence may exercise functional control over another. In the first, a response in one sequence controls a response in another sequence. Figure 4–9 presents a paradigm of this form of functional control. The paradigm presents a situation in which (A) is aversively stimulated (S^{av}) by the noise of his baby (C). His daughter's (B's) presence is the discriminative stimulus that combines with S^{av} to produce his initial response, "tell Johnny to be quiet," (R_{A1}). B's response of telling baby to be quiet (R_{B1}) is under the dual control of the discriminative stimulus of daddy's initial verbal command (S^D_{A1}) and the conditioned aversive stimulus (S^{av}) consisting of her father's implied threat of punishment for noncompliance. B's response (R_{B1}) of telling baby to be quiet constitutes both a discriminative stimulus (S^D_{B1}) and an aversive stimulus (S^{av}) for baby's stopping the noise (R_{C1}). Baby's stopping the noise is both a reinforcing stimulus (S^r_{C1}) to father and a discriminative stimulus (S^D_{C1}) for the withdrawal of threat to B by father. It also is a discriminative stimulus for daughter, which produces her response reinforcing baby (R_{B2}) and removing the threat of punishment. B's response (R_{B1}), unlike a response in simple dyadic relationships, is not directly reinforcing to A. Rather, A is reinforced by C's response (R_{C1}), C by B's response (R_{B2}), and B by A's response (R_{A2}). It is apparent in this example that a response in one sequence (the A-B sequence) is controlling a response in another sequence (the B-C sequence). Such "chain of command" response sequences are exemplified in the military and in many business organizations.

The second type of situation is one in which a response in one sequence is under the control of a *whole* other sequence. This situation is limited to the circumstance in which no individuals in the first sequence are also in the

FIGURE 4–9. Response-related authority sequences. (Reprinted with permission from J. S. Adams and A. K. Romney. The determinants of authority interactions. In N. F. Washburne (Ed.), *Decisions, values and groups.* Volume 2. New York: Pergamon Press, 1962.)

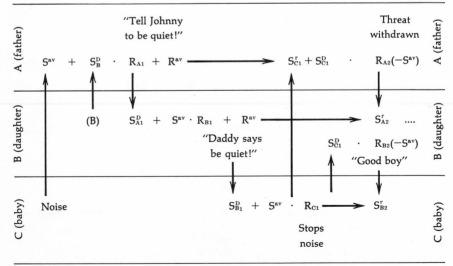

second. Adams and Romney maintained that a sequence most frequently controls a response in a second sequence through the mechanism of imitation. The first sequence serves either as a discriminative stimulus or as a conditioned aversive or deprivation stimulus for a response in the second sequence. They presented an example of a group of mothers and children; the children are playing in mud. The first authority sequence, in which one mother restrained her child from mud-playing, may constitute a conditioned aversive stimulus in that social disapproval may be implied to the second mother if she does not restrain her child. It is a discriminative stimulus setting the occasion for the second mother's response to her child. If the second mother commands her child also to stop playing in the mud and her child complies, the aversive disapproval of the first mother is withdrawn, and the second mother is thereby reinforced. The second mother's initial response is thus under the control of discriminative and aversive stimuli inherent in the authority sequence of the first mother and her child.

A COMMON VARIABLE EXERCISES FUNCTIONAL CONTROL OVER TWO OR MORE SEQUENCES   Adams and Romney presented two situational variants of this particular case. The first is concerned wtih the situation in which an individual exercises authority over a large number of other individuals. A particularly relevant example of this situation is depicted in Figure 4–10 in which a drill sergeant executes a command over a platoon of soldiers. The response, "attention," on the part of the drill sergeant specifies as its rein-

FIGURE 4–10.   One-to-many authority sequences. (Reprinted with permission from J. S. Adams and A. K. Romney. The determinants of authority interactions. In N. F. Washburne (Ed.), *Decisions, values and groups.* Volume 2. New York: Pergamon Press, 1962.)

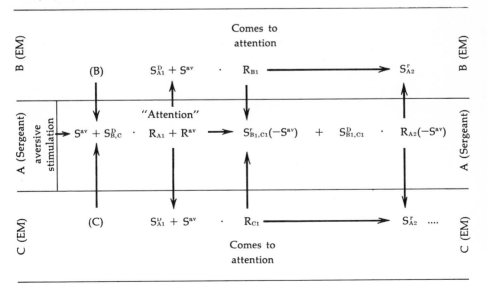

forcement the behavior of many individuals. Each pair of individuals made up of the sergeant and one other man can be thought of as an authority sequence. Each authority sequence is functionally related to all of the others since they are all under the control of those variables that determine the initial response of the sergeant.

The second situation fitting this case is one in which two or more individuals simultaneously initiate an authority sequence with a third. In this instance, both responses are identical in that they specify the same behavior to be performed by the third party. A very apt example offered by Adams and Romney is one in which both a mother and father simultaneously demand that their child stop being noisy. Their responses are functionally related because they are under the control of the child's presence and aversive noise making and because they both specify the same reinforcing response to be made by the child. In this situation, the mother and father may be viewed as a "coalition," and hence the child is under greater implied threat for nonresponse than in the simple authority sequence, and theoretically he should be more compliant.

Authority conflict. Authority conflict occurs when the superordinate persons in two or more authority sequences specify responses to the same subordinate that are either contradictory or cannot be performed simultaneously. In this case, the sequences interfere with one another. Adams and Romney gave the example of two bosses making simultaneous typing requests of a secretary late in the work day. Because of time limitations, the secretary could comply with only one of these requests. Thus, the three alternatives available to her are (1) she may fulfill boss A's request, (2) she may fulfill boss B's resquest, or (3) she may comply with neither request.

The first two of these alternatives constitute reinforcement for one of the bosses at the expense of the other. The sequence will tend to be reinitiated by the reinforced boss, but it probably will be extinguished with the nonreinforced boss. On the other hand, the reinforced boss may become a negative discriminative stimulus for the nonreinforced boss. In other words, on future occasions boss B will emit authority responses to the secretary only when boss A is not present in the field for, in this case, his responses have a greater probability of reinforcement. Where alternative 1 or 2 is selected by the secretary, many factors may have determined selection. The reinforced boss may have rewarded the secretary more frequently or more graciously in past similar circumstances; there may have been a disproportionality in the ranks of the two bosses; the reinforced boss might be more generally reinforcing than the nonreinforced boss (authority sequences may be enacted in several different interactions).

The third alternative open to the secretary is to reinforce neither response. In this case, both bosses initiating authority responses should undergo extinction or change. The most adaptive change would involve each boss using the other as a discriminative stimulus, and thus each would initiate requests to the secretary that do not occur in the other's presence or that are not incompatible with the other's requests.

Comment and Evaluation

The functional analysis of authority proposed by Adams and Romney is logically consistent, is stated in a testable form, and is not inconsistent with other accepted theories. In a sense, it is simply a conceptual application of Skinnerian principles to authority situations. However, the theorists advanced some fairly specific hypotheses about authority relations that can be subjected to independent empirical test. Until this testing is done, these hypotheses can be only tenuously accepted by virtue of their derivation from well-established principles drawn from other areas.

Although the hypotheses are stated in testable form, there seems to be no experimental evidence specifically designed to test them. However, the work of Mulder, Van Dijk, Soutendijk, Stelwagen, and Verhagen (1964) dealing with the effect of power is consistent with the theory. They defined social power as control of reinforcers and manipulated the power of one group member over others by varying the amount of monetary rewards or punishments controlled by him. They were able to show that liking relations in the group varied as a function of the magnitude of the power possessed by the most-powerful member. Since their definition of power is conceptually the same as Adams and Romney's definition of authority, the results from this study may be taken as support for their theory.

In sum, the major assets of Adams and Romney's approach to authority relationships are its clarity and conciseness in language and concepts. They operationalize all the terms in their analysis, thus considerably simplifying the experimental test of their hypotheses. Its major and most-telling weakness is that it has not been adequately substantiated by empirical research. Thus, one cannot establish the strengths and weaknesses of the analysis nor determine whether or not their simplification is an oversimplification.

THE FIELD-THEORETICAL ORIENTATION
PART 3

The field-theoretical orientation is most closely related to gestalt psychology, and many of the principles of field theory are identical with those found in gestalt theories. Because of this close affiliation, it will be helpful to review briefly the major tenets of gestaltism before considering field theory.

Gestalt psychology was founded as a school by Max Wertheimer, Wolfgang Kohler, and Kurt Koffka in Germany near the beginning of the twentieth century. According to Marx and Hillix (1963), it had its beginnings with a 1912 paper on apparent movement by Wertheimer. The founding of this school appeared to be a reaction against the atomistic approaches that were currently popular in Europe and in the United States. Its major emphasis was on the part-whole relationship, which was exemplified by perceptual phenomena. Briefly, their position may be stated as follows: parts or elements do not exist in isolation but are organized into units or wholes. For example, when we look at a building, we do not see bricks, lumber, glass, and similar parts; instead we see a house. The integration of the parts is determined by certain principles of organization, which lead the organism to perceive the best gestalt or figure possible under the given conditions. The principles of organization also determine which parts will be incorporated into which whole. The laws of science are thus the laws of systems and are equally applicable to diverse disciplines, such as physics and psychology.

Kurt Lewin, whose name is most frequently associated with field theory, was a student of the founders of the gestalt movement during its formative years. He was thus thoroughly indoctrinated with the principal viewpoints of the gestalt psychologists. It is not surprising, therefore, that these views should be recognizable in his own theorizing. However, the gestalt school was concerned primarily with perceptual phenomena, whereas Lewin soon became interested in problems of personality and social psychology. He considered the gestalt principles to be inadequate for the task of analyzing these new and different issues. New approaches were therefore necessary. Lewin's version of field theory is thus derived from early gestalt ideas, but his approach proceeds in a different direction and goes well beyond the gestalt school.

The reader may have gotten the impression that Lewin's theory is the only one that can properly be labeled as a field theory. This is not the case. The theories of Tolman (1932), Wheeler (1940), Lashley (1929), and Brunswik (1949a), to mention a few, have been called field theories (Marx & Hillix, 1963). Not everyone agrees with this classification, however, and none of these theories deals specifically with social behavior. For these reasons we have chosen Lewin's approach as the best representative of the general field-theoretical orientation, and the explication that follows is based largely upon his work. We have relied heavily on his journal articles that are reprinted in *Field Theory in Social Science* (1951). The expositions by Deutsch (1954), Cartwright (1959a), and Marx and Hillix (1963) have also contributed to our understanding of Lewin's constructs.

THE PRINCIPAL ATTRIBUTES OF FIELD THEORY

According to Lewin (1942), there are six attributes of field theory that are particularly important:

1. The use of a constructive method
2. A dynamic approach
3. An emphasis upon psychological processes
4. Analysis based upon the situation as a whole
5. A distinction between systematic and historical issues
6. A mathematical representation of psychological situations

An explication of these characteristics is necessary to provide a background for understanding field theory.

The *constructive method* is essentially an attempt to overcome the difficulties inherent in other methods that are designed to develop general concepts and laws of behavior. Lewin argued that once generalities have been abstracted from individual differences, there is no logical way to deal with the individual case. General categories such as "normal person," "average child," etc., are of little value for predictions of individual behavior. And he questioned whether they have any value if they do not permit such predictions. He proposed that psychology must shift from the "classificatory method" to a "constructive" or "genetic" method. In the first method, objects, persons, and events are grouped according to similarities; in the constructive method, they are grouped according to their relationships (that is, the way they can be derived from each other). The classificatory method uses elements of abstraction, whereas the method of construction uses elements of construction. Elements of abstraction are objects of the scientist's experience; elements of construction are his ideas (Cartwright, 1959a). An example drawn from studies of conflict behavior may serve to clarify the differences between these two approaches. Using the classificatory method, the scientist might observe that a given person revealed conflict when faced with a choice between apples and pears, a choice between chops and steaks, a choice between pie and cake, etc. He might then classify all these as *food conflicts*. Similarly, conflicts between various forms of entertainments might be grouped into a type called *entertainment conflicts*. Applying the method of construction to the analysis of conflict, Lewin showed how various types of conflict can be constructed from patterns of psychological forces. Two positive forces operating in different directions produce *approach-approach conflict;* a positive and a negative force operating in the same direction produce *approach-avoidance* conflict, and so on (see pp. 130–133 for a more-detailed presentation of the analysis of conflict).

In essence, the constructive method outlined by Lewin considers general laws as statements of empirical relations between constructive elements or certain properties of them. The "constructive elements" are really psychological constructs such as "position," "life space," "boundaries," and similar concepts. A consideration of the major constructs of field theory will be presented later in this chapter.

In applying the constructive method, Lewin maintained that the approach must satisfy several requirements. First, the approach must be *dynamic*. This refers to an interpretation of changes that are the result of psychological forces. He was critical of traditional approaches that emphasize the "static" aspects of behavior. In order to understand behavior in depth, it is necessary to formulate scientific constructs that deal with the underlying forces of behavior. Psychoanalysis is cited as the outstanding example of the dynamic approach, although it has not always met the requirements of scientific method.

In addition to being dynamic, the approach must at all times be *psychological*. Field theory is said to be behavioristic in the sense that concepts are defined operationally. However, field theory breaks with other behavioristic approaches that have "confused" the need for operational definitions with a demand for the elimination of psychological descriptions. Behavior must be described in terms of the psychological field as it exists for the individual at any given time. One might say that the description of the situation must be "subjective" rather than "objective." That is, the situation must be described from the viewpoint of the individual whose behavior is under consideration, rather than from the viewpoint of the observer. Scientific constructs must therefore represent psychological concepts.

In order to use scientific constructs in the dynamic analysis of behavior, field theory holds that the *analysis must begin with the situation as a whole*. Instead of beginning with isolated elements of the situation and later attempting to organize them into an integrated system, field theory begins with a description of the situation as a whole. After the initial characterization of the whole situation, it is then possible to examine it for specific elements and relations among these elements. This approach is presented as being analogous to the approach taken in physics. It presupposes that there are properties in the field that can be seen under certain conditions as a unit. The types of properties that are used (for example, "space of free movement," "social climate") in the analysis of the situation as a whole are seen as being similar to physical concepts (for example, "field of gravity," "electrical field").

Behavior must be analyzed in terms of *the field at the time* the behavior occurs. The approach must be systematic rather than historical in nature. This is one of the major distinctions between theories based upon the gestalt orientation and those derived from other viewpoints. Gestalt-like theories assert that it does not matter how the situation came to be the way it is at the present time; it has the same effect on behavior regardless of its historical antecedents. Lewin pointed out that few psychologists would accept the proposition that behavior can be derived from future events. But, he argued, derivation of behavior from past events is just as unacceptable because past events no longer exist and hence cannot affect behavior in the present. Of course, he recognized that the past can have an indirect effect on behavior via its effect on the psychological field. The past psychological field serves as an origin of the present field, and the present field in turn affects behavior. But in most cases the ways in which the past influences the present are not known in enough detail to be useful in the analysis of behavior. Although field theory may be applied to historical problems in order to understand the developmental process, the analysis of behavior per se should be ahistorical in its approach.

The language of scientific analysis must be logically strict and in line with the dynamic, psychological, constructive method of analysis. This meant, for Lewin, that the language must be *mathematical*. He rejected the common notion that mathematics cannot handle qualitative data. On the contrary, he maintained that certain forms of geometry, especially topology, are exceedingly useful in representing the structure of psychological events. (As we shall see later, topology is the major mathematical tool exploited by field theorists.) Topological and vector concepts are the most powerful and precise conceptual tools available to psychologists. Progress in psychological analysis can be made only if such conceptual tools are employed to represent psychological situations.

In summary, Lewin's formulation of field theory requires a dynamic, psychological application of the "constructive" method to psychological problems. The behavior must be viewed as a function of the situation as a whole as it exists at the moment for the individual. The psychological situation must be represented in the most-precise terms possible, and this task requires a mathematical representation.

With the general orientation of Lewin clearly in mind, we are now ready to examine the major theoretical constructs that he employed in attempting to explain social phenomena. The reader should also keep in mind that Lewin's constructs were introduced in piecemeal fashion, rather than as parts of a unified and integrated theory. That is, the various constructs were formulated as needed to handle the particular social problem of concern at the moment. If the following presentation appears somewhat disjointed, it is because, at least in part, of the fact that Lewin's ideas were presented in a series of papers and were never organized into a single integrated theory.

THE MAJOR CONSTRUCTS OF FIELD THEORY

Science is usually defined as systematized knowledge of any one department of mind or matter, and *scientist* is defined as one who is skilled in science. Thus, the scientist is one who systematizes knowledge. To Lewin this definition meant that the scientist's task consists of the process of conceptualizing; his task is to make appropriate translations from phenomena to concepts (Lewin, 1951). This is no easy job, since a useful scientific concept not only must represent both the qualitative and quantitative aspects of the phenomenon, but also must adequately represent its causal attributes. Furthermore, it should be formulated in such a way that operational definition is easy (or at least possible) and should permit the stating of general laws that may be applied to the individual case. As D. Cartwright pointed out (in foreword to Lewin, 1951), this calls for powerful concepts and a powerful method to generate them. Lewin believed that the method of construction was equal to the task. This method, first developed in mathematics, has been used successfully in other disciplines, such as physics. Elements of construction, such as ions and atoms, have been particularly useful in physical theories.

To apply the method of construction to psychological phenomena, one must also develop elements of construction and techniques for organizing these elements into a system (Lewin, 1944). In psychology, elements of construction are such things as "life space," "field forces," and "tension systems." Such scientific terms are not to be confused with popular terms such as "frustration," "hope," "aggression," and "learning." A popular term cannot be considered an element of construction because it lacks conceptual definition through coordination with mathematical concepts and refers to many different settings rather than to one conceptually definable situation. For example, the field-theoretical approach insists that it is impossible to investigate the laws of frustration without investigating at the same time what frustration *is* psychologically.

Lewin suggested that concepts like "learning" and "frustration" are related to easily observable but superficial properties, whereas more-adequate scientific constructs go beyond this level. One evidence of higher-level constructs is the possibility of defining their conceptual type and their conceptual dimension. Again appealing to physics for an example, Lewin indicated that speed and acceleration do not have the same conceptual dimension, since speed is distance over time and acceleration is distance over time squared. Everything that can be expressed as speed has the same conceptual dimension as do all things that can be expressed as force. This distinction is important, since only those things that have the same conceptual dimension can be compared as to magnitude; that is, quantitatively. Unfortunately, he did not develop the idea of concepual dimensions in detail. He did, however, indicate some psychological concepts that have the same conceptual dimension and some that are different. Psychological position, defined as a spatial relation of regions, has the same conceptual dimension as group belongingness, occupational position, and cognitive structure. Concepts having different conceptual dimensions include such things as locomotion (a relation of positions at different times), force (a tendency to locomotion), and goal (a positive valence).

The foregoing ideas underlie the development of formal constructs in Lewin's theoretical work. In the following pages we will attempt to identify and describe the major constructs proposed by Lewin and to show how these were applied to selected social problems. His most fundamental construct is, of course, "field." In psychology, the field that must be considered is the *life space* of the individual; hence, our first task will be a consideration of this psychological construct.

Life Space

The life space of an individual consists of the person and the psychological environment as it exists for him. It is the totality of all psychological factors that influence the individual at any given moment. In a similar manner, the life space of a group consists of the group and the environment as it exists for the group at the time. Before going into a detailed discussion of the nature of the life space, it will be helpful to consider some of the general characteristics of this construct.

The first important aspect of life space is that it includes all the things that have *existence* and excludes all that do not have existence for the individual or group at the time. For Lewin, a thing exists if it has demonstrable effects. The task of the scientist, therefore, is to determine specifically what things exist for the individual or group and to devise methods of observation and measurement adequate for representing the life space. Adequate representation of the life space will then permit the statement of laws concerning the properties of the life space and the changes of these properties. Lewin devoted much time to the question of what should be included in the life space and what should be excluded. It is relatively easy to decide many things that should be included, such as the needs and goals of the individual, and also many things that should be excluded, such as events occurring in remote parts of the world and unknown to the individual. However, there is a broad zone of ambiguity where the decision is not so easy. For example, there are many economic and political events that affect the individual's behavior, although the events occurred in remote places. These must be included in the individual's life space. There are also certain unconscious states that must be included, since these can be determined to have effects on behavior.

The various elements of the life space are characterized by *interdependence*, although the degree of interdependency may vary. This fact imposes many problems of conceptualization and measurement, which were never adequately solved by Lewin. However, his concern with these problems led to many useful insights, as we shall see later.

Finally, it is important to remember that Lewin regarded the properties of the field at any given time as the only determinants of behavior. This *ahistorical orientation* is often seen as a denial of the efficacy of learning, but such a view reflects a misunderstanding of the principle. Lewin recognized that the life space at any given time was partially determined by past events, but his position was that these past events were not directly related to behavior. For example, if a person is thirsty, he will drink—and it does not matter whether the thirst was produced by several hours of water deprivation or by one hour of hard work. The important thing for behavior is that the need for water is a part of the individual's life space at the time water is available to him. Similarly, if a person has "learned" that a wire is charged with electricity he will respond to it in the same way regardless of the source of this information, assuming, of course, that other parts of the life space remain constant.

We are now ready to examine the nature of the life space: its cognitive structure and its dynamic characteristics. We will look first at the life space of an individual and later show how this may be applied to the group. The first thing of significance is that the life space is *differentiated* into *regions*. A region (or life sphere) is any major part of the life space that can be distinguished from other parts of the life space. Examples of life spheres are needs, profession, family, friendships, and the like. These life spheres are further differentiated into smaller units. In practice, the degree to which the differentiated parts of the life space must be considered will depend upon the purposes of the analysis. In some cases it will suffice to identify only life spheres, whereas in others the differentiation of these spheres must be taken into account.

The degree of differentiation of the life space of an individual depends upon a number of variables, such as the age of the person, his intelligence, and the experiences that he has had. The life space becomes more differentiated as the child grows older; the more-intelligent person has a more highly differentiated life space than the less-intelligent person, and so forth. Figure 5–1 shows the life space of a hypothetical person as a child and as an adult. We can see that the adult's life space is considerably more complex than the child's, and thus his behavior is determined by more variables than the behavior of the child is.

The diagrams in Figure 5–1 also illustrate two additional dimensions of the life space: the *fluidity* of the system and its *reality-irreality* characteristics. The fluidity of the life space refers to the degree to which regions are distinguishable from each other, to the ease of moving from one region to another. The life space of the child is more fluid than the life space of an adult in that the various regions are less clearly defined and different regions are often only vaguely distinguishable. In the case of the newborn, for example, no region called "my own body" exists; only later in life does the infant begin to pay attention to his own body and to differentiate it from the environment (Buhler, 1939; Lewin, 1946). The relative fluidity of the various regions of the life space is due to the *rigidity* of the *boundaries* of the regions. This aspect of the life space is shown in Figure 5–1 by the width of the boundaries separating regions. The wider the boundary the more distinguishable the region, the more rigid the boundary, and the less fluid the system. This aspect of the life space will be of further interest in connection with our consideration of tension systems, presented in the next section.

The second aspect of the life space, the reality-irreality dimension, is indicated in Figure 5–1 by the two levels marked "I" (irreality level) and "R" (reality level). The level of irreality involves imagery and fantasy, whereas the level of reality involves more-objective aspects of the life space, such as the

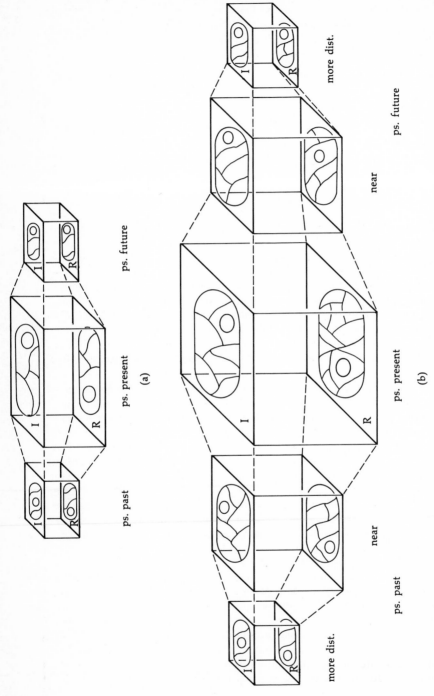

FIGURE 5–1. The life space at two developmental stages. The upper drawing represents the life space of a younger child. The lower diagram represents the higher degree of differentiation of the life space of the older child in regard to the present situation, the reality-irreality dimension, and the time perspective. (C = child; R = level of reality; I = level of irreality; Ps past = psychological past; Ps present = psychological present; Ps future = psychological future.) (Reprinted with permission from K. Lewin. *Field theory in social science.* New York: Harper and Row, 1951.)

toys in a playroom. The level of reality in the psychological future corresponds to what is expected, whereas the level of irreality corresponds to the hopes and fears for the future. Dynamically, the level of irreality is more fluid and more closely related to the central layers of the personality than the level of reality.

To conclude this section, we might note that the structure of the life space consists of the positional relations of its parts and is expressed by Lewin by the topology of the life space. Changes in structure may occur in a variety of ways:

1. By an increase in differentiation of a region
2. By a combination of two or more regions into one
3. By a decrease in differentiation
4. By breaking up a region into relatively independent regions
5. By restructuring; that is, by a change in pattern but no change in differentiation

Behavior and Locomotion

Behavior means any change in the life space. Behavior is coordinated to the movement of the person in the life space, but not all such movements are behavior. For example, if the person is moved from his office (professional region) to a hospital (health region) while he is unconscious, this would be movement in the life space but would not constitute behavior. On the other hand, if he went to the hospital for a checkup, this movement would be behavior.

Behavior may be regarded as a *locomotion* of the person in the life space, since locomotion refers to movement within the life space. Locomotion is not the only change in the life space, but Lewin states that it is the most important one (Lewin, 1936, p. 47). There are different kinds of locomotions: for example, a person may move about (bodily locomotion), or he may approach or avoid certain goals (psychological locomotion). But the person may locomote in only some parts of the life space; that is, only some parts of the life space are open to him from his present position. This *space of free movement* is usually a multiply connected region, limited by what is forbidden to the person and by what is beyond his abilities. Such a *barrier*, defined as a boundary that offers resistance to locomotion, limits the space of free movement when it is impassable or impenetrable.

Locomotion may be produced by a *need*, which corresponds to a tension system of the interpersonal region. The extent to which the need will produce locomotion depends in part upon the degree to which the interpersonal region is in *communication* with another region, where two regions are said to be in communication if a change of state in one region produces a change in the other region. If two regions are in communication, and a need is aroused in one of the two regions, locomotion from that region to the second occurs until a state of equilibrium is reached; that is, until the opposing forces in the two regions are equal in strength.

Force and Force Fields

When an individual moves from one part of his psychological field to another, locomotion occurs, but the structure of the life space determines what locomotions are possible at any given time. In handling this problem, Lewin invoked the construct *force*. A force is defined as that which causes change (Lewin, 1936). Its properties are direction, strength, and point of application. (In Lewin's diagrams, direction and strength are represented by a vector and point of application by an arrow.) Thus, for any given point in the life space, the construct force represents the direction of and tendency to change. A number of forces can act on the same point at any given time, and the combination of these forces is called the *resultant* force. This is the effective force operating to determine behavior. When the resultant force is greater than zero, there is either a locomotion in the direction of that force or a change in the cognitive structure that is equivalent to locomotion. Conversely, if a locomotion or change in structure occurs, resultant forces exist in the direction of that change (Lewin, 1946).

Psychological forces represent or correspond to relations between regions of the life space. This can be illustrated by the situation depicted in Figure 5–2. The force *fg* is acting on the person p in the direction of the goal G. The strength of this force depends upon the state of p and upon the nature of the region G. For example, if the person is very hungry and the goal region consists of food, the force is relatively strong; if the person is only slightly hungry, the force is relatively weak. In the example shown in Figure 5–2, the goal region is attractive to p and so is said to have a positive *valence* (indicated by the + beside G).

The term "valence," like many other concepts in Lewin's system, was adopted from the physical sciences where it is used to refer to the combining power of an element. Lewin used valence to describe a field of forces in the life space. Valences may be either positive or negative, depending upon the

FIGURE 5–2. An example of a field of forces corresponding to a positive valence. (Adapted with permission from K. Lewin. *Field theory in social science.* New York: Harper and Row, 1951.)

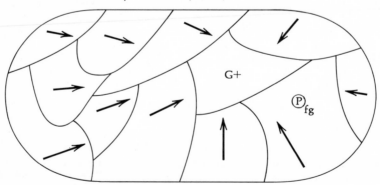

attractiveness or repulsiveness of the goal region; that is, forces may produce locomotion either toward or away from the goal region. If only one force exists, as in Figure 5–2, then p will locomote to G. More commonly, however, p is subjected to many forces, some of which are positive and some of which are negative with respect to any given goal region. This happens when the goal region both attracts and repels p, or when two or more mutually exclusive goal regions having positive valences are in the individual's life space. In such cases, the resultant force on p is some combination of all the forces acting on him.

The strength of force toward or away from a goal is a function of the strength of the valence and the psychological distance between the person and the goal. The strength of the valence, as we have indicated before, depends upon how attractive or repulsive the goal region is for p. The effect of psychological distance on force strength is somewhat complicated. In general, the closer p is to the goal, the stronger the force acting on p. However, it is important to remember that Lewin was talking about *psychological* distance, not physical distance. Although psychological and physical distance are correlated, they are not identical and it is the former that is important. The unattainable young lady may be only 3 feet away. Furthermore, the change in the strength of the force with distance to the goal (called *goal gradient*) is different for positive and negative valences. Force strength increases much faster as p approaches a negative goal than when he approaches a positive goal. More will be said about this effect when we discuss Lewin's analysis of conflict.

Lewin identified several types of forces: driving forces, restraining forces, induced forces, forces corresponding to one's own needs, and impersonal forces. Forces toward a positive or away from a negative valence are called *driving forces* because they lead to locomotion. However, locomotion may be hindered or prevented by physical or social obstacles or barriers. Such obstacles are called *restraining forces*. They do not lead to locomotion but they do exert an influence on the effects of driving forces. For example, if an individual sees a friend (positive valence) on the other side of a high fence (barrier acting as restraining force) and wishes to approach him (driving force), locomotion cannot be in a straight line; the individual must detour by way of a gate. Social barriers can be equally effective as restraining forces. A worker may wish to enter the boss's office and demand a raise, but social restraining forces prevent his doing so.

The kinds of driving forces used in the examples above might also be classified as corresponding to the person's *own needs*. There are forces, however, that do not correspond to the person's own desires but to the wishes of another person. Such *induced forces* are exemplified by the wishes of a mother for her child, of a foreman for his workers, etc. There are also forces that do not correspond to either an individual's own needs or to the wishes of another person but rather to the requirements of the situation. Social norms represent one example of such *impersonal forces*.

Finally, it should be noted that the point of application may be any part of the life space. Most frequently, perhaps, the point of application of a force is the region corresponding to one's own person, but it is sometimes the case that the point of application is a region of the life space of another person. For example, a child may experience that "doll wants to go to bed" (Lewin, 1951).

Tension and Tension Systems

In any life space or field there exist opposing forces; for example, two or more positive forces toward different goals or both positive and negative forces toward the same goal region. As a result, a state of tension exists. As evidence for the existence of tension, Lewin cited studies of the effects of interrupting subjects before they completed an assigned task. The general finding was that interrupted tasks are both recalled (Zeigarnik, 1927) and resumed (Ovsiankina, 1928) more frequently than completed tasks (the so-called Zeigarnik effect). Tension is aroused when the person accepts task completion as a goal. The tension associated with the task region presumably is discharged or reduced to an acceptable level by task completion. When the procedure is interrupted before the task is completed, the tension level remains relatively high and produces the drive toward resumption and the greater recall of incompleted tasks. The fact that resumption and recall rates are greater for incompleted than for completed tasks is therefore taken as proof of the existence of tension. (The reader will recall that for Lewin a thing exists if it can be shown to have effects.)

At this point it is necessary to digress from a consideration of the nature of tension systems and elaborate upon Lewin's idea of tension reduction. First, it is important to notice that he does not mean the same thing by tension reduction as Hull and other S-R theorists. For Lewin, tension reduction means that the tension associated with one region changes in such a way as to achieve equilibrium (or a quasi-state of equilibrium) with neighboring regions. Thus, when the tension level of a given region is the same as that of surrounding regions, tension reduction has occurred. Note that this does not imply a zero level of tension. In fact, the absolute tension level may remain relatively high after tension reduction has occurred. This has important implications for behavior change, as revealed by studies of group decision (Lewin, 1951). Change can be produced either by increasing the tension in the region where the behavior originally took place or by decreasing the tension in the region to which locomotion is desired. In the first instance, the overall tension level is increased, leading to dissatisfaction; in the second case, the overall level is decreased and satisfaction is relatively high.

Tension presumably has both general and specific effects. Lewin was never very clear on this point, but apparently the tension is associated with a particular region in some cases, whereas in other cases it is more pervasive and affects the entire system. The degree to which the tension level in one system can affect the tension level in another depends upon the *permeability* of the boundaries between regions. When the regions are highly differentiated and separated by rigid boundaries, the effects of events in one region on the tension level of another region are minor. However, when the regions are less clearly differentiated and the boundaries less rigid (and therefore more permeable), the interregional effects are great. This interregional exchange of tension reduction is referred to as *substitute satisfaction*.

Lewin suggested that the substitute value of an activity depends upon the degree of similarity of the substitute and the original activity and upon the degree of difficulty of the substitute activity. For example, if an individual is working toward completion of an arithmetic task and is interrupted, he may reduce the tension by completing other (substitute) arithmetic problems. Reduction of tension is greater if the substitute problems are more difficult than the interrupted ones. Lewin (1951) cited a study by Mahler (1933) as evidence. She found that talking could serve as a substitute for task completion when the task was to solve a problem (where talking could lead to solution), but talking was much less effective as a substitute when the task was construction of a material object (where talking could not lead to task completion).

Substitute effectiveness may also depend upon the degree of differentiation of the cognitive structure, as stated above. One might say that the possibility of substitution depends upon permeability of boundaries, but whether substitution is in fact effective depends upon similarity and difficulty. In the Mahler studies, the subjects ranged in age from six to ten years, and their cognitive structure was presumably less highly differentiated and the boundaries more permeable than in older persons (although Lewin reported that little differences are found between children and adults). The greatest differences in permeability of boundaries would be expected between normal persons and mentally deficient persons. According to Lewin (1935), the mentally deficient person is less highly differentiated than the normal, but the boundaries between regions are more rigid and less permeable than in the normal person. Therefore, the effects of activities in related regions upon tension levels should be less in mentally deficient persons than in normals. Evidence for this expectation has been provided by Shaw and Bensberg (1955), who demonstrated that success and failure on one task had greater effects on the level of aspiration for a different task when subjects were normal than when they were mentally deficient.

The psychological satiation of needs was cited as still further evidence of tension and tension reduction. It is well known that eating large amounts of food will lead to satiation of the hunger drive. Lewin suggested that similar satiation occurs with regard to other activities. He cited a study by Karsten (1928) which showed that repetition of tasks such as writing letters, drawing, and turning a wheel led to measurable evidences of satiation (or tension reduction).

In summary, Lewin proposed that regions of the life space are characterized by tension, and the relations among the various regions constitute tension systems. These systems function as forces toward action. Activities in one region *can* affect the tension in another system to the extent that the boundaries between regions are permeable. The degree to which the activities *do* influence the tension level in other regions is a function of the similarity of the activities and their relative difficulties. Repetition of an activity leads to psychological satiation or tension reduction.

The Relation of Tension and Force

Lewin was never very specific regarding the relation between psychological tension and psychological force. Force was defined as the cause of change and tension as a state of a region relative to surrounding regions. Tension was said to involve forces at the boundary of the region that tend to produce changes such that differences in tension are diminished (Lewin, 1936). This seems to imply that tension is the source of force. However, according to Cartwright (1959a), tension is more appropriately related to inner-personal regions. Thus, when an inner-personal region is in a state of tension, a related environmental region becomes the center of a force field (acquires positive valence). Which environmental region becomes the center of a force field depends upon the qualitative nature of the tension and of the region. If the tension system corresponding to hunger is aroused, the environmental region that acquires a positive valence will be that associated with eating. As Cartwright so aptly stated, the exact manner in which regions are selected has not been worked out in field theory.

APPLICATIONS OF THE THEORY

In the preceding pages we have given, for the most part, only abstract definitions and principles of field theory. The constructs described may become more meaningful if they are exemplified in concrete situations. Therefore, in this section we will give two examples of the way in which Lewin applied field theory to psychological phenomena. The first example, conflict, concerns individual behavior, and the second, aggressiveness in democratic and autocratic atmospheres, deals with a problem in group life. These examples are presented only as illustrations and are not intended to provide proof of the validity of the approach.

Conflict

A *conflict* situation is described as one in which the forces acting on the person are opposite in direction and about equal in strength (Lewin, 1946). Conflict situations may involve driving forces, driving and restraining forces, or own forces and various combinations of induced and impersonal forces. Driving forces may result in conflict when (1) the person is located between two positive valences, (2) the person is between two negative valences, or (3) a positive and negative valence are in the same direction with respect to the person. It may be noted that the first two situations correspond to what is usually called choice. Figure 5–3 depicts these three possibilities. For example, (a) might represent the situation in which p must choose between going to a

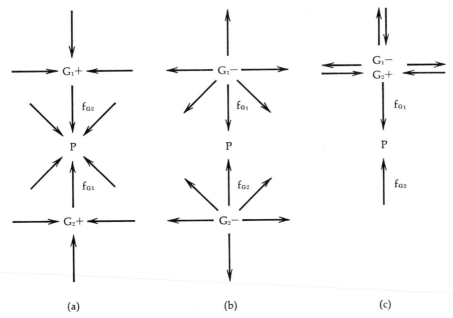

FIGURE 5–3. (a) A force field corresponding to two positive valences; (b) a force field corresponding to two negative valences; (c) a force field corresponding to a positive and a negative valence in the same direction. (Adapted with permission from K. Lewin. *Field theory in social science.* New York: Harper and Row, 1951.)

concert (G_1+) or attending a play (G_2+). In this example, fG_1 represents the force toward the concert (a positive valence) and fG_2 the force toward the play (also a positive valence). According to the goal gradient hypothesis (see p. 127) when the person p moves toward either G_1 or G_2, the strength of the force toward the chosen goal increases and the force toward the other decreases. Thus initially, the positive-positive (or approach-approach) (Miller, 1944) conflict is unstable, and any movement toward one goal region determines the direction of conflict resolution. In the second situation (b), an avoidance-avoidance conflict situation is shown. Here, forces are acting to cause p to move away from both G_1 and G_2. If he moves away from G_1, the strength of the force away from G_1 decreases, but the strength of the force away from G_2 increases (since he is moving toward it). When p reaches a position where the two opposing forces are equal in strength, a quasi-state of equilibrium has been achieved, and p tends to remain in that position. Actually, he may overreact and move beyond this position, correct by moving back in the opposite direction, etc., thus vacillating between the two negative goals. This is called a *stable* conflict situation because the conflict tends to remain unresolved. It should be clear that in order for this type of conflict situation to occur, there must be barriers or restraining forces that prevent the person from "leaving the field"; that is, moving away from both goal regions.

In the third situation (c), the two goals represent positive and negative valences in the same direction. This approach-avoidance conflict situation tends to be stable also, since movement toward G_1 (and consequently toward G_2) increases both fG_1 and fG_2. The strength of fG_2, being negative, increases more rapidly than that of fG_1 (which is positive), so the person moves to a quasi-state of equilibrium as in the avoidance-avoidance situation. Psychologically, the person is in the same position as a person in the avoidance-avoidance situation who is prevented from leaving the field. Experiments by Brown (1942) and Miller (1944) demonstrate these phenomena.

Conflicts involving driving and restraining forces occur when the person is surrounded by barriers with a positive valence outside or when a positive valence is surrounded by a barrier with the person outside. The first is a prison-like situation; in the second the person is free except with respect to the goal region. These situations are depicted in Figure 5–4. In diagram (a) the person p is surrounded by the barrier B which prevents him from responding to the force fG; whereas in diagram (b) the goal G is surrounded by barrier B which prevents the force fG from moving the person p to G. The conflict may be resolved by overcoming the barrier, but if the barrier is impassable the person may respond with aggression, hostility, frustration, apathy, or other nonadaptive behaviors. If the person attempts to overcome the barrier and fails, it may require negative valence, in which case the force field will extend beyond the barrier. In case (b) this will result in p leaving the field.

Each type of conflict mentioned above could be caused by the opposition of two forces corresponding to the person's own needs, by the opposition of two induced forces, or by the opposition of own need and an induced force. Many of the effects of conflict are independent of the differences

FIGURE 5–4.   Conflict situations deriving from opposed driving and restraining forces. (Adapted with permission from K. Lewin. *Field theory in social science.* New York: Harper and Row, 1951.)

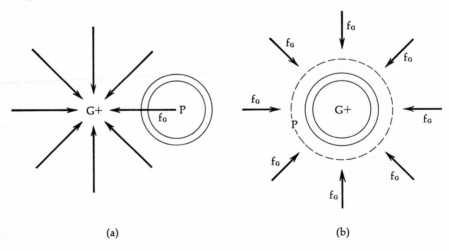

(a)   (b)

between own and induced forces, but there are some effects that are peculiar to these types of conflict. If a force is induced by another person A on person p, it is implied that A has power over p: he can change valences by giving orders, for example. Thus, there is always one additional way of resolving conflict that is not open to conflicts not involving induced forces: p may be able to undermine the power of A and thus change the force field.

Aggressiveness in Democratic and Autocratic Atmospheres

The amount of aggressive behavior among members of groups led by autocratic and democratic leaders has been studied in the well-known experiments by Lewin and his associates (Lewin, Lippitt, & White, 1939; Lippitt & White, 1943). Groups of boys were observed in group activities that were the same except that the boys were exposed to a leader who behaved autocratically or to a leader who behaved democratically. The average amount of aggression within the group was either very high or very low for the autocratic groups, whereas it was on a medium level in the democratic groups. Lewin (1947) used these data to illustrate certain principles of field theory.

Lewin began by assuming that each level of aggressiveness is a quasi-stationary equilibrium. The question, then, is what forces tend to raise or lower the level of aggressiveness. Forces against aggression include such variables as friendship, the character of the setting, and the presence of an adult leader; forces toward aggression include the type of activity (a wild game provides more opportunity than a quiet discussion) and the fact that a certain amount of aggressive interaction is fun for boys. The experimental data suggest that these opposing forces lead to an equilibrium in the democratic groups, as shown in Figure 5–5. In this diagram, the strength of the forces is indicated by the length of the vectors and the direction of the force by the arrows. Thus, the opposing forces in democratic groups are moderately strong and approximately equal. In the case of aggressive autocracy, the style of leadership and the irritation due to the restriction of free movement increases forces toward aggression, as shown by the long arrows in Figure 5–5. At the same time, the we-feeling, which tends to decrease aggression, is weakened in the aggressive autocrat groups. Thus, the increase in forces toward aggression and the decrease in forces against aggression produces the level indicated in the diagram.

The explanation of apathetic autocracy effects is less straightforward. Lewin had to assume that similar forces are operating in both types of autocracy, but that in apathetic autocracy there are additional forces against aggression, perhaps because of greater authoritarian control in these groups.

There are several conclusions that Lewin drew from this analysis of the effects of social climate on aggressive behavior. First, the level of inner tension is higher in autocratic groups than in democratic groups, a difference that holds even for the apathetic autocracy situation that appears quiet. This is because of the fact that the autocratic atmosphere produces two contradictory effects: it leads to frustration and thus increased forces toward aggression, and its restrictive nature is equivalent to restraining forces that inhibit aggres-

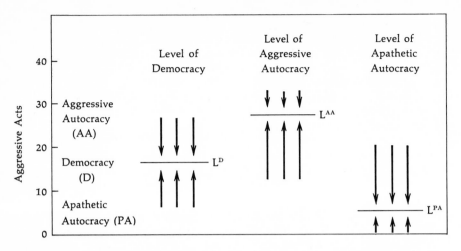

FIGURE 5–5. Force fields at different levels of aggressiveness in various social atmospheres. (Adapted with permission from K. Lewin. *Field theory in social science*. New York: Harper and Row, 1951.)

sion. The resulting quasi-stationary equilibrium is thus produced by relatively strong opposing forces.

A second conclusion, following from the first, is that aggression would increase in the apathetic autocracy if the restrictive leadership were removed from the situation. Lippitt and White (1943) reported precisely this effect when groups were shifted from autocratic leadership to a less-restrictive form of leadership.

This treatment of aggressive behavior in social climates has presented only the broad outlines of Lewin's analysis, but it indicates the way in which he attempted to apply the theory to a social problem. It should be clear that this represents a *description* of the forces that are presumed to operate in such situations, rather than a *demonstration* that these forces are in operation.

STRENGTHS AND WEAKNESSES OF THE THEORY

We will not attempt a detailed evaluation of field theory, but it is important to note some of the more-significant contributions and shortcomings of the approach.

Contributions of Lewin's Field Theory

Probably the greatest contribution of field theory to social psychology was that it provided a conceptual framework for controlled empirical studies of social behavior. Prior to Lewin's analysis it had been tacitly assumed that the major problems of social psychology could not be studied in the laboratory. His conceptualizations provided a basis for many empirical studies that revealed the falsity of the assumption. The theory also led to the formulation of many experimental techniques and procedures that have advanced the science of social behavior.

The concepts introduced in the theory have had broad significance for general psychology. Concepts such as life space, locomotion, and psychological force are common terms in the language of psychology. Thus, the theory has contributed to the integration of such diverse fields as learning, perception, motivation, development, social phenomena, and abnormal behavior.

Finally, the contributions of the theory to practical problems are numerous and significant. Lewin's channel theory (Lewin, 1951), dealing with food habits and food distribution, his studies of group decision (Lewin, 1952), and his concern with interracial problems (Lewin, 1948) are examples of such contributions.

Criticisms of Field Theory

Like most theories, field theory is open to a number of serious criticisms. These criticisms have been leveled by a number of writers (Leeper, 1943; London, 1944; Deutsch, 1954; Cartwright, 1959; Marx & Hillix, 1963); hence, we will review them only briefly.

A very serious criticism, for purposes of this volume at least, is that Lewin failed to state his system precisely enough to permit confirmation or disconfirmation. He has provided plausible descriptions of social situations, but he has not stated propositions in such a way that they can be refuted by empirical test. The lack of precision and specificity may be because Lewin never presented his entire system in any single publication. His contributions are in the form of papers published at various times and in various books and periodicals. In this chapter, we have tried to integrate his work into a single comprehensive system, but the lack of complete success is revealed by the disjointed presentation at several points in the discussion.

A related criticism is that he failed to define many of his key concepts in an unambiguous way. The definition of "behavior" is an outstanding example (see p. 125). He also often failed to present the empirical basis of his psychological concepts.

It has also been suggested that field theory places undue emphasis upon the perceptual and cognitive aspects of behavior and neglects the motor aspects. It deals too much with the deeper aspects of the person and not enough with overt behavior.

A final criticism that might be mentioned, although it is of minor significance for purposes of this book, is the charge that Lewin misused topological concepts (London, 1944), that he merely borrowed certain terms and concepts from topology and failed to use the full range of relationships available from that discipline. This is undoubtedly true, but one wonders whether it is necessary to use every tool that is available to benefit from the use of a few selected tools.

It is clear from this brief review that most of the criticisms of field theory are concerned with methodological problems. Such problems are, of course, extremely important for any theoretical approach, since the validity of a theory can be determined only if adequate methodological procedures are specified by the theory. In spite of these shortcomings, field theory has had great impact on theories in social psychology. In the next chapter we present a number of theories of social behavior that have as their basic orientation the field-theoretical approach.

The field-theoretical orientation exemplified by the Lewinian model has been attractive to a number of theoreticians. Its appeal probably derives from the emphasis upon humanistic and phenomenological concepts, without at the same time sacrificing rigor. Many social psychologists reject the apparent dehumanization reflected by the reinforcement and similar theories (see Chapters 2, 3, and 4). These psychologists seek a theoretical framework which is methodologically sound, but which gives cognizance to the richness and complexity of the phenomenal world of the individual. Field theory represents one attempt to meet these requirements. Although it has not been entirely successful in this respect, it is one of the few orientations which emphasize both the scientific and the humanistic viewpoints.

Field-theoretical analyses have been provided for many specific problems. In addition to the areas of conflict and aggression in "social climates" reviewed in the preceding chapter, this type of analysis has been applied to level of aspiration phenomena (Lewin, Dembo, Festinger, & Sears, 1944), learning (Lewin, 1942), regression (Lewin, 1941), social change (Lewin, 1943; Coch & French, 1948), and feeble-mindedness (Lewin, 1935), to mention only a few. Here, we are more interested in theories dealing with broader aspects of social behavior than that represented by the direct application of Lewinian principles to specific behavioral situations. We are concerned with theories which have adopted the basic field-theoretical orientation, but which have modified and adapted its principles to fairly broad social psychological phenomena. We have identified four theories which we believe approximate this objective: Heider's (1958) theory of interpersonal relations, Cartwright's (1959b) field-theoretical conception of power, French's (1956) formal theory of social power, and Deutsch's (1949a) theory of cooperation and competition. Each of these theories shows strong field-orientation influences, and each deals in a rigorous manner with a significant aspect of social behavior. None is merely a direct application of Lewinian principles, although Cartwright's analysis of power deviates only in minor ways. Cartwright's formulation is included because it does make a contribution to our understanding of social power and because it related directly to the French theory of power. Of the four, Heider's theory encompasses by far the broadest range of behavior and is derived least directly from Lewinian field theory.

A THEORY OF INTERPERSONAL RELATIONS

Heider's theory of interpersonal relations is spelled out in detail in his *Psychology of Interpersonal Relations* (1958).[1] Heider adopted Lewin's "method of construction," but he appealed to "common-sense psychology" as a source of insight into interpersonal behavior, maintaining that scientific psychology could learn much from common-sense psychology, which is important in at least two ways. First, common-sense psychology governs our behavior toward others, and hence it is an essential part of interpersonal phenomena. Second, it contains many truths concerning interpersonal relations.

In making use of common-sense psychology, Heider attempted to use the concepts of everyday language by sharpening them and relating them to each other. This process of *explication* (Carnap, 1953) is seen as a necessary stage in the development of scientific language. The reader will encounter many common terms, such as "can," "trying," and "wanting," but he should keep clearly in mind that Heider's use of such terms is usually more specific than their use in everyday language. We will try to give his definition each time a new "common-sense, scientific" term is introduced.

Following this common-sense approach, Heider considered several aspects of interpersonal behavior, including perceiving the other person, the other person as a perceiver, the analysis of action, the experiences of desire and pleasure, and the roles of environmental variables. We will consider the more-significant aspects of his theory in the following sections.

Perceiving the Other Person

Following Brunswik (1934), Heider assumed that the principles of person perception are essentially the same as the principles that govern the perception of impersonal objects, such as tables and chairs. However, it is not assumed that there are no differences between the perception of persons and things. Persons are seen as having abilities, emotions, intentions, wishes, sentiments, and other qualities that are not ordinarily attributed to physical objects. Other persons can act to benefit or harm us, they can act purposefully, and they can perceive us in turn. To fully understand person perception, then, it is necessary to consider the conditions that determine a person's perceptions of the environment and the people in it, as well as the consequences of the person's awareness that the other person (o) is perceiving his own environment, including the person (p).

In dealing with these problems, Heider resorted to phenomenal and causal descriptions. Phenomenal description refers to the nature of the contact between p and his environment as it is experienced by p, whereas causal description refers to the analysis of underlying conditions that give rise to

---

[1] Heider's theory appears to derive from field theory in all but one respect: his treatment of sentiments. Here, he resorts to a cognitive approach which is basically a balance theory. Therefore, his theory regarding sentiments is treated in Chapter 8.

perceptual experience. Phenomenally, p feels that he is in direct contact with persons and things in his environment. He sees objects as if they are "out there" and really accessible to him. People are perceived as having shape, size, color, and other spatial and physical characteristics, but they are also seen as having wishes, needs, intentions, and other intangible properties. These intangibles are also seen as being directly given. Causal analysis, on the other hand, distinguishes a number of steps in the perceptual process. According to Brunswik (1952) the perceptual process can be likened to a perceptual arc involving the object (called the *distal stimulus*) and the percept; that is, the way the object appears to us. The distal stimulus, then, is the thing that is outside p and at some distance from him. The distal stimulus is the starting point of perception, but does not directly affect p. Instead, the distal stimulus is mediated by light and sound waves that excite the sense receptors. The stimulus pattern which impinges directly upon the sense organs is called the *proximal stimulus,* since it is the stimulus that is in direct proximity to p.

Causal analysis of person perception also divides the perceptual process into steps. The other person (o) is the distal stimulus, and the perceptual construction within p that leads to an awareness of o is the proximal stimulus. The *mediation* consists of the manifestations of the personality of o that determine the proximal stimulus pattern. For example, p observes that o has a red face, speaks loudly, and makes hostile statements; these manifestations mediate the perception that o is angry. In many instances, the manifestations that serve as the mediation of person perceptions are obvious or, at least, open to p's awareness. In other cases, however, p may not be aware of the cues that lead to the perception. This is especially true when the cues involve the interpretation of expressive features, such as gestures and tone of voice.

Since mediation serves the important function of giving information about the distal stimulus (the environmental contents), it is necessary to consider the principles that govern the coordination of the mediation to the environmental contents. Mediation is seen by Heider as being either *synonymous* or *ambiguous* in its coordination to the distal stimulus. When the mediation is synonymous, each specific manifestation is coordinated to a specific content of the environment. In such instances, it is necessary only for p to learn these specific connections in order to perceive accurately the qualities of o. In the case of ambiguous mediation, a specific manifestation may derive from (be caused by) any one of several contents. For example, a raised eyebrow might indicate that the person is dubious, that he is amused, or that he does not understand. Figure 6-1 represents instances of synonymous and ambiguous mediations. In the figure, C_a (cause a) is synonymously (or equivalently) mediated by m_1, m_2, and m_3; m_3 is an example of ambiguous mediation since it can be caused by C_a, C_b, or C_c.

It is probable that most distal stimuli are represented by ambiguous mediation, since a given manifestation is rarely connected to a single environmental content. The coordination of mediation and distal stimulus is not a simple process. However, coordination is rendered less difficult when the manifestations of the distal stimulus are *embedded* in the total situation. In

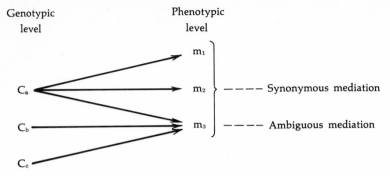

FIGURE 6–1. Ambiguous and synonymous mediation. (Reprinted with permission from F. Heider. *The psychology of interpersonal relations.* New York: Wiley, 1958.)

this connection, Heider distinguished between *local* and *total stimulus.* Local stimulus refers to the part of the stimulus pattern that is particularly relevant to the percept, whereas the total stimulus includes the surroundings as well. The term *embeddedness* is used to refer to the fact that in many cases the appearance of the local stimulus is determined, at least in part, by the stimuli that surround it. For example, a grimace by o would be interpreted differently by p depending upon the presence or absence of other persons in the immediate environment. The surrounding stimuli thus serve to reduce the ambiguity of at least some mediations.

Although Heider did not clearly identify the case of overlapping ambiguous mediations, it seems clear from his analysis that such situations may reduce the ambiguity of mediations. An example of overlapping mediations is shown in Figure 6–2. The mediations m_1 can be caused by either C_a or C_b, whereas m_2 can be caused by either C_a or C_c. If both m_1 and m_2 occur, the most economical interpretation is that the underlying cause (distal stimulus) is C_a, although, of course, it is possible that these mediations are caused by the simultaneous effects of C_b and C_c.

FIGURE 6–2. Overlapping ambiguous mediations.

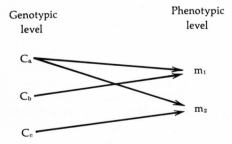

The Other Person as Perceiver

As we mentioned earlier in this chapter, p is aware that o is also a perceiver and that o's perceptions have effects on o. P's understanding of the way o's perceptions influence o have important effects on p. According to Heider, p is influenced in at least three ways: his actions are influenced, his expectations are affected, and his attributions are determined. For example, if p perceives that the effects of o's perception on o are desirable, p will try to produce those perceptions; if they are not desirable, p will try to prevent them. Similarly, if p knows that o has perceived something, he will expect that o will respond to that perception in appropriate ways; that is, p will expect the consequences of o's perception. Conversely, if p knows that the consequences have occurred, he will assume that the necessary perception has also occurred.

Heider gave special attention to selected instances of the common-sense recognition that o's perceptions have certain effects on o which in turn affect p in significant ways. The meaning of "o perceives x" and the way p reacts to this meaning are influenced by the beliefs that p holds concerning the effects on o when o perceives x. Common-sense psychology holds that when o sees x, his knowledge of x is improved, and Heider asserts that most of the effects of perception can be interpreted as the effects of this improved knowledge. These effects include the following:

1. control over the environment
2. evaluation of x
3. motivation for further action with regard to x
4. ability to report about x to others
5. communion with others

Let us consider the consequences of each of these effects for p.

When o can observe x, he has more control over it, and thus more control over the environment, than when he cannot observe x. His action possibilities are increased. Being aware of this, p may try to influence o's perceptions as a means of influencing his actions. For example, p may try to create conditions such that o perceives p as helpful, thus encouraging o to act in a favorable manner toward p. Or p may attempt to conceal his thoughts from o in order to avoid control by o.

Evaluation is a common tendency in everyday behavior. When o observes x, he is very likely to judge it as either favorable or unfavorable. Thus, p often tries to influence o's perceptions so that evaluation of p by o will be favorable. He will reveal qualities of himself and/or possessions that he believes will lead o to perceive him in a favorable light. Conversely, he may attempt to conceal those aspects of himself that may lead to unfavorable evaluations by o. Knowing that o is an evaluating perceiver may also lead to heightened self-consciousness on the part of p, which may be manifested by shyness or embarrassment. Therefore, p may try to avoid the conditions that give rise to this state, or he may deliberately try to create the conditions that will produce embarrassment in o.

The perception of x by o may produce motivation for o to act in a particular manner. Again, p may try to influence o's perceptions in order to arouse motivations toward actions that p wishes o to engage in, or to prevent the arousal of motivations toward actions that are not desired by p. For example, if p acts in a way that he knows will arouse anger in o, he will seek to prevent o's learning about the action.

If o perceives x, he can tell other people about x. This fact often leads p to try to influence o's perception so that he may report to another if x is favorable to p, or so that o cannot report to others if x is unfavorable to p. For example, p may try to ensure that o observes his good work if he thinks o will tell p's boss about it. On the other hand, if p has engaged in socially disapproved behavior, he will try to prevent o's perception of it, thus preventing o from reporting to others.

Finally, communion is an effect of mutual perception. Heider considers "communion through the eyes" as a unique form of interaction, since the eyes are the only organs that can both send and receive simultaneously. In this, he follows Simmel (1921), who asserted that the direct mutual glance represents the most-perfect reciprocity in the entire field of human relationships. Communion through the eyes is said to create such a deep interpersonal experience that the mutual glance is only maintained when a deep intimacy is desired. Thus, p allows this kind of communion with o when he desires intimacy and avoids it by deflecting his gaze when he does not wish to be intimate. Several interesting experimental studies have been reported concerning the conditions and effects of mutual communion through the eyes. (See Exline, 1963; Gibson & Pick, 1963; Exline, Gray, & Schuette, 1965; Nachshon & Wapner, 1967).

Naïve Analyis of Action

Interpersonal relations depend to a large extent upon a person's perceptions (interpretations) of the actions of others. According to Heider (1958), it is an important principle of both scientific and common-sense psychology that man understands reality by referring transient and variable behavior and events to relatively invariant underlying conditions. These relatively unchanging underlying conditions are called *dispositional properties;* that is, properties that "dispose" objects and events to manifest themselves in certain ways under certain conditions. It is these properties that make our world more or less stable, predictable, and controllable. For example, if an individual learns rapidly, solves problems easily, etc., it may be inferred that he is intelligent. The learning and problem-solving behavior are relatively transient events which become understandable when related to the more-permanent property called intelligence.

When a person observes the actions of another, therefore, he seeks to understand the action by referring it to certain dispositional properties. In general, the result of an action is seen as depending upon factors within the person and factors within the environment. The outcome of the action is thus a function of some combination of *effective* personal forces and *effective* environmental forces, where the term *effective* means the totality of forces deriving from the person or the environment. (Presumably, environmental forces can be either positive or negative with respect to personal forces. For example, task difficulty is seen as an environmental force that operates in opposition to the personal force directed toward the completion of that task.)

Effective personal force is analyzed into a power factor and a motivational factor. Power is determined primarily by ability, although other characteristics (for example, temperament) may also affect power. The motivational factor refers to a person's *intention* (what he is trying to do) and *exertion* (how hard he is trying to do it). Power and trying are related in a multiplicative manner, since effective personal force is zero if either power or trying is zero.

If a person has the power to do something regardless of the effective environmental forces, common-sense psychology perceives that he *can* do it. (*Can* is used by Heider to refer to the possibility of a given action being performed by a specific person.) Like "trying," *can* is also seen as a dispositional property—at least under most circumstances. In the naïve analysis of action, *can* and *trying* are said to be the necessary and sufficient conditions for purposive action. Thus, if person p can do x, but does not, he is seen as not trying; that is, he is not motivated to do x and hence is not exerting himself in that direction. Conversely, if p is seen as being unable to do x, his power is not sufficient to overcome the effective environmental forces with respect to x.

The motivational factor (trying) is the factor that propels and guides action; it is the thing that gives action its purposive quality. Heider regarded this factor as the major one that distinguishes personal and impersonal causality, which in turn are major determinants of interpersonal behavior. For this reason, he dealt extensively with the differences between personal and impersonal causality.

Personal and Impersonal Causality

The term *personal causality* was used by Heider to refer to those instances in which p intentionally produces x; that is, situations which he designated as purposive actions. Thus the intentions of the person are central to the attribution of personal causality, and it becomes important for a person to determine whether a given event is the result of an intention on the part of another person. In making such a determination the person makes use of the causal network in personal and impersonal causality. In the case of personal causality, the actions of the other person are directed toward the production of a single end result, and his actions change in response to altered circumstances. In Heider's terms, the means are variable, but the end is invariant (a situation which he labeled equifinality). Figure 6–3a depicts an instance of personal causality and its characteristic of equifinality. When p (a person with intention to produce a given effect, e) notes that circumstance c_1 exists, he employs means m_1; if c_2 obtains he employs m_2, etc., in order to produce e.

Impersonal causality, on the other hand, is characterized by multifinality. In this case the effects of an impersonal event vary with the circumstances

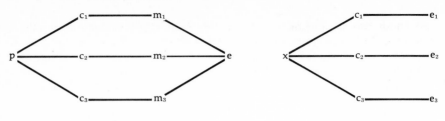

a. Personal causality   b. Impersonal causality

FIGURE 6–3. Equifinality and multifinality as characteristics of personal and impersonal causality. (Adapted with permission from F. Heider. *The psychology of interpersonal relations*. New York: Wiley, 1958.)

surrounding the event; if the circumstances change, so do the effects produced by the impersonal event. Figure 6–3*b* depicts an instance of impersonal causality.

As we indicated earlier, Heider stressed the fact that intention is the central factor in personal causality. Thus we hold a person more or less responsible for the outcomes of his actions, depending upon whether the act is seen as an indication of his motives. In the naïve analysis of action, a given outcome that is produced by p is not always attributed to p, but it is sometimes attributed to environmental factors. The concept of responsibility is used differently at different stages of development. As the individual develops (becomes socialized), he moves through successive levels of sophistication. At each level of development, he takes into account successively more variables or circumstances relevant to the situation. Heider identified five such levels:

Level 1 is the most primitive level and the concept of responsibility is such that the person is held responsible for any effect that he is associated with in any way. At level 2, the person is held responsible for any effect that is caused by actions ascribed to him, whether or not he could have foreseen the consequences of his actions. This corresponds to Piaget's (1932) objective responsibility stage. At level 3 the person is held responsible for effects resulting from his actions that could have been foreseen, except that the person was careless or unconcerned about the possible consequences of his actions. At the next level, the person is held responsible only for intentionally produced outcomes. This is what Piaget called subjective responsibility and corresponds to Heider's personal causality structure. Finally, at the most advanced stage (level 5) the person is held less responsible for intended outcomes if the circumstances justify his actions; that is, if most other people would have acted as the person did under the conditions that existed at the time.

Desire and Pleasure

In the preceding analysis of trying, intention and exertion were identified as the constituents of trying. The conditions that elicit trying were not specified, although Heider emphasized that man has a strong need to understand the conditions underlying the events that he experiences. *Desire* is seen as one of the important conditions of trying; *pleasure* as the experiential consequence of achieved desire. Heider admitted that desire is conceptually ambiguous, since it refers to motivational states variously labeled as desire, need, wish, want, etc. Desire differs from intention in that it refers to the motive that gives rise to the intention, whereas the intention is identified only by the structure of personal causality. Desire is one answer to the question, why does p intend to produce x?

Desire and action are often coordinated in that desire may arouse the person to action or that desire may be inferred from action. If p is seen as trying to do x, it is often inferred that p desires x. However, desire and action are not invariably coordinated. The person may desire x without engaging in any action directed toward the attainment of x. This event happens when x appears unattainable or when the other effects resulting from the action necessary to attain x are sufficiently undesirable as to negate the desire for x. Sometimes, of course, no action is necessary; the desire may or may not be realized quite independently of p's action. Furthermore, a given desire may lead to different actions, depending upon the environmental requirements. Actions are determined not only by desire but also by the way the person sees the causal structure of the environment. Nevertheless, desire has important implications for interpersonal behavior. If another person does something that most people like to do or if he appears pleased with a given effect, it will be assumed that he desired it. A person's reactions to various possibilities, occurrences, and actions regarding x will also be largely determined by the person's desires about x.

When the desire is fulfilled, common-sense psychology postulates that pleasure invariably follows. This a priori connection between wish fulfillment and the experience of pleasure cannot be contradicted by experience. Suppose p states that he desires x and subsequently obtains x, only to find that he does not experience the expected pleasure. Instead of concluding that desire fulfillment and pleasure are not invariantly related, the naïve observer concludes that p did not really desire x, or that the obtained x was not the one really desired, or that the apparent lack of enjoyment displayed by p is mere pretense—that p really experienced pleasure but wished to conceal this fact for his own purposes. The desire-pleasure principle remains unchanged by contrary evidence.

Conceptually, common-sense psychology postulates two relations between the person and the object of his desires: *value* and *distance*. The value relation refers to the sentiment and is reflected by statements of the form "p likes x." This implies that there is something about x that is positively valued by p, although it does not necessarily deny the existence of negatively valued characteristics of x. For example, a person may like to smoke, although he knows that smoking may have deleterious effects on his health.

The distance relation between the person and the object of his desire refers to the psychological distance between person and object. It includes relations such as contact, the possibility of wish fulfillment, and similar relations. In the case of desire, the person and the valued object are separated, whereas in pleasure they are in contact; that is, the distance relation is zero.

Thus, if p is seen as being in contact with a valued x, it is inferred that he is experiencing pleasure; if he values x but is not in contact with it, it is assumed that he will wish for x. Again, common-sense psychology presumes harmonious relations among desire, liking, contact, and pleasure, and apparently inharmonious events are reinterpreted to maintain the expected harmony.

Particularly significant effects result when a person almost obtains a desired x or almost loses an enjoyable x. A near success is said to lead to heightened frustration, whereas a near loss evokes a sense of relief or feelings of being blessed or warned. According to Heider, the intense negative reaction to a near success is partially because of the possibility of wish fulfillment: the perceived possibility of wish fulfillment increases as the distance to the goal decreases. (We might note in passing that the effects of a near success are consistent with the goal-gradient hypothesis discussed in Chapter 5, pp. 127 and 131.)

Sentiment

Sentiment plays an important role in Heider's common-sense psychology; however, in his treatment he adopted a position more closely related to cognitive theory than to field theory. For this reason, we give only brief attention to his treatment here and defer a more-detailed discussion to Chapter 8.

A sentiment refers to the way a person feels about a person or thing. This feeling may, of course, be either positive or negative, and Heider used the terms *liking* and *disliking* to indicate positive and negative sentiments, respectively. Whether a person likes another person or the other person's products has important implications for interpersonal relations. A liking relation between two persons is likely to increase interaction, to determine the quality of the interaction, and cause similar effects.

In his analysis of the effects of sentiments on interpersonal events, Heider employed two major concepts (in addition to liking): *unit formation* and *balanced state*. Unit formation refers to the quality of belongingness. Two or more objects (which may be persons) are in unit formation when they are seen as belonging together. For example, a person and his products are seen as forming a unit. When a number of persons and/or objects are considered, there is a strong tendency for the liking and unit formation relations to be such that a state of balance is achieved. A situation is said to be in a balanced state if the unit and sentiment relations can coexist without stress; that is, when there is no pressure toward change. In general, a situation is in a state of balance if the product of the signs of the relations is positive. For example, if p likes o, and p likes o's products, there are three positive relations: the two positive liking relations and the unit relation between o and his products. The product of three positive relations is positive; so the situation is balanced. But if p likes o, and dislikes o's possession, there are two positive and one negative relation and a state of imbalance exists. Pressure to change therefore exists and disharmony will result. Balance can be achieved either by changing one of the positive relations to negative or the negative relation to a positive one. (See page 189 for a more-detailed presentation of Heider's balance theory.)

Oughts and Values

In addition to the factors so far considered, the evaluation and determination of behavior and its consequences are also influenced to a great extent by the perceived requirements of the situation. According to common-sense psychology, we often feel that specific consequences should follow certain actions; the bad actor deserves his punishment and the doer of good deeds merits praise. Heider uses the term *ought* to refer to this requiredness (Wertheimer, 1935) of the situation.

Oughts are said to derive from perceived demands of the objective order; p feels that he ought to do x because of the demands of the environment rather than because of the demands of others. This indicates two important aspects of ought; oughts are impersonal, and they are dispositional in character. Hence, oughts have interpersonal validity: all people should perceive the same ought requirements in a given situation. Obedience or disobedience of ought requirements thus determines whether a person should be praised (or blamed) for his actions.

The concept of *value* also plays an important role in the determination and evaluation of behavior, as pointed out earlier in this chapter. Heider used the term *value* in two different, albeit related, ways. First, it was used to mean the property of an entity; second, it was used to mean a class of entities. In both cases there is the connotation of being objectively positive. Like oughts, values are impersonal and dispositional, and therefore they have interpersonal validity. But ought and value differ with regard to the force field. Ought is said to represent a field of forces, whereas value represents a potential force and thus results in action only under certain conditions. Heider stated the difference succinctly:[1]

> In brief, the ought can be considered a cognized force with objective validity; value can be considered a cognized positive property of something, a relevance with objective validity. These cognized forces and relevances have, of course, a great influence on p's own forces because in most cases there will be a strong tendency to be in harmony with them. (Heider, 1958, p. 226.)

Request and Command

Ought and value were described above as environmental forces that induce action, but action may also be evoked by personal forces. Heider listed five ways in which p may induce action in o:

1. p may change a valence for o, so that an unattractive x becomes attractive to o
2. p may show o the desirable consequences of x
3. p may create additional (derived valences) for o by promising him rewards or punishments

---

[1] Here it may be noted that Heider's theory is most directly related to Lewin's field orientation and that he used the concept of force field in the same sense that Lewin used it. See pp. 126–128 for a discussion of Lewin's treatment of force fields.

4. p may request o to do x
5. p may command o to do x.

The latter two instances which involve *request* and *command* are based on sentiments and power relations, respectively. When p asks o to do something, he is implying that he is dependent on o's good will. The other person should grant the wish because he has a favorable attitude (positive sentiment) toward p. On the other hand, when p commands o to do x, it is implied that o must comply with p's wishes. Therefore, the forces on o toward doing x derive from a power relation between p and o. However, the distinction between requesting and commanding is not always clear-cut, since the "request" of a person in a power position often has the force of command.

The conditions surrounding requests and the reactions to requests involve not only sentiments, but also oughts, can, values, power, and the consequences of the requested action. Ought forces play a role in that o may believe that he should comply with p's request. If o can do x and p cannot, o often believes that the objective order requires that he comply with p's request to do x, even though he has no positive sentiment toward p. For example, few adults would refuse to comply with a small child's request for a glass of water, even if they disliked the child. On the other hand, if o cannot do x, p ordinarily will not request that o do x. The value of x for p and for o also influences p's willingness to make the request and o's readiness to comply. For example, if x has great value for p, he is more likely to request that o do x, and o will be more likely to respond to the request by doing x. *Power* relations are involved to the extent that compliance implies the superiority or inferiority of o. If compliance to a request suggests that o is superior to p, he is apt to concede to p's wishes; if compliance can be viewed as a weakness on the part of o, he probably will not comply with p's request. Finally, the consequences of the action for p and for o influence compliance with the request. Desirable consequences create forces toward compliance, and undesirable consequences create forces against compliance.

Benefit and Harm

When o responds to a request or command by p, he *benefits* p if he complies or obeys and fails to benefit p, or he *harms* p, if he does not. More generally, o benefits p when he produces an x that has positive value for p and harms p when he produces an x that has negative value for p. Thus benefit and harm include a causal factor and an evaluative factor. The circumstances surrounding causality and evaluation are of course significant determinants of p's reactions to o's behavior. Heider invoked the concepts of *local* and *total* relevance in analyzing these effects. The local relevance of an event includes only the beneficial or harmful nature of x and the fact that o caused x. The wider implications of the circumstances surrounding the event are referred to as the total relevance of the event. The relative strength of local and total relevance varies with the level of development (maturation and socialization) of the persons involved. Total relevance becomes more salient with increasing maturation. (See pp. 143–144 for a review of Heider's five stages or levels of maturation with respect to attribution.)

The perception of and reaction to benefits and harms are also influenced by sentiments, power, and ought forces. If o likes p, he may be expected to benefit p; if p likes o, he tends to see o's actions as a benefit; the actions of a disliked o are prone to be perceived as a harm; and if a disliked o benefits p, his actions are suspect and p may look for ulterior motives. Similarly, a benefit produced by a powerful o is perceived as the result of o's own forces, whereas a harm by a powerful o may be accepted as the natural order of interpersonal relations. Thus, ought forces play a role in the acceptance or rejection of harm. Ought forces also influence p's feelings of obligation to o for benefits produced by o. If o ought to benefit p, p feels no obligation to o. In like manner, p may reject a benefit that he believes he does not merit and may resent an undeserved harm.

Reactions to the Experiences of Others

When another person experiences a benefit or harm, there are, according to Heider, four types of reactions that may occur:

(1) sympathetic enjoyment, in which o's positive experience is positive for p

(2) compassion, in which o's negative experience is negative for p

(3) envy, in which o's positive experience is negative for p

(4) malicious joy, in which o's negative experience is positive for p.

(Heider did not consider instances in which p is indifferent to the experiences of o.)

The first two types are said to be concordant reactions and the last two discordant reactions. In common-sense psychology, all these reactions are referred to as feelings or emotions.

Sympathetic enjoyment and compassion are both sympathetic reactions to the experiences of others. Heider pointed out that a number of writers (Becker, 1931; Westermarck, 1932; Asch, 1952; Scheler, 1954) have distinguished between true sympathy and emotional contagion. True sympathy has as its object the feelings of the other person, whereas emotional contagion takes place only in the presence of others. With true sympathy, the point of application is the other person, but with contagion the point of application is one's own person. A person who experiences sympathy will try to make a sad o happy (and try to see that a happy o remains so), whereas a person responding to emotional contagion will join a happy o but will avoid an unhappy o.

The reaction of p to the experience of o is influenced by (1) p's sentiment toward o: p tends to be sympathetic toward a liked o; (2) p's own experience: p's own state provides a background or standard against which o's experiences are evaluated, in accordance with the principles of contrast and assimilation; and (3) p's similarity to o: if p considers himself in the same class as o, his reactions to o's experiences are apt to be of the concordant type.

Comment and Evaluation

The preceding presentation is, at best, an abridged account of Heider's views and does not do justice to the richness of his formulation. His appeal to common-sense psychology yielded many insights into the complex realm of interpersonal relations. It is obvious even to the casual reader, however, that his analysis is far from being naive. His work is clearly a major contribution to social psychological theory, especially with regard to attribution theory and balance theory.[2]

The theory meets the minimal criteria for acceptance, but it is, of course, open to certain criticisms. The alert reader will have noted that it is primarily a theory about interpersonal perception and only secondarily a theory about interpersonal relations. It is concerned largely with an analysis of the processes by which one person perceives and interprets the behavior of another person. Although Heider noted the relevance of these perceptions and interpretations for interpersonal behavior, he failed to consider in detail the connections among perceptions, attributions, and interpersonal behavior. It is also easy to get the impression that Heider has considered a series of isolated topics concerning interpersonal perception and behavior. Although he made it clear that the various aspects of interpersonal relations are interrelated, he failed to spell out the nature of these interrelations in explicit detail. Furthermore, the reader is not prepared for the somewhat abrupt shift from attribution to balance theory. The first part of the theory apparently derives from a gestalt field orientation, whereas the second part adopts a more strictly cognitive position. Both analyses derive from his earlier work on attribution (Heider, 1944) and on balanced structures (Heider, 1946). (It is recognized that gestalt, field, and cognitive orientations have much in common and that Heider's two treatments are not necessarily incompatible. However, there are some important differences that are apparent in the two analyses.) Finally, theoretical propositions are often stated in a form that makes it difficult to test them empirically. The frequent appeal to statements such as "x tends to follow y" illustrates this point. When x does not follow y, the proposition is not invalidated. Nor did Heider specify the conditions under which y is not expected to follow x. In some cases, the consequences that theoretically may follow from a given set of conditions are so numerous and varied that one is led to conclude that "anything can happen."

Nevertheless, many significant and testable hypotheses may be found in or derived from Heider's analysis. Our purpose is not to review exhaustively the research relevant to the theory, but a few examples may be instructive. The bulk of experimental work has been directed toward hypotheses deriving from either balance or attribution formulations. Since we will deal more extensively with balance theory in Chapter 8, we will not review studies relevant to it at this point, but instead we will report some of the work concerning the attribution process. The studies cited below derive rather directly

[2] The interested reader is well advised to read the original version of Heider's *The Psychology of Interpersonal Relations.*

from Heider's theory and are representative of the research stimulated by the theory.

When we observe a change in a person's behavior or an effect produced by a person's actions, we may attribute it to internal or personal causes (personal causality), to external or environmental causes (impersonal causality), or to some combination of these two sets of factors (Heider, 1958). This general proposition has been tested in a number of ways. Jones, Davis, and Gergen (1961) tested the hypothesis that behavior that is appropriate to a well-defined social role is relatively uninformative about personal characteristics. Subjects were required to listen to an interview in which a person was heard being instructed to respond as if he very much wanted to qualify as an astronaut (in two treatments) or as a submariner (in two treatments). The interviewee responded in line either with the specified qualifications for an astronaut (inner-directedness) or with those specified for a submariner (other-directedness). Thus there were four experimental conditions corresponding to in-role behavior regarding the astronaut position and the submariner position and out-of-role behavior with respect to each of these two positions. As predicted, the out-of-role interviewees were perceived to be revealing their true characteristics more than the in-role interviewees.

Two experiments reported by Thibaut and Riecken (1965) also related to the same general hypothesis. The specific hypothesis tested was that the perceived locus of causality for a stimulus person's compliance with an influence attempt will be internal for a high-status person and external for a low-status person. Subjects attempted to influence the behavior of two paid confederates, one who posed as a high-status and the other as a low-status person. Both complied with the influence attempt. Subsequent interview and rating scale data supported the hypothesis.

Finally, two studies by Hastorf, Kite, Gross, and Wolfe (1965) dealt with the effects of locus of causality on the subsequent evaluation of the person and his behavior. Subjects listened to the recordings of a three-man group discussing two problems and rated the group after each problem. The two discussions were staged so that one group member talked much less in the second session, whereas another member talked much more in the second session than in the first one. Experimental subjects were told that reinforcement lights were used during the second discussion to produce this differential rate of talking. Control subjects were told that the group members did not receive reinforcement. In both studies, the experimental subjects saw less change in quality relative to change in amount of talking than did control subjects.

Another significant part of Heider's theory related to the development of "sophistication" in the attribution of responsibility. Presumably, persons advance through levels during their development (socialization); at each successive level the person considers additional variables (circumstances) in judging whether the person is responsible for the consequences of his actions. The rate of development is theoretically related to age and experience. Several studies have provided evidence on this point. Shaw and Sulzer (1964) devised questionnaires to describe situations representing the minimum variables needed to elicit attribution from an individual at each level of development and were able to demonstrate that children's attributions of responsibility were more "primitive" (showed less differentiation among variables) than the attributions of adults. Studies of cultural differences also support the general theory. For example, subjects from deprived environments develop at a slower rate than subjects from less-deprived environments (Shaw & Schneider, 1967; Garcia-Esteve & Shaw, 1968). Comparisons of subjects from Latin and American cultures also reveal differences in attribution that are consistent with differences in child-rearing practices in the two cultures (Shaw, Briscoe, & Garcia-Esteve, 1968). Several other studies provide general support for Heider's attribution theory (Aronfreed, 1961; Kohlberg, 1963; Sulzer, 1964; Lerner & Simmons, 1966; Lerner & Matthews, 1967). Jones and Davis (1965) adopted many of Heider's ideas in formulating their theory of attribution (see Chapter 11).

A FIELD-THEORETICAL CONCEPTION OF POWER

Cartwright (1959b) noted that the concept of *social power* has long played an important role in the analysis of social behavior, although there is little agreement regarding its precise nature. Writers on social power have employed a wide range of definitions, all which have elements in common but also significant differences (for example, Bierstadt, 1950; Lasswell & Kaplan, 1950; Simon, 1956; Dahl, 1957). For example, Lewin (1951) suggested that the power of person A over person B can be defined as the quotient of the maximum force which A can induce on B and the maximum resistance which B can mobilize in the opposite direction. Each of the several authors represented in Cartwright's monograph (1959b) used somewhat different definitions of power, although all agreed in viewing power as the ability of one person or group to influence or control some aspect of some other person or group. Considering these several definitions, Cartwright proposed a modified version of Lewin's definition: the power of A over B with respect to a change from x to y at a specified time is equal to the maximum strength of the resultant force which A can set up in that direction at that time. This definition is based upon the concept of forces, first formulated by Lewin. However, Cartwright's usage of force is somewhat unusual in that it is defined by seven "primitive" terms.

Primitives

The seven primitive terms used by Cartwright in defining psychological force are *agent, act of agent, locus, direct joining, motive base, magnitude,* and *time.* These terms were defined as follows:

> Agent is any entity that can produce effects or suffer consequences. This agent is most commonly a person, although it may be a committee, group, legislature, or other similar entity, or even subparts of persons.

Act of agent is any event that activates an effect. For an agent to produce effects, he must act in some way. Acts which produce effects in the life space of another person (agent) are usually called influence attempts.

Locus refers to a position in space. Cartwright used the term to refer to Lewin's concept of region, to a position in a group or organization, or to a position on a scale indicating an opinion, attitude, or other psychological quality.

Direct joining refers to the possibility of going directly from one locus to another. For example, if there are two offices in an organization such that it is possible to be promoted directly from one to the other (for example, from vice-president to president), the two offices are directly joined.

Motive base is defined as a "predisposition" that energizes behavior; for example, need, drive, or motive. A given motive base, according to Cartwright, is designated by the type of activity which satisfies it.

Magnitude refers to the strength of constructs. Cartwright assumed that it is possible to use positive and negative real numbers as magnitude indicators.

Time is the duration of any event. Physical time units may serve as indicators, although Cartwright believed that other units might be more useful in the study of power. He required only that the temporal order be specified.

These primitives were used by Cartwright to define *force*, and hence, *power*. Force was described as consisting of act of agent, motive base, directly joining pair of loci, magnitude, and time. Power was defined in terms of forces, as stated earlier, or alternatively, in terms of acts: the power of A over B with respect to a change from x to y at a specified time equals the maximum strength of any act which A can perform at that time. In this definition, strength is specified for the direction xy in B's life space.

Cartwright's definition differs from Lewin's in that Lewin defined power as the *ratio* of maximal forces, whereas Cartwright defined it as the maximal *difference*. It also differs in that Lewin's definition does not clearly specify the source of the resistance that B can muster against A, whereas Cartwright limited the resistance which B can offer to those forces which are activated by an act of A.

Cartwright also made a distinction between *power* and *control*. A person may be able to activate forces acting on another person and still be unable to change his behavior. For example, A may ask B to do something and B may experience a tendency to comply (waver, feel guilt, etc.) without actually doing so. In such cases, A has power over B but has not controlled his behavior. Therefore, Cartwright defined control as a situation in which an act of A results in combined forces in B's life space which change B's behavior in a direction corresponding to that intended by A. Control is thus seen as a special case of power; control depends upon other things in addition to ability to influence (power).

Conceptual Properties of Power

By defining power in terms of primitives used in general theories of behavior, Cartwright hoped that the concept of power could be more readily integrated into such theories. He also suggested that many of the conceptual properties of power derived from the primitives used in the construction of the definition of power. It is helpful to review the contribution that he believed each primitive made to the concept of power.

AGENT   Power may be conceived of as a relation between an ordered pair of agents. This conception leaves open the question of just what empirical entities may properly be considered agents. However, it is possible to consider the formal properties of the power relation. Cartwright considered the properties of symmetry, reflexivity, and transitivity, although his presentation implied that there are other important properties that should be considered. The power relation is conceived as being *nonsymmetric, nontransitive,* and *irreflexive.* The knowledge that A has power over B establishes no requirement concerning the power of B over A. Similarly, there is nothing in the definition of power that implies either transitivity or intransitivity; if A has power over B and B has power over C, nothing is implied about A's power over C. With regard to the third property, it is possible to think of a reflexive relation (A has power over A), but Cartwright considered such cases as implying two agents that are subparts of a single person (A).

ACT OF AGENT   Acts of agents may include such things as commands, requests, policy decisions, hints, and similar events associated with agents. Since acts of agent may be so diverse in nature, it is necessary to classify them in order that acts may be related to other phenomena. Acts may be classified according to their meaning for A or their meaning for B, and Cartwright suggested that both types of classifications are needed. He considered the following aspects of the meaning of an act: intensity, intentions, directional properties, motivational relevance, and temporal characteristics. Thus the act may be mild or strong; A may intend to act in such a way as to set up forces in B or the consequences of his act may be unintentional; the act may vary in clarity or direction; the act may fit certain motivational bases and not others; and, finally, an act may vary with respect to the duration of activated forces. All these factors have important consequences for the forces activated by acts of the agent and, hence, for power.

LOCUS AND DIRECT JOINING   Since the power of A over B must always be specified with respect to a pair of directly joining loci in B's life space, it is necessary to consider locus and direct joining as a unit. Three aspects of this relation are of interest: classification of loci, range of power, and visibility of loci. The abstract term "locus" may be applied to many different empirical phenomena; hence it is useful to specify the particular application in any given situation. It is important to note in this respect that forces may be activated at various types of loci and that A may have great power over B with respect to some loci and lesser or no power with respect to other loci. This fact makes it necessary to consider not only types of loci, but also the range of power of A over B. Cartwright defined the range of power in the following way: at any given time, the range of A's power over B is the set of directly joining pairs of loci in B's life space with respect to which A's power over B exceeds a specified magnitude.

In principle, the power of A over B with respect to a given locus may be independent of his power with respect to other loci. In practice, however, it appears that there are interpendencies such that power with respect to one locus implies power with respect to others. A boss who has power over a worker on the job may also have power over him in social affairs.

Finally, Cartwright noted that most social psychological research has been concerned with observable changes in B's life space. The degree of observable compliance has special significance for all forms of power in which B's need satisfaction is contingent upon A's evaluation of B's compliance.

MOTIVE BASE   The concept of motive base, as employed in Cartwright's conception of power, has several important consequences. First, it provides a basis for linking power theories with theories of motivation. Second, it calls attention to the fact that an act of an agent must be related to a motive base in order for it to activate a force; that is, unless A is able to relate his actions to some motive of B, he will have no power over B. Third, many important empirical questions are made apparent by relating power to motivation. Lastly, the fact that need satisfaction requires resources points to the further fact that A can have power over B only if he has access to resources that will satisfy a need (or needs) of B. This in turn suggests the need to examine the properties of resources and their relation to power.

MAGNITUDE   Little is said about magnitude, although there are two significant aspects worthy of mention: (1) it is assumed that the magnitude of a force may vary with variations in any of the other primitives and (2) the magnitude of power may assume negative values. Both of these assumptions raise important empirical questions.

TIME   Time serves to remind us that power is not static, that it changes from time to time. Further, by studying power structures over time it is possible to describe a given power relationship with regard to stability and the tendency to assume any given state.

Unsolved Problems

Cartwright stated that his purpose was to provide a conceptualization of power based upon terms common to more-general theories of behavior in the hope that such a formulation would facilitate its integration into a single conceptual system. He would seem to have accomplished his purpose, although his hope has not yet been realized. The various hypotheses are logically consistent and could be tested empirically, although they are stated in a form that does not immediately suggest a method for testing. It fits in quite well with other theories, perhaps its strongest point.

There are several problems which Cartwright recognized and to which he devoted some consideration. First, it might be objected that the proposed definition of power does not deal with what power "really" is. Cartwright suggested that this is a meaningless objection, since words have no inherent meaning and may be applied to any conceptualization if done so in a consistent manner. However, he took the position that most definitions of power can be encompassed in the system of concepts that he used.

A second problem or set of problems is concerned with the operational treatment of power. Because power is a complex phenomenon, we must be careful not to employ operations that are superficial or that refer to only one aspect of power. However, these problems are solvable; Cartwright cited operations used in several empirical studies as examples of possible techniques (for example, Lippitt, Polansky, Redl, & Rosen, 1952; Hurwitz, Zander, & Hymovitch, 1953). The findings of these studies are generally consistent with the theory.

Cartwright dealt primarily with relations between two persons, but he stated that most of the interesting empirical problems of power are found in social systems (for example, industrial organizations, political systems). These problems have scarcely been touched upon. Related to this area is the question of coalition formations, but again the present formulation has little to offer toward a solution.

A final criticism, not mentioned by Cartwright, may be in order. Many of the definitions and concepts employed are not clearly specified. For example, the definitions of "primitives" are generally vague; one must infer their meaning from the lists of entities to which they are applied. Again, the notion of *intention* employed in the distinction between power and control is left undefined, although it is said to be essential in any discussion of the effectiveness of an influence attempt.

Despite the unresolved problems and lack of clarity with regard to certain concepts, the formulation represents an important step forward in the social psychological study of social power. The definition proposed by Cartwright played a significant role in the theory of social power developed by French (1956) and described in the following section.

A FORMAL THEORY OF SOCIAL POWER

The French (1956) theory of social power is concerned with influence processes in groups, or more specifically, with influences leading to opinion change in N-person groups. Basically, the theory attempted to reduce influence to a summation of interpersonal influences involving three patterns of relations: the power relations among group members, the communication patterns in the group, and the relations among opinions within the group. Thus, the theory is restricted with respect to the range of social influences to which it is applicable, and it is not concerned exclusively with social power.

The Model of Social Influence

The model of opinion change formulated by French was derived from Lewin's (1951) theory of quasi-stationary equilibrium. Changes in opinion are conceptualized in terms of forces operating along a unidimensional continuum. Social influences are analogous to force fields induced by one person with respect to another. Power is coordinated to the strength of these forces; that is, A has power over B in proportion to the strength of the force fields which A can induce on B. This power is potential power that will be effective only if A communicates to B in some manner. For example, when A expresses his opinion or argues with B, then the forces which A can induce on B are activated in the direction of a central position corresponding to A's opinion. In groups larger than dyads, other group members may also have power over B that can be invoked through communication. The actual change in B's opinion will thus be a function of the resultant force from all these member forces and a force corresponding to B's resistance.

To demonstrate how the model can be used to derive the exact amount of influence that each group member will have over every other group member, French assumed a unidimensional continuum of opinion which can be measured by a ratio scale. Suppose two persons, A and B, hold the initial opinions represented in Figure 6–4. In Figure 6–4 the ordinate indicates the strength of the force that A can induce for B and the strength of the resistance that B can mobilize against A, and the abscissa indicates the opinion continuum. The solid line represents the forces that A can induce with respect to B, and the broken lines indicate the forces of resistance emanating from B against A. These two force gradients intersect at a point one-half the distance between A and B, where there is an equilibrium: the two forces are equal in strength and opposite in direction. At all points to the right of this point of equilibrium A's forces are stronger than B's resistance, and B will change his opinion in the direction of A. At all points to the left of the equilibrium point, B's resistance is stronger than A's forces and B will move toward the point of equilibrium (although it is difficult to understand how B could be in such a position). The effects of forces induced by other group members in larger groups can be derived in a similar manner.

FIGURE 6–4.   Force fields influencing opinion change by person B. (Adapted with permission from J. R. P. French, Jr. A formal theory of social power. *Psychol. Rev.*, 1956, **63**, 181–194.)

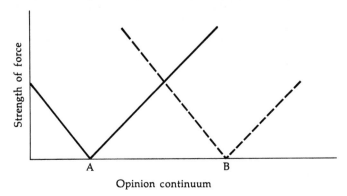

Influence in groups is a gradual process that requires time; therefore, French divided the influence process into units. He defined a unit as the time required for all members who are being influenced to change their opinions to the point of equilibrium of all the forces operating at the beginning of that unit. At the end of that unit, a new constellation of forces is in operation to produce a new equilibrium to which all members shift during the next unit. This process will continue until all group members have the same opinion or until the maximum change possible has occurred. (Conditions determining whether uniformity of group opinion can be achieved will be considered in a later section.) This analysis assumes that all persons change at the same rate.

French made a distinction between *direct* and *indirect influence*. Direct influence is mediated through direct channels of communication (A communicates directly with B), whereas indirect influence is mediated through other persons. According to the above formulation, direct influence always occurs during the same unit, whereas indirect influence requires two or more units.

The Bases of Social Power

As noted earlier, French adopted Cartwright's definition of social power, which he stated in a somewhat different form: "the power of A over B (with respect to a given opinion) is equal to the maximum force which A can induce on B minus the maximum resisting force which B can mobilize in the opposite direction" (French, 1956, p. 183). The basis for interpersonal power was defined as a more or less enduring relationship between A and B. Following an earlier analysis (French & Raven, 1959), five bases of power were identified:

> *Attraction power,* which is based on a liking or identification relationship, labeled by French and Raven as "referent power"
>
> *Reward power,* based on A's ability to mediate rewards for B; that is, A's ability to administer positive valences and to remove or decrease negative valences
>
> *Coercive power,* based upon A's ability to mediate punishments for B; that is, A's ability to administer negative valences and to remove or decrease positive valences
>
> *Legitimate power,* based on B's belief that A has a right to prescribe B's behavior
>
> *Expert power,* based on B's perception that A has greater resources (knowledge or information) within a given area

Reward and coercive power both lead to dependent behavior; that is, their effectiveness depends upon the presence of A. The other three types are less dependent in that the presence of A is irrelevant. For all types, the stronger the basis of power, the greater the power will be.

It should be noted that various bases of power are not independent, since a given person's power may have more than one basis. For example, one may believe that it is right that an informed person should have power over him (legitimate *and* expert power). The exercise of one type of power may also increase or decrease the basis for another type of power. For example, if A exercises reward power over B, it may be expected that B's liking for A will increase and thus increase attraction power.

Postulates

French formulated three postulates concerning power relations, opinion relations (discrepancies), and opinion change. The first postulate refers to all of the bases of social power outlined above.

Postulate 1. For any given discrepancy between A and B, the strength of the resultant force which an inducer A can exert on an inducee B, in the direction of agreeing with A's opinion, is proportional to the strength of the bases of power of A over B (French, 1956, p. 184).

Postulate 2. The strength of the force which an inducer A exerts on an inducee B, in the direction of agreeing with A's opinion, is proportional to the size of the discrepancy between their opinions (French, 1956, p. 184).

Postulate 3. In one unit, each person who is being influenced will change his opinion until he reaches the equilibrium point where the resultant force . . . is equal to zero (French, 1956, p. 185).

Postulates 1 and 2 state merely that the strength of the resultant force in situations similar to the one depicted in Figure 6–4 will be proportional to the strength of the bases of power and the discrepancy among opinions in the group. French cited experimental evidence supporting both of these postulates. Postulate 3 is an application of Lewin's assumption that locomotion will take place in the direction of any resultant force that is greater than zero. French stated that this assumption is consistent with empirical studies but cannot be tested directly.

Theorems

French selected certain representative theorems for consideration. We shall discuss those related to the power structure of the group, communication patterns, and patterns of opinions.

POWER STRUCTURE   In formulating theorems about the effects of the power structure on the influence process, French (1956) represented the power structure in terms of the mathematical theory of directed graphs. A directed graph (or digraph) is a finite set of points and a subset of the directed lines between these points. Points were coordinated to group members and directed lines to power relations. The property of a digraph labeled "degree of connectedness" was used to characterize the power structure of groups. To explicate this property it is necessary to define *complete digraph* and *directed path*. A digraph is complete if there exists a directed line from each point to every other point. Thus, for a power structure to be complete, each group member must have power over every other member. A directed path is a collection of points (for example, A, B, C,) together with a sequence of directed lines beginning at the first and ending at the last point; that is, there is a directed line from A to B and from B to C, but not directly from A to C.

In an unpublished work, Harary, Norman, and Cartwright defined four degrees of connectedness: strong, unilateral, weak, and disconnected. French adopted their definitions, which may be stated as follows:

1. A digraph is *strongly connected* if for every pair of distinct points, A and B, there exists a directed path from A to B *and* from B to A.
2. A digraph is *unilaterally connected* if for every pair of points, A and B, there exists a directed path from A to B *or* from B to A.
3. A digraph is *weakly connected* if it is impossible to separate its points into two classes such that no line of the digraph has one end point in one class and the other end point in another class.
4. A digraph is *disconnected* if its points can be separated into two or more classes of points such that no line goes from one class to another class.

From these definitions it is clear that all complete digraphs are strong, although not all strong digraphs are complete; that all strong digraphs are unilateral and weak; that all unilateral digraphs are weak; and that all weak digraphs are not strong. However, French used each label to mean digraphs that fit only the definition given for that particular degree of connectedness. For example, *strong* refers to a digraph that is strongly connected but is not complete, *unilateral* to a diagraph that is unilaterally connected but not strong, etc.

According to the model of opinion change and the postulates given above, French was able to specify the nature of opinion change in each type of power structure. In groups where each member communicates to all other members over whom he has direct power during every unit of the influence process, the following theorems may be derived:

Theorem 1. For all possible patterns of initial opinions, in a complete power structure the opinions of all members will reach a common equilibrium level, equal to the arithmetic mean of all initial opinions, in one unit.

Theorem 2. In a strong power structure, all members will reach a final common opinion at the arithmetic mean in an infinite number of units.

Theorem 3. In a unilateral power structure, group members will reach a final common opinion in an infinite number of units.

Theorem 4. In a weak power structure group members will not reach a common opinion except under special conditions in the distribution of initial opinions.

No theorem was stated for a disconnected structure, but French noted that when the final equilibrium has been reached, there will be at least as many different final opinions as there are classes of members (cliques), because no clique can influence any other. The power structure of each clique will determine the course of opinion change in that clique, in accordance with theorems 1 through 4.

The theorems presented thus far have considered power as an all-or-none relation. Theorem 5 refers to the effects of variations in power, derived primarily from postulates 1 and 3.

Theorem 5. The greater the bases of power of A over B, the more influence A will have on B and subsequently on any other person P for whom there is a directed path from B to P.

COMMUNICATION PATTERNS   It is clear that a person may not always communicate with everyone over whom he has power, but French assumed that communications stabilize so that they may be treated as consistent communication patterns. It is also obvious that the strength of the influence attempt can vary continuously, although a communication from A to B must be treated as an all-or-none variable in order to use digraph theory. Finally, in formulating theorems about the effects of communication patterns on opinion change, French considered only complete power structures with variations in degree of connectedness of communication channels. With these restrictions, theorems 1 through 4 also apply to communication patterns.

The model can also be applied to situations in which communication patterns are not stable, provided the interaction pattern is specified for each unit. French illustrated this in theorem 6, specifying the following interaction pattern: A exerts influence in the first unit, B and C in the second unit, A in the third unit, B and C in the fourth unit, and so on.

Theorem 6. In a three-person group in which A has power over B, B has power over C, and C has power over A, and the communication pattern is A, BC, A, BC, . . . , the final common opinion reached by the group members equals $(2a + b + 2c)/5$, where a, b, and c are the opinions initially held by persons A, B, and C, respectively.

The expression, "the communication pattern is A, BC, A, BC, . . . ," in theorem 6 means that person A exerts influence in the first unit, persons B and C exert influence in the second unit, etc. Two main consequences of the communication pattern and the power structure are at once evident: the person who speaks first in the interaction sequence has more influence than those who speak later in the sequence, and the person who has direct power over others has more influence than a person who has only indirect power over others.

PATTERNS OF OPINION   In his consideration of patterns of opinion, French analyzed only the case of a completely connected power structure with completely connected communication channels in which every member communicates to everyone else during each unit. Under these conditions:

Theorem 7. The amount of change of a deviate toward the opinions of the majority is proportional to the sum of the deviations of all other members from the opinion of the deviate.

In general, then, the more members in the group the more they will influence the deviate, and the larger the deviations the more the deviate will change his opinion. The studies by Asch (1952) are cited as an example, although French stated that the conditions of the Asch experiments do not fit the model very well.

Comments and Criticisms

The theory of social power presented by French is important in that it formalizes several conceptions of intragroup relations and makes fairly specific predictions about the outcome of influence attempts under specified conditions. Perhaps its most serious problem is the concept of *unit*. It is not at all obvious how one can determine the duration of a unit. The definition of unit suggests that a unit begins with communication among group members and ends when each member has maximally changed his opinion in response to those communications. It would appear that units can be specified only when the interaction process is strictly controlled; for example, when interactions are limited to discrete trials and each member is limited to a single communication to each person over whom he has direct power. Under these restricted conditions, it should be possible to test empirically the predictions inherent in the theorems. In other cases, one could probably obtain indirect evidence by observing the speed and degree of unanimity achieved under various structural conditions.

The analysis of the bases of social power also presents problems. It is obvious that the five bases (reward, coercion, attraction, legitimate, and expert) are not necessarily independent. In fact, all five can be conceived in terms of reward and punishment. Reward and coercion are types identified by French and Raven (1959) as having control of rewards and punishments as the basis of power; however, the other three appear to be merely special cases of reward power and coercive power. "Legitimate power" may be regarded as socially acceptable control of rewards and punishments; "attraction power" as ability to reward or punish deriving from the liking relation; and "expert power" as power based upon control of scarce rewards. The analysis of authority by Adams and Romney (1959) seems more accurate, although their analysis derives from a reinforcement orientation (see pp. 103–113).

There are few studies specifically designed to test French's theory. However, there are several experiments that are consistent with his analysis. With regard to opinion change, the studies by Sherif (1935) and by Asch (1952) are cited by French as being in general agreement with his analysis. Experiments by Shaw, Rothschild, and Strickland (1957) dealing with conformity and opinion change in different communication nets showed that subjects in a completely connected communication pattern achieved greater uniformity of opinion and required less time to do so than in patterns that were not completely connected. Studies reported by Mulder (1959, 1960), Shaw (1959), Lippitt, Polansky, Redl, and Rosen (1952), and Hurwitz, Zander, and Hymovitch (1953) are generally consistent with the theory.

The greatest amount of work appears to have been directed toward a study of the effects of power derived from different bases, as outlined by Raven and French (1959). The effects of legitimacy in power relations has been demonstrated by French and Raven (1958a, b) and by Shaw and Penrod (1964). Coercive power has been examined by French, Morrison, and Levinger (1960) and by Zipf (1960), and attraction power has been shown to be effective in a study by Wilson (1960). Thus, although the evidence for the theory is not always directed toward the major principles, it is nevertheless generally consistent with French's predictions.

In summary, the theory is logically consistent, testable, and agrees with known empirical data. It concerns important social phenomena and merits more-extensive empirical evaluation.

A THEORY OF COOPERATION AND COMPETITION

The theory of cooperation and competition outlined in this section was developed by Deutsch (1949a) and is based upon the Lewinian field orientation. In contrast to previous theories which dealt with the conditions for cooperation and competition (for example, May & Doob, 1937), the present theory is concerned with the *effects* of cooperation and competition upon small-group functioning. In his presentation of the theory, Deutsch began with a definition (or conceptualization) of cooperative and competitive situations. He then considered the implications of the definitions and formulated a set of hypotheses about the relative effects of cooperation and competition upon group process.

Definitions

In the process of defining cooperation and competition, Deutsch examined a number of definitions proposed by others (Maller, 1929; May & Doob, 1937; Mead, 1937; Barnard, 1938; Lewis, 1944) and noted that implicit in all definitions was the notion that the major difference between cooperation and competition was in the nature of goal regions in the two situations. His definitions are based upon this distinction and may be stated briefly as follows: A social situation is *cooperative* if the goal regions for each of the individuals or subunits in the situation are defined so that a goal region can be entered, to some degree, by any given individual or subunit only if all of the individuals or subunits under consideration can enter their respective goal regions, to some degree. (The term *promotively interdependent goals* was used to refer to situations in which individual goals are interrelated in the manner described.)

A social situation is *competitive* if the goal regions for individuals or subunits in the situation are such that if a goal region is entered by any individual or subunit, or by portions thereof, the other individuals or subunits will, to some degree, be unable to reach their respective goals. (The term *contriently interdependent goals* was used to refer to this type of goal interrelatedness.)

Implications

It follows from these definitions that persons who have promotively interdependent goals will come to have promotively interdependent locomotions in the direction of those goals; that is, each person in a cooperative group can achieve his goal (locomote to his goal region) only if other persons in the group achieve theirs. Similarly, persons with contriently interdependent goals will come to have contriently interdependent locomotions in the direction of their goals; that is, if one person in a competitive group achieves his goal (locomotes to his goal region), other persons in the group do not achieve theirs.

Deutsch pointed to the difficulties involved in going from these statements about objective social space to statements about psychological life space. Nevertheless, he believed that one could use the principles of learning and of perceptual and cognitive organization to make the jump more reasonable. He therefore assumed that all action is directed toward need reduction (that is, reduction or removal of tensions associated with needs), and that the significance of an object is developed during action. From these assumptions, he derived that an individual's perceptions and expectations are likely to be veridical to his objective environment, in proportion to the simplicity of his environment and to his capabilities and experiences. Thus, the perceptions of reasonably normal subjects with average abilities who are placed in reasonably obvious social situations should be veridical. Applying this logic to cooperative and competitive situations, the following hypotheses were proposed. Hypotheses have been restated for convenience, but we believe their meanings remain as intended by Deutsch (1949a).

Hypotheses

1. Individuals in cooperative situations will perceive themselves to be more promotively interdependent, and individuals in competitive situations will perceive themselves to be more contriently interdependent.

2. Substitutability for similarly intended actions will be greater in the cooperative than in the competitive situation. (Substitutability means that the acts of one person in the group can be substituted for the actions of another; two individuals need not perform the same act.)

3. A larger percentage of actions by fellow members will be positively cathected (become attractive or be regarded favorably) by members of cooperative than by members of competitive groups.

3a. A larger percentage of actions by fellow members will be negatively cathected (be regarded unfavorably) by members of competitive groups than by members of cooperative groups.

4. There will be greater positive inducibility (production and channeling of own forces in the direction induced by the inducing agent) with respect to fellow group members in the cooperative than in the competitive situation.

4a. There will be greater self-conflict among members of cooperative than among members of competitive groups.

5. Members of cooperative groups will help each other more than members of competitive groups will help each other.

5a. Members of competitive groups will exhibit more obstructiveness towards each other than will members of cooperative groups.

6. At any given time, there will be greater interrelation of activities (working together) among members of cooperative groups than among members of competitive groups.

6a. Over a period of time, there will be more frequent coordination of efforts in cooperative than in competitive situations.

7. Homogeneity with respect to amount of contributions or participations will be greater in cooperative than in competitive situations.

8. Specialization of function will be greater in cooperative than in competitive situations.

9. Specialization of activities will be greater in cooperative than in competitive groups.

10. Structural stability with respect to functions will be greater in cooperative than in competitive situations.

11. Change of roles to adapt to changing circumstances will be greater in cooperative than in competitive situations.

12. The direction of forces operating on members of cooperative groups will be more similar than the direction of forces operating on members of competitive groups.

13. There will be more achievement pressure in cooperative than in competitive groups.

14. The group force in the direction of the goal will be stronger in cooperative than in competitive situations.

15. Cooperative and competitive groups will not differ in total strength of forces (interest and involvement) operating on members in their respective situations.

16. When the task is such that the production of observable signs (participation) is perceived as a means for locomotion, total signs produced per unit time will be greater in competitive groups than in cooperative groups.

17. When locomotion is possible without the production of signs, total signs produced per unit time will be greater in cooperative than in competitive groups.

18. Attentiveness to the production of signs by others will be less in competitive than in cooperative groups.

19. Communication difficulties will be greater in competitive than in cooperative groups.

20. Communication difficulties will be greater, even when attentiveness is optimal, in competitive than in cooperative groups.

21. There will be more mutual agreements and acceptances of communications by communicators and communicatees in cooperative than in competitive groups.

22. Members of cooperative groups will have more knowledge about its active members than will members of competitive groups.

23. Group orientation will be greater among members of cooperative than among members of competitive groups.

24. Productivity per unit time will be greater for cooperative than for competitive groups.

24a. It will require less time for a cooperative group to produce a given amount than for a competitive group to produce that same amount.

25. The qualitative productivity of cooperative groups will be higher than that of competitive groups.

26.   Members of cooperative groups will learn more from each other than will members of competitive groups.

27.   There will be more friendliness among members of cooperative than among members of competitive groups.

28.   Members of cooperative groups will evaluate the products of their group more highly than members of competitive groups will.

29.   Percentage of group functions will be higher in cooperative than in competitive situations.

30.   Percentage of individual functions will be greater in competitive than in cooperative groups.

31.   The perception of attitudes of others toward one's own functioning in the group will be more realistic in cooperative than in competitive groups.

32.   The attitudes of each member toward his own functioning should be more similar to the attitudes of other group members toward his functioning in cooperative than in competitive groups.

33.   Members of cooperative groups will perceive themselves as having more favorable effects on fellow members than will members of competitive groups.

34.   Incorporation of the attitude of the generalized other will occur to a greater extent in cooperative than in competitive groups. ("Attitude of the generalized other" refers to the internal structure resulting from the introjection of mutually interacting attitudes of those persons with whom one interacts frequently.)

Comments and Evaluation

In the presentation above of Deutsch's hypotheses, we have omitted much of the reasoning that led him to formulate these hypotheses and thus have not shown how the various hypotheses are interrelated. It should also be kept in mind that the hypotheses were formulated with respect to a particular kind of social situation, namely, five-person groups of college students who are asked to solve particular kinds of problems. Nevertheless, it seems that he used unnecessarily obscure terminology that sometimes impedes understanding of the theory. We have tried to substitute simpler terms wherever we believed we could do so without distorting the intended meaning. On the other hand, the conceptualization of cooperative and competitive situations is clear and provides a firm basis for research, which had been lacking before Deutsch's theoretical analysis. The preciseness of the hypotheses also makes support or refutation relatively direct and unambiguous. The theory is internally consistent and generally satisfies the minimal criteria for a "good" theory.

Perhaps an empirical evaluation is more meaningful than logical or subjective considerations. Major empirical support is provided by Deutsch (1949b). Five-person groups were studied as they attempted to solve human relations problems and puzzle problems. Extensive observational data were obtained by four observers using formal rating scales, as well as data from subject ratings. The results provided impressive support for the theory.

Moderate to strong support was found for twenty-three of the thirty-four hypotheses; weak or ambiguous evidence was found relative to four hypotheses (8, 13, 16 and 26); and seven hypotheses were not tested (10, 11, 14, 20, 22, 31, and 32). Additional relevant data have been reported by Grossack (1954), who examined the consequences of cooperation and competition on small-group cohesiveness, social influence, and communication. He found that cooperative subjects showed significantly more cohesive behavior, more attempts at influence, greater exertion and acceptance of pressures toward uniformity, and more relevant communications than did competitive subjects. Raven and Eachus (1963) found that members of cooperative groups solved problems more rapidly, evaluated other group members more favorably, showed less hostility, were more attracted to the task, and showed greater concern about own performance than members of competitive groups did. All these findings except the "concern about own performance" are consistent with Deutsch's theory.

Other experimental studies adopting the Deutsch theoretical orientation (Gottheil, 1955; Shaw, 1958; Hammond & Goldman, 1961) also report results that are generally consistent with the theory. The large number of hypotheses stated by Deutsch almost ensures that some will be supported, but the high percentage supported by the experimental evidence is unusual for a social psychological theory.

THE COGNITIVE ORIENTATION
PART 4

Cognitive theory is a term used to refer to the general theoretical orientation that emphasizes central processes (for example, attitudes, ideas, expectancies) in the explanation of behavior. This orientation may be contrasted with behavioristic approaches that emphasize peripheral factors (that is, stimulus and response variables) as the major explanatory concepts. In fact, proponents of cognitive theory usually express their views in contrast to behavioristic principles. Scheerer (1954) apparently found it necessary to outline behavioristic principles in order to present the cognitive viewpoint. His statement of cognitive theory is largely a polemic against behaviorism in which he described what cognitive theory is *not*. Ausubel (1965a) stated explicitly that any exposition of cognitive theory must begin with an examination of contrasting views of cognitive and neobehavioristic theorists. He outlined several points of disagreement between neobehaviorism and cognitive theory:

1. Behaviorism deals with operant and classical conditioning and rote, instrumental, and discrimination learning, whereas cognitive theory is more concerned with concept formation, thinking, and the acquisition of knowledge.

2. Behaviorism tends to rely upon observable responses, whereas cognitive theory appeals to so-called mentalistic concepts, such as knowing, meaning, understanding, and similar conscious experiences, as the most significant data of science.

3. Behaviorism tends to assume a basically organismic process underlying psychological or "cognitive" events, whereas cognitive theory tends to "... define cognitive events in terms of differentiated states of consciousness—existing in relation to organized systems of images, concepts, and propositions in cognitive structure—and the cognitive processes on which they depend" (Ausubel, 1965a, p. 7).

To this list may be added:

4. Behaviorism tends to adopt a molecular form of analysis, whereas cognitive theory usually assumes a molar approach (Krech & Crutchfield, 1948; Scheerer, 1954).

5. Behaviorism reveals a genetic bias in that genetically early events are regarded as more fundamental than events that occur later, whereas cognitive theory rejects this view (MacLeod, 1947).

6. Behaviorism tends to assume that behavior is activated by specific primary or derived needs and that no learning occurs without the reduction of these needs, whereas cognitive theory holds that learning may occur without need or tension reduction (Allport, 1937).

Of course, not all behaviorists accept all of the beliefs and assumptions attributed to behaviorism in the list above (see Chapter 2), nor do all cognitive theorists reject them or make different assumptions. The cognitive position should become clearer after we consider cognitive explanations of specific psychological phenomena.

The cognitive theoretical orientation is most closely related to gestalt psychology and Lewin's field theory (see Chapter 5). However, there are significant differences in the nature of theoretical explanations offered by representatives of cognitive, gestalt, and field orientations. The major similarities and differences have been stated clearly by Ausubel (1965a, p. 5).

> Historically, the cognitive viewpoint is most closely identified with the theoretical position of *Gestalt* psychology insofar as it is nonmechanistic and focuses on organized and differentiated conscious experience such as is involved in perception and thinking. All cognitive theorists, however, do not necessarily endorse the *Gestalt* doctrines of perceptual nativism, psychophysiological isomorphism, the insightful nature of *all* problem solving, and the perceptual dynamics underlying the trace theory of forgetting. And, similarly, although Kurt Lewin was an extremely influential 'cognitive-field' psychologist, not all cognitive theorists necessarily subscribe to his concepts of life-space and psychological tension, to his topological diagrams, and to his insistence on the contemporaneity and invariable purposiveness of behavior.

As implied in Ausubel's statement, there is no set of general principles that is acceptable to all (or even most) cognitive theorists, nor is there general agreement regarding the classification of cognitive theorists. For example, Edward Chace Tolman is sometimes identified as a cognitive theorist (Scheerer, 1954), apparently because his theory makes use of cognitive elements such as "expectancy" and emphasizes the molar rather than the molecular approach (Tolman, 1932). On the other hand, Hilgard (1948) called Tolman's theory behavioristic, and Tolman's most recent statement (1959) is strongly behavioristic in flavor, despite his "mentalistic" concepts. Thus, it is clear that any exposition of cognitive theory must be either very brief or offensive to some who have different views concerning the "basic" principles of cognitive theory.

In the following sections of this chapter, we have attempted to reveal the essential flavor of the cognitive orientation through a discussion of the positions of individuals who are identified, by themselves or others, as cognitive theorists. In this discussion we consider cognitive definitions of some basic concepts in psychological theory and cognitive explanations of significant psychological phenomena. In the final section of the chapter, we present the cognitive principles formulated by Krech and Crutchfield (1948) as an example of cognitive theory related to social psychology. Their formulation is probably the most explicit statement of cognitive theory that is currently available.

COGNITIVE DEFINITIONS OF BASIC TERMS

It is always presumptuous to attempt to identify the "basic" concepts used in theories proposed by others. Nevertheless, it is necessary to identify and define concepts and terms that seem to be most central to cognitive theory, at least in the sense that they are used frequently. It is obvious that *cognition* and the related terms *cognitive* and *cognitive structure* are basic to cognitive theory. In addition, it will be helpful to consider cognitive-theory definitions of *stimulus, response,* and *meaning.*

Cognition and Cognitive Structure

Most cognitive theorists use the concept *cognition* without explicitly defining it, perhaps because they believe it is so frequently used as to require no definition. However, some writers have attempted to define cognition. For example, Scheerer (1954) referred to cognition as a centrally mediated process representing internal and external events. "It takes the form of phenomenal organization *which is centrally imposed between* the source of stimulation and the behavioral adjustment" (Scheerer, 1954, p. 99). Festinger (1957) identified "cognitive elements" as cognitions, which he defined as the things a person knows about himself, his behavior, and his surroundings. He used the term "knowledges" to refer to these things. Most recently, Neisser (1967) stated that the term refers to the processes by which any sensory input is transformed, reduced, elaborated, stored, recovered, and used. Thus, cognition seems to be that which is known or knowledge acquired through personal experience.

Cognitive structure, on the other hand, is usually explicitly defined. Zajonc (1960) defined cognitive structure as an organized subset of the attributes an individual uses to identify and discriminate a particular object or event. In a similar vein Scott (1963) used the term *cognitive structure* to mean those structures whose elements consist of ideas consciously held by the person or as the set of ideas maintained by a person and relatively available to conscious awareness (Scott, 1962). The content of experience is believed to be organized into more-complex structural assemblies, and it is these structures that give meaning to specific elements (for example, particular beliefs, knowledges, values, expectancies). These cognitive structures play a significant role in learning, perception, and similar psychological processes, as we shall see later.

Since cognitive structures are seen as consisting of various attributes and relationships among attributes, it is necessary to identify and describe the properties of these relationships. Zajonc (1960) identified the properties of cognitive structures as *differentiation, complexity, unity,* and *organization.* Differentiation refers to the number of attributes constituting a given cognitive structure, complexity to the degree of interrelatedness of attributes, unity to the degree to which attributes are functionally dependent upon each other, and organization to the extent to which one attribute or cluster of attributes dominates the whole.

A similar but somewhat more-detailed analysis of cognitive structure has been made by Scott (1962, 1963). He identified three major structural properties: *differentiation, relatedness,* and *integration.* Differentiation was used to refer to the distinctiveness of elements that contribute to the set of ideas maintained by a person. This usage contrasts with Zajonc's use of the term to refer to *number* of attributes, but it is quite similar to Bieri's (1955) concept of complexity of attributes and to the construct measured by Kelly's (1955) rep test. Differentiation is necessary before one can consider relations among elements.

Relatedness is used to refer to two aspects of the cognitive structure. On the one hand, it refers to types of relations, such as similarity, association, proximity, covariance, and so forth; on the other hand, it can refer to the phenomenal influence of one element on another. With regard to the latter, when two elements are correlated in this way the question always arises as to whether elements are causally related but independent or are merely undifferentiated. *Salience* of an attribute may also be regarded as an aspect of relatedness. Scott defined salience of an attribute as the likelihood of the attribute's being aroused by environmental cues. It is represented structurally as the number of concepts with which it is associated in a dependent fashion, and in this sense is similar to Zajonc's concept of unity. When a person's cognitive structure has many attributes with equal salience there exists a state of dispersion among saliences.

Integration is used to refer to the degree of connectedness among parts of the structure. When the cognitive structure is integrated, the relations among the various concepts or attributes are known to the person and are manipulable by him. He can therefore shift from one to the other and combine them in various ways in responding to his world.

Implicit in both the Zajonc and the Scott analyses is the notion of a structure consisting of differentiated parts (ideas, concepts, etc.), which are related to one another in such a way that an integrated organization exists. It is this cognitive structure that enables the person to deal with a complex environment in a meaningful way.

Stimulus

A *stimulus,* for the cognitive theorist, is a complex affair, and an adequate definition requires consideration of the whole perceptual process. This problem was examined by Scheerer (1954), who appealed to Heider's (1944) analysis of perception for purposes of explication. The reader will recall (see Chapter 6) that Heider analyzed the perceptual process into three elements: the distal stimulus (for example, physical objects), the mediation (for example, light waves reflected by an object), and the proximal stimulus (for example, the pattern of stimulation on the retina). Thus, we must rely upon the proximal stimulation for perception, but this pattern is not the object we perceive. Although the proximal stimuli are mutually independent, the perception is an organized whole. We see a table, for example, and not merely the pattern of light waves reflected by the object (table). This organization of independent local stimuli is induced by the relations among them. This analysis led Scheerer to conclude that there are at least three definitions of stimulus, roughly corresponding to the three elements in the perceptual process: (1) The stimulus consists of the physical objects which affect the organism through the medium of proximal stimulus relations. (2) The stimulus is the total proximal field distribution which elicits patterns of excitation in the central nervous system. (3) The stimulus is the phenomenal representation of the geographic object.

It is clear that cognitive theorists have used all three definitions of *stimulus,* although in practice (experimentation) the most common one appears to be definition (1). However, the stimulus in this sense is not merely an isolated object in the physical world, but a more-complex molar organization. A stimulus, for most cognitive theorists, would consist not only of the object, such as table, but also of other elements of the total situation and the relations among them.

Response

Response is another term that is not often defined by cognitive theorists, although Scheerer (1954) stated that cognitive theorists have not separated stimulus and response in the traditional manner. The response is viewed by Scheerer as a process of organization. For example, the configurational response to the relations among proximal stimuli is the phenomenal representation of the stimulus. The response is thus relational rather than specific, and its organization depends upon relations among stimulus elements.

An apparently similar view is expressed by Hunt (1962). According to his formulation, the adult person has learned a number of large information processing units. These units are specifically designed for the manipulation of an internally represented environment. This environment is, of course, symbolically coded. Using these learned information processing units, the individual is able to construct an internal model of the environment. This environment can then be used to predict external events. He concluded that these routines could be regarded as responses.

These two views of response agree in that the response is regarded as a complex event that is not clearly separable from the stimulus. Unfortunately, it is not made clear exactly how a response can be identified, if, indeed, this is possible, nor how it can be measured. Without such specification it is difficult to see how the response can be studied.

Meaning

Meaning is a central concept in cognitive theory and plays a role in theoretical explanations of almost all complex psychological processes. Ausubel (1965b) viewed meaning as an "idiosyncratic phenomenological product" of meaningful learning. In the learning process the potential meaning inherent in symbols (or in sets of symbols) is converted into differentiated cognitive content. No underlying organismic process is assumed, except, of course, for the organized system of images, concepts, and propositions (that is, the cognitive structure). It is the relation of new content to this cognitive structure that results in new meanings. Ausubel did not deny that neurophysiological events may underlie meaning as a cognitive phenomenon, but he viewed such events as bearing a substrate relationship to meaning. That is, there is no causal connection between meanings and neurophysiological events.

Bruner (1957a) reflected a similar view in his discussion of perceptual readiness. In his view, the meaning of whatever is perceived derives from the class of percepts with which it is grouped. Meaning is thus a consequence of a categorization process that is basic to perception. This conceptualization will be clarified when the cognitive view of perception is considered.

COGNITIVE EXPLANATIONS OF SELECTED PSYCHOLOGICAL PROCESSES

We will not attempt to present the cognitive view of all significant psychological processes that cognitivists have attempted to explain. Instead we have selected the ones which have been dealt with most extensively and which most clearly reveal the cognitive orientation; namely, *perception, learning,* and *reinforcement.*

Perception

Many cognitive theorists have accepted the gestalt conceptualization of the perceptual process, and all are strongly influenced by the gestalt position. For example, Scheerer (1954) reviewed the gestalt principles of perception, which hold that perception is the phenomenal representation of distal objects resulting from the organization of the distal stimuli, the medium, and the proximal stimuli, and concluded that this phenomenal organization is a cohesive structured field in which the units represent objects in the geographic environment.

Berlyne (1957) reviewed Piaget's work on perception in relation to thought, identifying several aspects of perception that set the perceptual process apart from thinking:

1.   The perceived properties of a stimulus vary according to the pattern of which it is a part.

2.   Perceptions are variable from person to person and from time to time.

3.   Perception varies with the direction (focus) of the sense organs.

4.   Perceptions tend to develop in a particular direction and are largely irreversible. For example, once a concealed object is discovered in a "hidden figures test," it cannot be ignored.

Krech and Crutchfield (1948) considered the determinants of perception and asserted that perception is determined by two major sets of factors or variables: structural variables and functional variables. The structural variables are those inherent in the physical stimuli and the neural events they produce in the nervous system. Functional factors are those that reside in the perceiver; for example, needs, moods, past experiences of the perceiver, and other individual characteristics.

These views of the perceptual process tell us something about the cognitive theoretical orientation, but they do not delve very deeply into the nature of perception. The analysis offered by Bruner (1957a) considered the problem in greater detail. According to Bruner, perception is a process of categorization. The organism is stimulated by some appropriate input (external object, event, etc.) and responds to it by relating it to a category of objects or events. This relating of input to category is an active process in which the person selects the appropriate category—the one which will provide identity and meaning for the new information. Thus, all perception is generic, since anything that is perceived is placed in and gets its meaning from the class of percepts to which it is related.

In addition to being categorical and inferential in nature, Bruner described perception as varyingly veridical. Historically, it has been assumed that what is perceived is to some extent a representation of the external world. This so-called representative function of perception has been a source of controversy among both philosophers and scientists, but the manner in which this representation is accomplished is still unclear. Most writers agree, however, that the degree to which the percept represents the external world varies with a variety of circumstances; for example, an object in a cloudy sky may be perceived as a plane when it is "really" a bird. It is this variable degree of correspondence between percept and object that Bruner referred to as "varying veridicality" of perception.

Since perception involves inference, Bruner concluded that it rests upon a decision process (see also Brunswik, 1949a; Tanner & Swets, 1954). Even the simplest perceptual event requires a decision; when the object in the cloudy sky stimulates the organism he must decide whether it is a plane or a bird. This decision determines to a large extent the category to which the input will be referred and, consequently, the meaning it has for the person. In many cases, however, there seems to be a sequence of decisions involved in the perceptual process. Having decided that the object in the sky is, indeed, a plane, the person may decide whether it is a commercial plane or a private one; whether it is preparing to land at the airport or fly past, etc. This example is what Bruner called a "bracketing" process in which there is a gradual narrowing of the category in which the object is placed. He identified four stages in the decision sequence:

1. *Primitive categorization* is a "silent" process in which the object or event is isolated and marked by certain spatio-temporal-qualitative characteristics. At this stage, meaning is minimal.
2. *Cue search* is a stage in which the perceiver is scanning the environ-

ment for additional information which will enable him to select the proper category for object placement. When the event is highly practiced or when there is high cue-to-category probability linkage, this second process may also be silent. In other cases the searching is a conscious experience.

3. *Confirmation check* occurs after the object has been tentatively placed in a category. At this stage the perceiver is no longer open to maximum stimulation; instead, the search is limited to additional confirmatory cues. Bruner referred to this as a "selective gating process" that reduces the effectiveness of irrelevant inputs.

4. *Confirmation completion* is the final stage in the process and is characterized by the termination of cue search. Openness to additional cues is greatly reduced and inconsistent cues are either "gated out" or modified to fit the category.

Bruner summarized his considerations about the general properties of perception in a series of propositions. These propositions may be briefly paraphrased as follows:

1. Perception depends upon a decision process.

2. The decision process involves the utilization of discriminatory cues which make it possible to assign inputs to categories.

3. The process of cue utilization involves the operation of inference, which leads to the placement of the object in a category.

4. A category is a set of specifications or rules concerning the kinds of events that will be grouped together.

5. Categories vary in the readiness with which a stimulus input will be identified in terms of the category; that is, in terms of accessibility.

6. A perception is veridical to the extent that the stimulus inputs are referred to the appropriate category.

7. When conditions are less than optimal, perception will be veridical to the degree that accessibility of categories reflects environmental probabilities.

The common thread running through the views expressed by the various cognitive theorists is that perception is not merely the passive reception and automatic interpretation of stimuli, but rather it is an active process in which the incoming data are selectively related to the existing cognitive structure. It is the relationship of the inputs (sensory data) to the organization of cognitive elements (cognitive structure) that determines and gives meaning to the thing perceived. The details of this perceptual process are viewed differently by different theorists, but there seems to be relatively good agreement concerning the general nature of the process.

Learning

The typical cognitive theorist recognizes more than one type of learning and holds that the principles that are adequate for the explanation of one type are not necessarily applicable to other types. Ausubel (1961) identified four types of learning, which he labeled *reception learning, discovery learning, rote learning,* and *meaningful learning.* These types are not independent, since both reception and discovery learning can be either rote or meaningful. The distinction between reception and discovery learning cuts across the rote versus meaningful learning classification, and the distinction between rote and meaningful learning cuts across the reception- versus discovery-learning classification.

In reception learning, the learner is required only to "internalize" materials that are available to him, so that it will be functionally reproducible at some time in the future. No discovery is required on the part of the learner, since all of the material is given. In discovery learning, however, the content to be learned must, for the most part, be independently discovered by the learner. Examples include concept formation (in which the thing to be learned is the set of attributes common to a number of diverse items or events), meaningful problem solving (in which the task is to discover the exact nature of a relationship between two events), and similar learning tasks. Discovery learning requires more than the mere internalization of content. Therefore, the learning process is one in which the information is reorganized and integrated into the cognitive structure, followed by further reorganization or transformation of the integrated combination. All of this occurs before internalization; afterward, the discovered content is internalized in the same way as in reception learning.

Ausubel also noted that repeated encounters with the learning materials produces different outcomes in reception and discovery learning. In reception learning repeated encounters primarily increase the degree and duration of retention, whereas in discovery learning repetition gives rise to successive stages in discovery.

The distinction between rote and meaningful learning was said by Ausubel to represent an entirely different dimension from the reception- and discovery-learning distinction. Rote learning refers to the situation in which the learner intends to memorize the learning material verbatim, as a series of arbitrarily related words. Meaningful learning, on the other hand, refers to situations that have at least two characteristics: (1) the material to be learned is potentially meaningful and (2) the learner's set is to relate substantive aspects of new concepts or information to relevant components of existing cognitive structures. Such integration makes possible "the incorporation of derivative, elaborative, descriptive, supportive, qualifying, or representational relationships" (Ausubel, 1961, p. 18). Learning material is potentially meaningful if the relation of concepts to the cognitive structure can be done on a nonarbitrary basis (a property of the material) and if it can be related nonarbitrarily to the particular cognitive structure of the particular learner (a property of the learner). It should be clear from the definitions above that reception learning is most likely to be rote, and discovery learning is most likely to be meaningful, although this is not necessarily so. When discovery is involved, rote learning corresponds to trial-and-error learning and meaningful learning to insightful problem solving.

The model of cognitive organization proposed by Ausubel (1963) for meaningful learning assumes that the cognitive structure consists of a hierarchical organization of conceptual *traces,* where the term "trace" is a hypothetical construct used to account for the continuing representation of past experience in the cognitive structure. That is, there exist highly inclusive traces under which less-inclusive traces are subsumed. As new information enters the cognitive field it interacts with and is subsumed under a relevant and more-inclusive conceptual system. At first, this serves to facilitate learning and retention by anchoring the new information to related materials. At this point, it can be dissociated from the subsuming concept and recalled as an individual entity. Later, however, a stage of obliteration begins. It is easier and more economical to retain a single concept than many specific bits of information; hence, individual items of information become progressively less dissociable from the subsuming system until finally they cannot be reproduced as specific entities. That is, they are forgotten.

The alert reader will have noted the similarity of Ausubel's subsumption theory of learning to Bruner's analysis of the perceptual process. In fact, it is difficult to make a clear distinction between Bruner's view of the perceptual process and his views of the learning process, at least insofar as meaningful learning is concerned. Distinctions among types of learning are implicit in the writings of Bruner and his associates, although he seems to consider meaningful learning and problem solving as the more-significant kinds of learning. For example, he stated that effective learning results when future use of the learned material is no longer bound to the specific situation in which the learning occurred (Bruner, 1959).

Bruner, Wallach, and Galanter (1959) asserted that much of learning and problem solving can be regarded as a task of identifying recurrent regularities in the environment. This task requires a model of regularity. The learner may employ an existing model or, if none exists, construct a new one. In either case, the problem is to identify the recurrent regularities and relate them to the model. Difficulties arise when the recurrent pattern is so complex that it exceeds the individual's cognitive span or when there are sources of interference. Sources of interference may be in the stimulus situation, in the pattern of responding, or in the organism. When interferences exist, learning consists largely in separating recurrent regularities from interferences. When there are no interferences and the memory span is not exceeded, learning is merely a matter of immediate recognition.

The information-processing theory proposed by Newell, Simon, and Shaw (1958) is similar in many respects to the viewpoints outlined above. They postulated an information-processing system with a large storage capacity holding complex programs or strategies. These strategies may be evoked by stimuli which determine which one or ones of the available strategies will be evoked. The content of these strategies is largely determined by previous experience. As a consequence of these storage systems and an active response to stimuli, the system is capable of responding in a highly selective and complex manner. Learning occurs when a response of the system to successive presentations of the same stimulus produces more or less lasting change in the response of the system.

The significant aspect of the various proposals by cognitivists is that different kinds of learning are recognized. Rote learning, conditioning, and similar types of learning occur but these are regarded as relatively unimportant forms of learning, at least for complex human behavior. The kind of learning that Ausubel (1961) labeled "meaningful learning" is emphasized as the type of learning that is most useful and most likely to lead to advances in human knowledge and welfare. This sort of complex learning requires active participation on the part of the learner and involves complicated internal processes such as subsumption, identification of recurrent regularities, and evocation of strategies.

Motivation and Reinforcement

The cognitive orientation generally deemphasizes the role of motivation and reinforcement in learning and in behavior. A careful reading of their writings, however, reveals that this deemphasis is more apparent than real. At minimum, most cognitive theorists implicitly assume the existence of a need for cognition or for cognitive structure. This assumption has been made explicit by Cohen, Stotland, and Wolfe (1955), who defined need for cognition as a need to structure relevant situations in meaningful and integrated ways. The person needs to understand his world as he experiences it; he needs to make his world reasonable. (Incidentally, it is probably the assumption of such a need that underlies the cognitive consistency hypothesis discussed in Chapter 8.) In order to demonstrate this need, Cohen et al. devised two independent measures of cognitive need that yielded consistent results. The subjects indicating either high or low need for cognition were presented either an ambiguous or a structured situation. The ambiguous situation produced more frustration than the structured one, and this effect was greater for high- than for low-need persons. These findings were taken as evidence of the existence of a need for cognition.

Perhaps what is really being objected to by cognitive theorists is the concept of motivation as tension and the proposition that all reinforcement consists of tension reduction. Scheerer (1954) pointed out that although drive reduction may be satisfying under some circumstances, it is just as often the case that the organism seeks drive intensification. He proposed that capacity fulfillment may be a more important source of gratification than tension reduction. When an individual sets a goal for himself, he is in effect creating a state of tension for himself. Moreover, goal attainment is satisfying (reinforcing) because it leads not so much to tension reduction as to the cognitive enrichment resulting from goal attainment. This cognitive enrichment leads to a changed, differentiated state of the organism, which produces satisfaction.

This view of reinforcement as a consequence of capacity fulfillment is similar to Maslow's (1948) view of self-actualization as gratification deriving from the fulfillment of higher needs. According to this view, needs constitute a hierarchy ranging from the lower needs, which are related to survival and propagation of the species, to the higher-level needs, which are related to actualizing one's potentialities. The lower needs demand satisfaction before the higher needs become operative. Satisfaction of these higher needs is unrelated to tension reduction. Allport's (1947) notion of intention as an "ultimate" motive that guides behavior is also consistent with Scheerer's formulation.

The most-notable examples of the use of reinforcement by cognitive theory are found in the theories of cognitive balance. Heider (1946) proposed that the person's (p's) cognitive structure representing his sentiments toward another person (o) and o's products (x) tend toward a balanced state. If the relations are unbalanced (for example, if p likes o but dislikes x), a state of tension results, and forces to restore balance are generated. A balanced state is preferred and is more pleasant; hence, reduction of imbalance is pleasant and satisfying to the person. Other consistency theories posit a similar mechanism. Newcomb (1953) postulated a strain toward symmetry in interpersonal communication. The principle of congruity advanced by Osgood and Tannenbaum (1955) holds that judgmental frames of reference tend toward maximal simplicity. Festinger's (1957) theory of cognitive dissonance also posits a form of tension reduction. According to his theory, two cognitive elements are dissonant if the obverse of one follows from the other. Such a state of cognitive dissonance is asserted to be psychologically uncomfortable and hence will motivate the person to achieve consonance.

All these cognitive-balance or consistency theories assume, either explicitly or implicitly, that imbalance or inconsistency creates a psychological state that is psychologically unpleasant, the reduction of which relieves the unpleasant state. This proposition is in no essential way different from the behavioristic principle of tension reduction. The cognitive consistency theories are discussed in greater detail in Chapter 8.

KRECH AND CRUTCHFIELD'S COGNITIVE THEORY

The most ambitious attempt to formulate a cognitive theory of social psychology is that by Krech and Crutchfield (1948). In this attempt, they began with a presentation of the basic principles of cognitive theory, which were then applied to social behavior. Their presentation is also probably the most explicit and precise statement of cognitive theory that is available. For these reasons, it will be instructive to examine their propositions as an example *par excellence* of cognitive theory. These propositions were grouped into those dealing with the dynamics of behavior, the perceptual process, and the reorganization of perceptions. We have followed their organization.

The Dynamics of Behavior

The first set of propositions presented by Krech and Crutchfield (1948) was concerned with the basic principles of motivation. The term "motivation" was used rather broadly to include emotions as well as needs and values. This first set of propositions also included statements concerning methodological questions that were seen as being intimately related to cognitive analysis. For the most part, the propositions are self-explanatory; each one is discussed here, only briefly.

Proposition I. *The proper unit of motivational analysis is molar behavior, which involves needs and goals* (p. 30).

This proposition clearly reveals the concern for method and reflects the molar bias of cognitive theory. The authors assert that only by considering all the behavior of an individual occurring at a given time can one really under-stand the complex effects of motivational factors. Molar behavior consists not only of overt actions but also of thoughts, perceptions, needs, etc., and the relations among these units of behavior. Since the person is a unit, these elements are interrelated and cannot be arbitrarily separated.

Proposition II. *The dynamics of molar behavior result from properties of the immediate psychological field* (p. 33).

Two problems are involved in this proposition: the immediate dynamic problem and the genetic problem. The first problem deals with the needs and goals of a given person in a given situation. The genetic problem deals with the question of how these needs and goals have developed. Krech and Crutchfield emphasized that motivational analysis need not look for the causes of behavior in the past; instead, all motives can be treated as con-temporaneous. The analysis of motivational behavior then becomes an analysis of the dynamics of the psychological field.

Proposition III. *Instabilities in the psychological field produce 'tensions' whose effects on perception, cognition, and action are such as to tend to change the field in the direction of a more stable structure* (p. 40).

At any given moment the organization of the psychological field is likely to involve inconsistencies that give rise to tensions. These tensions produce conscious correlates such as vague feelings of restlessness, feelings of needs, and perceived demands of the environment. Tensions persist until resolved and evoke behaviors that may be actions toward a goal, cognitive reorganiza-tion, or a general restructuring of the field.

Proposition IV. *The frustration of goal achievement and the failure of tension reduction may lead to a variety of adaptive or maladaptive behaviors* (p. 50).

When motives are blocked so that the person cannot achieve the goal, frustration results. Frustration of motives may result from environmental fac-tors (physical or social) or personal factors (biological or psychological). The person may respond with adaptive behaviors such as intensification of effort to achieve the goal, reorganization of the perceptual field, or substitution of an accessible goal for the unattainable one. On the other hand, the person's responses to frustration may be maladaptive in the sense that they interfere with the healthy functioning of the individual. Maladaptive reactions include aggression, regression, withdrawal, rationalization, autism, and similar responses.

> Proposition V. *Characteristic modes of goal achievement and tension reduction may be learned and fixated by the individual* (p. 66).

Although Krech and Crutchfield assumed that instabilities in the psychological field give rise to tensions that evoke behaviors oriented toward tension equilibrium, they maintained that this process is not static or mechanical. Instead, it is an active process that often leads to successively higher levels of organization. Since the psychological field of an individual is highly complex, organization of the person's needs and goals is necessary to avoid chaotic behavior.

Perceptual and Cognitive Structure

Krech and Crutchfield maintained that all man's molar behavior is shaped by his private conceptions of the world. Therefore, it is necessary to describe the social world as perceived by the individual and to discover the general principles of perception and cognition. The propositions stated in this section are concerned primarily with the second problem, that is, the formulation of the laws of perception and cognition. No attempt was made to demonstrate the validity of the propositions, although Krech and Crutchfield believed that each proposition has a firm experimental foundation. Neither was an attempt made to distinguish between structural factors (physical stimuli and the neural reactions they evoke) and functional factors (needs and past experiences of the individual). Both sets of factors are encompassed in the following propositions:

> Proposition I. *The perceptual and cognitive field in its natural state is organized and meaningful* (p. 84).

This proposition is illustrated by the tendency of people to form integrated impressions of others, to jump to conclusions, and to resist changes in attitudes.

> Proposition II. *Perception is functionally selective* (p. 87).

The individual is exposed to a vast array of stimuli that might be perceived, but it is manifestly impossible to attend to all of them. Instead, only certain objects play an important role in perception—those which are functionally significant to the person. In this way, the individual is able to integrate his perceptions into the existing cognitive structure with the least threat to stability.

> Proposition III. *The perceptual and cognitive properties of a substructure are determined in large measure by the properties of the structure of which it is a part* (p. 94).

This proposition states merely that any given perception has meaning only in relation to the cognitive structure in which it is embedded. It supposedly says something about the nature of relationships between a given perception and the cognitive structure of that perception. Two reformulations were given to clarify the general proposition.

1. *When an individual is apprehended as a member of a group, each of those characteristics of the individual which correspond to the characteristics of the group is affected by his group membership, the effect being in the direction either of assimilation or of contrast* (p. 96).
2. *Other things being equal, a change introduced into the psychological field will be absorbed in such a way as to produce the smallest effect on a strong structure* (p. 98).

The first of these is exemplified by the effects the tendency to group people according to race, religious beliefs, social class, etc., has on our perceptions of individual persons. The second one points to the fact that the strongest cognitive structures are least susceptible to disruptive influences. For example, a man's strongest beliefs are least subject to change in the face of contradictory evidence.

Proposition IV. *Objects or events that are close to each other in space or time or resemble each other tend to be apprehended as part of a common structure* (p. 102).

This proposition is clearly based on the gestalt principles of similarity and proximity as determinants of perception. However, Krech and Crutchfield did not accept the gestalt view that these are purely structural variables. Instead, culture and training are significant factors in the determination of what will be seen as "similar" and, hence, in the determination of perceptual organization. Nonstructural aspects of proximity are perhaps not so evident, but Krech and Crutchfield believed that social factors also play a role here. For example, in some primitive cultures the birth of twins and a disastrous earthquake occurring at the same time could be organized into a single event caused by the devil.

Cognitive Reorganization

Cognitive structures are constantly changing in response to the individual's changing experiences. Changes may result from situational changes (learning), from changes in the person's physiological state, or from the effects of dynamic factors involved in retention (forgetting). The propositions discussed in this section deal with cognitive reorganization and include the reorganization involved in learning, thinking, problem solving, forgetting, and physiological change.

Proposition I. *As long as there is a blockage to the attainment of a goal, cognitive reorganization tends to take place; the nature of the reorganization is such as to reduce the tension induced by the frustrating situation* (p. 112).

This proposition states that the effects of frustration will continue over time until tension is reduced by cognitive reorganization. The nature of the reorganization is determined by several factors, including strength of needs, the person's characteristic mode of response, and his perception of the block to the goal. When the need is very intense or when the block to the goal is misperceived, maladaptive reorganizations tend to occur. The person's characteristic mode of response may also be nonadaptive or maladaptive.

Proposition II. The cognitive reorganization process typically consists of a hierarchically related series of organizations (p. 117).

This proposition points to the fact that each successive step of the learning process is meaningfully organized. This fact has several important implications regarding the learning experience: (1) repeated situations provide the opportunity for continued cognitive reorganization rather than producing a gradual build-up of the final structure; (2) the experiences that influence the reorganization are the perceived experiences of the individual; and (3) consciously directed education is vitally important in shaping the cognitive reorganization.

Krech and Crutchfield also asserted that although the reorganization process constitutes a series of separately organized structures, these are frequently related to each other in a uniform manner. This sequence proceeds from the more-general to the more-specific organizational structure. The main point that they emphasized, however, is that the reorganization process is unified and interdependent.

Proposition III. Cognitive structures, over time, undergo progressive changes in accordance with the principles of organization (p. 125).

The major point of this proposition is that cognitive reorganization may occur independently of needs; that is, not all cognitive reorganization is because of blocking of the goal and subsequent tension reduction. Some important changes occur during the time between the formation of the structure and the moment it functions again in the person's behavior. Essentially, this proposition asserts that forgetting may occur and usually does. However, not all forgetting is regarded as merely decay of the original structure. The principles of organization that determine the original structure operate over time to produce the same effects as they did originally.

The specific changes in cognitive structure over time were attributed to the structural and functional properties of the original cognitive organization and to the relation between the properties of the original structure and intervening perceptions.

Proposition IV. The ease and rapidity of the cognitive reorganization process is a function of the differentiation, isolation, and rigidity of the original cognitive structure (p. 135).

Krech and Crutchfield took the point of view that the problems of speed of reorganization and of individual differences in ease and rapidity of reorganization can best be handled by an analysis of the properties of the cognitive structure rather than through an analysis of the biological characteristics of the person. In general, simple and isolated structures are more easily reorganized than differentiated and interdependent structures. Krech, Crutchfield, and Ballachey (1962) used the term *multiplexity* to refer to this dimension of the cognitive structure.

The factors that determine multiplexity of cognitive structures include (1) biological capacities of the person, (2) the principles of organization, (3) the conditions producing the original structure, and (4) needs and emotions. The most important conditions in the determination of the original structure are the manner in which the stimulus situation was presented and the frequency with which it was presented. Needs and emotions have their greatest effect on the rigidity of the cognitive structure.

SUMMARY

The major viewpoints of cognitive theory should now be apparent, although the definitions and explanations may not be so clear as we would like them to be. Let us restate briefly the chief cognitive tenets:

1.   Complex behavior can be understood only by considering the so-called mentalistic concepts such as percept, idea, image, and expectancy. One must analyze these central processes in order to adequately conceptualize the more complicated and more important forms of human behavior.

2.   The proper method of analysis is the holistic, or molar, approach. It is impossible to understand unitary behavior by studying molecular elements.

3.   Not only is behavior organization molar but cognition is the most important element in this organization. Thus, perception is seen as a process of relating incoming data to existing cognitive structure and learning as a process of cognitive reorganization.

4.   Learning and other behavior may be a consequence of tension and tension reduction, but capacity fulfillment is at least equally important in the determination of behavior.

5.   Neurophysiological events may underlie psychological phenomena, but there is no necessary causal relationship between physiological and psychological events.

Perhaps all these can be subsumed under the general proposition that behavior is organized, that this organization is molar, and that the most important element in this organization is cognition.

8 ‖ COGNITIVE CONSISTENCY THEORIES

The term *cognitive consistency theories* refers to a host of proposals based upon the general proposition that inconsistent cognitions arouse an unpleasant psychological state which leads to behaviors designed to achieve consistency which is psychologically pleasant. The inconsistent relation among cognitions is referred to variously as cognitive imbalance (Heider, 1946), asymmetry (Newcomb, 1953), incongruence (Osgood & Tannenbaum, 1955), and dissonance (Festinger, 1957). Similarly, these inconsistent relations arouse either tension, strain toward symmetry, pressure toward congruity, or psychological dissonance, respectively. There are wide variations among theories concerning the identification of cognitions that are psychologically inconsistent, the nature of the psychological state resulting from inconsistent cognitions, and the kinds of behavior leading to consistency. Theories also differ in scope of application. Perhaps the most limited theory is the principle of congruity (Osgood & Tannenbaum, 1955), which is concerned only with attitude change. Without question, the most extensive theory is the theory of cognitive dissonance (Festinger, 1957), which deals with behavior in general, both social and nonsocial.

Historically, Heider (1946) appears to have been the first person to use the concept of cognitive inconsistency (imbalance) in a social psychological theory. Later theories are largely variations, modifications, and/or extensions of his formulation. The basic notion that inconsistent cognitions lead to behaviors directed toward the achievement of consistency appears as a central proposition in all theories. All these theories represent the general cognitive orientation (see Chapter 7) in that they appeal to central factors such as attitudes, expectations, knowledges, and beliefs as basic elements in the explanation of behavior.

In this chapter we have chosen to discuss four consistency theories that appear most prominently in social psychology and that reflect the major conceptualizations that have grown out of this general theoretical approach. These are Heider's (1946, 1958) p-o-x theory, Newcomb's (1953) A-B-X system, Osgood and Tannenbaum's (1955) principle of congruity, and Festinger's (1957, 1964) theory of cognitive dissonance. Festinger's theory is not, strictly speaking, a social psychological theory, but it is included here because it has been highly influential with respect to research in social psychology. Related approaches that are not reviewed in this book include those proposed by Abelson and Rosenberg (1958), Cartwright and Harary (1956), and Pepitone (1958).

THE p-o-x THEORY

The p-o-x theory was first proposed by Heider in 1946 and was later elaborated in *The Psychology of Interpersonal Relations* (Heider, 1958). As originally proposed, it was concerned with the sentiments of a person (p) toward another person (o) and an impersonal object (x) "belonging" to o. The later formulation was expanded to include more-general interpersonal relations; for example, the x element could be not only an impersonal object but also another person who is related to o in some way.

In general, the theory holds that separate entities (for example, p, o, and x) constitute a unit when they are seen as belonging together. When the unit has the same dynamic character in all respects, a balanced state exists and there is no pressure to change. When the various elements cannot coexist without stress, tension is aroused and there is pressure to change the cognitive organization to achieve a balanced state. This general proposition is simple enough, but the identification and description of the elements that result in either a balanced or an imbalanced state and the explication of methods of achieving balance become complicated processes.

Relations Among p, o, and x

Heider proposed two types of relations in the p-o-x system: unit relations and sentiment relations. *Unit relations* are of only two types: U and notU; that is, two or more elements are seen either as belonging together (U) or as not belonging together (notU). The concept of unit formation plays a critical role in Heider's theory, since the notion of a balanced state is most relevant when entities are seen as forming a unit. For example, if p likes o and dislikes x, the question of balance is of no great concern so long as o and x are seen as entirely separate entities. Heider considered the U relation as positive and the notU relation as negative, but he recognized that the notU relation is ambiguous.

According to Heider, unit formation is governed largely by the gestalt principles of perceptual organization. The major unit-forming factors are therefore similarity, proximity, common fate, good continuation, set, and past experience. It follows that two or more separate elements (entities) will be seen as belonging together if they are similar in some respect, if they are together in space and time, if they experience the same consequences, and so on. For example, two dogs walking along together are more likely to be perceived as belonging together (in unit formation) than a dog and an elephant walking in different directions. In the case of interpersonal relations, a person is often seen as being in unit formation with others of the same nationality, religion, family, and so on. Similarly, a person and his actions, his property, and his products are seen as belonging together. Prelinger (1959) has demonstrated experimentally that a person sees some things related to self and others to nonself.

The formation of a unit may also depend upon surrounding factors. Whether two things are seen as being in unit formation varies with the properties of other entities in the environment, and an existing perceptual unit may be either strengthened or weakened by the presence of other factors. For example, if two girls are playing together, they are likely to be seen as a unit; if they are joined by a boy, the unit may be strengthened (if the girls are seven-year-olds) or weakened (if the girls are eighteen-year-olds).

Sentiment relation refers to a person's evaluation of something. It includes such relations as liking, admiring, approving, rejecting, disliking, condemning, worshipping, adoring, and similar evaluative reactions. As in the case of unit relations, sentiment relations may be either positive (designated L) or negative (designated DL). It is relatively easy to classify sentiment relations: such relations as liking, approving, and admiring are positive; disliking, disapproving, and rejecting are negative.

With regard to the sign character of relations, Cartwright and Harary (1956) pointed out that it is desirable to distinguish between the opposite of a relation and the complement of a relation. For example, the DL relation has been taken as the opposite of L, whereas the notU relation has been used as the complement of the U relation. They suggested that notU is best conceived as neutral rather than negative, and their analysis supports this view, as we shall see later.

Balanced and Imbalanced States

Heider (1958) defined a balanced state as a situation in which the relations among the entities fit together harmoniously and in which there is no stress to change. His basic assumption was that unit relations and sentiment relations tend toward a balanced state. In general, dyads are balanced when the relations between the two elements are all positive or all negative. Imbalance arises when one relation is positive and the other is negative. Triads are balanced when all three relations are positive or when two of the relations are negative and one is positive. Imbalance results when one relation is negative and two are positive. When all three elements are negative, the situation is ambiguous. (It is important to remember that the situation is always considered from p's viewpoint. Balance and imbalance result from p's cognitions.)

Examples of balanced and imbalanced situations will illustrate these proposals. If p likes x and p owns x, the dyad is balanced since two positive relations are involved; if p owns x but dislikes x, the dyad is imbalanced. Similarly, in the case of triads, if p likes both o and x, and o produced x, there are two L relations and one U relation; so the triad is balanced. If p dislikes both o and x, and o produced x, the situation is also balanced, since there are two negatives (DL's) and one positive (U) relation. If p likes o but dislikes his product (x), the triad is imbalanced.

Consequences of the Tendency toward Balance

Heider proposed that there are at least three kinds of effects resulting from the tendency toward a balanced state: preference for balanced states, induction of relations, and change of imbalanced to balanced states.

PREFERENCE FOR BALANCED STATES   Heider's phenomenal analysis of balanced and imbalanced situations led to the conclusion that balanced states are preferred over imbalanced states. When the situation is imbalanced, the cognitions seem to be pulling in different directions, leaving the person with a disturbed feeling. Heider recognized that unbalanced situations may sometimes arouse pleasure, as in the case of certain puzzles, magic tricks, and the like. However, the most common reaction is a preference for balanced states. From this proposition he inferred that balanced states would also be more stable and hence better remembered. Experimental studies have generally supported these hypotheses. Jordon (1953) presented subjects verbal descriptions of balanced and unbalanced triads and found a significant preference for balanced situations. Zajonc and Burnstein (1965) reported that balanced triads were learned more rapidly than imbalanced triads when the situation involved relevant issues, but there was no significant difference when the issue was of little concern to the subjects.

INDUCTION OF RELATIONS   Given a particular relation, the tendency toward balance induces other relations that result in a balanced state. For example, p tends to dislike a person dissimilar to himself; therefore p dislikes o induces p dissimilar to o. Other examples include p in contact with o induces p likes o; p likes o induces p in contact with o; p likes o induces o familiar to p; p owns x induces p likes x; and so on. Experimental studies have generally supported the induction hypothesis. Association between similarity and liking was demonstrated by Fiedler, Warrington, and Blaisdell (1952), and antagonism between dissimilar ethnic groups is a well-known phenomenon. Homans (1950) reported that persons who interact frequently tend to like one another. Persons who have opportunity to interact frequently were found to be more likely to be friends (Festinger, Schachter, & Back, 1950). Darley and Berscheid (1967) reported that subjects increased the attractiveness of an assigned partner before personal contact with that person.

CHANGE TOWARD BALANCE   Perhaps the major consequence of the tendency toward balanced states is that imbalanced states arouse pressure to change cognitive relations. In general, balance can be achieved by a change in either sentiment relations or unit relations. Consider an unbalanced triad consisting of an L relation, a DL relation, and a U relation. A balanced state can be attained by changing the L relation to DL, the DL relation to L, or the U relation to notU. For example, Joe might see a painting that he admires very much (L relation), but later he learns that the artist (U relation) is a person he detests (DL relation). He might decide that the painting is not very good after all, or that the artist is really a likable person, or that he probably is not the real artist but is only claiming credit for something he did not do.

In addition, there is one other way that imbalance can be changed to balance: a change in unit relations through differentiation. That is, p can resolve imbalance by differentiating o into parts, some of which are positive and some of which are negative. In our example, Joe might decide that the part of the artist that is in unit formation with the liked painting is acceptable, but his other characteristics are still detestable. This relatively sophisticated method of achieving a balanced state is probably used infrequently. In fact, in a study by Esch (1950) in which subjects were asked to judge what a person would probably do in a situation like this, it was found that only about 2 percent of the subjects thought differentiation would occur, compared with 75 percent who thought a sentiment relation would change and 5 percent who believed the unit relation would be challenged; 18 percent failed to resolve the imbalance.

Strengths and Weaknesses of the p-o-x Theory

The p-o-x theory is logically consistent, simple, and generally testable. It fits known data reasonably well and is not inconsistent with other accepted theories in social psychology. According to the usual criteria, then, the theory is at least minimally acceptable.

Perhaps the strongest point of the theory is that it has provided a basis for the development of other systems and has, directly or indirectly, stimulated a tremendous body of research. Although there are some notable exceptions, the support for the theory has been generally favorable. Related to this support is the fact that it provides a wealth of testable hypotheses; however, this also represents a weakness, since the predictions are not always precise. In fact, Heider stated most of his hypotheses in the form "x tends to produce y," and he maintained that exceptions do not invalidate the hypothesis of a tendency toward balance. For example, exceptions might result from uncontrolled factors that have nothing to do with the hypothesis. There may also be factors relevant to the hypothesis that have not been considered or fully analyzed. It should be evident, however, that well-designed experiments would not permit the first possibility as an attractive alternative. The second condition is of course an admission of the limitations of the balance hypothesis, at least as formulated by Heider.

The ambiguity of the notU relation has already been referred to, but it remains one of the difficulties with the p-o-x system. It can be treated as a neutral relation as suggested by Cartwright and Harary (1956); their reanalysis of Jordan's data treating notU as neutral increased the significance of the preferences for balanced triads. Perhaps another alternative would be to limit the theory to situations involving U relations; indeed, treating the notU relation as neutral has this effect in many situations.

Heider also pointed out that the case of all negative relations is ambiguous. For example, if p dislikes o, p dislikes x, and o is not in unit formation with x, it is difficult to see why this should be unharmonious. In fact, it is difficult to see why the three relations should be considered simultaneously. On the other hand, suppose that p dislikes x, p dislikes o, but learns that o also dislikes x. In this case, some disharmony might be expected. Thus two apparently identical situations, in terms of relations, appear to produce different cognitive experiences.

Finally, it is important to note that the relations proposed by Heider are all-or-none in nature; that is, a given relation is regarded as either positive or negative with no provision for degree of positivity or negativity. Intuitively, it would be expected that the *degree* to which the relation is positive or negative would be an important determinant of balance. The principle of congruity (Osgood & Tannenbaum, 1955), which is discussed in a later section of this chapter, does take degree into account, thus providing for varying degrees of system balance-imbalance. The Cartwright and Harary (1956) extension of Heider's theory also provides a basis for degree of system balance. Both approaches demonstrate that the p-o-x theory would be improved if degree of positivity and negativity were considered.

Recent experimental studies (for example, Price, Harburg, & Newcomb, 1966; Gerard & Fleischer, 1967; Rodrigues, 1967) are generally supportive, but they point to the need to differentiate between positive and negative relations and to consider nonbalanced situations as well as balanced and unbalanced systems. A situation is said to be nonbalanced when a state of relative indifference exists.

THE A-B-X SYSTEM

The A-B-X theory had its beginnings in an early study by Newcomb and Svehla (1937), but it was not formalized until much later (Newcomb, 1953). Over the years, the theory has undergone minor modification (Newcomb, 1959, 1961), but the basic assumptions and principles have remained unchanged. For this reason, we have chosen to present the original system and refer to later discussions whenever it seems appropriate.

The theory is based upon the general hypothesis that there are lawful relations among beliefs and attitudes held by a given individual and that certain combinations of beliefs and attitudes are psychologically unstable, resulting in events leading to more stable combinations. To this extent, the theory does not differ from the p-o-x theory. However, Newcomb extended this hypothesis to include communication among individuals and relations within groups. His concept of system strain, discussed later, has much in common with field theory concepts and could be considered as representing that general orientation as readily as the cognitive orientation. We elected to present it here because of its obvious similarities to other consistency theories that are more truly representative of the cognitive approach.

Newcomb (1953) began with the initial assumption that communications perform the necessary function of enabling two persons to maintain simultaneous orientation toward one another and toward objects of communication. He then presented a rationale for this assumption and derived a set of propositions from it. Before considering the system in detail, it is necessary to define certain terms that are basic to the theory.

Basic Definitions

The key concepts in the A-B-X system are communicative act, orientation, coorientation, and system strain. A *communicative act* is a transmission of information from a source to a recipient. Information consists of stimuli that are associated with a thing, state, property, or event and that enable a person to discriminate the thing, state, property, or event from other things. These stimuli were called "discriminative stimuli (see Chapter 2 for a fuller discussion of stimulus and response concepts). According to Newcomb's analysis, the simplest communicative act is the case in which one person (A) transmits information to another person (B) about something (X). He represented this act as AtoBreX.

Orientation was used by Newcomb to refer to individuals' "cognitive and cathectic habits of relating themselves" to others and to the objects around them. This is conceptually identical to the usual definition of attitude as an organization of affective and cognitive processes about some aspect of the individual's world (for example, see Krech & Crutchfield, 1948). However, Newcomb distinguished between orientations toward persons and orientations toward things. An orientation toward another person was called *attraction* and orientation toward an object was called *attitude*.

Orientations were categorized in terms of both cathectic and cognitive aspects. The cathectic aspects refer to approach-avoidance tendencies; hence, orientations vary in sign (direction) and strength. The cognitive aspects of orientations refer to the ordering, or structuring, of attributes of the object of the orientation. Discrepancies among cognitive orientations constitute the system variables of interest.

Coorientation or simultaneous orientation was used to refer to the interdependence of A's orientation toward B and toward X. The definition of coorientation was not stated explicitly, but Newcomb apparently intended it to mean that a given person orients toward another person and an object at the same time and in the same context. For example, when A attributes to B an attitude toward X, and A himself holds an attitude toward X, A is coorienting toward B and X. In this case, an individual A-B-X system exists for A.

System strain or *strain toward symmetry* refers to a state of psychological tension resulting from perceived discrepancy of self-other orientations or from uncertainty as to the other's orientation. This concept is similar to Heider's (1958) notion of tension arising from imbalanced states and resulting in a tendency toward balance. According to Newcomb (1959), the amount of system strain varies with the degree of perceived discrepancy, the sign and degree of attraction, the importance of the object of communication, the certainty of the person's own orientation, and the relevance of the object of orientation. The notion of system strain will become more meaningful when A-B-X systems have been considered in greater detail.

Systems of Orientation

Newcomb was really concerned with two kinds of systems: individual systems that are "within the person" and group systems that involve relations among persons. In both cases, the minimal components of an A-B-X system are (1) A's attitude toward X, (2) A's attraction to B, (3) B's attitude toward X, and (4) B's attraction to A. For convenience, Newcomb identified attitudes as either favorable or unfavorable (measured in terms of both sign and intensity) and attraction as either positive or negative. Thus, A and B may have similar attitudes toward X (both favorable or both unfavorable) or different attitudes toward X (one favorable and the other unfavorable). The same is true with regard to attraction. When the attitudes and/or attractions of A and B are similar, they are symmetrical; when they are dissimilar, they are asymmetrical.

In individual systems, the relations are those perceived by one person. If person A is being considered, the relations are A's orientations toward B and X and A's perceptions of B's orientations. For example, if A has a favorable attitude toward X and is attracted to B, and A perceives that B has an unfavorable attitude toward X, the system relations are asymmetrical, and there exists strain toward symmetry.

The group system was designed to fit two-person communication with several limitations imposed:

1.   Communicative acts were treated as verbal acts in face-to-face situations.

2.   Initiation of communication was assumed to be intentional.

3.   It was assumed that the communicative act is attended to by the recipient.

4.   A and B were assumed to be group members in the sense of continued association.

Coorientation was assumed to be essential to human life because orientation of A toward B seldom occurs in an *environmental* vacuum and orientation of any person toward X seldom occurs in a *social* vacuum. That is, persons rarely are able to maintain a relation between themselves without reference to others, and few objects are so private that the person's attitude toward them is uninfluenced by the attitudes of others. Therefore, Newcomb concluded that orientation toward objects and toward other persons oriented toward these same objects is a necessary process. Furthermore, to the extent that A's orientation toward either B or X depends upon B's orientation toward X, A will be motivated to discover B's orientations toward X and/or to influence B's orientation toward X. For example, if A's friend B has an unfavorable attitude toward an X that A is favorable toward, A may try to influence B in the direction of a more favorable attitude toward X.

In general, then, there is a tendency or strain toward symmetry in A-B-X systems. At any given moment the system may be conceived as being in a state of balance, but a change in any of the four relations described above may lead to changes in any of the others. Newcomb further assumed that the system is subject to forces from without which produce strains toward certain states of equilibrium in preference to others. This assumption, of course, is not inherent in the model.

Values of Symmetry

Symmetrical relations were seen by Newcomb as having several advantages or values to the person. The first advantage is that cognitive symmetry permits an individual to calculate (or predict) the other's behavior. If A and

B have similar orientations toward X, there is less need for either of them to translate X in terms of the other's orientation and thus less chance of error. Coorientation thus becomes less difficult.

Second, there is the advantage of consensual validation of attitudes toward X. If A and B have similar attitudes toward X, each person is more confident of his own orientation toward X. Newcomb suggested that communicative acts that result in symmetry should be rewarding (because of the advantages of symmetry) and that symmetry should acquire secondary reward value. He therefore postulated that the stronger the forces toward A's coorientation with respect to B and X, the greater will be A's strain toward symmetry with B regarding X, and the greater the probability that communicative acts will lead to increased symmetry.

This postulate led to the formulation of several hypotheses. First, under conditions in which the orientation toward either B or X demands orientation toward the other, the greater the intensity of the attitude toward X and of attraction toward B, the greater the force toward coorientation. From this, it follows that the greater the intensity of the orientations toward B and X, the greater the likelihood that they will result in symmetry. In support of this hypothesis, he cited the studies of Festinger and Thibaut (1951), Back (1951), and Schachter (1951), which indicated that attempts to change others toward one's own opinion vary as a function of attraction.

A second hypothesis asserted that the likelihood of perceived symmetry increases with attraction and with intensity of attitude. This proposition was based upon the view that judgments of symmetry are influenced by autistic and reality factors, which are a function of attraction and attitude and which lead to increased perceived symmetry. Communication is the strongest reality factor, and the studies cited above reveal that this varies with attraction. Autistic factors presumably lead to distortion of perception, and these factors are stronger the greater the attraction and intensity of attitude. Thus, both reality factors and autistic factors exert pressure toward the perception of symmetry.

The third hypothesis proposed by Newcomb is based upon the second one: perceived symmetry is a determinant of symmetry-directed communication. For example, Festinger (1950) reported that tendencies to communicate to others in a group concerning X increased with opinion discrepancy, relevance of the opinion to the group, and cohesiveness of the group. Newcomb asserted that these data are consistent with the hypothesis.

Consequences of Asymmetry

As we have already noted, asymmetry leads to tension, which activates behaviors directed toward the achievement of symmetry. It is not entirely clear whether the motivation is directed toward tension reduction or toward the advantages resulting from symmetry or both. The amount of strain toward symmetry, however, was postulated to vary with a number of factors (Newcomb, 1959):

1. Degree of perceived attitude discrepancy between A and B
2. Sign and degree of attraction between A and B
3. Importance of X (the object of communication)
4. Certainty of own orientation (the degree of commitment of A and B)
5. The relevance of X to the system

These system-strain variables were categorized as accompanying either positive or negative attraction. Since this distinction is of theoretical importance, strain was labeled positive or negative strain in accordance with the sign of the attraction. For example, any time A is positively attracted to B and there is a perceived discrepancy between A's and B's attitude toward a relevant X, the system is in a state of cathectic strain, from A's viewpoint.

Newcomb identified seven ways in which an individual can reduce strain. He may (1) reduce the strength of his attraction to B, (2) reduce the relevance of X, (3) reduce the perceived relevance of X to B, (4) reduce the importance of X, (5) reduce the perceived importance of X to B, (6) change his own attitudes, or (7) change his perception of B's attitude toward X. All these can be accomplished without communication, although the process may be facilitated through communication. As we have already indicated, A may communicate to B in an attempt to change B's attitude toward X.

At the interpersonal level, Newcomb was concerned with the relationships among orientations, system strain, and communicative behavior. He proposed that several group properties are outcomes of its communicative practices. These include *homogeneity of orientation toward certain objects, homogeneity of perceived consensus,* and *attraction among members.*

Homogeneity of orientation means that group members are in agreement with regard to expectations; for example, each person is expected to assume a particular role but not necessarily that all members will act alike. The group becomes aware of these expectations through a process of communication (verbal or nonverbal), and communication varies according to the dynamics of the A-B-X system.

Homogeneity of perceived consensus refers to agreement in judgments of the homogeneity of orientation. Newcomb cited the study by Schanck (1932) as evidence that homogeneity of judgments are not coextensive with homogeneity of orientations. Schanck reported that many persons in a community disagreed with a perceived norm but that each one believed that he was the only one who did not agree with the norm. Newcomb proposed that any degree of accuracy in degree of homogeneity of perceived consensus is the result of communication.

Attraction among members is usually regarded as a necessary state if the group is to continue to exist. Newcomb suggested that interpersonal attraction varies with the degree to which the demands of coorientation are met by communicative acts.

Strengths and Weaknesses of the A-B-X System

In many ways, Newcomb's theory is identical with Heider's p-o-x theory. It also meets the minimal criteria for acceptability as a theory. Its strongest point is probably the extension of the balance principle to relations among persons. His analysis has clarified many aspects of the interpersonal situation and has provided interesting and testable hypotheses concerning interpersonal behavior. The evidence deriving from the research by others and cited by Newcomb generally supports the theory. There have been a number of studies relevant to the theory since it was first presented in 1953. Newcomb (1961) reported an extensive study of the acquaintance process based upon the A-B-X system. Two sets of seventeen male students were provided a rent-free house in return for their services as experimental subjects. In each case, the students were observed, tested, questioned, rated, and so on for several hours per week over an entire semester. The subjects had been selected as total strangers at the beginning of the semester. He found a strong tendency for those who were attracted to one another to agree on the way they perceived themselves, their ideal selves, and their attractions to other group members. Both real and perceived similarities tended to increase over time, in agreement with predictions from the theory. In a later report (Newcomb, 1963), however, he noted that estimates of others' attraction toward oneself did not become more accurate with increasing acquaintance, contrary to theoretical expectations.

Experimental studies by Burdick and Burnes (1958) also yielded results in support of the theory. In one study they found that measures of the galvanic skin response, assumed to be an index of emotional reaction, were significantly different when the subject agreed with a well-liked experimenter than when he disagreed with the same experimenter. The results of a second study showed that subjects who liked the experimenter changed their opinions in the direction of agreement with him and those who disliked the experimenter changed their opinions in the direction of disagreement.

The experimental evidence regarding the A-B-X system is not extensive, but the available evidence is generally favorable when relations are positive.

There are two major weaknesses of the theory. The first is a lack of clarity in some definitions and some postulations. The conception of strain and the process of strain reduction are not precisely formulated. As we noted earlier, it is not clear whether the motivation derives from a desire to achieve the advantages presumably deriving from symmetry or from the satisfying consequences of tension reduction. In several instances, it is also unclear what prediction would be made from the theory. For example, Newcomb suggested that although system strain leads to change, it does not necessarily do so. There is a strong need for a specification of the circumstances under which strain does and does not lead to system change.

Another problem is related to one of the theory's strengths: the application of balance theory to interpersonal situations. Osgood (1960) criticized Newcomb for sliding too easily from the individual to the group situation. In his explication of the theory, Newcomb did not clearly distinguish between individual and group systems. The reader cannot always tell whether a given principle applies to the individual system, to the group system, or to both. The problem of negative relations raises special difficulties when the elements in a triad are three persons. Price, Harburg, and Newcomb (1966) reported a failure to verify balance theory predictions concerning affective reactions to triads involving two or more negative relations. They proposed the concepts of *uncertainty, ambivalence,* and *engagement* to account for their findings. They suggested that when relations among persons are positive, assumptions of reciprocity can be made with confidence; however, when relations are negative, such assumptions cannot be made dependably. Paralleling this uncertainty is a degree of ambivalence toward disliked others (negative relation). As a consequence of these factors, there is less engagement in situations involving negative relations than in those involving positive relations. That is, in a situation involving negative relations among three persons, A, B, and X, each is unconcerned with the attitudes, beliefs, and feelings of the other two. This concept of engagement is similar to Heider's unit relation and might be considered as merely a fourth relation in the total situation. However, Price et al. considered uncertainty, ambivalence, and engagement as additional variables that must be taken into account when the joint object of A's and B's concern is another person and when the A-to-B relation is negative.

In spite of these shortcomings, the theory has called attention to some significant aspects of social behavior. The fact that it stimulated Newcomb's (1961) longitudinal study of the acquaintance process is probably sufficient to earn it an important place among social psychological theories.

THE PRINCIPLE OF CONGRUITY

The congruity theory (Osgood & Tannenbaum, 1955) is a theoretical model that was designed to account for the most significant variables in attitude change. The theory was concerned with prediction of attitude change in a typical experimental situation in which a communication from an identifiable source urges a person (the subject) to adopt a particular attitude toward some object. The variables that were deemed as most important in this situation included the existing attitude toward the attitude object,[1] the existing attitude toward the source of a message about the attitude object, and the evaluative nature of the assertion relating source and attitude object. Osgood and Tannenbaum believed that their model would permit predictions of the directions and amounts of attitude change toward both the source and the attitude object. Thus the congruity theory attempts to explain attitude change in greater detail than many attitude-change theories (see Insko, 1967), but it applies to a more limited range of behaviors than either the p-o-x theory or the A-B-X system.

Underlying Assumptions

The congruity theory grew out of research concerning the meaning of concepts. The general view emerging from this research was that the con-

---

[1] Osgood and Tannenbaum used the term "concept" in referring to the thing toward which persons hold attitudes; we have used "attitude object" because we believe this term is more descriptive than concept.

notative meaning of a concept could be defined by its location in space by a number of dimensions (Osgood, 1952). Osgood began by attempting to measure the meaning of concepts by means of the *semantic differential scales*. These consist of a set of descriptive bipolar rating scales of the following sort:

good: :   :   :   :   :   :   :bad

The concept is rated by checking one of the seven spaces. These scales were applied to several concepts and the results subjected to a factor analysis. The results revealed three factors, which Osgood called evaluative, activity, and potency. The evaluative factor represents scales such as good-bad, fair-unfair, valuable-worthless, and the like. It was found that scores on the evaluative factor correlated highly (.74 to .82) with scores on Thurstone attitude scales; therefore, Osgood assumed that the evaluative factor represented the rater's attitude toward the concept being rated. Hence, *attitude* toward an attitude object (concept) is its projection onto the evaluative dimension of semantic space. That is, attitude toward an object is an evaluation of that object.

A second underlying notion was that judgmental frames of reference tend toward maximal simplicity. This notion led to two correlated assumptions: first, it was assumed that extreme all-or-one judgments are simpler than more finely discriminated judgments of degree. If this is true, it suggests that there is continuing pressure toward polarization along the evaluative dimension; that is, there is a tendency for objects to be viewed as either all good or all bad. Second, Osgood and Tannenbaum proposed that the assumption of identity is a simpler process than maintenance of distinction; therefore, there should be a continuing pressure toward the elimination of differences among objects which are evaluated in the same direction. That is, all objects that are viewed as good in any degree should be viewed as the same or at least similar, and all those viewed as bad to some degree should be grouped together.

The set of assumptions regarding judgmental simplicity led to the conclusion that the simplest frame of reference is one that consists of two tight clusters of polarized, undifferentiated concepts that are diametrically opposed on the evaluative dimension. This frame of reference operates to push any new concept toward one or another of the two clusters. The less sophisticated the person, the more likely it is that he will adopt this simplistic judgmental frame.

The Congruity Principle

The principle of congruity, as formulated by Osgood and Tannenbaum, states that changes in evaluation always occur in the direction of increased congruence with the person's frame of reference. That is, when two or more attitude objects are linked by an assertion, there is a tendency for the evaluation of one or both of the objects to change so that the evaluations of the two objects are more similar. For example, if President Nixon (positively evaluated) praises (associative assertion) Ho Chi Minh (negatively evaluated), there is a tendency for Nixon to be evaluated more negatively and for Ho Chi Minh to be evaluated more positively.

In applying the principle to specific situations, it was necessary for the theorists to consider (1) situations in which congruity is an issue, (2) the directions of change that lead to congruence, and (3) the amount of stress created by incongruity and its distribution among attitude objects.

THE ISSUE OF CONGRUITY   Osgood and Tannenbaum asserted that the issue of congruity arises only when two or more attitude objects are related by an assertion. So long as objects are not linked by an assertion it is possible to have varying attitudes toward them without any pressure to change; that is, the issue of congruity simply does not arise. Unfortunately, they did not give a precise definition of "assertion." However, they did classify assertions according to complexity and direction. Three degrees of simplicity-complexity were identified. The simplest assertion is a *descriptive statement,* such as "modern art is interesting." This may create some pressure to change if parts of the assertion are different in evaluation; that is, if "modern art" is evaluated negatively and "interesting" is evaluated positively. *Statements of classification,* such as "John is a senator," may arouse stress similar to that produced by descriptive statements. More-complex assertions are those in which a *source makes a statement about an object,* such as "university administration denies tenure to advocate of civil rights." This is the situation that has been most widely investigated; therefore, Osgood used it to evaluate congruity predictions.

Assertions were also classified as associative (positive) or disassociative (negative). An associative assertion is a statement such as "John is intelligent," "Tom likes Mary," and the like. Statements such as "John is not intelligent" or "Tom does not like Mary" are disassociative assertions.

Assertions may reflect evaluations of (attitudes toward) an object, and in these cases the issue of congruence arises. Attitudes, according to Osgood and Tannenbaum, can be positive, negative, or neutral. When attitudes toward both the source and the attitude object are polarized, the nature of the assertion determines congruence or incongruence. The general notion propounded by Osgood and Tannenbaum is that sources that we evaluate favorably should support the things that we support, like the things that we like, and so on. Similarly, sources that we dislike should attack the things we support and dislike the things we like. For example, if a university president (positive) supports academic freedom (positive) this would be consistent with the frame of reference of most university professors and hence attitudinally congruent. On the other hand, if the university president (positive) came out in opposition to academic freedom (negative), it would be incongruent.

If the evaluations of both the source and the object are neutral, the issue of congruence between them does not arise. Any change in evaluations will be determined completely by the nature of the assertion. For example, if John praises Tom (neither of whom is known, hence neutral), the evaluation of Tom is likely to increase because the assertion was positive. That is, Tom gains in value through the simple process of "being praised." The effect of the assertion is on the recipient rather than on the source.

THE DIRECTIONS OF CHANGE   From these considerations, Osgood and Tannenbaum stated the following principle of congruity:

> Whenever one object of judgment is associated with another by an assertion, its congruent position along the evaluative dimension is always equal in degree of polarization (d) to the other object of judgment and in either the same (positive assertion) or opposite (negative assertion) evaluative direction (Osgood & Tannenbaum, 1955, p. 45).

This principle asserts that if two attitude scores toward two attitude objects AO_1 and AO_2 are assigned a value d representing degree of polarization, the congruent position can be defined as follows: When AO_1 is positively related to AO_2, the congruent position of AO_1 is equal to the polarization of AO_2. When the two attitude objects are negatively related by the assertion, the congruent position of AO_1 is equal to that of AO_2 but in the opposite direction.

Since attitude scores were derived from the semantic differential, they ranged from 1 to 7, with 4 treated as neutral.[2] For convenience, negative scores were assigned values of -1, -2, and -3 and positive scores values of $+1$, $+2$, and $+3$; the midpoint was assigned a value of zero. Thus three degrees of polarization in each direction are possible. When a source and an attitude object are linked by a positive assertion, and the polarization score of the source is $+2$, congruence requires that the polarization score of the attitude object be -2. The degree to which the polarization scores depart from the congruent position is a measure of incongruity.

AMOUNT AND DISTRIBUTION OF PRESSURE   The total amount and distribution of pressure toward congruity may be derived from principle 1, as stated in principle 2:

> The total available pressure toward congruity (P) for a given object of judgment associated with another by an assertion is equal to the difference, in attitude scale units, between its existing location and its location of maximum congruence along the evaluative dimension; the sign of this pressure is positive (+) when the location of congruence is more favorable than the existing location and negative (−) when the location of congruence is less favorable than the existing location (Osgood & Tannenbaum, 1955, p. 46).

Principle 2 thus asserts that the total pressure to change an evaluation of either the attitude object or the source is equal to the difference between its polarization and the point of maximum congruence. For example, if source and attitude object are related by a positive assertion, and the initial polariza-

___

[2] The assumption that the midpoint of a rating scale represents a neutral attitude is open to question, as we shall see later.

tion of the source is +3 and the initial polarization of the attitude object is +1, the total pressure to change the evaluation of the attitude-object is +2. That is, there is a pressure of two units to change the attitude in a more favorable direction. The pressure to change the evaluation of the source is of the same magnitude but in the opposite direction; that is, −2.

The third principle was based on the assumption that intense attitudes are more resistant to change than less-intense attitudes:

> In terms of producing attitude change, the total pressure toward congruity is distributed between the objects of judgment associated by an assertion in inverse proportion to their separate degrees of polarization (Osgood & Tannenbaum, 1955, p. 46).

Principle 3 may be stated alternately in the following formula:[3]

$$AC_{ao} = \frac{d_s}{d_{ao} + d_s} P_{ao}$$

where AC_{ao} is change in the evaluation of the attitude object (attitude change), d_s is the degree of polarization of the source with direction ignored, d_{ao} is the degree of polarization of the attitude object without regard to direction, and P_{ao} is the total pressure to change the evaluation of the attitude object. Similarly, the predicted amount of change toward the source is

$$AC_s = \frac{d_{ao}}{d_s + d_{ao}} P_s$$

The formulas above make the implicit assumption that assertions are credible. However, Osgood and Tannenbaum noted that not all assertions are believable, especially in an experimental situation. For example, a statement such as "Hitler loved Jews" is not likely to be accepted at face value. Principle 4 attempted to take the variable of credulity into account:

> The amount of incredulity produced when one object of judgment is associated with another by an assertion is a positively accelerated function of the amount of incongruity which exists and operates to decrease attitude change, completely eliminating change when maximal (Osgood & Tannenbaum, 1955, p. 47).

Incredulity is limited to situations in which incongruity arises; that is, when similarly evaluated objects are associated by a positive assertion. According to principle 4, the amount of incredulity in such situations increases with the total amount of pressure toward congruity. The predicted attitude change (AC) must therefore be corrected for incredulity. The exact

---

[3] The symbols have been changed to make them consistent with our terminology, but the formula is essentially the same as that given by Osgood and Tannenbaum.

nature of the incredulity function was regarded as an empirical question, although the following function was proposed as an approximation:

$$i = \frac{1}{40}(d_s^2 + 1)\,(d_{ao}^2 + d_{ao})$$

where i refers to incredulity and 1/40 and 1 are constants; d_s and d_{ao} refer, of course, to degree of polarization of source and attitude object, respectively. In predicting attitude change, the correction for incredulity (i) is always added to predicted negative change and subtracted from predicted positive change; that is, the effect of the correction is always a reduction in the amount of predicted change.

Still another correction was proposed for the prediction of change in attitude toward the attitude object: a correction for the direction of the assertion. It was pointed out that in the typical case, the assertion is directed toward the attitude object rather than toward the source. If A praises B, the praise applies primarily to B. Similarly, when A denounces B, the denunciation applies chiefly to B. Therefore, Osgood and Tannenbaum proposed an "assertion constant" ($\pm$ A) which must be added when predicting attitude change toward the attitude object. The sign of the constant is always the same as that of the assertion. The value of this constant was determined empirically to be approximately ⅛ of a scale unit.

Application of the Osgood and Tannenbaum formulas leads to some interesting predictions. For example, if a positive source attacks a positive object, both become more negative. On the other hand, if a negative source attacks a negative object, both become more positive. One is also led to the interesting conclusion that the highly negative person can only gain by interaction with another, whereas the highly positive person can only lose.

Corollaries of the Congruity Principle

Five corollaries were derived from the principle of congruity. These may be paraphrased as follows:

1. Changes in evaluation are always in the direction of equalization of polarization of objects associated by an assertion. Thus, the more-polarized object tends to become less polarized and the less-polarized object tends to become more polarized.

2. With a given degree of pressure toward congruity, it is easier to change toward greater polarization than toward lesser polarization. This prediction is consistent with the general notion that evaluative frames of reference tend toward maximum simplicity, but the prediction is not intuitively obvious.

3. Amount of attitude change is an inverse function of the intensity of the initial attitude toward the object. Weakly held attitudes are less resistant to change than strongly held attitudes are.

4. Attitude change toward an attitude object (or source) in the direc-

tion of an assertion is an approximately linear function of degree of favorableness of the initial attitude toward the source (or attitude object) with which it is associated. This proposition generally holds that the more "room to change," the greater will be the change resulting from a given amount of pressure.

5.   When two differently polarized, nonneutral objects are related by a congruent assertion, the more-polarized object becomes less so. As an example, Osgood and Tannenbaum suggested that when Eisenhower (+3) praised golfing (+1), he lost some prestige while producing a large increase in the positive evaluation of golfing.

Evaluation of the Congruity Principle

Like the two previous theories, the congruity principle is logically consistent and testable. It is moderately simple and is easily understood by anyone who takes the trouble to read its principles carefully. It has served a useful purpose in stimulating research and in articulating variables that have been neglected by other theories. However, it agrees with known data only moderately well. The theory appears to predict direction of attitude change, but it is less than adequate in predicting degree of change.

The congruity theory has accomplished at least one very significant advance over previous attempts to predict attitude change: it has provided a method for making precise mathematical predictions of the amount and direction of change. This exact formulation makes explicit the implications of the theory and permits direct testing of predictions. However, there are, as usual, certain criticisms that may be directed toward the theory. We have already mentioned the lack of a precise definition of "assertion" and the problem of treating the midpoint of a rating scale as reflecting a neutral attitude. Although it is clear that an assertion is a statement linking two things (usually a source and an attitude object), the treatment of types of assertions and how these affect pressure toward congruity was not spelled out in detail. The distinction between associative and disassociative assertions is especially vague.

The problem of "neutral attitude" is well known but unsolved. Theorists disagree widely about even the *existence* of a neutral attitude (see Shaw & Wright, 1967, for a discussion of this controversy). However, in connection with the congruity theory, we are more concerned with the meaning of a particular point on a rating scale. To identify any particular score as a neutral point it is necessary to show, at minimum, that persons who earn such a score do in fact perceive themselves as being neutral toward the object being evaluated. There seems to be no evidence that the midpoint on the semantic differential meets even this minimal requirement (or that it does not).

Several other problems should be considered. First, the precision achieved by considering degree of evaluation was not extended to assertions. It seems intuitively clear that the intensity of the assertion should be a factor in attitude change. Faint praise would not be expected to have as much effect as a highly laudatory commendation.

Second, the importance and relevance of the attitude for the person is ignored. It is possible that an individual may hold an intense attitude toward an object that is of little importance to him and/or is of little relevance to him. The effect of these variables is not clear, as we shall see later, but there is some evidence (Kerrick, 1958) that the congruity theory predicts better for relevant than for nonrelevant sources.

Third, the theory may be criticized for limiting the resolution of incongruity to changing evaluations of the source and attitude object (Brown, 1962). This is legitimate criticism, although in a later report that considered other consistency theories as well as the congruity model, Osgood (1960) listed six methods of achieving congruity:

1. The sign or existence of a relationship may be changed.
2. The sign or existence of a cognitive element may be changed.
3. Other cognitive elements that are in a relation of balance with the dissonant elements may be added (bolstering).
4. Other cognitive elements that are in a relation of imbalance with the dissonant elements may be added (undermining).
5. One or more of the dissonant elements may be divided so that one part is in balance with the other cognitions (differentiation).
6. Dissonant elements may be combined into a larger unit which is balanced (transcendence).

These methods, of course, do not apply exclusively to the principle of congruity. The general problem of determining when each of the various modes of resolution will be utilized also remains unsolved. This problem is discussed more fully in a later section of this chapter.

Fourth, polarity and intensity appear to be used interchangeably. Although it is true that more-extreme (highly polarized) attitudes are usually more intense, it is possible to hold an extreme attitude of low intensity, and vice versa. However, the degree of correspondence between polarity and intensity is sufficiently close that failure to distinguish between them probably introduces little error of prediction.

Finally, Insko (1967) objected to the corrections for incredulity and assertions. He correctly noted that these corrections do not follow from the principle of congruity; however, his suggestion that they were introduced to "patch up" the implications of the congruity principle does not seem warranted. There is no reason why more than one principle should not be used in formulating a theory; in fact, it appears that the congruity theory could be much improved by a consideration of still more variables that are known to affect attitude change.

Osgood and Tannenbaum (1955) cited a number of experimental studies that are consistent with their theory, including one conducted in their own laboratory. In addition, a number of studies have been conducted since the formulation of the theory with generally supportive results. For example, Jones and Kohler (1958) found that subjects with prosegregation attitudes learned plausible prosegregation statements and implausible antisegregation statements more rapidly than implausible prosegregation and plausible antisegregation statements. The opposite was found for subjects holding anti-segregation attitudes. This finding supports the notion of incredulity. However, Waly and Cook (1966) failed to replicate the Jones and Kohler results. As noted above, Kerrick (1958) presented evidence supporting the theory when the situation was relevant to the subjects. A later study (Kerrick, 1961) compared informed and uninformed subjects with respect to attitude change. Kerrick reported that attitude change was in the expected direction in all cases when subjects were uninformed (which, of course, is the situation to which congruity theory applies). Tannenbaum and Gengel (1966) produced changes in experimentally created attitudes in a manner consistent with the congruity principle. Fishbein and his associates (Triandis & Fishbein, 1963; Fishbein & Hunter, 1964; Anderson & Fishbein, 1965) applied the model to evaluations of composite stimuli with varying degrees of success. It is questionable, however, whether the theory was intended to apply to this kind of situation.

In summary, the experimental evidence for the congruity theory is generally favorable, although the obtained scores do not always agree with the predicted scores. That is, the data are in the predicted direction in most cases, but they do not always agree in magnitude. Revisions of the theory may overcome this deficiency.

A THEORY OF COGNITIVE DISSONANCE

The theory of cognitive dissonance (Festinger, 1957) follows in the tradition of Heider (1946, 1958) and other consistency theorists in that the essential principle is the tendency toward cognitive consistency or balance. However, the theory differs from other theories in two important respects: (1) it purports to deal with cognitive behavior in general and hence is not primarily a theory of social behavior and (2) its influence on social psychological research has been much more dramatic than that of any other consistency theory. It is probable that this latter effect is because of Festinger's genius in formulating intriguing hypotheses rather than to the characteristics of the theory per se.

The basic core of the theory of cognitive dissonance is deceptively simple: there may exist "nonfitting" relations among cognitive elements that give rise to cognitive dissonance; cognitive dissonance creates pressures to reduce dissonance and to avoid increases in dissonance; the results of such pressures are manifested by changes in cognition, behavior changes, and selective exposure to new information and opinions. However, problems related to the nature of the "nonfitting" relations, the nature of dissonance, and the modes of dissonance reduction are complex problems indeed. Furthermore, the various revisions and modifications that have been introduced by Festinger (1964) and others yield a confusing picture of the current status of the theory.

In this presentation, we begin with an outline of the model as originally presented in 1957, followed by a consideration of the more-significant modifications of the theory. An evaluation of the theory is attempted, although a detailed evaluation that does justice to the mass of experimental data that have accumulated is beyond the scope of this book.

Definition of Dissonance

Believing that "consistency" and "inconsistency" possess unwanted logical connotations, Festinger substituted the terms "consonance" and "dissonance," respectively. Dissonance and consonance were used to refer to relations which exist between pairs of elements. It was therefore necessary to define "elements" and "relations" before defining dissonance and consonance.

Elements were identified as cognitions; that is, the things a person knows about himself, his behavior, and his environment. The term *cognition* was used to refer to any knowledge, opinion, belief, or feeling about oneself or one's environment. Elements, then, are knowledges a person has about his psychological world. Festinger raised two questions in connection with the notion of elements of cognition: (1) When is an element of cognition a single element and when is it a group of elements? (2) How are cognitive elements formed and what determines their content? The first question was left unanswered, but Festinger asserted that this lack poses no problem of measurement. In answering the second question, he proposed that the most important determinant of cognitive elements is reality. In general, elements of cognition correspond to what actually exists in the environment and in the individual's psychological world.

Relations were classified as irrelevant, dissonant, or consonant. If two elements have nothing to do with each other, then one cognitive element implies nothing about the other. A relation of irrelevance exists between them. For example, suppose that a person "knows" that it never snows in Florida and that jet airliners can fly faster than the speed of sound. The two cognitions have nothing to do with each other; hence, an irrelevant relation exists between them. (Most persons would probably say that there is *no* relation between them.) A relation of irrelevance is similar to Heider's notU relation. On the other hand, there are cognitions that are related in such a way that one implies something about the other. The relation between them is relevant and may be either consonant or dissonant.

Dissonance was defined in the following way: Two elements are in a dissonant relation if, considering the two alone, the obverse[4] of one would follow from the other. For example, if a person is standing in the rain, it would follow that he should get wet. Therefore, cognitions of a person standing in the rain and not getting wet would be in a dissonant relation. A *consonant* relation exists when two elements are relevant and not dissonant;

---

[4] Festinger apparently used the word "obverse" in a highly specialized way. Obverse usually refers to an opposite view of the same fact. For example, the obverse of "A is B" would be "notA is notB." Clearly, this is not what Festinger meant when he used the term; instead, he used obverse to refer to the negation of a given fact. For example, according to his usage, the obverse of "A is B" would be "A is not B."

that is, when one cognition follows from the other. It is not always easy to determine whether the "obverse" of one element follows from the other, and in this respect the definitions of dissonance and consonance are ambiguous. To complicate the situation further, Festinger asserted that motivations and desired consequences may also be factors in the determination of dissonance. For example, he cited the case of a person who might continue playing and losing money in a card game despite the fact that he knows the other players are professional gamblers. His continuing to play is dissonant with his cognition about the other persons in the game, but if for some reason the person wanted to lose, the relation would be consonant.

The phrase "follows from" may take on different meanings; so Festinger suggested that dissonance could arise from several sources:

1. *Logical inconsistency.* The obverse of one cognition may follow from another on logical grounds. The belief that water freezes at 32 degrees is logically inconsistent with the belief that a chunk of ice will not melt at 100 degrees.

2. *Cultural mores.* The culture often defines what is consonant and what is dissonant. Festinger suggested that eating chicken with the fingers is dissonant with the person's knowledge of formal dinner etiquette; it is probably not true in the Deep South where etiquette does not censure this chicken-eating technique.

3. *Opinion generality.* Dissonance may arise because an opinion is included in a more-general opinion. A Democrat's preference for a Republican candidate should arouse dissonance because being a Democrat implies a preference for Democratic candidates.

4. *Past experience.* If a cognition is inconsistent with knowledge based on past experience, dissonance will arise. In the example of standing in the rain but not getting wet, dissonance is based on the fact that in past instances a person standing in the rain has always gotten wet. An inexperienced person probably would not experience dissonance.

Magnitude of Dissonance

Since not all dissonant relations are of equal magnitude, Festinger attempted to identify the determinants of the strength of dissonant relations between two elements and between two clusters of elements. His general proposition was that the magnitude of dissonance between two elements is a function of the importance of the elements to the individual. Two elements that are of little consequence are not likely to arouse much dissonance, regardless of how inconsistent they may be. On the other hand, two very important dissonant elements may be expected to arouse considerable dissonance.

The definition of dissonance involves two elements taken alone; however, it is unlikely that the individual ever considers only two elements. Instead, any given element is relevant to many others, and some of these are likely to be consonant and others dissonant. Festinger noted that it is rare for no dissonance at all to exist within a cluster of elements. It is therefore necessary to consider the total amount of dissonance between any given element and other cognitive elements relevant to it. Accordingly, he asserted that the total amount of dissonance between a given element and other cognitions will depend upon the weighted proportion of relevant elements that are dissonant with the one in question. "Weighted proportion" was meant to indicate that each relevant relation should be weighted in proportion to the importance of the elements involved in the relation. Unfortunately, he provided no way of determining relevant relations or degree of importance.

The maximum amount of dissonance possible was said to be equal to the total resistance to change of the least resistant element. When dissonance reaches this level of magnitude, the element will change and dissonance will be reduced. Of course, it is possible that changing the least-resistant element will create greater dissonance in some other system, in which case the element would not be changed.

Consequences of Dissonance

The general consequences of dissonance were indicated by two basic hypotheses: (1) Dissonance is psychologically uncomfortable and motivates the person to reduce dissonance and achieve consonance. (2) When dissonance is present, the person not only tries to reduce it, but also will actively avoid situations and information that are likely to increase it. These hypotheses thus assert that the existence of "nonfitting" relations among cognitions is a motivating factor. This motivation influences behavior in a variety of situations.

REDUCTION OF DISSONANCE   As noted above, the existence of dissonance gives rise to pressures to reduce or eliminate the dissonance. The strength of this pressure is a function of the magnitude of the dissonance. Festinger suggested three possible ways of reducing dissonance: changing a behavioral element, changing an environmental cognitive element, and adding new cognitive elements. For example, suppose that a person owns a car that his friends call a "lemon." One way of reducing or eliminating dissonance would be to sell the car (changing a behavioral element). But perhaps he cannot find a buyer, or he must take a large financial loss. In this case, it might be preferable to try to convince his friends that the car is really a fine piece of machinery (changing an environmental cognitive element). Friends, however, are not always easily convinced; so perhaps he would fail there also. He might then seek favorable opinions of others regarding the quality of the car (adding new cognitive elements). Of course, it is not proposed that an individual is more prone to use one mode of reduction rather than another nor that he systematically tries all methods of dissonance reduction. On the contrary, one weakness of the theory is that it does not provide a way of predicting which method of dissonance reduction will be chosen under a given set of circumstances.

AVOIDANCE OF DISSONANCE   Festinger stated that under some circumstances there are strong tendencies to avoid increases in dissonance or to avoid dissonance altogether. The avoidance of increases in dissonance was said to be due to the existence of dissonance, and it manifests itself when the person seeks support for changing a cognition or for adding a new cognition. Under these conditions, the seeking of new information must be done in a highly selective manner. Festinger suggested that the individual will initiate conversation with those who may be expected to support the new cognition, avoid those who may be expected to disagree, seek out supporting and avoid nonsupporting information, and so on.

When there is no dissonance, there is little motivation to seek new supporting information or to avoid negative information. However, Festinger suggested that experience may cause a person to fear dissonance, and this fear will cause him to avoid anything that might give rise of dissonance.

Implications of the Theory

According to Festinger, the theory has important implications for many specific situations. He considered implications for decisions, forced compliance, exposure to information, and social support.

DECISIONS   Festinger asserted that dissonance is an inevitable consequence of decision. This proposition is based upon the notion that an individual must be faced with a conflict situation before a decision can be made; that is, a "decision" between an alternative that is all good and one that is all bad cannot properly be called a decision. Therefore, there may be decisions between two completely negative alternatives, two alternatives having both positive and negative aspects, or among several alternatives. (Festinger did not indicate that a decision may also be between two completely positive alternatives, but it seems apparent that this decision is at least theoretically possible.) In each of these cases, the choice of one alternative results in a dissonant relation between the knowledge that a choice has been made and one or more aspects of the two alternatives. In the typical case, the dissonant elements are the negative aspects of the chosen alternative and the positive aspects of the rejected alternative.

The magnitude of postdecision dissonance, according to Festinger, is determined by the importance of the decision, the relative attractiveness of the unchosen alternative, and the degree of cognitive overlap of the alternatives involved in the decision. The more important the decision and the more attractive the unchosen alternative, the greater the dissonance. The effect of cognitive overlap is perhaps less evident. The consideration here is that many elements may be common to the two alternatives. Such common elements would not be expected to contribute to dissonance; hence, the greater the cognitive overlap, the less the dissonance created by the decision.

Pressure to reduce postdecision dissonance may be manifested by revocation of the decision, altered attractiveness of the alternatives, or the creation of cognitive overlap. Festinger cited experimental data demonstrating that following a decision (1) there is active seeking of information that produces cognitions that are consonant with the decision, (2) there is increased confidence in the decision or an increase in the discrepancy in attractiveness between the alternatives, or both, and (3) there is increased difficulty in reversing a decision once it is made; this difficulty varies with the magnitude of dissonance.

FORCED COMPLIANCE   The application of dissonance theory to forced compliance situations is limited to public compliance without accompanying change of private opinion at that time. Such public compliance is brought about either through threats of punishment or promises of reward. The source of dissonance is the person's awareness that he has behaved publicly in a manner that is inconsistent with his private opinions. The magnitude of dissonance is a function of the importance of the private opinions and the magnitude of the punishment or reward. The more important the opinions, the greater the dissonance; but the *smaller* the punishment or reward, the greater the dissonance. (Of course, the reward or punishment must be sufficient to elicit the desired compliance.) Dissonance resulting from forced compliance can be reduced by subsequent change of private opinion or by magnification of the reward or punishment. Festinger cited experimental evidence showing both these effects.

EXPOSURE TO INFORMATION   As stated earlier, dissonance results in selective exposure to information: the individual will seek consonance-producing information and avoid dissonance-producing information. Festinger hypothesized that active information seeking is curvilinearly related to the magnitude of dissonance. If there is little or no dissonance, the person will neither seek consonant nor avoid dissonant information. Moderate amounts of dissonance lead to maximum information-seeking/avoidance behavior. With near-maximum dissonance there is again a decrease in selective exposure, and the person may actually seek out dissonance-producing information. This latter is based upon the assumption that the person will try to increase the dissonance to an intolerable level that will bring about a change in some aspect of the situation and, ultimately, dissonance reduction.

In cases of involuntary exposure to dissonance-producing information, the individual may reduce dissonance by the usual methods, but he may also set up defensive processes that prevent the cognition from becoming firmly established as a part of the person's cognitive system.

Festinger cited experiments related to selective exposure, but the results were equivocal. Evidence concerning defenses against the effects of forced exposure yielded more convincing results. These indicated that such information is often misperceived or its validity is denied by the individual.

SOCIAL SUPPORT   Cognitive dissonance may be produced by a person who knows that another person holds an opinion that is contrary to his own. This aspect of the theory is closely related to Festinger's social comparison theory (Festinger, 1950, 1954; see Chapter 11). The magnitude of dissonance produced by the lack of social support is a function of (1) the extent to which objective, nonsocial cognitive elements that are consonant with the person's opinion exist, (2) the number of persons known to the individual who have the same opinion, (3) the importance of the elements, (4) the relevance of the disagreeing person or group to the opinion, (5) the attractiveness of the disagreeing person or group, and (6) the extent of the disagreement. Such dissonance may be reduced by changing one's own opinion, by influencing those who disagree to change their opinion, or by making those who disagree not comparable to oneself. The most dramatic example of attempted reduction of dissonance created by lack of social support is a case of mass proselyting following prophecy failure (Festinger, Riecken, & Schachter, 1956). A group of religious fanatics were convinced that the world would end on a given date and had taken strong action in accordance with this conviction. The reaction was one of trying much more strongly than before to convert others to the religious order. However, we might note that a later study failed to replicate these findings (Hardyck & Braden, 1962).

Modifications of Dissonance Theory

Research findings have led to several suggested changes in the theory that are primarily restrictive in nature; that is, they suggest that the theory applies only under certain conditions. The most notable modifications and limitations are those proposed by Brehm and Cohen (1962), Festinger (1964), Aronson (1968), and Bramel (1968).

Brehm and Cohen emphasized the role of *commitment* and *volition* in the arousal of dissonance. They maintained that whether one cognition is the obverse of another, or follows from another, depends upon the degree of the person's commitment. For example, when a person makes a decision but is free to change his mind, he is not committed and should experience no dissonance. On the other hand, once a person has engaged in an irreversible behavior (for example, destroying a valuable painting) or makes a decision that he must "live with," he should experience dissonance, and dissonance-reducing behavior should occur. However, volition or choice is also deemed an important variable in the arousal of dissonance. According to this view, the individual must believe that he has made the choice or acted *voluntarily;* otherwise he is unlikely to experience dissonance. Unfortunately, Brehm and Cohen did not offer a precise theoretical formulation as to how these variables operate in the arousal of dissonance. Later, Festinger (1964) accepted the commitment variable and tried to specify its role more clearly. Linder, Cooper and Jones (1967) experimentally demonstrated the importance of volition in the arousal of dissonance by insufficient reward for compliance with a request to act counter to one's own attitudes.

In his 1957 version of the theory, Festinger was concerned primarily with what happens following a decision. His position was that prior to a decision, the individual is faced with a conflict situation during which he impartially and objectively seeks and evaluates information relevant to the decision. When he has accumulated enough evidence to be confident about the correctness of a given decision, the decision is made. After the decision is made, the individual experiences dissonance and attempts to reduce it in order to achieve consonance. The only presumed consequence of the prior conflict was in its effect on the magnitude of dissonance: the greater the prior conflict, the greater the dissonance following a decision. Maximum dissonance was presumed to occur immediately following the decision, becoming less intense with the passage of time. By 1964, enough evidence had accumulated to lead Festinger to change his thinking in at least three respects. First, he came to the conclusion that predecision activity probably has some effect on postdecision behavior, although the nature of this effect could not be specified at that time. Gerard (1967) has now reported data verifying this conclusion. Second, he accepted the notion of commitment proposed by Brehm and Cohen. However, he proposed that a person is committed to a decision if the decision unequivocally affects subsequent behavior. He rejected the notion that the decision must be irrevocable in order for the person to feel committed to it. Thus, his 1964 version limited dissonance theory (at least as applied to decisions) to the situation in which the individual experiences commitment. Third, he changed his view of the course of dissonance following a decision. His modified view was that there is a period immediately following the decision in which the decision maker experiences regret. This is the period after the decision and before dissonance reduction becomes effective. Although he is not very clear on this point, it appears that he believed dissonance and regret are experienced simultaneously. In his monograph (Festinger, 1964) he cited ten experiments that provided evidence generally supporting these modifications.

Aronson (1968) suggested that dissonance theory had neglected several variables of importance. First, the theory assumes, at least implicitly, that all persons respond in the same way to dissonance and that no one has much tolerance for dissonance. Aronson argued that dissonance may be tolerated and that people differ in degree of tolerance. He suggested that individual differences need to be considered. His major point, however, was that Festinger mislocated the source of dissonance. According to Aronson, what is dissonant is the relation between cognitions and self-concept. An individual typically regards himself as a sensible person, and the knowledge that he has behaved in a nonsensible manner is inconsistent with this conception of himself. For example, if he regards himself as an honest person, the knowledge that he has lied to a fellow human being is dissonant with this view of himself as a person. Thus, expectancy plays an important role in the production of dissonance: the individual expects that he will behave in a certain way, and behavior that contradicts that expectancy arouses dissonance.

Bramel (1968) took a similar position, although he did not agree with Aronson on all points. He asserted that dissonance arises when (1) the individual encounters information which disconfirms an expectation and/or when (2) he discovers that he has chosen incompetently or immorally. He proposed that dissonance is a feeling of personal unworthiness—a type of anxiety. This feeling probably can be traced to rejection of the person by others either in the present or in the past. He also suggested that the reason dissonance is greatest when a person feels responsible for his behavior is that this corresponds to the situation under which rejection most frequently occurs. The basis for these speculations was the observation that experimental results which most strongly and consistently support dissonance theory predictions have been found in situations in which both disconfirmation of expectation and incompetent or immoral behavior occurred.

One might conclude from these suggested modifications that dissonance is limited to the situation in which the individual feels committed, he believes he is responsible for his conduct, and an expectation is disconfirmed and/or he perceives that he has behaved incompetently or immorally. If Aronson is right, the net result is that the person's cognitions are inconsistent with his self-concept and these are the nonfitting relations which arouse dissonance.

Evaluation of Dissonance Theory

Of all the consistency theories, the theory of cognitive dissonance has been by far the most popular—and the most unpopular. It has been tested, questioned, applied, modified, vilified, accepted, and rejected. The reasons for this furious reaction to a basically simple theory are not easy to identify. The supporters of the theory are obviously active researchers, and their penchant for predicting nonobvious results undoubtedly contributed to its popularity. Perhaps it has aroused so much negative reaction because it threatened many pet theories. Whatever the reasons, it has stimulated massive research, and for many this research is sufficient justification for greatness.

Dissonance theory is logically consistent, permits the formulation of testable hypotheses, and is basically simple. Some of its predictions are not consistent with widely accepted theories (for example, reinforcement theory), but it is necessary to point out that these other theories are not universally accepted. It is also not always evident just what the theory would predict in certain relevant situations. Perhaps the best evaluation of the cognitive dissonance theory is in terms of its agreement with known data. As noted earlier, a complete review of the research findings is not feasible in a work of this sort. However, a number of reviews are available for the interested reader (for, example, Chapanis & Chapanis, 1964; Freedman & Sears, 1965; Insko, 1967). We will consider only some of the major areas of research and try to indicate the trend of the results.

REVALUATION OF CHOSEN AND UNCHOSEN ALTERNATIVES   The most common type of research is one in which the individual evaluates two objects, "freely" chooses one of them, and then reevaluates the two objects. Dissonance theory predicts that the evaluation of the chosen object should increase and the unchosen decrease. In spite of difficulties in interpretation due to the usual procedures of discarding subjects who choose the lower-valued object, who are suspicious, and so on, the results are generally in accord with theoretical predictions.

FORCED COMPLIANCE   Compliance with the wishes of the experimenter can be induced either by promise or reward, threat or punishment, or other justification for the behavior. The theory predicts that the greater the justification for an overt act that is inconsistent with private opinion, the less will be the subsequent attitude change. The results of the research in this area are extremely difficult to evaluate because of the difficulty of inducing compliance without at the same time inducing opinion change, the elimination of subjects, and other problems of design. It is clear, however, that the results are inconsistent and generally inconclusive. These are the findings that led Brehm and Cohen (1962) to conclude that choice or volition is a necessary condition for arousing dissonance through forced compliance. However, it is difficult to show that a person can be forced to comply with the experimenter's wishes and still believe that he acted on his own volition. The evidence for Brehm and Cohen's contention is limited and inconclusive, leading Insko (1967) to the conclusion that the necessity for volition is still unproven.

Playing a role that is counter to one's own attitude might be considered an example of forced compliance because the subject is behaving overtly in a manner that is contrary to his own attitudes. The theory predicts that the role player will subsequently change his own opinion to bring it into agreement with the role that he has played. Although research is relatively limited in quantity, the results are much more consistent than in other areas and generally support the theory.

SELECTIVE EXPOSURE   The general prediction of dissonance theory is that the existence of dissonance will lead the individual to seek consonant information and to avoid dissonant information. Freedman and Sears (1965) conducted an extensive review of the research on selective exposure and concluded that the evidence does not support the dissonance theory prediction.

SOCIAL SUPPORT   Dissonance may be aroused through lack of social support; this dissonance can be reduced by changing one's own view, by seeking to change the views of those who do not support one, or by finding others who do support one's own position. Some research on this point, that dealing with mass proselyting after belief disconfirmation, was reviewed earlier. The two studies cited yielded different results, one supporting the dissonance prediction and one failing to support the theory. Other relevant studies have been just as inconsistent; hence the evidence regarding the effects of lack of social support is ambiguous.

This brief survey is perhaps sufficient to indicate the unsettled state of research relevant to the theory. Generally supportive evidence exists for the revaluation of alternatives following a choice, and certain kinds of justifications in forced compliance studies. The evidence concerning the effects of punishment and of choice in forced compliance studies is inconclusive, and the evidence regarding selective exposure fails to support the theory. The many failures to find unambiguous support for the theory suggests that it needs modification in several respects. The attempts by Brehm and Cohen (1962), Aronson (1968), and Bramel (1968) are indicative of the kinds of revisions that are required.

There are also several problems of definition and conceptualization associated with the theory of cognitive dissonance; however, most of these are not limited to this theory but apply to most or all consistency theories. Therefore, we reserve the discussion of these for the following section.

GENERAL PROBLEMS OF CONSISTENCY THEORIES

The difficulties inherent in consistency theories fall into three general classes: inadequate definitions, multiple modes of resolution, and oversimplification.

PROBLEMS OF DEFINITION   The major sources of ambiguity with regard to definition center around the concepts of *elements, inconsistency, relations,* and *relevance.* Although the various consistency theories differ in the terms used to refer to the concepts and the definitions given them, all are alike in assuming that there are elements (attitudes, cognitions) that are mutually relevant and that may be related in psychologically inconsistent ways. Precise definitions are often lacking and usually are reduced to operations that are only partially coextensive with the conceptual definitions. (For a discussion of the general problem of correspondence of conceptual and operational definitions, see Shaw, 1966).

The problem of definition of elements is probably most serious with respect to dissonance theory, because Festinger's definition is so broad: an element is a cognition, and a cognition is "knowledge" about the individual's world. Pepitone (1966) noted the problems that this has caused in experimentation relative to dissonance theory.

The definition of inconsistency creates fully as many problems. In Heider's p-o-x theory, a major problem arises with regard to unit formation, since only elements in unit formation are either consistent or inconsistent. But this problem is tied in with the problem of relations, since it is not clear when a given relation is to be considered in the determination of inconsistency or even when two relations are regarded as inconsistent. These latter problems are particularly obvious when negative relations are involved.

The question of relevance is no clearer. In Heider's theory, relevance is defined in terms of unit relations, but, as we have seen, the basis for unit formation is less than equivocal. In other theories, there is no clear specification of relevance; there is no way of determining when two cognitive elements are mutually relevant.

MULTIPLE MODES OF RESOLUTION   All the consistency theories assume that inconsistency can be resolved by a variety of methods, but none specifies the conditions under which a given method will or will not be employed. Festinger (1957) hinted that the change will occur in the weakest element or relation when he asserted that the maximum possible dissonance is equal to the total resistance to change of the least resistant element; however, he did not elaborate this point. In practice, experimenters have implicitly assumed that inconsistency will be reduced by whatever means is available to the individual. Hence, they have attempted to block all modes of resolution but the one of interest. Change in elements related to this one mode is then measured. This procedure is reminiscent of the attempt to isolate the sense modality employed by white rats in learning to negotiate a maze (Moss, 1946). It will be recalled that one sense modality after another was eliminated, but the animal always successfully negotiated the maze.

What is called for here is a specification of all the ways in which inconsistency can be reduced in a given situation and behavior relevant to all these methods examined. It should then be possible to determine whether the individual attempts to resolve inconsistency by *any* method. It is possible that some individuals can tolerate inconsistency and make no attempt toward resolution, a view recently espoused by Aronson (1968). Evidence of individual differences in dissonance reduction has been reported by Harvey and Ware (1967). Such a procedure would also permit specification of the conditions under which given modes of resolution will be adopted. Some progress has been made in this direction in the studies by Harvey and Ware (1967) and by Walster, Berscheid, and Barclay (1967).

OVERSIMPLIFICATION   By oversimplification is meant the failure to consider relevant variables in the situation to which the theory is supposed to apply. It is overly optimistic to expect a theory to handle all aspects of a complex phenomenon, but some of the more-obvious ones should be considered. For example, only the congruity principle considered the degree of positivity-negativity of a given relation, and even that theory neglected to consider the strength of an assertion. The confidence that a person has in his attitudes, beliefs, and so on is surely an important variable in dissonance aroused, as demonstrated by Walster (1965). The neglect of the variables of commitment, volition, and self-esteem is evident in most consistency theories, as noted by Brehm and Cohen (1962), Aronson (1968), and Bramel (1968). Pepitone (1966) noted that the consistency theories had failed to relate to theories of general psychology and that findings relevant to dissonance may be explained by other formulations. Although true, it does not appear that these are valid criticisms of inconsistency theories per se.

In general, consistency theories have contributed much to our understanding of social behavior. The theories are especially relevant to problems of attitude formation and change, interpersonal attraction, person perception, mass action, communication in groups, and similar types of social behavior. The problems cited above point to the fact that consistency theories need to be stated much more precisely than they have been to date. It is also clear that further modifications are very much in order if such theories are to continue to play a vital role in social psychology.

THE PSYCHOANALYTIC ORIENTATION
PART 5

9 | THE PSYCHOANALYTIC ORIENTATION

A comprehensive review and analysis of psychoanalytic conceptualizations are well beyond the scope and purpose of the text. Instead, the goal in this chapter is to provide the reader with a fundamental view of the general structure of the analytic orientation. The discussion is restricted to concepts, constructs, and principles within the orientation that have some relevance to theories within the discipline of social psychology. The problems involved in organizing Freud's prolific writings into a unitary system are almost unsolvable. Freud's formulations changed constantly so that his views must be dated to be completely understood. In this chapter we have attempted to distill the basic aspects of the psychoanalytic orientation and have avoided extensive discussion of minor variations and controversial issues. In addition to the primary sources relative to Freud's group psychology (for example, *Group Psychology and the Analysis of the Ego; Civilization and Its Discontents*), we have relied heavily on selected secondary sources as an expository base for articulating the general system and basic constructs. The predominant seconday sources that are used in this chapter include Rapaport's (1959) presentation in Koch's compendium, *Psychology: A Study of a Science;* Hall and Lindzey's (1957) presentation of Freud's theory of personality; and Blum's (1964) book on psychoanalytic theories of personality.

Rapaport's work was perhaps the most ambitious endeavor. His predominant goal was to impose a systematic structure upon the divergent writings of Freud. His final product is indeed an ingenious synthesis of Freud's orientation or, more appropriately, Freud's orientations. Rapaport accurately noted that there are several models that emerge from Freud's writings, and many misinterpretations of his propositions occur because it is often difficult to specify which model is operative in any given presentation. Other misinterpretations occur because Freud proclaimed psychoanalysis to be several things at once: (1) a system of conducting inquiry into human functioning, (2) a system of psychotherapy, and (3) a theory of human behavior. Again, it is often difficult to specify which of these functions is being elucidated by a particular construct or model. We hope that the treatment in this chapter is not simply one more misinterpretation, although it is clear that the following discussion is incomplete and considers only the major aspects of the orientation.

The aspects of the psychoanalytic orientation reviewed in this chapter include the following: Freud's conception of intrapersonal variables and the psychic apparatus, his concept of stage development, the conception and articulation of ego defenses, Freud's group psychology, and the several models of psychoanalysis and the assumptions of psychoanalysis based upon these models. A final section considers some of the criticisms and misinterpretations of the psychoanalytic orientation.

In Chapter 10, several theories in social psychology are presented that have, at least in part, been derived from the analytic framework. These include Sarnoff's (1960) theory of attitude formation and change, Bennis and Shepard's (1956) theory of group development, Schutz's (1959) theory of interpersonal relations, and Bion's (1950) theory of group process.

INTRAPERSONAL VARIABLES AND THE PSYCHIC APPARATUS

The psychic apparatus as conceived by Freud may be said to consist of three categories: a vital energy of life force (called *libido*), the mental life of the individual, and the personality of the individual.

Libido

One of the most fundamental concepts of psychoanalysis is that every person possesses a store of vital energy (libido). The libido is considered to be entirely mental in nature and should not be confused with physical energy that derives from biological needs such as hunger and thirst. Freud asserted that the libido has one source and one nature: it is sexual. His usage of the term "sexual" differs greatly from the common meaning of the term, however, and it was the misunderstanding of this term that created much of the negative reaction to his propositions.

The construct of psychic energy was postulated to account for the dynamic properties of human functioning. In Freud's system, the sources of psychic energy may be identified as instinctual impulses. He proposed that all instincts are reducible to two general classes: the life instincts or the self-preservative instincts (that is, the sources of libido) and the death instincts, or the self-destructive instincts. (He had no special label for the energy generated by the latter class of instincts.) Libidinal energy, then, results from the biological tensions which are predominantly sexual in nature. Hall and Lindzey (1957) noted that Freud considered the ubiquitous sexual instinct to be many instincts. The many instincts that were said by Freud to reflect sexual tension were linked to bodily zones which he referred to as erogenous zones. When stimulated, these zones produce pleasurable feelings in the individual; hence the label "sexual." The zones which Freud viewed as most salient in the fulfillment of sexual instincts are the mouth, anus, and genital region. However, as Freud's system developed, sex gradually became represented as the basis of most tensions and most pleasurable sensations, regardless of the involvement of bodily zones.

The strength and nature of the libido and the channels which it follows are important factors in the determination of man's mental life and his personality. This is one of the reasons why childhood events were regarded as so critical in the psychic life and personality structure of the adult.

Structure of the Mind

According to Freud, the mental life (mind) of the individual is divided into three parts: the conscious, the preconscious, and the unconscious. The *conscious* is that state of man consisting of behavioral determiners within his awareness; it is that mental content of which the individual is aware at any given moment. The conscious functions on the basis of a set of laws which Freud referred to as *secondary process*. Secondary process is that level of functioning that is characteristic of man's customary mode of logical thought, and it is reality-oriented. The content of the conscious is constantly changing. Some of it comes from the external world, but much of it comes from the lower levels of the mind; that is, the preconscious and the unconscious.

The *preconscious* is that part of the mind that is readily available to the conscious. The contents of the preconscious can be easily brought into the conscious realm through the association of ideas. Freud posited no particular process for this aspect of the mind, and it played a relatively minor role in his system.

The *unconscious* is the most extensive region of the mind and plays the most significant role in Freud's system. It consists of a multitude of mental processes that are unknown to the individual but that nevertheless influence his behavior. In the unconscious, antagonistic impulses can exist without conflict. It is characterized by emotion, desire, and instinct; reality has no place in the unconscious. The unconscious functions on the basis of *primary process*. In contrast to secondary process, primary process consists of non-logical, symbolic, and fantasy-laden components of "thought." The symbolism of dreams is a prime example of primary process thought.

Freud considered the unconscious and its primary process mode of ideation as the most significant aspect of mental functioning. As a consequence, he proposed that the understanding of overt human behavior is predicated upon valid inferences about the contents of the unconscious. Blum (1964) noted that Freud inferred the existence of the unconscious on the basis of several factors. Some of the more-prominent ones are the following:

1. The evidence from demonstrations of posthypnotic suggestion
2. The discovery of the latent meaning of dreams
3. Memory slips, speech slips, and the like
4. The "fact" that the psychoanalytic technique has revealed that behavioral symptoms are not explainable by the conscious components of the subjects' thinking
5. The assumption of the existence of the unconscious has led to an adequate practical method for altering the course of conscious processes

Blum (1964) also articulated five attributes of the unconscious:

1.   Wishes based upon instinctual impulses reside in the unconscious. These wishes exist independently and may be incompatible or contradictory since the unconscious is not backed by rules of logic.

2.   The processes within the unconscious are insensitive to and unaltered by the passage of time. Time is a dimension of the conscious.

3.   The contents of the unconscious are absolute. There is no doubt, no negation, and no uncertainty in the unconscious system. Thus, the unconscious is uncensored from within.

4.   The unconscious bears little relation to external reality and operates on the basis of the *pleasure principle* to seek pleasure and avoid pain. Thus, the unconscious is amoral and insensitive to situational constraints from the environment.

5.   The energy which emanates from unconscious ideas is highly pliable. Blum pointed out that since the unconscious is unfettered by rules of logic, time or reality, the energy generated by unconscious ideas may be discharged in a number of undifferentiated ways. The conscious on the other hand generates energy that can be discharged only upon specific and differentiated objects, and energy discharge must obey the very rules that do not bind the unconscious.

Structure of the Personality

The personality of the individual is closely related to the mental processes and the libido. Libidinal energy "circulates" in a closed intrapersonal network and is distributed among the three major structural systems in Freud's theory of personality. These three systems were called the id, the ego, and the superego.

The id was conceptualized as the reservoir of all psychic energy. The id system is wholly unconscious and functions on the basis of primary process thought. At birth, the id system constitutes the totality of man's psychological energy system. Instinctual impulses based upon biological needs are the sole moving principle of the neonate's psychological make-up, and hence, these impulses are the contents of the id system. Since the id is an unconscious system, all the characteristics applying to the unconscious also apply to the id. Therefore, it is amoral, unaltered by the passage of time, not oriented to reality, uncensored from within, and operates on the basis of the pleasure principle to strive for the reduction of tension generated by instinctual impulses. Freud (1923, 1938) described the id as a "seething cauldron" of instincts that constitutes the hidden essence of man's being. It is wholly inaccessible to the observer except through the use of intuitive inference based upon the reality-oriented behavior of the observed. Thus, for example, if an individual is eating, one might assume that he is operating on the basis of hunger needs and self-preservative instincts within the id system. However, if that individual engulfs large amounts of food every hour on the hour, one might assume that eating is a compensatory activity reducing the tension from some other instinctual impulse or impulses within the id (for example, dependency needs, self-destructive needs, etc.). Thus, the behavioral expression does not always define the underlying tension state of the id. Many behaviors may more or less reduce the tension from a single id impulse. The id does not differentiate between the reality objects used to reduce tension because it does not converse with reality.

Since the id does not converse with reality, and since most objects necessary for the satisfaction of instinctual impulses are located in the real world, then some mechanism that does converse with reality must evolve from the id in order for the individual to gratify his needs. For this reason, Freud posited that a mechanism, which he referred to as the *ego*, evolves from the all-encompassing amorphous id very early in the infant's development. Blum (1964) notes that the beginnings of ego functioning occur when the infant is confronted with the realization that the outside world is an indispensable agent of his tension reduction. Therefore, the ego develops as a functional consequence of the individual's primary desire for pleasure through the reduction of tension.

The ego derives its energy from the id, and in the course of development it functionally differentiates itself from the id. In general, its primary function is to interpret the reality surrounding the person and, when the time is appropriate, to exploit that reality in the most efficacious way to reduce the tensions of the id. Thus, ego functioning is said to be based upon the *reality principle*. It functions in reference to the external world and is therefore constrained by considerations such as time and place. The reality principle temporarily supplants the pleasure principle in human functioning (Hall & Lindzey, 1957). That is the ego might deter the tension-reduction goals of the id until the reality situation deems tension reduction as appropriate and tenable.

The ego, as well as operating on the basis of the reality principle, also operates on the basis of secondary process thought. Thus, the ego utilizes logical inference and organization to interpret the contextual reality surrounding the individual. The processes of perception and cognition are integral features of secondary process thought. The ego is responsible for the perception of objects in the real world, particularly those which facilitate tension reduction. Furthermore, it is responsible for the conceptual organization and interpretation of objects and events in the surrounding environment. To this end, the ego engages in *reality testing*. Reality testing is the process whereby the ego gains information about the relevance of particular actions toward particular objects. This dimension of relevance is defined by the success of the tested actions in providing a judicious and workable means of reducing the tensions of the id.

From these considerations it is obvious that the ego is at one time the servant and the ruler of the id. That is, it serves the id's pleasure-directed strivings but dictates the circumstances under which these strivings might in reality be achieved. Hall and Lindzey (1957) noted that although the ego is the "executive" of the personality, it nevertheless derives its energy and its very existence from the id. According to Freud, the reason for its coming into being is to promote the aims of the id, and, as such, it never becomes completely independent of the id. However, some revisionist proposals of the ego psychologists have assigned independent status to the ego as the integrative mechanism of personality (Kris, 1950; Hartman, 1958).

As well as coordinating the demands of the id with the conditions available in the external environment, the ego must also cope with the requirements of the third structure in Freud's personality theory, the *superego*. Hall and Lindzey (1957) referred to the superego as the "moral arm" of personality. It consists of cultural norms, societal values, and strictures that have been internalized (introjected) by the individual. Although its energy, like all psychic energy, is derived from the id, it is a differentiated part of the ego (Rose & Abrams, 1965). The superego is a predominantly unconscious system; like the id, it is basically unresponsive to reality factors such as time and place. The unconscious nature of this system is purported to result from the conditions of its formation. That is, the superego is formed through rule internalizations that occur beyond the level of awareness of the internalizer.

The superego develops in response to the rules of appropriate behavior held by the society. These rules are communicated to the child by the parents through subtly operating mechanisms of reward and punishment. These "dos and don'ts" of behavior are, in time, incorporated into the child's own repertoire through the process of introjection. Freud (1948) noted that the superego is the heir of the Oedipus conflict. That is, with the resolution of the Oedipus conflict the child's behavior is no longer predominantly guided by factors, such as castration fear and loss of love, which have an external origin, but rather his controls begin to emanate from within. Instead of being inhibited in his behavior by fear of reprisal from others, he is inhibited by self-criticism and guilt. Thus, the superego is the mechanism whereby the individual makes moral demands upon *himself* and sets his own limitations for appropriate behavior. As noted, these self-imposed limitations evolve from the introjection of parental and societal norms which previously were enforced by external control. Thus, the formation of a healthy superego is the primary goal of socialization as that process is defined by Freud. The socialized person is one who has accepted the rules of society as his own rules for appropriate behavior. The storehouse of these incorporations of moral standards is the superego system.

The superego is usually characterized by Freud and others as the harsh and unequivocal censor of impulse-directed behavior. Although the id strives for pleasure, the superego strives for perfection. In the many areas on which id strivings conflict with the goals of "moral" perfection, the superego and id are opposing forces. Both let their demands and wishes be known to the ego. A major task of the ego is to integrate the demands of both the id and the superego and arrive at a behavioral strategy that satisfies both. As well as responding to the divergent demands of the id and superego, the ego, because it is reality-oriented, must also conform to the external environmental content with which the person is confronted. Understandably, then, the ego executive is under considerable strain. Thus, in order to perform its many functions adequately, it must command sufficient portion of the energy available in the intrapersonal system. The distribution of psychic energy is an all-important factor in the level of functioning of the personality system. An overbalance of energy in the superego system results in an inhibited person whose needs are suppressed and secondary to his moral ideals. An over-balance of energy in the id system results in the impulse-laden person who seems unrestricted by self-imposed moral standards and societal standards.

Under most normal conditions, the personality is not a complex of war-ring factions but functions as a totality which executes its expression through the ego's contact with the environment. Freud's trisystem structural and dynamic theory of personality is a metaphorical one and should not be inter-preted literally. What he has basically proposed is that the subsystems within the personality system form in order to fulfill those functions that are indis-pensable to the optimally functioning personality. In this context, the id is viewed as the biological basis of personality, the ego as the psychological basis of personality, and the superego as the social basis of personality (Hall & Lindzey, 1957). The concepts of id-superego opposition and ego-executive functioning are convenient models that were used by Freud to account for the final behavioral product of personality and the underlying motivational and unconscious determinants that result in that product.

EGO DEFENSE

As we have noted, the ego, as the executive arm of personality, is often in a state of strain. As such, for its own preservation it must take steps to reduce the strain and at the same time accommodate the id's pleasure seeking and the superego's moral sanctions. To accomplish these goals the ego has at its disposal several subterfuges and deceptive maneuvers that "disguise" reality and the objects within it so as to simultaneously reduce the tension of the id and conform to the moral tenets of the superego. In this process, the ego not only deceives the id and superego concerning the conditions of reality or the nature of the individual's interaction with that reality but also deceives itself. Freud referred to these maneuvers of the ego as *defenses* because their goal is to defend the individual and his ego system from intolerable tension and anxiety. Hall and Lindzey (1957) articulated two characteristics of all ego defenses: (1) they all deny or distort reality and (2) they operate on an unconscious level.

Ego defenses can distort both internal and external reality. Thus, for example, the ego may defend itself by not acknowledging the existence of a particular need or instinct, or it may defend itself by not acknowledging the existence of an external object. Defensive maneuvers take on many forms ranging in their subtlety. Sigmund Freud articulated some of the forms that ego defense takes, and Anna Freud (1946) expanded upon the conceptual definitions of several ego defenses. In the following paragraphs, we define several kinds of ego defenses.

Repression

In the development of Freud's concept of personality, repression was initially ascribed independent status as *the* defense available to the ego (Freud, 1894). In this early presentation, repression was considered to be synonymous to defense (Blum, 1964). Although Freud's views concerning the defensive properties of the ego expanded with time, and although he postulated several other specific defenses, repression was always considered by him as the basic defense and one that operates in the functioning of all other defensive processes.

Repression involves the expulsion of disturbing and painful ideas from the individual's conscious perception. Those ideational components that are repressed become part of the unconscious system and remain beyond the awareness of the individual. The ego represses ideas, wishes, actual external events, memories, and the like if the recognition of these leads to a disruptive increase in energy-produced tension in the personality system. Thus, from a Freudian viewpoint, a child may repress his sexual desires toward his mother, his hostile impulses toward his father, his fear of castration by his father, and so forth. Once repressed, the ideational components may remain tightly entrenched in the unconscious system, or the energy that these components generate may be channeled toward different objects or activities. Therefore, repression may lead to the utilization of other defenses, to the displacement of the unacceptable idea or impulse onto an object that is not as threatening as the original one, and/or to behavioral symptoms. These three possible products of repression do not necessarily occur independently of one another, but any two or all three might be represented in a single behavior or idea.

Displacement is prone to occur in the situation in which an idea or wish is repressed, but the energy generated by that idea or wish continues to "circulate" in the personality system and seek discharge. Thus, the child's "idea" of expressing hostility toward his father may find expression in the hostility he shows toward his older brother. This allows for at least the partial discharge of hostile energy without the concomitant severe consequences that might occur upon the expression of the original impulsive idea.

Even though the initial basis for repression is generally the threat generated by an unacceptable wish or "idea," it does not follow that when the threat is removed, the repression is lifted. Hall and Lindzey (1957) noted that once repressions are formed, they are very difficult to abolish. They reasoned that for repressions to be lifted, the individual must test reality and determine that the initial threat no longer exists. However, to test reality, the repression must first be abolished and thus removed from the non-reality-oriented unconscious. Thus, a vicious circle is created and nearly precludes the abolition of repressions. For this reason, Freud maintained that adults carry with them many childish fears. One of the prime goals of Freud's therapeutic technique is to provide a means for the individual to expose childhood repressions and to test the reality of the threats upon which they are based.

Projection

Projection involves the attribution of one's own unacceptable wishes, impulses, or ideas to an external object, usually another person. In using this defense, the ego protects itself from intolerable anxiety by admitting that certain unacceptable impulses exist, but disowning these impulses. Hall and Lindzey (1957) pointed out that projection serves a dual defensive purpose: (1) it reduces anxiety by substituting a lesser danger for a greater one and (2) it allows for the expression of unacceptable impulses under the guise of protecting the person against his enemies.

A simple example of these dual defensive purposes of projection can be drawn from a possible father-son relationship. If the son during the period of Oedipal conflict builds up a unconscious hate against father that defies expression because of its unacceptability to the sanctioning superego, he may *project* this hate onto the father and thus consciously accept the proposition, "Father hates me." Although this proposition is threatening to the son, according to Freud, it is not as threatening as the self-realization of his own hate for the father, which implies the retaliation of father as well as the loss of his love. Furthermore, once the son projects this feeling of hate on to his father, his acts of hostility toward father are construed by him as protective measures rather than offensive behaviors.

There are innumerable examples of projection that might be cited here. They may range from everyday instances of projection, such as seeing a fear that one unconsciously experiences as being experienced by others, to the extreme of paranoid projection that involves the attribution of persecutory motives to others in order to disguise one's own feelings of self-hate. However, such detailed examples are beyond the scope of this text.

Reaction Formation

The ego may defend itself against the acknowledgement of an unacceptable feeling or impulse by repressing it and then acknowledging its opposite. Thus, hate is converted into love, depression to ebullience, the desire to soil to excessive cleanliness, and so forth. With this defense mechanism, the original inacceptable impulse is disguised and the energy that it generates is invested in an impulse that is its opposite. The premise here is that the diametric opposition between the original and expressed impulse disguises the original one to such an extent that it precludes its recognition on a conscious level. Hall and Lindzey (1957) implied that for the individual to accept his expressed reactive impulse, he generally overexpresses it. Thus, an unconscious hate impulse might be expressed in the form of extreme displays of affection. This overreaction embodies the individual's unconscious attempt to completely camouflage the unacceptable impulse.

Denial

When an external object or person connotes an extreme threat to the individual's psychic economy, the ego might defend itself by denying the presence of this object. This particular defense is probably the most primitive and penetrable defense of the ego because it is highly subject to consensual invalidation by others. Blum (1964) pointed out that denial and reality are incompatible; hence, with the development of the person's perceptual capacities, denial becomes increasingly difficult to maintain. Denial involves the perceptual distortion of reality, and in its extreme form it is most characteristic of young children and psychotics. Although all defenses can be lifted by reality testing by the ego, denial and projection are most vulnerable to reality-testing processes. In otherwise quite "normal" individuals, denial may occur under conditions of extreme environmental threat. Sarnoff (1960) offered the example of some German Jews' denial of impending doom under the Nazi regime.

Sublimation

Freud characterized sublimation as one of the most salient bases for the advancement of civilization. It involves the ego's desexualization of instinctual energies from the id. This libidinal drive energy is then channeled to socially acceptable and often socially and individually beneficial drives and activities. Freud viewed sublimation as the harbinger of artistic creativity, skilled technical activity, vocational excellence, and so forth. Hence, sublimation is a culturally and individually adaptive defense. In its use, the ego protects itself from the expression and recognition of unacceptable impulses through the engagement in acceptable alternative activities. For example, a psychoanalytic formulation might maintain that a surgeon is engaging in the sublimation of underlying aggressive impulses. Thus, a by-product of the ego-defensive maneuver of sublimation is the progress of civilization. It constitutes the one defensive posture that Freud viewed as having generally positive societal and individual outcomes.

The five defenses above should provide the reader with an adequate sampling of the defenses enumerated by Sigmund Freud and expanded upon by Anna Freud (1946). In addition to these, we have also discussed the process of introjection, which is defensive in nature, and will discuss the processes of fixation and regression in the next section. Furthermore, the additional defense of identification with the aggressor is dealt with in the context of the presentation of Sarnoff's theory in Chapter 10.

Freud's conceptualization of ego defense has found substantial application in several areas of social psychology. Two of the more-notable instances of application have been Sarnoff's (1960) and Katz and Stotland's (1959) attitude change theories, and experimental research on the motivational and social bases of perception. The latter area of application is most apparent in studies of perceptual defense (Bruner & Postman, 1947; McGinnies, 1949; Eriksen, 1951).

PSYCHOSEXUAL DEVELOPMENT

Freud believed that personality develops through an orderly sequence of sexually and dynamically based stages. The stages of development that he proposed are differentiated from one another on the basis of the predominance of particular bodily regions. As the child progresses from one of these stages to another, the bodily focus of his pleasure-directed strivings changes. Along with the change in zonal focus, there occur changes and developments in the structure of the id, ego, and superego, as well as changes in the dynamic properties of human psychological functioning. Although Freud's theory implicitly or explicitly considered psychological development from the "womb to the tomb," it was his firm conviction that the first five years of life are the most significant ones in the formation of personality.

An excellent exposition of Freud's theory and other analytic theories of development has been made by Blum (1964). In addition Erikson (1963) has articulated a Freudian-based theory of psychosexual development that is enlightening with regard to many psychoanalytic propositions. We commend these works to the reader who has more than just a passing interest in Freud's developmental theory. Our goals in this section are not nearly as extensive as those of Blum and Erikson. Instead, we shall attempt to provide the reader with a skeletal scheme of Freud's stages of development, including only the most significant aspects of these stages.

Before we begin our discussion of specific developmental stages, it should once again be noted that from an analytic viewpoint the source of change in the personality system is the distribution of psychic or libidinal energy. As such, the change from one developmental "zonal" focus to another in the course of the individual's development is based upon the efficacy of a given bodily region in producing tension and providing the organ for the reduction of sexually based tension states. In the following paragraphs, we discuss five stages of development. From Freud's point of view the three most important stages are the first three "pregenital" phases, the *oral*, the *anal*, and the *phallic*. The second two stages, although instrumental in the development of adult personality and "sexuality," are not regarded as important as the first three. They are the *latency* stage and the *genital* stage.

The Oral Stage

This stage encompasses approximately the first year or eighteen months of life. The newborn infant is predominantly a biological organism. Hence, his major experiences are sensations of pleasure or pain and changes in tension (Blum, 1964). He is id-controlled, and neither the ego nor the superego has taken its place in the personality structure.

The primary region of pleasurable sensations within this developmental era is the mouth. The infant's major source of pleasure in the first four to eight months of life is the incorporation of food and the sucking of objects.

Thus, during this period the source of libidinal energy is centered around the mouth, lips, and tongue, as well as around the skin senses. During this stage the infant is in a state of utter dependency, so dependent in fact that he does not make fine distinctions between himself and external reality. According to Blum (1964), self-other distinctions begin to be made by the infant only when he is confronted with the nonfulfillment of his oral needs. Thus, deprivation is a necessary precondition in the development of ego functions. The realization that self and environment are not one develops from the infant's realization that his every demand is not met by the capricious external world. These initial realizations of self-environment distinctions, then, result in the formation of the "archaic" ego.

With the passing of the substage of complete oral incorporation the infant moves toward a substage of "aggressive incorporation" or oral sadism. In this second portion of the oral stage the infant begins engaging in oral activities such as biting and chewing. In both portions of the oral stage, however, the infant is primarily moved by pleasure-directed strivings for which the mouth serves as the primary zone.

Orthodox analytic formulations consider the acts of sucking and biting as the beginning expression of the sexual instinct (Blum, 1964). The act of sucking, since it often occurs without food objects, is seen as resulting in some satisfactions that are not based on hunger. Freud chose to refer to these non-hunger-related needs of oral activity as sexual, and he related them historically to later genital sexuality.

The first object with which the infant forms relationships is the mother or mothering figure. Since the newborn infant is not capable of making self-other distinctions, his early relationship to the mothering figure is one of "symbiosis." Through the gradual development of the perceptual processes of the ego, the oral infant begins to have impressions of mother as an independent object. His first impressions are guided by considerations of trust and mistrust of this object. The oral period is considered by Freud to be the basic era for the establishment of feelings of trust toward others and, as such, has lasting effects on subsequent social behavior. Insofar as mother can be "trusted" to fulfill the infant's oral needs, she is loved and the infant seeks oral union with her (for example, mouth-breast contact) (Blum, 1964). In the oral-sadistic phase of this era, the infant begins to develop attitudes of hostility. The development of these attitudes, coupled with the love and "trust" of the incorporative period, lead to the development of relationships of ambivalence (to suck or to bite; that is the question). The emotions of love and hate are later derivatives of this ambivalence (Blum, 1964).

Blum (1964) notes that orthodox analytic formulations posit six basic mechanisms of the newly formed ego that are characteristic of the oral stage of development. They are introjection, primary identification, projection, fixation, regression, and denial. In the early stages of ego development, the ego is confronted with judgments of whether or not to incorporate objects. An object that is incorporated or accepted is introjected, and one that is unacceptable and thus not incorporated is projected. Since the primary functions of the oral period center around the mouth, the prototype of introjection is viewed as sucking and swallowing, and the prototype of projection is viewed as spitting out. The decision to introject or project is based upon the pleasure principle. Thus, all objects that result in tension reduction are incorporated, and those objects resulting in tension increase are projected or "spat out." These two processes are recapitulated in the child's subsequent development in the forms of the introjection process of the superego and the ego-defensive process of projection. To project is to say, "it does not belong to me" or "it shall not be part of me, it belongs to the external environment."

Blum (1964) noted that the *state* of *identification* is enforced by the *process* of introjection. To incorporate an object into the ego is to identify oneself with that object. Thus, object relationships characterized by identification have their beginnings in the oral period. The identificatory state in the oral period is primary because it represents the infant's first relationships to objects. Identification in this period is the forerunner of the very important identifications that occur in the child's social development (for example, sex-role identifications).

Fixation and regression are the mechanisms through which some of the characteristics of prior developmental stages are carried into subsequent stages. Fixation and regression, therefore, are two of the major mechanisms that render psychosexual development continuous. The arresting of development, with respect to any or all characteristics, at any stage is referred to as *fixation* (Blum, 1964). The process by which the individual returns to a previous mode of behavior, interaction, perception, or emotional conflict is referred to as *regression*. Regression usually occurs in response to a stressful, tension-producing situation. Thus, the child who perceives that he is extremely threatened by the loss of love or favor of his mother might regress to orally fixated behaviors reflecting dependency needs (for example, sucking of the thumb, refusal to eat unless fed, etc.). Fixation and regression function complementarily. Thus, the stronger the fixation, the greater the probability that regression to the fixated mode will occur. Freud regarded the many adult behaviors involving oral stimulation as regressive and as evidence of the earlier formation of a fixation. Hence, smoking, alcoholism, excessive eating in times of stress, and many other behaviors are viewed as regressions to oral modes of functioning upon which the individual is fixated. Blum (1964, p. 49) citing Fenichel (1945) enumerated some notable causes of fixation:

1.   Fixation might be caused by the simultaneous satisfaction of instincts and the need for security. Thus, an oral fixation might be established by providing a child with a bottle each time he awakens in the middle of the night. In this case, the child's instinctual hunger drive and need to suck is being fulfilled, simultaneously with the fulfillment of his need for security embodied by the environment's responsiveness to his needs.

2.   It may be caused by excessive overindulgence of the infant so that he finds it difficult to relinquish the particular developmental stage.

3.   Excessive deprivation leading to the individual's continual search for gratification of his frustrated needs of the stage in question might also lead to fixation.

4.   Last, inconsistency in the response of the mothering one might result in fixation. That is, she either alternates between excessive gratification and excessive deprivation, or she makes an extreme and sudden shift from one to the other.

Fixations occur at all stages of development, but they initially come into being with the oral stage.

Since denial and projection are the two most primitive forms of ego defense, both make their initial appearances in the most primitive stage. The denial of reality by the oral infantile ego is generally characterized by the unwillingness to acknowledge those aspects of reality which do not satisfy the ubiquitous pleasure principle. Hence, the oral infant denies the painful elements in his experience.

The Anal Stage

This stage extends from sometime after the first year of life until approximately four years of age. The erogeneous zone that is prominent during this stage is the anus. During this stage the child and his parents become concerned with the eliminative and retentive functions of the bowels and sphincter.

Blum (1964) noted that orthodox analytic concepts indicate that ego development during this stage is represented by the development of an active mastery over objects, the realization and tolerance of anxiety, the development of speech and thought, and the development of defenses against impulsivity. All these ego developments are related to one another and arise from the experiences characteristic of the anal stage. Active mastery occurs in two forms: (1) mastery over the motor functions of the body—walking, talking, bowel retention—and (2) the growth of judgment and reasoning that is greatly facilitated by the emergence of language. (Blum, 1964). Mastery over motor functions such as sphincter control constitutes the basis for independence in the child, and the appearance of speech functions facilitates the development of reality testing.

The development of speech that allows the child to engage in the concrete testing of reality also renders the child capable of anticipating the future through the mechanism of imagination. (Blum, 1964). Thus, the ego at this stage begins to become capable of anticipating the occurrence of anxiety. Anticipatory anxiety is not as likely to flood the ego system as anxiety that is situationally experienced without any forewarning. Thus, the child's ego builds up its tolerance for anxiety by experiencing it in small preparatory doses. Some major sources of anxiety during this stage are the fear of loss of love because of the violation of parental sanctions (particularly those related to toilet training) and the fear of loss of self esteem (particularly from the inability to master objects). A further development of ego functioning occurring in this stage is that the ego acquires the ability to postpone or permanently deter the gratification of id impulses. This development results from the child's adaptation to the threats from the external world that appear during this stage (for example, parental "penalties" for soiling).

A further significant development of the anal stage is the rudimentary appearance of the adult superego. During this period the child has his first intense experience with socialization. The many strictures of the toilet-training regime of the parents must be internalized if sphincter control is to be established. Although the internalizations reflecting superego development in this stage are probably not organized into a consistent set of internalized rules and sanctions, they nevertheless establish the foundation of the superego system.

There are two psychosexual phases of the anal period: the anal-expulsive and the anal-retentive phases. Classical psychoanalysis maintains that in the anal-expulsive phase, sexual gratification results from the pleasurable sensations derived from the process of excretion. Further pleasure is derived from the interest and attention afforded to the child's excretory functions by the parents. In the anal-retentive phase, the child derives sensual pleasure from retaining feces. In the context of the toilet-training regime the child may express hostility and defiance toward his parents by expelling feces when he should retain them and retaining feces when he should expel them (Blum, 1964). According to Freudian theory, the adult character traits of stinginess and generosity derive from the child's experience with expulsion and retention during the anal period. Other adult traits that are often attributed to the conflicts of the anal period are cleanliness, compulsivity, and sloppiness.

Blum (1964) characterized the object relationships of the anal period as being ambivalent and sadomasochistic. Again, these characteristics are attributed to the nature of the socializing experiences during this period. The child's ambivalence stems from the conflict between the hostility or love he might express by either retaining or expelling feces. The sadomasochistic tendencies derive from the sexual gratification gained from withholding or expelling feces as well as the physical punishment he might experience upon violating the toilet-training regime. Furthermore, Blum noted that the child's act of surrendering his feces to his parents is the first indication of object love.

The unstructured beginnings of the ego defense of reaction formation appear sometimes during the anal phase. It generally manifests itself as a protective response to the ambivalence so characteristic of this phase. Lastly, Anna Freud (1946) postulated that a more-sophisticated form of denial evolves in the anal period. She referred to it as "denial in word and act," and it involves a more-reality-based denial than was apparent in the oral phase. Thus, the child may deny the existence of toilet-training rules in order to protect himself against the anxiety generated by his fears of reprisal by his parents.

The Phallic Stage

The movement of the child from the anal stage to the phallic stage usually occurs in the third or fourth year of life. At this time, the genital region becomes the principal psychosexual zone. Correspondingly, the child's interest in sexual matters is greatly enhanced. Blum (1964) noted that the orthodox analytic view ascribes three major developments to the phallic stage: (1) accelerated sexual interest, both within the family in the form of the Oedipus complex and within the inner life and fantasy of the child,

(2) the major evolution of the superego, and (3) the expanded utilization of ego-defensive processes.

The behavioral manifestations of accelerated sexual interest in this stage are the increased incidence of masturbatory activities, heightened needs for body contact with members of the opposite sex, and exhibitionistic tendencies (Blum, 1964). Most of the events and changes of the phallic stage center around the Oedipal conflict. According to orthodox psychoanalytic formulations, the Oedipal conflict arises when the child directs his (her) newly awakened sexual impulses toward his (her) opposite-sexed parent and, in turn, perceives his (her) same-sexed parent as a rival who jeopardizes the satisfaction of these impulses. In the male child, this state of affairs generates a fear of retaliatory action on the part of the father. Since the conflict is generated by sexual motives, the boy's fear of retaliation takes the form of castration fear or castration anxiety. The conflict for the female child is somewhat different. The principal object for the male child has always been the mother, and in the phallic period the mother remains the principal object but takes on sexual significance. The female child, however, must shift the focus of her object strivings from mother to father. Once this shift in identification takes place the mother is viewed as a rival. Because of the genital endowment of the female, she is not prone to castration anxiety, but rather she perceives herself as having already been castrated by her rival mother. Furthermore, Freud concluded that one potent basis for the female child's attachment to father is her *envy* of his genital organ.

Freud characterized the overcoming of the Oedipal conflict as a prerequisite for normal adult sexuality (Blum, 1964). This conflict is resolved when the child reconciles himself to the invincibility of his rival same-sex parent and relinquishes the full sexual possession of his opposite-sexed parent to him. This "surrender" results in the child's identification with the same-sexed parent and is viewed as a prerequisite of sex-role learning.

The above is at best a sketchy outline of what Freud considered one of his most important "discoveries." It should be noted that many of the ramifications and conditions of the Oedipal conflict are almost totally within the fantasy of the child and, for the most part, are beyond his conscious awareness.

As a result of the identifications consequent upon the resolution of the Oedipal conflict, the superego becomes highly defined in this stage. The child's identification with his same-sexed parent leads to the introjection or internalization of his values, attitudes, and sanctions. Blum (1964) notes that the child does not identify with his parents as they are or with the manner in which they themselves are bound by moral sanctions, but instead he identifies with an idealized version of his parents. Hence, he identifies not so much with the person of his parent as with the parent's superego. This idealization of the parents with regard to moral standards leads the child to strive for perfection in his own moral behavior. Thus, as we mentioned earlier, Freud maintained that the superego is the heir to the Oedipus conflict.

Because of the intensity of conflict and tension buildup during the duration of the Oedipal situation, the ego in the phallic period forms a good part of its defensive armamentarium. The defenses of repression, reaction formation, and displacement are particularly well formed in this period. Repression forms in order to protect the ego from an awareness of the complex of negative emotions and instincts that the child feels toward his same-sexed parent. It also protects him from the awareness of his sexual drives toward his opposite-sexed parent. Hence, repression becomes fully established as a defensive process in order to ward off the conscious perception of the events and feelings of the Oedipal period. Displacement arises as a defense in order to channel the excess of libidinal energy generated by the Oedipal conflict toward more-acceptable aims and objects. This channelization protects the personality system against excessive increments in psychic energy.

The defense of reaction formation, which had its beginnings in the anal period, reaches a more-complete development in the phallic period. Reaction formation accompanies the resolution of the Oedipal period. That is, hate and hostility toward the same-sexed parent are converted to love for and identity with that parent. Hence, the utilization of reaction formation is a necessary prerequisite for the satisfactory climax of the phallic period.

The Latency Stage

Freud conceptualized the latency stage as a plateau in the child's development. After the intensity of conflicts in the three previous stages, the child now is in a period in which he consolidates his position (Blum, 1964). He begins to relate more openly to objects in the outside world and particularly extrafamilial objects.

By the time the child has reached the period of latency he has learned to sublimate his sexual and libidinal urges, largely as a function of the events of the phallic period. In the latency stage sexual love toward parents is sublimated and manifests itself as respect. Intrapersonal conflict is at a low ebb during this period, and there are little if any transformations in the intrapersonal subsystems. While the defenses of repression, reaction formation, and sublimation are frequently utilized as protective measures during this phase, no new defensive postures are formed.

The function of the latency period is the consolidation of the events, conflicts, and resolutions of the three earlier stages so that the child might prepare for the upcoming events of adolescence.

The Genital Stage

The genital stage is the bridge between childhood and adulthood. The child emerges from his relatively quiescent latency period into an explosive period of physiological and psychological development. This emergence occurs in phases. First, the child steps out of latency into a prepubertal phase. Orthodox analytic formulations (A. Freud, 1946) point out that although the transition to prepuberty is accompanied by few qualitative changes, there are quantitative changes in the form of increments of libidinal energy. Thus, the sexual and aggressive instincts that were so prominent during the pregenital phases of development are once against awakened with renewed vigor. In the prepubertal phase, the aims of these instinctual strivings are not differentiated. Therefore, the preadolescent is in the position of having much sexual energy at his disposal with few environmental objects to discharge it upon.

A second phase of the genital period is the onset of pubescence. The stormy events characteristic of the child's becoming an adolescent are well documented in both the popular and scientific literature. There are the physiological developments of the appearances of secondary sexual character- istics, the growth of orgastic potency, the onset of menstruation in females, and so forth. Concomitant psychological changes occur in the newly crowned adolescent's desire for independence, adherence to peer rules, rebellion against parents, thought confusion, and the like.

Freud characterized most of the changes of the adolescent era as being based upon the reestablishment of the lines of battle between the id and superego. The id at this phase has accumulated alarming abundances of libidinal energy. Society imposes negative sanctions against the reduction of the resultant tension. That is, taboos have been constructed against adolescent sexual expression as well as incest. Thus, the adolescent must turn to himself for the gratification of his libidinal impulses. He withdraws from the family circle and at first isolates himself from peers. The adolescent in the early phases of puberty becomes as narcissistic and self-loving as he had been in the pregenital stages. Masturbation is his most frequent form of sexual activity and libidinal "release."

After recovering from his sudden thrust into the pubertal phase, the adolescent begins to adapt to his newly formed genital sexuality. Narcissism transmutes into altruistic love, first with same-sexed peers and later with opposite-sexed peers. Furthermore, even though the parental agents are still rebelled against, the adolescent will often seek out a parental substitute (for example, teacher-confidant). In this progression from narcissism to altruistic love, the ego begins to gain control over the id impulses. It becomes capable of channeling the adolescents intense sexual drives into appropriate sublima- tions, such as friendships, clubs, sports, and creative endeavors.

Normally, the genital period ends when the adolescent is converted into a socialized adult. That is, the ego usurps control of the personality system and the individual becomes reality and socially oriented. Pregenital sexuality is transformed into genital and adult sexuality, and the adult character struc- ture emerges. Hall and Lindzey (1957) noted that the adult character structure is a fusion or synthesis of the all-important events of the pregenital phases with the sublimations and ego alterations of the genital period.

FREUD'S GROUP PSYCHOLOGY

Freud's group psychology bears the mark of social and cultural anthropology rather than social psychology. For this reason it has been more readily embraced as a quasi-theoretical framework by anthropologists than by social psychologists. In Aristotelian fashion, Freud viewed society or culture as the product of the conglomeration of the individual personalities within it. Fur- thermore, he regarded the social systems to be macrocosmic version of the personality system. The neoanalytic theories of Sullivan, Adler, Horney, and Fromm dealt more explicitly with social psychological variables, for they became concerned with the social determinants of individual behavior and personality as well as the effect of personality on social-interaction processes. In fact, most neoanalytic theories, although using many of the basic tenets and points of view of classical psychoanalysis, deviate from the orthodox framework in their movement away from the intrapersonal and toward the interpersonal.

Nevertheless, in keeping with the foregoing presentation we will concentrate in this section on Freud's group psychology. Although Freud made frequent references to social factors such as family structure, political structure, social conflict and war, and the like throughout his writings, there are four major works within which his principles of group psychology are presented: (1) *Group Psychology and the Analysis of the Ego* (1922), (2) *Civilization and its Discontents* (1930), (3) *Totem and Taboo* (1913), and (4) *The Future of an Illusion* (1928). Below we have stated the principles of group functioning that emerge from these four works:

1. The principal thesis which Freud continually iterates throughout his writings on group psychology is that society functions to inhibit and repress the instinctual impulses of the individual. Social order is predicated on the adaptation of the ego to the demand's of social reality. A corollary to this thesis is that social order and society in general would be destroyed or at least become chaotic if individual men were allowed full and unmitigated expression of their impulses.

2. The family is the fundamental agent of society. As such, it enforces the individual's orientation toward the social order at the very early stages of his existence. With the development of the child, the family imposes ever more-intense restrictions on the expression of his instinctual wishes. These impositions are based on the demands and rules of the prevailing social order. The goal of the parental agents is to have the child accept society's rules and strictures as his own. The process of socialization, then, involves the child's introjection of parentally administered social dictums and therefore the eventual formation of the superego.

3. Even before the formation of an organized superego, the child in his attempt to cope with the conflict between his instincts and an uncompromising reality forms an ego. As we have frequently noted, the ego serves as a mediator between societal limitations and the instincts. It conjures up many techniques of defense and control to satisfy both agencies. In Freud's view a well-functioning ego system is a necessary precondition for survival in the social environment.

4. Because of the oppositional nature of man's needs and society's demands, Freud conceptualized man and his environing society as in a constant state of conflict. Since it has been observed that most men abide by societal limitations, it was concluded that society holds the upper hand in this conflict. Men repress their instinctual needs in deference to a harsh social reality. The motivating factors in man's submission to the social order are said to be the pressure of external force and the fear of destruction by that society. Furthermore, Freud maintained that with the tearing down of societal limitations and strictures, man would become an instinctual animal. Thus, he

visualized man and society as enemies with irreconcilable differences. Reconciliation results only from forced external control and the induction of fear by social agents.

5. Freud proposed that societies and groups are formed and men are bound together as a subsequent reenactment of the individual's libidinal ties toward his parents. The child makes his initial social contacts in the family, and this unit serves as the prototype for all later social relationships. The parental agents are his first interpersonal objects and they administer to his needs and impose socially dictated limitations on their expression. Parents protect, feed, and punish, and in Freud's view, they are the child's prototypes of leaders. Their protection and nourishment set up conditions of dependency, and their suppression and frustration of instincts create feelings of hostility and fear.

In deference to the child's helplessness in the face of his powerful "leaders," the child identifies with them and incorporates their values. This serves to minimize his hostility and curb his aggressive impulses against the parental figures. The Oedipal conflict is particularly relevant to this process of identification with the "leader." Freud viewed all group ties as being based upon the process of identification with the powerful leader or quasi-leadership group. Thus, if several children identify with the same powerful leadership objects, then these children are "tied" together by their common identifications. This holds for both familial and social leadership. The tie that binds people together into groups is their common identification with a leader or leader-surrogate.

6. In his characteristically pessimistic view of social institutions, Freud maintained that social justice arises from the feelings of envy and hostility that group members experience toward one another. This envy and hostility is based upon the competition for the favor of the leader. Since the expression of envy and hostility is blocked and sanctioned by society, rules of justice are set up to guarantee that one man receives no more or no less than the next man, particularly with regard to the favor of the leader (or his laws). Sibling rivalry that leads to the later tie between siblings is an example of the conversion of envy to justice. In short, Freud proposed that social justice is a reaction formation to envy.

7. Social institutions such as law and religion are formed in order to protect man and society against man's own aggressive, hostile, and sexual impulses. Freud therefore viewed social institutions in their negative roles as inhibitors of individual expression. Legal standards and agents as well as beliefs in deities arise as replacements for parental restrictions.

8. Last, it should be noted that Freud did not represent common identification with powerful objects as the sole basis for group cohesion and formation. He also noted that since society through repressive mechanisms limits the expression of man's sexual impulses to one or only few individuals, the libidinal energy directed at forbidden objects is desexualized and sublimated into friendship bonds. Thus, the sphere of man's friendships well exceeds the sphere of his sexual relationships.

While the eight propositions above are not a complete exposition of

Freud's group psychology, they encompass its basic tenets. It should be noted that these tenets are consistent with his conceptualizations of the psychic apparatus, the ego defenses, psychosexual development, and assumptions about human functioning. In the following chapter, we consider some theorists who have extrapolated constructs from the Freudian framework and applied them to relevant sociopsychological phenomena. These constructs may or may not be based upon his group psychology, but in all cases they are derived from his general psychological theory.

THE STRUCTURE AND ASSUMPTIONS OF PSYCHOANALYTIC THEORY

From the foregoing material, it should become apparent to the reader that psychoanalysis as a system cannot be represented by any single point of view. Rather, Freud proposed a psychological system based upon multiple assumptions and multiple points of view about human functioning. He viewed personality as a structural and dynamic system, and he viewed it in historical and genetic perspective. The many currents of thought that run silently and deeply beneath the manifest aspects of Freud's system were not always coherently articulated by him. Rapaport (1959) has attempted to portray Freud's metapsychology through the systematic presentation of the several points of view and several assumptions upon which the psychoanalytic system is based. In the following paragraphs we present Rapaport's specification of the points of view and assumptions of Freudian theory.

The Empirical Point of View

This point of view holds that the subject matter of psychoanalysis is behavior. Rapaport pointed out that Freud's definition of what constitutes a behavioral pattern is considerably broader than that of other psychological systems. Freud included feelings, thoughts, symptoms, normal and pathological manifestations, and unconscious wishes or ideas in the universe of human behavior. Thus, Freud did not limit his investigations or theory to observable aspects of human behavior.

Underlying the empirical point of view is the assumption of psychological determinism. That is, *all* behavior is viewed as determined by both genetic and historical antecedents. Furthermore, Freud placed great stress on the unconscious determiners of behavior as the predominant forces motivating the individual's external actions, symptoms, and environmental adjustments. The view that unconscious factors are the crucial determiners of behavior has been referred to by Rapaport as the topographic point of view.

The Gestalt Point of View

Here Rapaport alluded to Freud's belief that no single factor, personality structure, conflict, or the like fully determines the expressed behavior of the individual. That is, a given behavior cannot be referred to simply as id-, ego-, or superego-determined, but rather, all behavior is the total expression of the contribution of all the structures and forces in the individual's personality system. Although behavior may be conceptually divided for purposes of analysis, in reality these divisions are artificial. Therefore, although one may speak of the id aspects of a given behavior, he would be violating Freud's assumptions about the *multiple determination* of behavior if he used clearly defined categories for id behavior, ego behavior, and superego behavior. From the point of view of the actor, any given behavior is indivisible. From the point of view of the psychoanalyst, all behavior is a multiply determined whole that results from the coalescence of the relative contributions of the various determiners.

In addition to the gestalt point of view, Rapaport noted that Freud also went one step further by espousing an organismic view of behavior. That is, Freud believed that no single behavior occurs in isolation. Instead he implied that the personality must be considered as an indivisible totality. Each specific behavior, then, is viewed only in terms of its place in the total behavioral and personality system of the individual. In summary, then, Freud maintained that both the individual and his behavior are each indivisible entities.

The Genetic Point of View

This point of view maintains that all behavior occurs in an epigenetic sequence that is governed by both the inherent laws of maturation and the experience of the individual. Thus, Freud maintained that every behavior occurring in the present has a history. Rapaport noted that the genetic point of view refers to (1) the history of the drive process, particularly with regard to the changes in object focus that occur in the progression from one stage to the next; (2) the history of the structures of personality; and (3) the history of the individual's relationship to the real environment. These three historical sources are by no means independent of one another. The distribution of drive energy and the processes of tension increase and reduction are related to both the structural and environmental determiners of personality.

Ross and Abrams (1965) indicated that two assumptions underlie Freud's genetic point of view: (1) mental phenomena have historical antecedents and (2) there are maturational and genetic sequences to behavior such that earlier forms of behavior may be reactivated to influence later behavior. The concepts of fixation and regression definitely presuppose the assumption of an epigenetic sequence in human behavior.

The Dynamic Point of View

The assumption of this point of view is that all behavior is ultimately drive determined. The primary drive that Freud concerned himself with was a broadly defined sexual drive. He maintained that all other drives are ultimately reducible to sexual or libidinal forces. He viewed drives as one of the more-important givens of genetic and phylogenetic inheritance. Rapaport noted that Freud's attribution of such a crucial role to drive functions stemmed from his observations of infantile sexuality and his observation that behavior can always be interpreted as goal-directed. Since Freud was very concerned with questions about the teleology of behavior, he proposed that if movement toward goals and objects occurs, then there must exist moving principles or sources of movement. Thus, he concluded that for any purposive behavior to occur, man must be driven to perform it. Furthermore, because he interpreted much of infant behavior as sexually or libidinally determined, he maintained that the earliest and most-basic drive is sexual.

Rapaport implied, however, that one should be cautious in accepting the thesis of the ultimate drive determination of behavior as it was stated in early analytic formulations. The many other points of view of the psychoanalytic system serve to qualify the concept of total drive determination. For example, the effects of drives are often mollified by the ego defenses, by epigenetic considerations, or by other unconscious factors. In the light of Freud's assumptions about the multiple determination of behavior, it would be incompatible to ascribe complete and utter drive determination to behavior.

The Economic Point of View

This point of view holds that all behavior is regulated by the distribution and flow of psychic energy in the personality system. An implicit assumption of this view is that there is for each individual a level of psychic energy that is desirable for optimal psychological function. Overabundancies of psychic energy in the system lead the organism to seek methods and objects for energy discharge. An insufficiency of energy in the system leads the organism to seek stimulation in order to build up tension energies. The economy of the individual personality is said to be dependent upon the conservation of needed psychic energy and the discharge of excess energy. Energy buildup and discharge are processes that operate within the structures of the personality system. Thus, the tension buildup usually occurs in the id system. When the tension reaches an excess, the id system seeks discharge of the tension by the investment of some or all of the energy in an object in the external environment. Since the ego is the structure that converses with reality, it is responsible for seeking out methods and objects for energy discharge that reduce the tension of the id without raising the tension level of the superego.

The ego and its defenses develop in the interest of the individual's psychic economy. The relatively immediate and spontaneous discharge of tension in the young infant is later moderated by the delaying and reality-oriented tactics of the ego. The ego, along with its defenses and controls, tends to neutralize the positive or negative valence of psychological energy.

The Structural Point of View

The concept that personality consists of relatively well-defined structural systems arose from the "observation" that drives and drive energies do not singularly determine behavior. There is usually a gap in time between the buildup of drive energy to a discharge point and the investment of that energy in an external object. Furthermore, often enough, the object in which energy is invested does not logically correspond to the underlying drive. For these reasons, Freud posited that structural systems that serve to mold, contain, and direct psychological energy intervene between energy arousal and investment.

Freud differentiated three structures of personality—the id, the ego, and the superego—on the basis of their differing contributions to the channeling, containment, and investment of psychological energy. The id was conceptualized as the source of drive energy, the ego as the reality-testing system that organizes and interprets reality in order to arrive at the most efficacious means of tension reduction, and the superego as setting internalized limits for energy discharge. Thus, the concept of multiple-personality structures was evolved as a point of view from Freud's commitment to the economic and dynamic models. Furthermore, the genetic point of view is quite relevant to the structural point of view, for Freud postulated that the ego, id, and superego are slowly transformed and differentiated in the course of psychological development.

The Adaptive Point of View

Simply, this point of view embodies the assumption that all behavior is to some extent determined by the reality surrounding the individual. This includes both environmental reality as well as the individual's bodily reality, excluding, of course, the somatic basis of drives. This point of view is predicated on the assumption that man must orient himself and his behavior to the demands of physical and social reality in order to survive. The ego, as the personality subsystem that is responsive to the reality principle, is the responsible agent of the individual's adaptation to the environmental surround. Thus, in development the individual must progress from the primary process modes of thought characteristic of the id system to the secondary process mode of thought of the ego.

The interchange between reality and the ego is a two-way street. Therefore, the ego is shaped by and shapes external reality. The ego must arrive at effective ways of coping with reality demands while at the same time responding to "internal" demands. If the ego does not adequately adapt its strivings to the surrounding reality, it will be severely hampered in efficiently discharging its role as the personality's link to tension-reducing objects.

It should be noted that Rapaport's discussion of the points of view and assumptions of analytic theory goes into much greater detail than our condensation of his discussion. The interested reader would do well to consult Rapaport's (1959) comprehensive discussion of these issues. Furthermore, although Rapaport also discussed the analytic conception of the social determiners of behavior, this discussion was based predominantly upon the neoanalytic proposals of Hartmann, Horney, Sullivan, Adler, and Erikson. Thus, it is not included in our presentation, which is predominantly concerned with Freud's theory.

CRITICISMS AND MISINTERPRETATIONS

Throughout this chapter we have noted that the interpretation of the psychoanalytic orientation is not easy. The many difficulties that American psychologists experience in interpreting Freud's system stem from several sources:

1.   Although Freud exposited a massive theory with many constructs, he did not provide an adequate systematic structure linking these constructs.

2.   The historical concern in American psychology with the quantification and observability of psychological processes precluded careful attention to Freudian constructs, which often deal with unobservables and which are loosely defined. In short, his theoretical system is not subject to traditional forms of empirical testing, and some would maintain that it cannot be tested by any acceptable procedure.

3.   Early translators often did not do justice to the clarity of his original statements, and sometimes they even made factual errors in translation. For example, the translations of A. A. Brill were often unwieldy and difficult to read and understand.

4.   Although Freud was not very receptive to criticism by others, he was very self-critical and was constantly modifying his formulations. Hence his theoretical propositions were mutable and underwent considerable change during his lifetime. This changeability is reflected in the tendency of some of Freud's critics to attack concepts that he had already altered or completely discarded (for example, his early conceptions of the ego and the id).

5.   Freud's controversial proposals concerning the predominant role that sex has in human functioning, the death wish, the Oedipal conflict, and the like led to much resistance to his system.

6.   Some of Freud's concepts, although in general agreement with the constructs of other systems, were rejected because they were said to contain much surplus meaning. For example, his conception of the "pleasure principle" was quite similar to Thorndike's "law of effect" and the derived principle of reinforcement, but it was rejected as imprecise. Today it is recognized that both formulations were imprecise and were not firmly based on antecedent and consequent conditions.

We have presented only a small sampling of the many criticisms of Freud's system. We have tried to indicate that many criticisms were (and are) justified, but at the same time we have tried to indicate that some of the rejection by experimentally oriented psychologists has been based on essentially irrelevant criteria. It may be noted, however, that this rejection was frequently more apparent than real. Indeed, most psychologists recognize that Freud has made an intractable and pervasive contribution to the field. Although his theoretical constructs were untestable in their original form, many psychologists have revised his constructs either to subject them to empirical testing (for example, Sarnoff, 1960) or to link them to another body of psychological theory (for example, Dollard & Miller, 1950). Even though such attempts at revision of psychoanalytic theory have often been questioned by both antirevisionist psychoanalysts and anti-Freudians, these attempts have nevertheless led to some productive propositions and hypotheses about human behavior. In the following chapter some consequences of the psychoanalytic orientation for social psychological theory are presented and discussed in greater detail.

10 | PSYCHOANALYTICALLY BASED THEORIES IN SOCIAL PSYCHOLOGY

The many attempts to apply psychoanalytic principles to a wide range of problems in the social and behavioral sciences have met with much controversy. As we have noted in Chapter 9, the methods and underlying points of view of the psychoanalytic approach to behavior diverge from the "mainstream" of psychological thought and method. Nevertheless, we believed it important to present psychoanalytically based theories of social psychology in order to provide the reader with a wide view of socio-psychological theorizing.

The four theories that we have chosen for consideration in this chapter take a portion or several portions of psychoanalytic principles and interrelate them with interactional and group phenomena. Sigmund Freud's classical dictums are not the only bases for the theories subsequently presented. The neoanalytic approaches of Sullivan, Adler, Fromm, Horney, and the ego psychologists also enter into the theories presented in this chapter. However, the varying approaches of these neoanalytic theorists are each derived from Freud's basic point of view, and although specific propositions differ, the general approach to human behavior is the same. Therefore, an understanding of the psychoanalytic formulations discussed in the preceding chapter should provide the reader with an adequate foundation for the following theoretical expositions.

The theories summarized in this chapter are Bion's (1948–1951) psychodynamic theory of group function, Bennis and Shepard's (1956) theory of group development, Schutz's (1955, 1958) three-dimensional theory of interpersonal behavior, and Sarnoff's (1960) psychoanalytic theory of social attitudes.

A DYNAMIC THEORY OF GROUP FUNCTION

Bion (1948–1951) published a series of papers in which he proposed a theoretical framework for the evaluation and remediation of groups. These papers were jointly published in a collected work in 1959. His theory is based upon his observations of and participation in therapy groups. Nevertheless, the observations that he made were held to be applicable to the functioning of all groups. Although his theory is linked to the psychoanalytic orientation, he used few explicit psychoanalytic concepts. However, implicit psychoanalytic assumptions about group functioning underlie his postulates.

Basically, Bion tended to view the group not only as an aggregation of individuals but also as a unit with emotional and dynamic properties all its own. He proposed that the functioning of a group is dependent upon the assumptions which that group makes about its reason for being. In line with the analytic framework, Bion tended to regard these group assumptions as functioning on an unconscious level. He also tended to link group assumptions to the basic motivations and anxieties under which humans operate. Although he never explicitly stated it, it becomes apparent throughout his works that he regarded the group as a macrocosmic version of the individual. It therefore has needs and motives (id functions), goals and mechanisms (ego functions) and boundaries (superego functions). The group is also said to undergo conflicts equivalent to the individual's Oedipal conflicts.

Our presentation of Bion's theory is brief and concentrates on articulating his concepts of *work group, basic assumptions of groups, group mentality, group culture,* and the *protomental system.*

The Work Group

A work group is one that meets for the purpose of performing a specific task and to that end uses a set of rules and procedures. The work group sets up the administrative machinery for accomplishing its ends and for achieving the cooperation of the individual members. Bion alternately referred to the work group as the sophisticated group. He did so in recognition of the relatively emotionless and reality-oriented fashion with which the work group procures its goals. He noted that every group has a sophisticated structure, which is most manifest in the formative stages. Thus, every group establishes the rules of order and the goals for assembling. Furthermore, the sophisticated structure of the group persists in one form or another for as long as the group exists.

The emotional properties of the group emerge when the group makes certain assumptions about its reason for being. These emotional components act in combination with the work group function, but it is highly unlikely that a group could survive if there were not an underlying sophisticated structure to focus the goals of the group. Thus, an important aspect of the work group function is the preservation of a cohesive group. To implement its self-preservative function, the work group has to restrict the emotions experienced by the group at any given time to those involved in a single basic assumption of that group. This suppressive function prevents the sophisticated structure from being overwhelmed by conflicting emotional states. Work group function, then, is very much like ego function in the individual. Like the ego, (1) it is governed by the reality principle, (2) it is activated by self-preservative needs, (3) it channels emotional expression so as to prevent conflict while allowing tension reduction, and (4) it responds to both the rules and boundaries of the group (superego) and the emotional demands of the group (id).

The Basic Assumptions of Groups

Bion asserted that there are three basic assumptions under which groups operate. These assumptions must be interpreted from the emotional climate of the group as reflected in the expressed emotions of the group members. Thus each of the basic assumptions is linked to the emotions which characterize it. The three assumptions proposed are the *dependency assumption,* the *pairing assumption,* and the *fight-flight assumption.*

THE DEPENDENCY ASSUMPTION   The assumption made under the dependency condition of the group is that the group has met in order to be nurtured and supported by a leader upon whom it is dependent. The accompanying feelings of the dependency assumption include inadequacy and frustration. The expressed behavior is the group's imploring of the leader to exert his omnipotence in directing and sustaining the group and the interaction therein. In a structured group, such as the therapy group, where there is a "natural" leader, initial dependency assumptions invoke him as the nurturant one. However, other leaders might emerge from the membership. This emergence is dependent upon the "natural" leader's failure or refusal to assume an omnipotent role and the situational factors that determine the appropriateness of another in assuming the nurturant role. The overriding characteristics of the group operating under the dependency assumption are immaturity in interpersonal relationships and inefficiency in group relationships. It is implied that inefficiency stems from the lack of direct interpersonal communication except of the member-leader type.

THE PAIRING ASSUMPTION   When any two group members form a pair by establishing a solid line of communication, the group makes the assumption that the pair has formed for sexual purposes. This assumption is said to hold despite the sex of the pair members. The interacting pair is accepted by the group without accompanying feelings of exclusion by the other members. Bion presented a rather obscure discussion of this particular group assumption. It appears that he proposed that the sexual purposes of pairing in the group are perceived on an unconscious level by the portion of the group not involved in the pairing. The basic emotion within the pairing group is hope. That is, the group will allow the pair to continue the involved interaction indefinitely because it suffuses it with the hope of preservation through the formation of sexual bonds. Bion characterized the emotion of hope peculiar to this group as a Messianic hope. Thus, the imagined leader of the pairing group is seen as the savior or messiah who will maintain the relationship bonds within the group and reduce the possibility that the group will be destroyed. The formation of a pair creates in the group the hope that other pairs may be formed. Thus, it creates in the group the hope that intensive sexual relationships will bind them together. The hope for intensive, close, and binding relationships is seen by Bion as the manifest assumption which obscures the latent and most-basic sexual premonitions of the group.

THE FIGHT-FLIGHT ASSUMPTION   This is the assumption made by the group that they have assembled for the purpose of fighting something or fleeing from something. Fight and flight are proposed as the only techniques the group knows of to promote self-preservation. The function of the accepted leader of the fight-flight group is to provide the mechanisms whereby the individual may express avoidance and aggression. Thus, the motives and emotions underlying the fight-flight group are anger, fear, hate, and aggression. For the sake of optimal preservation, the group must cohere to reduce the tension from any of these emotions. Thus, the accepted leader of a fight-flight therapy group might set the conditions in which the individual members may flee into obscurity and melt into the group structure. He may ensure that the individual members do not become known to the therapist or any other observers. Furthermore, he may set the stage for the expression of aggression toward the therapist or outgroups. A unified group, then, as well as providing a haven for its members can also become a cohesive unit for warding off "foreign" intruders.

Bion did not propose that his basic assumption groups were the only ones that could be conceptualized. Rather, he maintained that these group assumptions appeared most frequently in his own experiences with groups. Throughout his book, he maintained that, although groups can continuously shift from one assumption to another, each assumption occurs apart from the other two. Thus, for example, at any point in time a group might operate on the dependency assumption but not on both the dependency and pairing assumptions. The emotional states belonging to any single assumption exclude the emotional states belonging to either of the other assumptions. However, any of the basic assumptions usually exists contemporaneously with the sophisticated structure of the group. In this coactive relationship, functions of the work group are either obstructed or facilitated by the basic assumptions of the group. Conversely, the reduction of tension from the emotions that spawn a given basic assumption can be obstructed or facilitated by the sophisticated group.

Group Mentality

Bion defines the concept of group mentality as "*the unanimous expression of the will of the group, contributed to by the individual in ways of which he is unaware, influencing him disagreeably whenever he thinks or behaves in a manner at variance with the basic assumptions*" (Bion, 1959, p. 65. Italics ours). Its relationship to the basic assumptions is a supportive one. Group mentality is the mechanism whereby group function is ensured of being in accordance with the basic assumptions. Thus, when an individual's behaviors in the group violate operating assumptions, he is violating the will and purpose of the group's existence. The establishment of a group mentality provides an inhibiting influence for the individual's deviation through the singular expression of his own will. In this sense, it serves a superego function for the group.

Group Culture

This construct is conceptualized as the product of the conflict between individual will and group mentality. It is the *"structure of the group at any given moment, the occupations it pursues, and the organization it adopts"* (Bion, 1959, p. 102. Italics ours). Thus, an egalitarian group is an example of a group culture, as is an aggressive group, a striving group, a decision-making group, etc. Any group may have several structures, and the one which achieves prominence at any moment is the one which expresses the current basic assumption of the group.

Protomental System

The emotional states that lead to the expression of a given basic assumption are in turn based upon a *protomental system*. The protomental system is that abstract entity which contains the prototypes of all three basic assumptions. It is the matrix, made up of all mental and physical elements available to the group. In fact, it is a level of group functioning in which the mental and physical are undifferentiated. When the protomental system is distressed by the disruption of group function, the emotions characteristic of the relevant basic assumption group emerge—and so the basic assumption emerges.

While one basic assumption is operating in a group, the others are, in a sense, stored in the protomental system until a shift in basic assumptions takes place, and a different set of emotions emerges and leads to a different basic assumption. The protomental system provides a reservoir for the basic assumptions and also prevents the group from experiencing conflicting assumptions. Thus, it serves an important role in the preservation of the sophisticated structure.

Comment and Evaluation

Bion's theory of group formation and functioning appears to be the product of the astute and sensitive insights of a fine therapist. Nevertheless, for the most part, it is untestable. Assessing the basic assumption under which a group is operating at any given time in the flow of interaction would appear to be a very difficult task. Clinicians will attest to the difficulty involved in inferring the emotional state of even a single individual. Therefore, Bion's basic assumption propositions are interesting and insightful but immeasurable. The clinician dealing with therapy groups would do well to understand Bion's basic assumption proposals, but they have little relevance for the experimental social psychologist.

Bion's concepts of work group, group mentality, group culture, and protomental system are similar to some of the proposals of Cattell's group syntality theory presented in Chapter 12. As we will note in that chapter, Cattell and his associates have garnered some tenuous experimental support for concepts such as "group personality." Their experimental findings might also serve as indirect and weak support for some of Bion's concepts.

Last, two points should be noted: (1) Bion's theory seems to subscribe fully to Freud's conception of the relationships between groups and individuals. That is, the members of a social group form bonds (pairing) toward one another because of their common identification with a leader (dependency) and as a reaction formation to their competition for the leader's affection. (2) Bion's theory has been cited by Schutz (1958) and Bennis and Shepard (1956) as a partial basis for their theories.

In summary, then, Bion's approach to group formation and function has not been experimentally tested, and it probably could not be. It is an organized presentation of the exquisite insights of a group psychoanalyst that might be useful to the group therapist. However, its utility for social psychologists is, at best, limited.

A THEORY OF GROUP DEVELOPMENT

The theory of group development proposed by Bennis and Shepard (1956) is basically psychoanalytic in orientation, although the authors were also influenced by other approaches. The writings of Sullivan (1953a, b), Lewin (1947), and Schutz (1955) were especially influential in the formulation of the theory. The theory is concerned with the processes of group development in human relations training groups. Since human relations training groups represent a special kind of group situation, it is necessary to specify their major characteristics before the theory can be presented.

Characteristics of Human Relations Training Groups

The human relations training groups observed by Bennis and Shepard were participants in training programs at the National Training Laboratory for Group Development at Bethel, Maine. Participants in these programs are selected to represent a broad spectrum of backgrounds and personalities. Teachers, ministers, supervisors, administrators, social workers, sociologists, and psychologists are typical participants. Generally, they are strangers to each other at the time they report to the training laboratory. Small groups of six to eight persons are formed early in the training program. Each group is assigned a trainer who follows well-defined procedures in dealing with the group. Group meetings are held several times a week over a period of several weeks.

The major goal of this training in a group setting is to assist the trainee in developing an understanding of his own motivations for responding to others as he does and to help him predict more accurately the consequences of his actions. Secondary goals, related to the first, include (1) an improved understanding of situational and group forces operating during interpersonal behavior, (2) increased control over interpersonal communication, and (3) an increase in the range of social behavior available to the trainee. At the group level, the goal was said to be the establishment of valid communication (Bennis & Shepard, 1956). In general, valid communication means that each group member is able to communicate accurately and freely about his own feelings, motivations, intentions, and so on. Valid communication is recognized by the fact that each member's perceptions of his place in the group agree with the perceptions of other group members, that the announced goal of the group and the member's efforts are congruent, and that members are able to share many levels of communication.

To bring about this desirable state of affairs, the trainer encourages free expression in the group, but he refuses to assume the traditional role of the leader. In effect, he abdicates leadership and insists that the group members must decide for themselves how they want to function as a group, what the group goal(s) shall be, and so on. During the course of this training procedure, the trainer may be rejected and asked to leave the group. In such cases, he complies readily, since he regards this request as a sign of progress. Later, he may be asked to rejoin the group, but at this point his role of "nonleader" is accepted by the group. According to the theory guiding the training procedure (Shepard & Bennis, 1956), the trainer is now in a position to assist the group more effectively toward the goal of valid communication.

The theory of group development is concerned primarily with the processes of change within the group leading to the goal of valid communication. The following sections describe the obstacles to this goal and the stages of development that the theory holds to be necessary to overcome them.

Obstacles to Valid Communication

When strangers assemble as a group, there are areas of internal uncertainty regarding relations among individuals. These internal uncertainties interfere with the communication process, since each person hesitates to express his true feelings as long as he is unsure about the reactions of others. According to Bennis and Shepard, the two major areas of uncertainty are dependence and interdependence. In the area of dependence the uncertainty concerns authority relations. Questions concerning who has authority over whom, who will be the group leader, and who will be followers are predominant. The area of interdependence involves personal relations among group members. The uncertainties here are related to questions of affection and emotional closeness.

To achieve valid communication, therefore, the group must resolve these uncertainties. Decisions must be made about power and authority structures and about the affectional-emotional relations within the group. The theory proposed by Bennis and Shepard asserts that orientations toward authority are prior to, and partial determinants of, orientations toward members. That is, during the process of group development authority relations are established first, followed by the formation of interpersonal relations.

Phases of Group Development

In its development, then, the group moves from a preoccupation with authority relations to a preoccupation with personal relations. Thus, there are two major phases in group development: the authority phase and the personal phase. Within each major phase of development, Bennis and Shepard posited three subphases that characterize the developmental process.

AUTHORITY PHASE   The three subphases of the authority phase are characterized by (1) preoccupation with submission (dependence), (2) preoccupation with rebellion, and (3) resolution of the dependence problem. In subphase 1, the expectations of group members are that the trainer will assume a position of leadership and will establish rules governing group behavior. These expectations are not realized, since the trainer refuses to accept this role. Consequently, there is much aimless activity. Group members try to get the trainer to tell them what the goals of the group are, but when this fails, they are likely to engage in many superficial activities. There is much discussion about what the group should be doing, the inadequacy of the trainer, and so on.

After a time, group members become dissatisfied with this situation and counter-dependent expressions take over. This represents the beginning of subphase 2. Disenthrallment with the trainer proceeds rapidly, and he is often asked to leave the group. Typically, two opposed subgroups develop around the question of leadership and structure. One subgroup favors the establishment of a strong leadership structure with an elected leader who will perform the duties of the abdicated trainer. The other subgroup argues for a less-structured group atmosphere. They see no need for a strong leader or for rigid rules to govern group behavior. During this subphase, there is relatively great hostility and dissension among group members.

In subphase 3, either resolution occurs rapidly or there is a long period of vacillation and indecision. (According to Bennis and Shepard's statement, there appears to be low probability of an intermediate level of resolution.) In the case of rapid resolution, agreement is reached concerning authority relations and the group moves on to the personal phase. If there is vacillation and indecision, the group is fragile and breaks into conflicting subgroups. This may continue for an indefinite period of time. However, unless the group dissolves, resolution is eventually achieved and the group enters the personal phase.

PERSONAL PHASE   The group developmental process during the personal phase proceeds from a preoccupation with intermember identification, through a period of preoccupation with individual identity, to a resolution of the interdependence problem.

In subphase 4, the group is happy, relaxed, and highly cohesive. Harmony is the order of the day. All decisions must be unanimous and disagreements are regarded with disfavor. Group members are likely to spend hours planning parties and other social activities that include all members of the group. They are just one big happy family. As time passes, however, this extreme harmony becomes more and more illusory, and many persons begin to be concerned that they are being swallowed up by the group. They fear that they are losing their personal identity. At this point the group enters subphase 5.

As group development continues into subphase 5, the group typically separates into two subgroups. One of the subgroups is still enchanted with the notion of group harmony and wishes to continue close interpersonal relations. The members of the other subgroup become concerned that they are losing their identity as individuals and anxious lest their self-esteem be destroyed by overidentification with the group. This subgroup is therefore opposed to continued close relations and insists upon less group and more individual activity. There is much conflict between these opposing factions during this period.

If group development proceeds according to the usual pattern, the conflict betwen subgroups is eventually resolved. Subphase 6 involves the resolution of interpersonal problems. Each person verbalizes his own private conceptual scheme for understanding human behavior, including both his own behavior and that of others. When this stage of development has been reached, group evaluation leads to greater understanding and hence more-valid communication. The process of group development is complete.

Although the developmental sequence described above was said to be typical, Bennis and Shepard recognized that not all groups achieve the final goal. Some groups become "fixated" at an earlier phase of development and may remain at that stage indefinitely or until the group dissolves. It is also possible for the group to remain at one stage for an unusually long period of time and then continue its development through the usual pattern. In short, just about anything can happen.

Comments on the Theory

The theory of group development consists of a set of interrelated hypotheses concerning the *course* of group development. These hypotheses are internally consistent, are testable, and agree reasonably well with the data from which they were derived. However, it is important to keep in mind that the theory was based upon the observation of training groups and that Bennis and Shepard did not claim that it represents the development of groups in general. The theory is thus a description of group development under highly specialized conditions. Nevertheless, it has been viewed as applicable to a broader range of groups. For example, Harvey, Schroder, and Hunt (1961) relied heavily upon the Bennis and Shepard analysis in their formulation of a theory of conceptual systems. The present theory has also been incorporated into Schutz's (1958) theory of interpersonal relations, which is outlined in the next section of this chapter.

That the extension of the theory is hazardous is revealed by studies of task-oriented groups. For example, Bales and Strodtbeck (1951) examined the interaction patterns of task-oriented groups and found that the course of interaction proceeded from problems of *orientation* to problems of *evaluation* to problems of *control*. Although not directly comparable to the Bennis and Shepard phases, problems of control are clearly in the area of authority relations rather than in the area of personal relations. According to the present theory, problems of control should have been considered first instead of last. The results of studies on personality changes in groups reported by Mann and Mann (1959, 1960) also appear to be inconsistent with the developmental sequence proposed by Bennis and Shepard. Thus, the theory may be adequate to describe the development of human relations training groups, but it probably cannot be extended to other types of groups without revision.

Finally, it may be noted that the authors specified only the *sequence* of phases in group development. They did not indicate how long each phase may be expected to last, what variables influence the rate of development or determine whether the group will move from one phase to the following one, or what variables determine the form of resolution of the dependence and interdependence problems. The predictive value of the theory therefore appears to be quite limited.

FIRO: A THREE-DIMENSIONAL THEORY OF INTERPERSONAL BEHAVIOR

The FIRO in the name of this theory is an abbreviation for "Fundamental Interpersonal Relations Orientation." This phrase summarizes the basic concern of the theory of interpersonal relations proposed by Schutz (1955, 1958); that is, the theory attempts to explain interpersonal behavior in terms of the orientations of individuals to others. The basic idea of the theory is that every person orients himself toward others in characteristic ways and that these orientations are the primary determinants of interpersonal behavior.

The initial impetus for the theory was an interest in the construction of effective work groups. In attempting to deal with this problem, Schutz was influenced primarily by the writings of Bion (1949) and Redl (1942). It is not surprising, therefore, that the theory has a strong psychoanalytic flavor. The theory was developed over a number of years, becoming more formal with the passing of time but not necessarily more precise.

The theory may be summarized briefly as follows: The patterns of interaction of individuals can be explained largely in terms of three interpersonal needs: inclusion, control, and affection. These needs are developed during childhood through interaction with adults (usually parents). In adulthood, the need for inclusion depends upon the degree to which the child was integrated into the family group; the need for control depends upon whether the parent-child relation stressed guidance, freedom, or control; and the need for affection varies according to the degree to which the child was emotionally approved or rejected. To the degree that these needs are not satisfied during childhood, the individual feels, respectively, insignificant, incompetent, and unlovable. In order to cope with these feelings, he develops defense mechanisms which are manifested in characteristic behavior patterns that can be observed in interpersonal interaction. When two people enter into an interpersonal relation, their characteristic behavior patterns may be either compatible or incompatible. That is, their behaviors may be such that the two persons work well together, or they may be such that the two persons cannot work well together. Of course, dyads may vary in degree of compatibility anywhere between the two extremes. Thus, Schutz specified that interpersonal compatibility is a property of a relation between two or more persons; it refers to the degree to which they can work together harmoniously and mutually satisfy their interpersonal needs. In groups, the group atmosphere and the effectiveness of group action are determined in large part by the degree to which the behavior patterns of various group members are compatible or incompatible.

These ideas were formalized in four postulates and related theorems. The first postulate concerns interpersonal needs, the second postulate considers the role of early childhood experiences in the development of these needs, and postulates 3 and 4 deal with the consequences of interpersonal needs for group compatibility and group development. The postulates and related principles are stated in the following section. Later sections describe the implications of the postulates for the development of needs, the associated behavior relative to others, and the effects of this behavior on group processes.

The Postulates

Postulate 1. *The Postulate of Interpersonal Needs.*
(a) Every individual has three interpersonal needs: inclusion, control, and affection.
(b) Inclusion, control, and affection constitute a sufficient set of areas of interpersonal behavior for the prediction and explanation of interpersonal phenomena (Schutz, 1958, p. 13).
Postulate 2. *The Postulate of Relational Continuity.* An individual's expressed interpersonal behavior will be similar to the behavior he experienced in his earliest interpersonal relations, usually with his parents, in the following way:
Principle of Constancy: When he perceives his adult position in an interpersonal situation to be similar to his own position in his parent-child relation, his adult behavior positively covaries with his childhood behavior toward his parents (or significant others).
Principles of Identification: When he perceives his adult position in an interpersonal situation to be similar to his parent's position in his parent-child relation, his adult behavior positively covaries with the behavior of his parents (or significant others) toward him when he was a child (Schutz, 1958, p. 81).
Postulate 3. *The Postulate of Compatibility.* If the compatibility of one group, *h,* is greater than that of another group, *m,* then the goal achievement of *h* will exceed that of *m* (Schutz, 1958, p. 105).
Postulate 4. *The Postulate of Group Development.* The formation and development of two or more people into an interpersonal relation (that is, a group) always follows the same sequence.
Principle of Group Integration. For the time period starting with the group's beginning until three intervals before the group's termination, the predominant area of interaction begins with inclusion, is followed by control, and finally by affection. This cycle may recur.

Principle of Group Resolution. The last three intervals prior to a group's antici-pated termination follow the opposite sequence in that the predominant area of interpersonal behavior is first affection, then control, and finally inclusion (Schutz, 1958, p. 168).

The Three Interpersonal Needs

Postulate 1 states merely that there are three interpersonal needs and that the areas of behavior related to these needs are sufficient to predict and explain interpersonal phenomena. Schutz (1958) pointed to the close parallel between biological needs and interpersonal needs. Three aspects were noted:

1. Biological needs are requirements to establish satisfactory relation-ships between the organism and the physical environment, whereas inter-personal needs are requirements to establish satisfactory relationships be-tween the person and his human environment. Just as biological needs require an optimum amount of gratification, so do interpersonal needs. Either too much or too little gratification produces unsatisfactory consequences.

2. Physical illness and sometimes death result from inadequate satis-faction of biological needs; mental illness and sometimes death result from inadequate satisfaction of interpersonal needs.

3. The organism has modes of adapting to lack of complete satisfaction of both biological and interpersonal needs that are temporarily successful.

When the child is deprived of adequate satisfaction of needs (that is, either too little or too much gratification) during childhood, he develops characteristic patterns of adapting to this lack of complete gratification. The characteristic behavior patterns formed in childhood persist into adulthood and determine the characteristic adult pattern of orientation to others. Let us examine this process relative to inclusion, control, and affection.

Inclusion was defined by Schutz as related to belongingness in a group situation, and the associated need was defined as the need to establish and maintain a satisfactory interactive relation with others. Inclusion behavior may range from intensive interaction to complete withdrawal and detachment. Parent-child relations may be either positive (the child has much contact and interaction with the parents) or negative (the parent ignores the child and there is minimum contact). The child's anxiety is that he is not a worthwhile person and that perhaps he does not even exist. He needs to be taken into account by the group, and he is concerned that he will be left behind, ignored and unnoticed. If the child is adequately integrated into the family group, his anxieties will subside. If he experiences inadequate inclusion, he may try to cope with his anxiety by either withdrawing into a shell or by making intensive efforts to integrate himself into the group.

Control refers to the decision-making aspect of interpersonal relations. The interpersonal need for control was defined by Schutz as the need to establish and maintain satisfactory relations with others with respect to authority and power. The expression of control behavior may range from too much discipline and control to too much freedom and lack of discipline. Extremes of the parent-child relation range from constraining actions (parents maintain complete control over the child, make all his decisions) to licensing actions (parents allow the child to make all decisions, give no guidance). The child's anxiety is that he will not know what is expected of him in a power hierarchy, that he is incapable of handling problems and therefore is not a responsible person. As in other areas, ideal parent-child relations reduce the anxiety; however, either too much or too little control leads to defensive behaviors. He may attempt to cope with the anxiety by following rules closely and dominating others, or he might withdraw and refuse to control or be controlled by others.

Affection is based on the building of emotional ties with others; hence Schutz defined the associated need as the need to be liked and loved. The expression of affection may be either positive (ranging from attraction to love) or negative (ranging from mild disapproval to hate and revulsion). Consequently, parent-child relations may involve either positive affection (characterized by warmth, approval, love, etc.) or negative affection (characterized by coldness, reserve, rejection, etc.). The anxiety associated with this relation is that the individual will be disliked and rejected. If the child has adequate emotional acceptance, he may cope with the anxiety by a variety of behaviors such as withdrawal (that is, avoidance of close interpersonal relationships), superficially friendly behavior, overly friendly or deferent behavior, or overly possessive behavior.

Types of Interpersonal Behavior

The parent-child relations within each interpersonal need area can involve either an ideal amount, too much, or too little need satisfaction. Schutz described three types of interpersonal behavior within each area, corresponding to the degree of need satisfaction experienced in the parent-child relation. He also described pathological behavior within each area.

TYPES OF INCLUSION BEHAVIOR   If the child fails to experience an adequate amount of inclusion satisfaction (either insufficient integration into the family or too much inclusion in family affairs), he is prone to either *undersocial* or *oversocial* behavior in interpersonal relations.[1] The undersocial type tends toward introversion and withdrawal. He avoids associating with others, refuses to join groups, and generally maintains distance between himself and others. This behavior may take the form of nonparticipation and noninvolvement, or it may be expressed more subtly by being late for meetings, missing meetings altogether, falling asleep during discussions, and so on. Schutz asserted that the deepest anxiety of the undersocial type is that he is a worth-

[1] Schutz originally related too much inclusion, control, and affection on the part of parents to oversocial, autocratic, and overpersonal behavior, respectively; too little inclusion, control, and affection to undersocial, abdicrat, and underpersonal behavior, respectively (Schutz, 1958, p. 89, Table 5–1). Later (Schutz, 1967, and in personal communication), he asserted that either type of behavior could result from either too much or too little gratification of the associated need during childhood. We have followed his later formulation in this respect.

less person. Unconsciously, he believes that no one will find him worthy of attention. By avoiding association with others, he can avoid verification of this belief.

The oversocial type tends to be an extrovert. He constantly seeks out others and wants them to reciprocate. Direct expression takes the form of intensive exhibitionistic behavior: he is loud, demands attention, forces himself upon the group, and so on. On the other hand, he may try to inject himself into the group by subtle means, such as making an excessive show of skills and knowledge, name dropping, or asking startling questions. According to Schutz's analysis, the interpersonal dynamics are the same as those of the undersocial, but the expression is just the opposite.

Adequate integration into the family group during childhood leads to the ideal type, the *social*. The social type has no problems relative to interaction. He can be happy alone or with people; he can be either a high or low participator; and he can commit himself to a group or not, depending upon the situation. Unconsciously, he feels that he is a worthy person and that others are interested in him and will include him in their activities.

TYPES OF CONTROL BEHAVIOR   Control behavior refers to the decision-making process between people. Three characteristic types of control behavior were labeled "the abdicrat," the "autocrat," and "the democrat" (Schutz, 1958). The abdicrat tends to be submissive and abdicates power and responsibility in dealing with others. He prefers a subordinate role, wants others to assume responsibility, and never makes a decision that he can avoid making. Unconsciously, he feels that he is not capable of making responsible decisions and that others are aware of this deficiency. By refusing to make decisions, he can at least conceal the extent of his incapacity.

The autocrat tends to dominate others. He prefers a power hierarchy with himself in the top position. He wants to make all decisions, not only for himself but for everyone else as well. Schutz indicated that the underlying dynamics are the same as for the abdicrat; however, the abdicrat's anxiety leads to persistent attempts to prove that he is capable and responsible.

The democrat is, of course, the ideal. He has successfully resolved problems associated with interpersonal relations in the control area; hence power and control are not at issue. He is comfortable in either a superior or subordinate position. He can give orders or take orders, depending upon the demands of the situation. Unconsciously, he believes that he is capable of making responsible decisions and feels no need to prove this to others.

Control pathology develops when the individual refuses to accept control of any kind. Schutz proposed that this describes the typical psychopath who refuses to respect the rights of others or to obey social norms. The obsessive obedience to norms may also reflect control pathology.

TYPES OF AFFECTION BEHAVIOR   Affection refers to close emotional feelings between two people (Schutz, 1967). Again, three characteristic types of behavior may result from childhood experiences. Inadequate parent-child relations in the affection area can result in either *underpersonal* or *over-*

personal behavior, whereas the ideal parent-child relation produces *personal* behavior. The underpersonal type tends to avoid close personal relations. He is superficially friendly but maintains emotional distance and prefers that others do the same. The expression of this behavior may be either active rejection and avoidance of others or, more subtly, the appearance of being friendly to everyone while remaining distant. Schutz asserted that the basis for this behavior is a deep anxiety about being loved; the person believes that he is unlovable and that others will discover this fact if he allows them to get close to him.

The overpersonal type desires very close emotional relations and attempts to create such relationships. He may approach this goal directly by being extremely personal and intimate or subtly by "devouring friends and trying to punish them for establishing other friendships." According to Schutz, this behavior is based on the same underlying dynamics as underpersonal behavior. Both types are motivated by a strong need for affection and both involve strong anxiety about being loved and unlovable.

For the person who has successfully resolved problems associated with affection relations with others in childhood, close emotional relations with others is not a problem. His characteristic type of expression is *personal* behavior. He can function adequately and comfortably in either close or distant emotional relationships. He has no anxieties about being loved and unconsciously believes that he is a lovable person.

Schutz suggested that neuroses are pathological behaviors attributable to the need for affection.

RELATIONAL CONTINUITY   The postulate of relational continuity asserts that the behaviors that develop in childhood persist in adulthood in specified ways. In the preceding section we have described the characteristic ways that adults are expected to behave as a consequence of their childhood experiences. The principles of constancy and of identification attempt to specify when the adult will behave as he did as a child and when he will behave as his parents did toward him. Generally, the postulate states that an individual will behave as he did when he was a child when he perceives himself to be in a position similar to his childhood position. On the other hand, when he feels that he is in a position similar to his parents' role, he will behave as his parents did toward him. Unfortunately, Schutz did not indicate what circumstances lead to the perception of one's own position as "childlike" or as "parentlike." Such specification is, of course, necessary if one is to predict from parent-child relations to adult behavior.[2]

The postulate of relational continuity is essentially the same as the fundamental assumption of psychoanalytic theory that present perceptions and behaviors are traceable to childhood experiences. Schutz stated that he was interested in specifying that the principle held for interpersonal behavior in particular; that the most common reaction to childhood interpersonal rela-

---

[2] This has been dealt with more extensively by Schutz in a forthcoming book, *Leaders of Schools* (personal communication, 1968).

tions is to continue the same pattern in adulthood; and that the particular areas in which such continuities occur are inclusion, control, and affection. Schutz (1958) cited a considerable amount of evidence, both from his own studies and from those by others, to support the postulate of relational continuity.

Compatibility

Postulate 3 states that compatible groups will be more effective in achieving group goals than incompatible groups. "Compatibility," as used by Schutz, refers to a relation between two or more persons. Two persons were said to be compatible if they could work together in harmony. Thus, his definition of compatibility corresponds with the usual dictionary definition of the term.

However, in order to test the implications of postulate 3, it was necessary to identify types of compatibility and to specify ways of measuring them. The identification of compatibility types was based upon expressed behavior and behavior wanted from others in each of the three areas. These elements were measured by a set of six Guttman scales (FIRO-B) designed to reveal expressed and wanted behavior in each of the three interpersonal need areas. Compatibility scores reflecting each type of compatibility were then computed by means of formulas developed for this purpose.

TYPES OF COMPATIBILITY   Schutz (1958) identified three types of compatibility in each of the three need areas: interchange compatibility, originator compatibility, and reciprocal compatibility. *Interchange compatibility* refers to the mutual expression of affection, control, or inclusion. Maximum interchange compatibility between two persons occurs when the amount of expressed and wanted behavior by one person is the same as that of the other person; the two persons are incompatible to the extent that they differ with respect to amount of expressed and wanted behavior in the area in question.

Originator compatibility is based on the originate-receive dimension of interaction. Originator compatibility occurs in the affection area when those who wish to express affection interact with those who want to receive affection. In the control area, originator compatibility exists when those who wish to dominate others interact with those who wish to be controlled. Originator compatibility in the inclusion area occurs when those who initiate group activities interact with persons who desire to be included in these activities. Incompatibility arises to the extent that group composition deviates from the ideal situation in each area.

Reciprocal compatibility refers to the degree to which each person's expression of inclusion, control, or affection meets the desires of others with respect to each need area. For example, two persons are compatible in the affection area if the amount of affection expressed by each person is consistent with the amount of affection wanted by the other. The greater the discrepancy between the behavior expressed by one person and the amount wanted by the other, the more incompatible the dyad will be.

Schutz further suggested that overall originator, interchange, and reciprocal compatibilities could be computed by summing across areas. Similarly, overall compatibility within each need area might be determined by summing across types of compatibility. Finally, a total compatibility score might be obtained by summing across both need areas and types of compatibility. Thus, using the FIRO-B scales and the compatibility formulas, Schutz derived sixteen compatibility indices.

COMPATIBILITY THEOREMS   Schutz proposed nine theorems relative to the postulate of compatibility. He presented evidence for three of the theorems (1, 2, and 9) and partial support for three others (3, 7, and 8). The theorems may be summarized as follows. (Some of the theorems were formulated with respect to specific experimental situations; we have restated these so that they are understandable without reference to the particular study.)

1.   If two dyads differ in compatibility, the members of the more-compatible dyad are more likely to prefer each other for continued personal contact.

2.   If two groups differ in compatibility, the productivity goal achievement of the more-compatible group will exceed that of the less-compatible one.

3.   If two groups differ in compatibility, the more-compatible group will be more cohesive than the less-compatible one.

4.   If a group consists of two or more incompatible subgroups, each member should prefer to work with a member of his own subgroup more than with any member of an antagonistic subgroup or with a neutral member.

5.   In incompatible groups, members of overpersonal subgroups will tend to like each other more than members of underpersonal subgroups will.

6.   In incompatible groups, overpersonal subgroup members will tend to overestimate the competence of the person they like best, whereas underpersonal subgroup members will not have this tendency.

7.   In compatible groups, persons predicted to be focal persons (key members) and those predicted to be main supporting members should rank each other high on the relation "work well with."

8.   Focal persons (key members) will be chosen as leaders by group members in all groups.

9.   The effect of compatibility on productivity varies as a function of the degree of interchange in the three need areas required by the task.

Group Development

Postulate 4 asserts that every interpersonal relation follows the same course of development and resolution, namely, that development begins with a concern for inclusion needs, followed by a concern with control and finally by a concern for affection. Resolution follows the reverse order. In formulating this aspect of the theory, Schutz relied heavily upon the Bennis and Shepard (1956) theory of group development described in the preceding section of this chapter. It may be recalled that their theory of group development was based in part on an earlier formulation by Schutz. Thus, the two analyses of group development have much in common. The main difference between them appears to be the addition of the inclusion phase by Schutz.

As soon as a group is formed, the inclusion phase begins. When people are confronted with one another, they are concerned about being in or out of the group. Each person is deciding whether he should become a member of the group. This decision involves questions about one's place in the group, the importance of the group, one's personal identity, how much he shall commit himself to the group, and so on. This phase of group development is often characterized by much discussion of issues of little interest to anyone. According to Schutz, such discussions are inevitable and serve the important function of working through problems related to inclusion needs.

After problems of inclusion have been sufficiently resolved, control problems become the center of concern. At this point, the issue of decision making arises. This involves a variety of problems concerning the distribution of responsibility, power, and control. Each person in the group is attempting to structure the situation so that he has just the right amount of responsibility and influence in the group. This phase corresponds roughly to the Bennis and Shepard authority phase.

Assuming that the control problems are resolved successfully, the group moves to the affection phase. At this point, the group has been formed, and problems of responsibility and power distribution have been worked out; all that remains is the problem of emotional integration. At this stage of development expressions of hostility, anger, and the like are common. Each member is attempting to establish for himself the most comfortable position possible with regard to affectional interchange.

The three phases are not discrete; all types of behavior occur in all phases. However, the phases represent periods in the group's history in which particular problem areas are emphasized. The various phases may also be repeated so that a given group may go through the inclusion, control, affection sequence several times. When the group approaches dissolution, the concern is first with affection, followed by control and inclusion (or perhaps one should say exclusion!).

Schutz used the analysis of group development to derive certain theorems concerning compatibility at various stages in the life history of the group. In general, he proposed that the members of a given group would be most compatible when the group is in the stage corresponding to greatest overall compatibility; that is, if the group is high on inclusion compatibility and low on control and affection compatibility, the members will be most compatible during the inclusion phase; if they are high on control compatibility and low on the other two, they will be most compatible in the control phase; and so on. Evidence for this was largely inferential.

Comments and Evaluation

The theory proposed by Schutz is an interesting set of hypotheses concerning interpersonal behavior. The theory is internally consistent, its predictions are amenable to test, and it agrees reasonably well with available evidence concerning interpersonal behavior.

The theory actually concerns three somewhat different aspects of interpersonal behavior: (1) the existence of three needs and the development of patterns of interpersonal behavior relative to these needs (postulates 1 and 2), (2) the consequences of these patterns of behavior for group compatibility and its effects on group effectiveness (postulate 3), and (3) the relation of the three interpersonal needs to group development and resolution (postulate 4). The portion dealing with the existence of needs and related behavior patterns reveals the psychoanalytic orientation most clearly, but, interestingly enough, this part of the theory is not really necessary for predicting behavior in groups. The particular behavior pattern that the individual enacts in interpersonal situations is the critical factor; why he behaves this way is not important for the prediction of group processes, although it may be of interest in its own right. The point here is that the patterns of behavior could have been determined without reference to past experience, and the predictions about adult behavior would be unchanged. The first part of the theory is therefore useful for "explaining" why the person behaves as he does, but it cannot be readily used as a predictor of interpersonal behavior. Perhaps the greater specification of variables determining the adult's perception of the position in which he finds himself will improve this aspect of the theory (see footnote 2, page 260).

Schutz relied upon two kinds of evidence to support his theory: the writings of other theorists and experimental data. The first kind of evidence was used to establish the "plausibility" of the postulates. Observational studies of parent-child relations (Champney, 1941; Baldwin, Kallhorn, & Breese, 1945; Sewell, Mussen, & Harris, 1955) and theoretical statements by psychoanalysts (Horney, 1945; Fromm, 1947; Freud, 1950) were cited as evidence of the plausibility of postulates 1 and 2. Some of his own empirical studies were also reported in partial support of postulate 2. Postulate 3 was evaluated primarily in terms of experimental data from his own studies (Schutz, 1955, 1958). In the first study, he was able to demonstrate that compatible groups are more effective on certain kinds of tasks than incompatible groups, but as we noted above, only three of nine theorems were unequivocally supported by later investigations. The final postulate concerning group development and resolution was supported by the data from Bennis and Shepard (1956), which was based upon observations of groups undergoing sensitivity training, as indicated earlier in this chapter.

Since the original formulation of the theory, numerous studies have been reported that are in general agreement with the theory. We shall cite two in order to indicate the kind of evidence available. Schutz (1961) reported a study in which five 14-person groups were formed on the basis of their responses to questionnaires designed to measure behavior relative to the three interpersonal needs (FIRO-B questionnaire). After six meetings, three of the five groups were able to identify their own group descriptions significantly better than chance, one was partially accurate, and one failed to do better than chance. Behavioral differences were also in agreement with theoretical expectations. Yalom and Rand (1966) examined the relationship between compatibility and cohesiveness in outpatient therapy groups. They found that high-compatibility groups, as measured by the FIRO-B questionnaire, were significantly more cohesive and were better satisfied than low-cohesive groups. These findings are in good agreement with the theory. In general, then, the experimental evidence for the theory is supportive.

Finally, it should be noted that Schutz has more recently applied the theory to problems of "expanding human awareness" (Schutz, 1967). He pointed out that the problems of group development occur in everyday life and that failure to resolve problems associated with the three interpersonal needs often leads to unhappiness and dissatisfaction in day-to-day interpersonal relations. In an interesting application of the theory, he shows how the individual who may have difficulty in the three interpersonal need areas can develop techniques for dealing with these more adequately. However, our main concern in this book is with the understanding of social behavior; therefore, we will not deal extensively with this use of the theory. Application is one result of science, and in this respect Schutz's work is exemplary.

A PSYCHOANALYTIC THEORY OF SOCIAL ATTITUDES

Sarnoff (1960) proposed a theory of attitudes based upon the psychoanalytic conceptions of ego-defensive mechanisms. Basically, he maintained that many attitudes are held to serve the function of defending the ego against internal and external threats. He posited a relationship between the motives underlying and impelling the individual's actions and that individual's expressed attitudes. Sarnoff began his discussion of his theory by defining the four basic concepts in the theoretical framework, followed by a consideration of the discrepancies and congruities between attitudes and motives, as well as the defensive maneuvers utilized to resolve various forms of motive-attitude discrepancy.

Basic Concepts

Sarnoff depicted the constructs of *motive, conflict, ego defense,* and *attitude* as the anchor points of his theory of social attitudes. He designated his theoretical task as the integration of these concepts through the use of a psychoanalytic framework.

MOTIVE   A motive was defined as *"an internally operative, tension-producing stimulus which provokes the individual to act in such a way as to reduce the tension generated by it and which is capable of being consciously experienced"* (Sarnoff, 1960, p. 252). Sarnoff expanded upon three elements of this definition for purposes of clarity. First, the proposition that a motive is an internally operative and tension-producing stimulus indicates that although a stimulus external to the organism may induce a motive, this motive functions largely within the organism. Its primary function is to induce an energy state in the organism which is referred to as tension. Second, accepting the proposition that a motive produces internal tension and adding to it the assumption that internal tension is uncomfortable for the individual, Sarnoff concluded that individuals will act to reduce the discomforts which result from internal tension. He added that in evaluating tension-reducing actions, account must be taken of the appropriateness of specific responses to the reduction of specific tensions. Third, Sarnoff assumed that tension-inducing motives, while sometimes beyond the consciousness of the individual, also may be consciously experienced. Following this, the individual may reduce tension through covert or overt responding.

CONFLICT   *"Whenever two or more motives are activated at the same time, their coalescence produces a state of conflict"* (Sarnoff, 1960, p. 253). Here, Sarnoff was assuming that individuals can only act to reduce the tension of one motive at a time. Thus, if two motives arouse tensions in the individual and each of the motives requires a specific and different tension-reducing activity, conflict will result. If the conflict that is consequent upon the arousal of two motives requiring differential tension-reducing activities is not resolved, the state of conflict will become chronic and the individual might become the passive victim of his own opposing motives. This will lead to the enactment of inadequate tension-reducing activities for each motive, and as a result, tension will chronically remain in the motive system of the individual. Sarnoff proposed that to avoid conflict, one is obliged (1) to establish the priority of his responses to the motives involved in the conflict and (2) to postpone his responses to all other motives while he is responding to a single motive within the conflicting hierarchy.

A hierarchy of conflicting motives is rather easily established in the case where the tensions aroused by different motives within the hierarchy are of discrepant intensities. Here, of course, the tension-reducing responses corresponding to the most-intense motives will have the highest priority of occurrence. However, Sarnoff noted that simultaneously acting motives are usually relatively equal in the tension they arouse. Nevertheless, if the individual is to reduce effectively the tensions created by any of the motives, he must respond to one at a time. Thus, Sarnoff made the somewhat circular implication that since the establishment of a hierarchy of motives is a necessary precedent to adequate reduction of the tension aroused by those motives, the individual functionally (and arbitrarily) establishes a hierarchy.

While the individual is making appropriate tension-reducing responses corresponding to a single motive, he must postpone making responses to reduce the tensions produced by motives lower on the established hierarchy. He may do this in three ways: (1) He may utilize ego defenses in the situation in which a postponed motive arouses intolerable fear. Thus, he may deny the existence of the motive, repress its importance and intensity, project it on to someone else, and so forth. In the situation in which the deferred motive is consciously acceptable, (2) he may voluntarily *inhibit* the responses necessary to reduce the tension aroused by that motive, or (3) he may temporarily *suppress* the perception of that motive. With the process of suppression, the individual is aware of his attempts to focus his attention on the reduction of tension from a single motive. Both suppression and inhibition lead to the orderly reduction of tensions produced by conflicting motives in a hierarchy.

EGO DEFENSE   The configuration of perceptual and motor skills which helps the individual to *"maximize the reduction of the tension of his motives within the scope of the constraints of his environment"* (Sarnoff, 1960, p. 255) is referred to as the ego. Thus, the perceptual function of the ego involves the accurate perception of both the individual's own motives and the social prescriptions for acceptable tension-reduction maneuvers. Threatening events exert a strain on the perceptual functioning of the ego and induce the motive of fear. When the level of induced fear is intolerable and the individual cannot separate himself from the feared object, he defends his ego. That is, he attempts to remove from consciousness both the fear motive and other motives associated with it in order to maintain the perceptual functioning of the ego. It is these protective responses which are referred to as *ego defenses.*

Individuals not only differ in the strength of their egos to withstand threatening stimuli, but also differ in the kinds of ego defensive responses they use when overwhelmed by fear. Thus, there are several ego defenses, and some are more characteristic of certain individuals than others. Although all ego defenses function to obliterate consciously unacceptable motives, two of them, *denial* and *identification with the aggressor,* perform this function by distorting the perception of objects in the *external* environment. Thus, Sarnoff noted that one way to avoid the threatening aspects of the environment is to fail to acknowledge their presence. These ego-defensive processes differ from *suppression* in that the individual is not aware of his expenditure of effort to obliterate the perception of external motive-producing stimuli. Ego defenses function on an unconscious level, whereas suppression involves the conscious expenditure of energy to avoid perceiving certain stimuli.

Some ego defenses function to eliminate the perception of the *internal* stimulus of the threatening motive. Sarnoff, following Freud, characterized *repression* and *projection* as serving this function. As noted in the previous chapter, repression tends to eliminate threatening internal impulses (motives) from the individual's conscious perception. When the individual cannot fully remove an internal motive from conscious perception through repression, he might then acknowledge the existence of that motive, but instead of attributing it to himself, he *projects* it on to others.

For an ego-defense to perform its function fully, it must result in an *overt* response to tension which cannot be logically related to the unacceptable motive. Overt responses of this type are referred to by Sarnoff as *symptoms.* Thus, although an ego defense eliminates the perception of threatening motives and their objects, symptomatic behavior reduces the tension generated by an unacceptable motive. A symptom was therefore defined as "an overt, tension-reducing response whose relationship to an unconscious motive is not perceived by the individual" (Sarnoff, 1960, p. 260). Attitudes, as overt behavioral expressions, are often symptomatic of more-basic underlying motives that are unacceptable to the individual. As we shall see in the subsequent discussion, this view of attitudes is the crux of Sarnoff's theory.

ATTITUDE   Like several other social psychologists, Sarnoff defined an attitude as a disposition to react favorably or unfavorably to a class of objects. He reasoned that since attitudes are inferred from overt responses and overt responses are made in order to reduce motive-generated tensions, then attitudes are the emergent product of the tension-reducing responses that are made to a class of objects. In line with this reasoning, Sarnoff stated that *"an individual's attitude toward a class of objects is determined by the particular role those objects have come to play in facilitating responses which reduce the tension of particular motives and which resolve particular conflicts among motives"* (Sarnoff, 1960, p. 261). Additionally, it is noted that since the tension generated by a motive may be reduced by several different overt responses (ego-defensively based or not), then the divergent attitudes held by different people toward the same class of objects may simply reflect the different overt responses used by those people to reduce motive-generated tension. On the other hand, identical attitudes held by several people toward the same class of objects may mediate the reduction of a different motive for each person. Thus, not every attitude can be considered as a reliable indicator of its underlying motive.

Sarnoff asserted that any investigator probing the motivational bases of attitudes must make educated guesses about the relationships among a specific attitude, a specific motive, and a specific behavior. He presented a four-step process for arriving at such educated guesses:

1.   The investigator must carefully examine the behavior from which the attitude is inferred.

2.   He must postulate all the motives which might possibly be reduced by the observed behavior.

3.   He must make an independent assessment of the individual's customary tension-reduction strategies with several attitudinal objects.

4.   If the assessment suggests that the individual is usually aware of his motive and the tension-reducing function of his response, then the attitude can be said to be truly reflected by the response. If the individual is neither customarily aware of his motive nor of his attempts at tension reduction, then the attitude should be regarded as an ego-defensively mediated symptom.

Thus, the attitudes arising from consciously acceptable motives are conceptualized differently than attitudes arising from consciously unacceptable motives.

Attitude-Motive Congruency

Sarnoff injected the concept of congruence into his psychoanalytic theory of attitudes. An attitude may be consonant with or discrepant from the motive whose tension it serves to reduce. An attitude congruent with its underlying motive is an anticipatory response that precedes the overt activities utilized to reduce the tensions generated by a consciously acceptable motive. Thus, under conditions of attitude-motive congruency, the individual is both aware of his motive and aware of the tension-reducing nature of his activities.

Where motives and attitudes are discrepant, the individual is neither aware of the underlying motive, nor is he aware of the goals of his overt response. In the latter case, the attitude reflects the functioning of covert ego-defensive responses which, although protecting the individual from the perception of an anxiety-producing motive, still preclude the maximal reduction of tension.

ATTITUDES AND CONSCIOUSLY ACCEPTABLE MOTIVES   Sarnoff noted five factors which prevail when motives are consciously acceptable to the individual:

1.   The overt responses to the motive will maximally reduce the tension generated by it.

2.   These overt responses will directly reflect the underlying motive.

3.   The responses will persist for a length of time which is proportional to the motive's intensity.

4.   The individual will be aware both of his motives and of the relationship between his motives and the overt responses.

5.   The individual's awareness of his motives will *not* arouse anxiety or result in ego-defensive responses.

When these factors prevail, the individual will orient himself toward objects in the environment so as to maximally reduce motive-produced tension. Attitudes, then, since they are response dispositions to environmental objects, should be determined by the role that certain objects play in reducing motive-produced tensions. Thus, Sarnoff proposed that in the case of consciously acceptable motives the individual will have positive attitudes toward objects that facilitate his tension-reducing responses and negative attitudes toward objects that hinder his tension-reducing responses. He offered the example of an individual who has a strong achievement motive which he recognizes. First of all, this individual should have a positive attitude toward work, since it is a situation necessary for achievement. Secondly, he should have a positive attitude toward objects such as prizes, medals, and the like, which by their very nature facilitate the reduction of tension generated by the achievement motive. And last, he should have a negative attitude toward objects such as low pay, which indicate failure to achieve and therefore hinder the reduction of tension generated by the achievement motive.

Several motives that are consciously acceptable to the individual may still conflict with one another. As we have noted, motive conflict resulting from consciously acceptable motives necessitates the inhibition or suppression of some of the motives so that the tension produced by one motive may be optimally reduced before overt tension-reducing responses are made to other motives. These "postponing responses" (inhibition and suppression) may be facilitated by the formation of attitudes. Thus, Sarnoff stated that "the disposition to respond favorably or unfavorably to an object may be determined by the extent to which a given disposition is required if the individual is to avoid making an overt, tension-reducing response to the inhibited motive" (Sarnoff, 1960, p. 265). For example, if an individual is driven by a prepotent motive of getting ahead on his job, he may have to respond favorably to objects that his boss favors. If in order to get ahead he must wine and dine an important client who engenders in him an aggressive motive, then assuming a publicly favorable disposition (attitude) toward that client will both reduce the tension generated by his prepotent motive and inhibit the tension-reducing responses (for example, punching the client in the nose) generated by his conflicting aggressive motive.

ATTITUDES AND CONSCIOUSLY UNACCEPTABLE MOTIVES   Motives that are consciously unacceptable to the individual result in attitudes that facilitate both covert ego-defensive responses and overt symptomatic responses. As noted earlier, the ego-defensive responses preclude the individual from becoming aware of his unacceptable motives, and the symptomatic responses allow him to reduce the tension produced by unacceptable motives.

In the case of attitudes which stem from unacceptable motives, the relationship between the attitude and the underlying motive cannot be articulated simply. Thus, an individual's "unacceptable motive" cannot be predicted solely on the basis of his expressed attitude. The prediction of the underlying motive involves the process of inference. That is, the predictor must infer what combination of motive and ego defense could most likely have led to the observed overt response and its accompanying attitude. Following upon this inference, he must then test the proposed relationship between the motive-ego defense combination and the attitude. Sarnoff cited *The Authoritarian Personality* (Adorno, Frenkel-Brunswik, Levinson, & Sanford, 1950) as an example of a correlational approach to testing the relationship between motive, ego defense, and attitude.

Sarnoff attempted to demonstrate the manner in which logical inferences might be made concerning the relationship between attitudes and ego defenses. His basic proposition appears to be that the form an attitude takes may facilitate a specific ego-defense. He cited examples including five defenses. The first two of these defenses, denial and identification with the aggressor, involve the perceptual obliteration of *external* stimuli, and the last three, repression, projection, and reaction formation, deal with the perceptual obliteration of *internal* stimuli. In both cases, all defenses were presumed to function *unconsciously*.

ATTITUDES FACILITATING DENIAL   The most common manifestation of denial is the individual's unwillingness to admit the degree of threat that an external object or situation holds for him. Denial may be inferred as occurring when the overt attitude of the individual is either favorable or neutral toward an object which should logically threaten him. Sarnoff cited the example of the rather apathetic attitude of some German Jews toward Nazi persecution that was noted by Allport, Bruner, and Jandorf (1953). In this case, the individual would be operating on the basis of a fear motive, which leads to a denial of the extreme threat of the Nazis and which is reflected in the expressed attitude, "they will not persecute me." Many other examples of how attitudes facilitate denial might be cited.

ATTITUDES FACILITATING IDENTIFICATION WITH THE AGGRESSOR
Identification with the aggressor is characterized by the individual's assumption of the beliefs, attitudes, and behaviors of a person or group that constitutes an intolerable threat to him. In the process, he no longer sees the person or group as a foe, but rather as similar to him. The inference that the ego defense of identification with the aggressor is mediating an underlying fear motive might quite logically be drawn from externally expressed attitudes. For example, some Jews in Nazi Germany might have displayed both their intolerable level of fear and identification with the aggressor through their espousal of anti-Semitic attitudes. Freud characterized the Oedipal conflict resolution process as the male child's identification with the aggressor (the father) through the assumption of his attitudes, norms, and behaviors. In the latter case, the underlying unacceptable motive being defended against was said to be fear of castration.

ATTITUDES FACILITATING REPRESSION   As noted in the previous chapter, Freud considered repression to be the most basic defense against intrapersonal threats. Repression may be inferred in the case of motives when the individual cannot recall a motive of which he had previously been aware. Sarnoff noted that, because of the very internalized nature of repression, it would be difficult to infer a functional relationship between a repressed motive and an attitude. He suggested that hypnosis might be one means of experimentally determining repression-facilitating objects. Theoretically, when repression is being used to defend the ego against unacceptable motives, the individual should hold positive attitudes toward objects that facilitate this defense. Very often the mechanism of repression is not wholly effective at maintaining an unacceptable motive at an unconscious level. When this is the case, several second-line ego-defenses, such as projection and reaction formation, must be invoked.

ATTITUDES FACILITATING PROJECTION   Projection is the means of ego-defense whereby the individual projects his own unacceptable motives on to another. Sarnoff depicted projection as the predominant ego-defense mediating prejudicial, antiminority group attitudes. Projection always presupposes that repression of a given motive has occurred. With regard to antiminority prejudices, Sarnoff proposed that to ensure that given motives remain unconscious to the individual, he will often attribute them to out-group members. Thus, if the individual has strongly repressed sexual motives, he might facilitate the repression of these motives by attributing sexual promiscuity to an ethnic or racial out-group. Therefore, a negative attitude toward a given minority group might facilitate the attribution of one's own undesirable traits to that minority group. Projection has been experimentally shown to be the ego-defensive strategy which renders antiminority attitudes most resistant to change (Katz, McClintock, & Sarnoff, 1957).

ATTITUDES FACILITATING REACTION FORMATION   Reaction formation involves the individual's performing of overt responses that are directly contrary to his underlying motives. Thus, he makes responses counter to the responses necessary to reduce the tension from a given motive. A male with an intense fear of sexual contact might utilize reaction formation to keep this fear from awareness and hence behave like a Don Juan. Similarly, an individual with strong aggressive motives might exhibit behavior or attitudes indicating tolerance, patience, and timidity.

The expression of attitudes counter to one's motives is a manifestation of reaction formation in the service of the ego. In making inferences about the relationship between attitudes and reaction formation, the observer must be cautious to distinguish between attitudes that reflect motives and those that reflect countermotives. This distinction might be a difficult one because, for example, affectionate attitudes based upon aggressive motives may appear quite similar to affectionate attitudes based upon affectionate motives. One basis for making a distinction is the level of manifest anxiety induced in the individual when tension from the unacceptable motive is aroused. Thus, the individual with unacceptable aggressive motives should become very anxious when confronted with aggression-inducing stimuli. This high level of anxiety is precisely the factor that eventually leads to reaction formation.

Attitudes Facilitating Overt Symptomatic Responses

As we have noted, Sarnoff proposed that attitudes can facilitate both ego-defensive processes and symptomatic responses that tend to be disguised tension-reduction responses for an underlying unacceptable motive. According to Sarnoff, symptomatic responses, to be effective, must allow the individual to reduce the tensions from a repressed motive, while remaining unaware of that motive. The mechanism that aids the individual in accomplishing this dual objective is the ego-defense of *rationalization*. Rationalization "permits the individual to misinterpret the motivational aim of those perceived aspects of his behavior which reduce the tension of a consciously unacceptable motive" (Sarnoff, 1960, p. 277). Rationalization may either maximally or partially reduce the tension from an unacceptable motive. It can be inferred when the individual views his behavior as indicative of his consciously acceptable motives, although the behavior is actually promoting the reduction of tension from unacceptable motives.

With maximally tension-reducing behaviors, the individual actually enacts the behavior consonant with the underlying repressed motive, but he interprets it in the light of consciously acceptable motives. For example, many wars have been waged in the name of Christian love and brotherhood. In this case, man's unacceptable aggressive motives receive full vent through the medium of war, but he interprets his aggressive activities as stemming from the love of God, the defense of God, the love or defense of humanity, and so forth. Attitudes can facilitate the symptomatic behavior by providing a basis for the rationalization of that behavior. Therefore, some wars are waged under the banner of a highly positive attitude toward God, man, communism, democracy, etc.

Partially tension-reducing symptomatic responses do not directly mirror the underlying unacceptable motives. Thus, a guilt motive about masturbation might be expressed through compulsive hand washing. In this case, the hand washing indirectly and partially reduces the guilt of the masturbatory motive. The facilitating attitude here might be positive attitudes toward cleanliness and sanitation and negative attitudes toward germs and dirt. Again, it is these attitudes that provide a rational basis for the tension-reducing symptomatic behavior.

Comment and Evaluation

Sarnoff has rendered a rather interesting and well-thought-out adaptation of some elements of psychoanalytic theory to the phenomena of social attitudes. As with many translations, be they from one language to another or from one universe of thought to another, the finished product differs somewhat from the original. Sarnoff (1966) noted that psychoanalytic theory may be a difficult model to apply to attitudinal processes because of its concentration on the involuntary and unconscious components of an individual's behavior. Indeed, much of attitude formation and change occurs quite within the conscious perception and with the conscious sanction of the individual.

Insofar as attitudes do reflect underlying motives, Sarnoff has articulated an effective, internally consistent model for inferring this relationship. Nevertheless, because of the very nature of analytic theory, alternative and more behaviorally linked interpretations of the functions of social attitudes can better account for the formation and change of attitudes. This is not to say that psychoanalytic theory cannot explain attitude phenomena, but rather that the explanation rendered might be less parsimonious and less testable than some others that have been proposed. Sarnoff's theory contains much that is irrelevant to the concept of social attitudes. The theory has much excess baggage, which tends to lead to a clouding of its major propositions.

The research that has supported the theory should be interpreted with this latter point in mind. Katz, Sarnoff, and McClintock (1956) have shown that an analytic interpretation of one's prejudicial attitudes is more effective in altering those attitudes than a rational argument. They also found that a group consisting of individuals of low and intermediate defensiveness were more prone to undergo attitudinal change than a group high in defensiveness. The authors' interpretation of these findings implies that psychoanalytic interpretations of prejudice serve to disarm the subject of his defenses and render him pliable to change. Insko (1967) noted that an alternative interpretation of these findings might be that interpretive communications are more conducive to conformity than informational ones. Several other alternative interpretations might be that (1) the interpretive communicator is seen more as a "tacter" (see Bem in Chapter 2) than an informative communicator is. That is, rendering a dynamic interpretation of another's behavior requires more-specialized knowledge than simply invoking rational arguments and hence might infuse the communicator with added credibility. (2) Attitude statements leading the subject to make self-reference may lead to more dissonance and hence more attitude change than objective nonself relevant statements (see Chapter 8).

A follow-up study by Katz, McClintock, and Sarnoff (1957) replicated the finding that individuals intermediate and low in defensiveness with regard to their prejudicial attitudes were more prone to change those attitudes in response to a communication than individuals high in defensiveness. The interpretation that can be made on the basis of the theory is that high-defensive individuals are more threatened with the awareness of their unacceptable motives than individuals lower in defensiveness. Since prejudicial attitudes are seen by Sarnoff as facilitating the repression of these motives, they are less subject to change with increasing levels of defensiveness. Findings similar to those stated above were reported by McClintock (1958) and Stotland, Katz, and Patchen (1959). In addition, findings by Janis and Feshbach (1953) indicated that although strong threat appeals increase the anxiety of the subject, he is more prone to display attitude and behavior changes to low-threat appeals. These findings further support the plausibility of the proposition that when one arouses the defenses of an individual the individual mobilizes his ego defenses and this lessens the probability of inducing attitude change.

Although the studies above all seem to lend support to Sarnoff's analytic propositions, the unequivocality of that support cannot be determined because the theory has not been tested against alternative interpretations that seem equally plausible and more parsimonious. Until the theory proposed by Sarnoff receives less-questionable experimental support, the process of making inferences about ego defenses and motives from expressed attitudes is no more than what Sarnoff calls "educated guessing."

TRANSORIENTATIONAL APPROACHES
PART 6

In the preceding chapters we have outlined some of the more-general theoretical orientations and have presented some of the theories that have been derived more or less directly from these general orientations. In addition, there are several important theories that are not clearly related to any one of the major theoretical systems in particular. Some of these other theories are eclectic in that elements of two or more general approaches are utilized; others appear to adopt an independent orientation. We have grouped both kinds of theories under the general rubric, "transorientational approaches." In this chapter we present theories concerning social-judgment processes and the process of attribution. Transorientational approaches concerning group processes are considered in Chapter 12.

SOCIAL COMPARISON THEORY

The social comparison theory was formulated by Festinger (1950, 1954). Development of the theory began with a consideration of the effects of social communication on opinion change in social groups (Festinger, 1950) and was later extended to include the appraisal of abilities as well as the evaluation of opinions. Basically, the theory holds that social-influence processes and certain kinds of competitive behavior stem directly from a need for self-evaluation and the necessity for this evaluation to be based on comparisons with other persons. Although the process is essentially the same for both opinion evaluation and ability appraisal, there are some important differences between the two processes. First, there is a unidirectional upward push in the case of abilities that is lacking with regard to opinions. Second, opinion change is relatively easy when compared with performance or ability change.

The major principles of the theory of social comparison processes were presented by Festinger (1954) in the form of hypotheses, corollaries, and derivations. These statements concerned the need to evaluate, sources of evaluation, the choice of persons for comparison, factors influencing change, the cessation of comparison, and pressures toward uniformity.

The Drive to Evaluate Opinions and Abilities

The basic assumption underlying the theory of social comparison is that *there exists a drive to evaluate one's opinions and abilities* (hypothesis 1 in

Festinger, 1954). That is, people need to determine whether or not their opinions are correct and to obtain an accurate appraisal of their abilities. The individual's opinions and beliefs, as well as his evaluation of his abilities, are important determinants of his behavior. Correct opinions and accurate appraisals of ability are likely to lead to satisfying or rewarding behavior; incorrect beliefs and/or inaccurate appraisals of ability lead to unpleasant consequences (punishment).

Festinger (1954) made a distinction between situations in which evaluations of ability function like opinions and situations in which they do not. Since abilities are reflected in performance, their manifestation varies in clarity. For example, a person's weight-lifting ability can be appraised directly in "objective reality," but in evaluating his ability as an abstract artist he must rely on the opinions of others (that is, on "social reality"). In the latter instance, evaluations of ability are really opinions about ability; however, in the first instance the appraisal depends more on a comparison of one's performance with that of others than on the opinions of others. Festinger was concerned with relatively unambiguous ability appraisal.

The existence of a drive to evaluate opinions and abilities implies that people will behave in ways designed to satisfy this need; that is, in ways which enable them to accurately evaluate their opinions and abilities. How people attempt to do this becomes an important question.

Sources of Evaluation

Festinger asserted that, in general, a person will use objective reality as a basis for evaluation when this means is available, but he will rely on the opinions of others (social reality) when objective reality is not available. Thus, hypothesis 2 stated that *people evaluate their opinions and abilities by comparison with the opinions and abilities of others, respectively, to the extent that nonsocial means are unavailable.* For example, a person cannot readily test by objective means his belief that democracy is the best form of government in existence, because there is no known way of doing so; hence he relies on the opinions of others. Similarly, one might measure the time required to solve a particular problem, but this would reveal little about his problem-solving ability unless one knew something about the time required for others to solve the same problem.

As a corollary of hypothesis 2, Festinger proposed that *subjective evaluations of opinions and abilities are unstable when there is neither a physical nor a social basis for comparison* (corollary 2A). Evidence for this proposition was drawn from studies of level of aspiration which show that judgments of the quality of performance are stable when there is a comparison standard (Gardner, 1939; Gould, 1939), but they are unstable when such a standard is absent (unpublished study by J. W. Brehm).

It was also proposed that *evaluations of opinions will not be based upon comparisons with others when an objective basis is available* (corollary 2B). Festinger cited the study by Hochbaum (1953) as evidence for this corollary. This study showed that subjects who were persuaded that their ability to judge the issue under consideration was very good did not change their opinion very often when others in the group disagreed with them, whereas those subjects who were persuaded that their ability was poor changed their opinions frequently when others disagreed with them. The results of this study seem to support Festinger's proposition; however, it may be noted that the conformity studies by Asch (1951) yielded contrary results. Subjects exposed to a unanimous majority who made obviously incorrect judgments of length of lines agreed with the majority about 30 percent of the time.

Choice of Persons for Comparison

Given that there is no objective basis for comparison, then the person will seek to evaluate his opinions and abilities by comparison with others. But there are usually many others that might be chosen for comparison. Festinger hypothesized that *the tendency to compare oneself with another decreases as the discrepancy between one's own opinion or ability and that of the other person increases* (hypothesis 3). The point here is that a person will choose to evaluate his opinions and abilities by comparing them with his peers or near peers. For example, a college student will choose other college students for comparison rather than prison inmates; teen-agers will choose other teen-agers rather than adults. Corollaries 3A and 3B follow: *Given a choice, a person will choose someone close to his own opinion or ability for comparison* (3A). *If only a divergent comparison is available, the person will not be able to make a precise evaluation of his opinion or ability* (3B).

Evidence for this set of hypotheses comes from a study by Whittemore (1925) which showed that in group-task situations subjects almost always reported the selection of someone whose performance was close to their own as a competitor.

Using hypotheses 1, 2, and 3, Festinger was able to derive a number of further predictions. Derivation A held that evaluations are stable when others close to one's own opinion or ability are available for comparison. Derivation B stated the other side of the coin: evaluations will tend to change when the available comparison group has opinions and abilities which differ from one's own opinions or abilities. Data from the level of aspiration studies cited above also tend to support these propositions.

Derivation C states that an individual will be less attracted to situations in which others have different opinions and abilities than to one in which others have opinions and abilities similar to the individual's own. This suggests that persons will be attracted to groups or persons who provide the most acceptable basis for comparison. Thus derivation C follows directly from hypothesis 1 and corollaries 3A and 3B.

Derivation D asserts that a discrepancy in a group with respect to abilities or opinions will lead to action designed to reduce this discrepancy. This follows from hypotheses 1, 2, and 3. Since there is a drive to evaluate opinions and abilities, it should produce behavior directed toward producing a state in which an acceptable evaluation can be made. This is a situation in which discrepancies are small or absent. Therefore, the behavior should be directed toward reducing discrepancies in the group.

Factors Influencing Change

There are two major factors that influence change of abilities as compared with opinions: the unidirectional upward pressure with respect to abilities and the relatively greater ease of changing opinions. Thus Festinger's hypothesis 4 states that *there is a unidirectional drive upward in the case of abilities which does not exist in the case of opinions.* At least in the American culture, high-performance scores are valued; therefore, there is pressure to continually improve performance. In the case of opinions, however, there is no inherent basis for comparison and hence no general pressure to change in any particular direction.

The second factor is considered in hypothesis 5, which states that *there are nonsocial factors which make it difficult or impossible to change one's abilities, but such factors are largely absent for opinions.* The person may believe that he should be able to lift a heavy weight but be physically unable to do so. No amount of effort can enable him to lift the weight. On the other hand, if a person decides that his opinion about a particular issue is incorrect, he ordinarily can change his opinion without too much difficulty.

Reconsidering derivation D, it is now clear that the behavior toward reducing intermember discrepancies in opinions is a simple pressure toward uniformity. The action with regard to abilities, however, is more complicated, since the pressure to reduce discrepancies interacts with the unidirectional upward push toward better performance. The net result of these forces is pressure toward uniformity up to a point where the individual is just slightly better than others—at which point the pressure toward uniformity ceases to operate. Thus, when a discrepancy exists with respect to opinions or abilities there will be tendencies to change one's own opinion or ability in the direction of others (derivation D_1) and to change others in the group to bring them closer to oneself (derivation D_2). Festinger suggested that when opinions are involved the expressed action will be primarily social; that is, persons will try to influence each other. In the case of abilities, the action will be primarily toward the environmental restraints. For example, the person who has little weight-lifting ability in comparison with others may practice weight lifting in order to improve his performance. Festinger cited data from experimental studies to support these two derivations (Back, 1951; Festinger & Thibaut, 1951; Gerard, 1953).

Cessation of Comparison

Under certain conditions an individual will cease to make comparisons with others; that is, comparability can be achieved by changing the composition of the comparison group. Derivation D_3 postulated that there will be tendencies to cease comparing oneself with persons in the group whose opinions or abilities are greatly discrepant from one's own.

Festinger believed that the consequences of cessation of comparison would be different for opinions and abilities. This was based upon the fact that opinion discrepancy implies that one's opinions are incorrect, whereas no such negative implications necessarily accompany ability discrepancy. This general view is stated as hypothesis 6: *To the extent that continued comparison with others implies unpleasant consequences, the cessation of comparison will be accompanied by hostility or derogation.* Corollary 6A states that *cessation of comparison will be accompanied by hostility or derogation in the case of opinions but not in the case of abilities.*

Festinger cited evidence from studies by Festinger, Schachter, and Back (1950) and by Schachter (1951) to support the prediction regarding opinions. These studies revealed a tendency of the group to reject group members who had very divergent opinions. The data relative to the abilities prediction came from a study by Hoffman, Festinger, and Lawrence (1954). One of three subjects was made to score higher than the other two on an intelligence test. When the situation permitted, the two low scorers competed with each other but ceased to compete with the high-scoring subject.

Pressures toward Uniformity

In several of the preceding propositions it was indicated that the drive to evaluate abilities and opinions gives rise to pressures toward uniformity. The strength of these pressures is determined by a number of factors. From hypotheses 1, 2, and 3, Festinger derived that any factor that increases the drive to evaluate an opinion or ability will also increase pressures toward uniformity with respect to that opinion or ability (derivation E). Similarly, hypothesis 7 states that *any factor which increases the importance of a group as a comparison group for an opinion or ability will increase pressure toward uniformity with respect to that opinion or ability.*

Several corollaries to the above two propositions were formulated to specify some of the factors determining strength of pressures toward uniformity. Corollary to derivation E asserts that *pressures toward uniformity will increase with an increase in the importance of an opinion or ability, or with an increase in the relevance of an opinion or ability to immediate behavior.* The position here is that an opinion or ability that is regarded by the person as of little importance will arouse little or no drive toward evaluation and that the greater the relevance of the opinion or ability to behavior, the greater will be the drive to evaluate the opinion or ability.

Corollary 7A states that *the pressure toward uniformity with respect to opinions and abilities will vary with the strength of attraction to the group.* The more attractive the group is to a person, the more important it will be as a comparison group. Therefore, the pressures to reduce discrepancies between himself and the group will be stronger. These pressures should be manifested as (1) a tendency to change own position, (2) an increased effort to change others, and (3) a greater tendency to make others noncomparable. Back (1951) showed that members who were highly attracted to a group made more influence attempts; Festinger, Gerard, Hymovitch, Kelley, and Raven (1952) found that members of highly cohesive groups changed their opinions more than members of low-cohesive groups; and Festinger, Torrey, and Willerman (1954) found that feelings of inadequacy regarding task performance were greater in low-attractive than in high-attractive groups. Corollary 7A thus appears to be in agreement with the experimental evidence available at the time it was formulated.

Corollary 7B holds that *pressure toward uniformity varies with the relevance of the opinion or ability to the group*. Despite some lack of clarity of the concept "relevance," Schachter (1951) was able to create differences in perceived relevance and to demonstrate that rejection of deviates was greater in high-relevance than in low-relevance conditions.

In addition to factors that influence the three forms of pressure manifestation, there are some factors that affect these manifestations differently. Thus, Festinger hypothesized that the tendency to narrow the range of comparability becomes stronger when persons whose opinions or abilities are divergent from one's own are perceived as also being different on attributes consistent with the opinion or ability divergence (hypothesis 8). Evidence supporting this hypothesis was taken from studies by Gerard (1953) and by Festinger and Thibaut (1951). In both studies group members were led to believe that the group held either homogeneous or heterogeneous opinions on a given issue. Actually, there was considerable variation in opinions held by group members in both conditions. During discussion there was less communication directed toward deviates in the heterogeneous than in the homogeneous groups. Festinger interpreted these results as showing that the perception of heterogeneity enabled subjects to narrow the range of comparability.

Hypothesis 9 is rather long and involved, so perhaps it is best cited verbatim:

> When there is a range of opinion or ability in a group, the relative strength of the three manifestations of pressure toward uniformity will be different for those who are close to the mode of the group than for those who are distant from the mode. Specifically, those close to the mode of the group will have stronger tendencies to change the positions of others, relatively weaker tendencies to narrow the range of comparison and much weaker tendencies to change their own position compared to those who are distant from the mode of the group (Festinger, 1954, pp. 134–135).

There is little direct evidence for this hypothesis, although results from the Festinger et al. (1952) experiment are consistent with it. In comparison with conformers, deviates were found to change their opinions more frequently, to show less tendency to influence others, and to show a greater tendency to redefine group boundaries to exclude those with divergent opinions.

Implications for Group Formation

The preceding sections have dealt primarily with the effects of the drive for evaluation on behavior in groups. However, the drive for self-evaluation also has important implications for group formation and the changing of group memberships. In the first place, since comparison can be accomplished only in groups, the drive for self-evaluation should cause the person to belong to groups and to associate with others. Secondly, the groups that provide the greatest promise of satisfaction are those which hold opinions near the person's own. Therefore, individuals will be more attracted to groups holding similar opinions and will tend to move out of groups that hold different opinions. This move will more or less guarantee that extant groups will be composed of persons whose opinions and abilities are similar. Festinger suggested that the segmentation into groups that are similar with respect to abilities gives rise to status in a society.

Consequences of Preventing Incomparability

We stated earlier that individuals will tend to redefine groups to render incomparable those whose opinions and abilities are too divergent from their own opinions and abilities. Festinger identified two kinds of situations in which this may not occur; that is, in which comparability is forced. The first situation is one in which the attraction to the group is so strong that the person continues to remain in the group in spite of divergencies of opinions and abilities. In this case, the power of the group over the individual is strong and differences in opinion will probably be eliminated. There will also be strong group pressure on the individual to improve his performance. Since he cannot change his abilities, he would be expected to experience feelings of inadequacy and failure.

The other situation in which incomparability is not possible is one in which the individual is constrained from leaving the group. For example, if the person is in prison he cannot leave his group. There are, of course, social restraints that may be equally effective in preventing the person from leaving the group. If a person must work in order to support his family, he may continue in a group he dislikes. In such cases, the group should have little power over the individual and uniformity would be expected only when coercion is used. This case would lead to public compliance but private resistance.

Current Status of the Theory

The social comparison theory is internally consistent and the hypotheses are stated in a form readily amenable to empirical evaluation. The theoretical propositions agree reasonably well with known data, but until recently the empirical evidence concerning the theory was limited almost entirely to that cited by Festinger in his presentation of the theory. However, a number of experiments were conducted in 1966 and reported in a special issue of the *Journal of Experimental Social Psychology*. These experiments were concerned with three aspects of the theory: (1) the hypothesis that there exists a drive to evaluate opinions and abilities, (2) the role of similarity in the choice of a comparison person or group, and (3) the assumption of a universal drive upward in the case of abilities.

The drive to evaluate was studied by several investigators with generally positive results. Gordon (1966) and Hakmiller (1966b) found that the desire to affiliate for social comparison purposes increased as opinion discrepancy decreased and that the desire was greater when the group had been shown to be correct than when it had been incorrect. Darley and Aronson (1966) reported that subjects threatened with electric shock preferred to be with persons who reported being slightly more nervous than themselves. Latané and Wheeler (1966) found results from a field study of an airplane crash that were inconsistent with the Darley and Aronson results, but this could have been because of the lack of control over relevant variables in the field study. The evidence thus generally supports the assumption of a drive toward self-evaluation.

The role of similarity in the choice of comparison persons was investigated in at least six studies, yielding only partial verification of Festinger's hypotheses. Two major hypotheses were tested: (1) social comparison can yield accurate and stable self-evaluation only when a person compares himself with a similar other (corollary 3B and derivations A and B) and (2) a person will choose for comparison others who are similar with respect to the characteristics being evaluated (derivation C). In testing the first hypothesis, Radloff (1966) demonstrated that subjects judged their performance on a pursuit rotor task more accurately when similar comparison scores were provided. In the absence of similar comparison persons, self-evaluation was found to be inaccurate and unstable. Thus the hypothesis was supported by the empirical results.

The experimental findings are less supportive with respect to the second hypothesis. Similar others are chosen for comparison when the characteristic to be judged is positively valued (Wheeler, 1966) and when the subject is unsure of his ability (Gordon, 1966; Hakmiller, 1966b). Similar others are not chosen more frequently than dissimilar others when negative characteristics are being evaluated (Hakmiller, 1966a) or when relatively unfamiliar characteristics are being judged (Thornton & Arrowood, 1966). In the latter instance, it appears that a person who is a positive example of the attribute being judged will provide a more accurate evaluation than a similar other. These findings, taken together, indicate a need to specify the conditions under which a similar other will or will not be chosen for comparison.

The assumption of a unidirectional drive upwards in the case of abilities was said to be a determinant of the choice of a comparison person (Festinger, 1954), but just how the choice is affected was not clearly stated. As Latané (1966) noted, it is not clear whether Festinger believed that the person would choose for comparison another person who had higher ability or one who had less ability than the person himself. Wheeler (1966) found that, given a choice, subjects elected to compare themselves with persons of slightly higher rank. Since this upward comparison correlated with assumed similarity to someone higher in the rank order, Wheeler interpreted his results in terms of motivation leading to assumed similarity, which in turn led to comparison choices that were expected to confirm this assumption of similarity. He viewed his findings and interpretations as supporting Festinger's theory.

Hakmiller (1966a) proposed that comparison with someone worse off than oneself can lead to self-enhancement, especially when the person feels threatened about the characteristic in question. His findings indicated significantly greater downward comparison among highly threatened subjects than among mildly threatened subjects. However, Thornton and Arrowood (1966) found that comparisons were upward when the characteristic being evaluated was positive, whereas there was no directional preference when the characteristic involved was negative. The results of these several studies support the general notion that direction of the drive to evaluate is a determinant of the choice of a comparison person, but the direction of the effect seems to depend upon other variables.

In summary, the overall results of the most-recent studies provide considerable support for Festinger's hypotheses, although there are some interesting findings that are at variance with the theory. The general conclusion that must be drawn is that there is a need for a clearer specification of the conditions under which the proposed relationships do and do not hold. Perhaps such specification must await further empirical evidence.

THEORY OF CORRESPONDENT INFERENCES

The theory of inference developed by Jones and Davis (1965) attempts to explain a perceiver's inferences about what another person is trying to do by a given action. The theory relies heavily on the work of Heider (1958), which is described in Chapter 6, especially on his analysis of the attribution process. Thus it might seem appropriate to consider this theory as deriving from field orientation. On the other hand, the theory is concerned with cognitive elements such as "intentions" and "inferences"; hence, it might also be considered a cognitive theory. We have avoided this issue by calling it a trans-orientational approach.

From Heider's analysis, Jones and Davis formulated the following description of the process of inferring personal characteristics (dispositions) from behavior. It is assumed that the perceiver begins with the observation of an overt action of another person. He then makes certain decisions about the person's knowledge and ability, which in turn permit him to make inferences about the person's intentions. For example, if the person had no knowledge of (could not foresee) the consequences of his actions, the inference of intention could not be made. Similarly, if the effect produced by his actions required a level of skill (ability) greater than that believed to be possessed by the person, intention would not be inferred. Knowledge and ability are thus preconditions for the attribution of intention. If both knowledge of consequences and ability to produce them are in evidence, intentions are inferred which are used to infer stable personal attributes (called "dispositions" by Jones and Davis).

The theory of correspondent inferences attempts to account for the attribution of specific intentions and dispositions on the basis of particular actions, and to this extent it represents an extension of Heider's analysis. The general thesis is that the intentional significance of an action derives from a consideration of the alternatives open to the actor. That is, the perceiver can understand the motives (intentions) underlying an action only by relating it to other possible actions and effects. For example, Jones and Davis cited an instance in which A and B are working together. It is observed that A gives orders and monitors and criticizes B's work. If the situation is entirely free, one might infer that A is domineering. But if it is known that A has been ordered to play a directive leadership role, there would be less likelihood that his behavior would be viewed as evidence of a personal quality of dominance. In Jones and Davis' terms, inferences about dominance from actions would be less *correspondent*.

The Concept of Correspondence

The term *correspondence* was used by Jones and Davis to refer to the extent to which the act and the underlying attribute are similarly described by the inference. In the preceding example, the most correspondent inference is the one which holds that the domineering behavior is a direct reflection of the intention to dominate and hence of a disposition to be dominant. In short, correspondence of inference varies directly with the degree to which the action appears to be constrained by the situation in which it occurs.

The formal definition of correspondence can now be stated: *"Given an attribute-effect linkage which is offered to explain why an act occurred, correspondence increases as the judged value of the attribute departs from the judge's conception of the average person's standing on that attribute"* (Jones & Davis, 1965, p. 224). Thus the attribution of an attribute or trait on the basis of a given action implies that the action departs from normative expectations.

Acts and Effects

Jones and Davis defined *act* rather broadly as a molar response that reflects choice on the part of the actor and that has one or more effects on the environment or on the actor. The choice of the actor may be only between action and inaction, although it is usually between alternative actions. *Effects* were defined as discriminable changes produced by actions.

The act of concern to the theory is the terminal act in an action sequence. For example, if a man rises, crosses the room, and closes the door, the act of interest is "closing the door." The act may have only one effect or it may have several effects. When multiple effects are produced, inference becomes more difficult. However, it is usually the case that certain effects are common to both the chosen and the unchosen alternatives. The theory assumes that these common effects could not have been helpful to the actor in his choice of action and hence do not give information about his intentions. But there may be (and often are) multiple noncommon effects; that is, the action may produce several effects which would not have occurred if the actor had chosen any other alternative action. Jones and Davis asserted that the perceiver usually assumes that some effects are more desirable to the actor than others and therefore are more indicative of his intentions. In general, effects that are seen as desired by most people are seen as being desired by the actor.

In most cases, a chosen action will produce both positive (desirable) and negative (undesirable) effects. The perceiver usually assumes that the actor acted as he did in spite of the negative consequences of his actions. Jones and Davis went further and stated that the importance of nonnegative effects increases in direct proportion to the negativity of other effects produced by the action. Therefore, inferences about intentions to produce desired effects increase to the degree that negative outcomes are also involved.

But Jones and Davis found a problem: to know that a person chooses a universally desired effect tells little about his unique characteristics. The theory holds that an inference must characterize the person as deviating from the norm if it is to be considered as correspondent. The authors concluded, therefore, that actions whose effects are no more universally desired than those of other possible actions provide the greatest amount of information regarding intentions and dispositions.

Determinants of Correspondence

Two aspects of the inference process were identified by Jones and Davis. When an observed action leads to multiple effects, the perceiver first assumes that certain effects are more likely to be the goal than others. If all effects are negative except one, the perceived probability that this one positive effect was the actor's goal is 1.00. In other cases, the probability of any given effect being the actor's goal varies directly with the assumed desirability of the effect and inversely with the number of other positive effects produced by the action. The attribution of intention reflects some combination of assumed desirability and number of noncommon effects.

The second part of the inference process is the attachment of personal significance to the effect(s) identified as the actor's goal. According to the definition of correspondence, relative extremity of the action is the crucial variable. As noted earlier, assumed desirability positively affects the judgment of relative extremity. Therefore, an inference from an action to a disposition is an inverse function of the number of noncommon effects of the action and the perceived desirability of these effects. It follows that the most correspondent situation is one in which both the number of noncommon effects and the assumed desirability of these effects are low. Hence, it is important to consider the factors influencing assumed desirability and the assessment of commonality of effects.

Factors Determining Assumed Desirability

Jones and Davis asserted that there are a number of conditions that might influence the perceiver's assumption that the actor desires the same effects as people in general. They suggested that these factors might include such things as the actor's appearance, the perceiver's stereotypes about identifiable groups, and/or shared perspectives relative to the situation in which the action occurs. Unfortunately, they did not analyze these factors in any detail.

Calculation of Commonality

Two sets of problems concerning the calculation of the commonality of effects were considered. The first set concerned the identification of effects and the determination of commonality of effects, and the second was concerned with the task of sorting out the noncommon effects of the action from all others. Jones and Davis concluded that the first set of problems could be resolved only through research; hence, they did not deal with them in their analysis.

The process of sorting out noncommon effects after common and noncommon effects have been identified was seen as consisting of three stages. The first stage constitutes identifying the different action alternatives that are likely to be noted by the perceiver. The next step is to pool all the effects supposedly produced by the unchosen actions and to compare these with the effects of the chosen action. In the final stage, the noncommon effects of the unchosen alternatives are considered as effects that the actor wishes to avoid. These are then treated in the same manner as positive effects produced by the chosen alternative action. The negative noncommon effects of the unchosen alternatives plus the positive effects of the chosen action provide the basis for inferring correspondence.

Jones and Davis presented this analysis as a guide for research and did not suggest that the perceiver proceeds in this manner, although presumably the results of the perceiver's responses to the situation should correspond to the results produced by the researcher's analysis.

A complicating factor in calculating the noncommon effects of an action is the fact that the actor has made choices among action alternatives prior to the action choice under consideration. For example, a person who chooses to attend law school A rather than law school B has already chosen his field, whereas a person who chooses to attend law school rather than medical school has not. The former is therefore at a later stage of the total choice process than the latter. Knowledge of preceding choices may provide information basic to the inference process.

Correspondence and Personal Involvement

In addition to the factors discussed to this point there are certain variables associated with the perceiver's involvement which affect the attributions of dispositions. Jones and Davis distinguished two levels of involvement, *hedonic relevance* and *personalism*. An action has hedonic relevance for a perceiver if it either promotes or interferes with the perceiver's goal; that is, if the action is either gratifying or disappointing to the perceiver. An action is personalistic if the perceiver believes that he is the intended target of the action; that is, if the perceiver believes that the action was intended either to gratify or to spite him. Thus an action can be either relevant or irrelevant to the perceiver; if it is relevant, it may be either personally relevant or impersonally relevant.

The theory holds that correspondence generally increases with increasing relevance, and hence relevance is a determinant of the attribution of dispositions. Jones and Davis went a step further and asserted that evaluation of the actor by the perceiver will also be a joint function of relevance and correspondence. If the effects of an action are positive, the perceiver's favorable impression of the actor will increase with increasing correspondence; if the effects are negative, the converse will be true.

Under conditions of personal relevance, the effects of correspondence and relevance on evaluation are enhanced. Jones and Davis believed that a condition of personalism and positive relevance would guarantee a positive evaluation of the actor because this set of circumstances would insure a correspondent inference of focused benevolence. Similarly, personalism and negative relevance should insure a negative evaluation of the actor.

Comment and Evaluation

The theory of correspondent inferences satisfies the minimal criteria for acceptance as a theory; it is internally consistent, testable, does not contradict the principles of other accepted theories, and agrees reasonably well with known data.

Several experimental investigations were cited by Jones and Davis in support of their theory. It will be instructive to review some of these as well as other relevant research. The first study cited (Jones, Davis & Gergen, 1961) tested the hypothesis that behavior which conforms to role expectations will be seen as uninformative regarding the actor's attributes, whereas out-of-role behavior will provide considerable evidence about the actor's characteristics. This hypothesis was derived from the notion that people are generally expected to behave in accordance with role requirements and hence in-role behavior does not lead to confident correspondent inferences simply because such behavior has multiple effects that are generally high with respect to cultural desirability. Subjects were exposed to recorded interviews of applicants for training as either a submariner or an astronaut. The job requirements were outlined in some detail during the first part of the interview. In the second part, applicants either responded in a manner consistent with the role (job) description or in a manner distinctly out of line with the role description. Subjects were then asked to rate the applicant as a person and to indicate their confidence in their ratings. The results indicated clearly that the ratings of out-of-role applicants were more extreme and subjects were more confident of their judgments than those of in-role applicants, thus supporting the hypothesis.

A study designed for a different purpose also provides support for this aspect of the theory. Briscoe, Woodyard, and Shaw (1967) found that impressions of a hypothetical person based on unfavorable descriptions of that person were less susceptible to change when contrary information was given than were impressions based on initially favorable information. These results were interpreted in terms of the relative meaning of favorable and unfavorable behaviors. Since the individual is expected to behave in a positive (favorable) manner in our culture, such behavior tells us little about his true nature. Negative behavior, on the other hand, cannot be accounted for in terms of cultural desirability and hence is seen as evidence of the person's basic personality.

Several experiments are related to the hypothesis that relevance increases correspondence in the inference process. Jones and deCharms (1957) conducted an experiment in which one member of a four- or five-member group was an accomplice who failed the assigned task while all other group members succeeded. The relevance of the failure was either minimized (individual fate) or emphasized (common fate). In the individual fate condition the rewards were based on individual performance, whereas in the common fate condition rewards were based upon pooled performances. The accomplice was judged by other group members as less competent and less dependable in the common fate than in the individual fate condition. Differences in relevance failed to produce the expected differences in perceived likeability and friendliness.

Several additional studies may be cited as giving general support to the hypothesis that relevance increases correspondence. Kleiner (1960) varied the probability of group failure and found that the greater the group's need for help, the greater the importance attributed to a helpful confederate and the more favorable the confederate was viewed by his fellow group members. The results of Deutsch's (1949) study of cooperation and competition are also in accord with this hypothesis (see Chapter 6 for a more detailed consideration of Deutsch's study).

Portions of the Jones and deCharms (1957) study support the hypothesis that evaluation is a joint function of relevance and correspondence. Half the subjects in each condition were led to believe that task failure was caused by lack of motivation and the other half that it was caused by lack of ability. Since lack of ability does not provide a choice, it cannot be a basis for correspondent inference. Under this condition, variations in personal relevance did not lead to differential changes in evaluation. Similarly, a study by Thibaut and Riecken (1955) showed that benevolent acts on the part of a high-status person led to greater attractiveness than similar acts by a low-status person.

The role of personalism has also been investigated in a number of experiments. Deutsch and Solomon (1959) found that subjects who believed they had done poorly on a task were less negative in their appraisal of another person who rejected them as work partners than subjects who had succeeded on the task were. The rejection is seen as less personal when it appears justified. The experiment by Strickland, Jones, and Smith (1960) also demonstrated that group support led to greater negative evaluation of a person who had attacked the subject's integrity. However, a study designed specifically to test the hypothesis that positive, supportive behavior will be taken as evidence of sincerity and good intentions to a greater extent when the actor is not dependent than when he is dependent on the perceiver failed to support the hypothesis (Jones, Gergen, & Jones, 1963).

In conclusion, it appears that the theory of correspondent inferences is supported very well by the experimental evidence, despite a few negative findings. The negative results of the Jones, Gergen, and Jones study, however, call for a modification of the theory, or at least a reexamination of the prediction. It may well be that positive behaviors are seen as a reflection of culturally approved roles regardless of the dependency of the actor on the target of the action. The results of studies by Strickland, Jones, and Smith (1960) and by Briscoe, Woodyard, and Shaw (1967) suggest that only negative behaviors provide unambiguous information about the true nature of the individual.

A THEORY OF EXTERNAL ATTRIBUTION

An analysis of the attribution process proposed by Kelley (1967) is related to the theory of correspondent inferences in that both derive from Heider's work. However, Jones and Davis were concerned with the circumstances under which an actor is seen as the cause of given effects, whereas Kelley was concerned with attribution to the environment. His analysis considered the problem of ruling out personal causes rather than identifying and accounting for them. The similarity of the two analyses is not great, therefore, although both claim to have been based on Heider's concepts. Kelley's theory is also less extensive than Jones and Davis' theory. The theory of external attribution can be regarded as complementary to the theory of correspondent inferences.

The Attribution Process

Kelley (1967) defined attribution as the process of perceiving the dispositional properties of entities in the environment. He accepted Heider's analysis of the perceptual process and especially his view that attribution may be either to the person or to the environment. In the perception of dispositional properties, then, there is a choice between external attribution (to the environment) or internal attribution (to the self). For example, if a person enjoys a television program, he may attribute this enjoyment to the intrinsic nature of the program (external attribution) or to his idiosyncratic tastes (internal attribution). The variables determining this choice are the ones Kelley attempted to identify.

In his analysis, Kelley adopted J. S. Mills' method of differences as the basic analytic tool: the effect is attributed to that which is present when the effect occurs and is absent when the effect does not occur. This basic notion of covariation was used to examine variations in effects with respect to entities, persons, time, and modalities of interaction with the entity. The general hypothesis is that attribution to the environment rather than to the self requires that the actor respond *differentially* to the thing (entity), that he respond *consistently* over time and over modalities, and that his response be in *agreement* with the consensus of other persons' responses to the entity. For example, enjoyment of a television program (entity) is attributed to the environment (the program) if the person does not enjoy all programs (differential response), if he enjoys it a second time (consistency over time), if he enjoys it not only at home but also at the home of friends, in the bar, and/or in black and white as well as in color (consistency over modalities), and if others also enjoy it (consensual agreement). To the degree that these conditions are not met, the enjoyment will be attributed to the self.

Informational Dependence and Influence

The four criteria for external validity mentioned above may now be defined more precisely:

Distinctiveness: an effect is attributed to the external environment (the entity) if it uniquely occurs when the entity is present and does not occur when the entity is absent.

Consistency over time: an effect is attributed to the entity if the effect is the same or nearly so each time the entity is present.

Consistency over modalities: an effect is attributed to the entity if it occurs even when the mode of interaction with the entity varies.

Consensus: an effect is attributed to the entity if the entity is experienced the same way by all observers; that is, if the entity produces the same effect on everyone.

According to Kelley, the degree to which a person's attributions fulfill these four criteria determines how confident he feels that he has a valid picture of his external world. If his attribution meets all of these criteria, he feels confident, makes judgments quickly, and takes action with vigor; if his attributions do not satisfy these criteria, he is unsure and hesitates to take action. Thus, these criteria provide an index of the person's state of information regarding his world. The index is based primarily on differentiation and stability. The information level is high if an individual can make highly stable but differentiated (distinctive) attributions.

Information level provided Kelley with a basis for the analysis of information dependence. His general view was that a person (A) is informationally dependent on another person (B) if B can raise A's level of information to a higher level than A can attain from other sources. (This is analogous to Thibaut and Kelley's analysis of outcome dependence. See Chapter 4.) Information dependence may be defined in terms of actual or potential effects or in terms of anticipated or experienced effects. Anticipated and potential effects refer to the future, whereas actual and experienced effects refer to the present or past. When future reference is involved, A may seek information from B in order to raise his information level. In general, an individual may be expected to seek information when his information level drops below the level that he expects to be able to attain. These information-seeking activities lead to increased interaction with other persons upon whom the individual is informationally dependent.

Attribution and Persuasion

These concepts were used by Kelley to describe the conditions determining susceptibility to persuasion and the immediate effects and persistence of persuasion. In general, he hypothesized that the more variable a person's prior attributions have been, the more susceptible he is to social influence. Attributions will be unstable when the person has had little social support, poor or ambiguous prior information, views that have been disconfirmed, and/or other experiences that lower his self-confidence.

One person A will be successful in persuading another person B if B's communication enables A to increase the distinctiveness and stability of his attributions. The factors relevant to this influence and the persistence of its effects vary with the method of persuasion. On the one hand, B may try to increase stability of attributions for A by increasing either the consistency or the degree of consensus with respect to A's attributions. The first method is usually called education and involves a more rational approach, whereas the second (the consensus aspect) is usually called persuasion and is more dependent on A's evaluation of B.

Kelley asserted that these propositions are consistent with what we know about persuasion, but he pointed out that few experimental studies have been done that are directly relevant to them.

Comment

Kelley has provided many interesting ideas and hypotheses about the attribution process and its relation to other aspects of social behavior. The preceding discussion of course does not do justice to the theory, nor have all of his views been presented in detail. Like other theories in this chapter, it meets the minimal criteria for a good theory. However, the evidence for the theory derives exclusively from studies designed for other purposes and is therefore indirect and inferential.

The proposed relationships among the four criteria for external validity and the attributor's behavior are amenable to test under controlled conditions. Such tests would contribute much to our understanding of the attribution process. However, a common situation with regard to social attribution is one in which the information regarding these criteria is minimal or lacking. For example, an experience with another person may occur only once, in only one setting, and with no evidence regarding the reactions of others to the person. Nevertheless, confident and speedy attributions are often made to the person. The theory provides no way of explaining this type of attribution.

There is also a practical problem with the concept of information level.

Kelley admitted that we do not have an adequate way of indexing this level, but he assumed that psychologists would ultimately provide one. Until such an index is available, the propositions involving information level remain untestable.

Despite these problems, Kelley has outlined some important considerations about the problem of external attribution. His conceptualizations provide a necessary complement to the theory of correspondent inferences, and the approach promises to be a significant contribution to attribution theory. As Kelley pointed out, the theory has implications for a broad range of social problems, such as the process of gaining information about self, the assignment of credit and censure, the role of language in the attribution process, the establishment of interpersonal trust, and similar problems. The theory provides at least a starting point for the theoretical analysis of a broad spectrum of social phenomena.

SOCIAL JUDGMENT THEORY

Social judgment theory (Sherif & Hovland, 1961; Sherif, Sherif, & Nebergall, 1965) derives directly from the general approach originally espoused by Sherif (1935, 1936). Sherif's approach could be considered as an orientation rather than as a theory, since it embodies a conceptual framework that he has applied to such diverse situations as norm formation, attitude change, and intergroup conflict. We have chosen to treat it as a theory for the following reasons:

1. The approach is not unique but "borrows selectively" from other theoretical orientations (Sherif, 1967).

2. The approach is articulated most clearly in connection with specific social phenomena such as attitude expression and change.

3. The approach has not had the pervasive influence on psychology that characterizes such broad frameworks as the psychoanalytic, reinforcement, and field orientations. Nevertheless, it is important to understand the basic concepts of the general approach in order to comprehend fully the theory of social judgment.

From the beginning, Sherif was concerned with an attempt to bring together data from the work of psychologists on judgment, perception, learning, and memory, as well as data from the work of anthropologists and sociologists. The basic proposition underlying all his work is that man structures situations that are important to him. This structure includes both internal (attitudes, emotions, motives, the effects of past experiences, etc.) and external factors (objects, persons, etc. in the physical surround) that are operative in the situation at any given time. The interaction of these internal and external factors constitutes the "frame of reference" of any given behavior or act, which can only be understood within this frame of reference. However, Sherif stressed the fact that there is no such thing as a frame of reference in the abstract (Sherif & Sherif, 1956). Instead, he insisted that one should consider only the frame of reference of behavior at a given time. The frame of reference at a given time includes all those factors, internal and external, that influence behavior at that time. Sherif argued that behavior is not directly determined by internal and external factors; rather, behavior follows a central patterning of these factors. This conception is of course quite compatible with both cognitive and field theory formulations (see Chapters 5 and 7).

Sherif emphasized that internal and external factors are not additive in their influences upon the patterning process. Their relative influence depends upon the degree of stimulus structure and the intensity of the motive state. In general, the greater the stimulus ambiguity and the more intense the motive state, the greater will be the influence of internal factors. Conversely, the more structured the stimulus and the less intense the motive, the greater will be the relative influence of external factors.

Although behavior can be understood only within the total frame of reference, there are reference points or anchors within the total frame of reference that may be more influential than other parts. Much of Sherif's work has been concerned with the identification and analysis of the main anchors which individuals use in making judgments. This work led to the social judgment theory that concerns us here.

Social judgment theory is concerned primarily with the psychological processes underlying the expression of attitudes and the change of attitudes through communication. A basic assumption underlying the theory is that the principles governing basic judgmental processes in general also apply to attitude expression and change. Therefore, Sherif et al. began with a consideration of the principles derived from psychophysical studies of judgment. These principles were then related to attitudinal processes and additional principles derived from studies designed specifically to study attitudes.

The basic assumption of judgment theory is that it involves discrimination and categorization of stimuli, whether these be neutral or attitudinal in nature. Discrimination and categorization involve comparison between alternatives. One of these alternatives may be (and often is) an internal frame of reference or standard of judgment. The formation and use of such standards depend upon the range of experiences that the person has had with the universe of stimuli, anchoring effects, degree of ego involvement, the person's own categories (latitudes of acceptance, rejection, and noncommitment), and assimilation and contrast effects. The social judgment theory consists of a set of interrelated hypotheses or propositions concerning the effects of these variables on the judgment of social events.

Judgment Scales

When an individual is faced with the necessity of making a judgment concerning a particular stimulus (for example, whether to accept or reject an attitude item), he can do so only by comparing the stimulus (item) with *something*. This "something" may be another stimulus, a frame of reference, or other judgment scale. Judgment thus requires discrimination or choice between two or more alternatives, which involves a comparison between these alternatives (Sherif, Sherif, & Nebergall, 1965). For example, when a person chooses to attend one school rather than another, a process of judgment is involved. This judgment is based not only on the merits of the two schools, but also on the person's own interests, values, and goals.

Sherif and Hovland (1961) suggested that judgment could be studied either in order to determine the discriminative capacity of a particular sense modality or to analyze the placement or categorization of particular stimuli in a series. Their analysis was concerned primarily with the process of placement. Since they were interested in attitude formation and change, their analysis dealt with the person's placement of attitude items such as those used in attitude measurement (for examples, see Thurstone & Chave, 1929; Likert, 1932; Shaw & Wright, 1967).

The major principles concerning the development of judgment scales derive from experimental studies using neutral stimuli, such as weights, tones, and lines. The general conclusion drawn from such studies is that an individual who is confronted with a series of stimuli from a given universe of stimuli tends to form a psychological scale of judgment. In a typical experiment the subject is presented with a series of stimuli (for example, weights), one at a time, and asked to make a judgment (for example, whether the weight is heavy or light). Under such conditions, subjects quickly develop a subjective standard or judgment scale which is near the center of the range of stimuli being judged. Those stimuli above the subjective standard are judged heavy and those below light. Similarly, if the subject is asked to place the stimuli into more than two categories, category thresholds are established; that is, the judgment scale consists of several subjective standards which delineate categories and determine the placement of specific items. These effects have been demonstrated in a number of experiments (Wever & Zener, 1928; Fernberger, 1931; Volkmann, 1951). These same effects have been shown to occur even when the stimulus series is not well graded by objective standards. For example, McGarvey (1943) demonstrated that all the effects found with physical stimuli could be reproduced with social stimuli (that is, social acts such as "lying to mother," "spitting on the crucifix," and "committing murder").

The particular nature of a judgment scale is largely determined by the conditions under which it is formed. When the scale is established on the basis of an unambiguous stimulus series with well-graded stimulus differences and with explicit anchors provided within the series, stimulus values, and scale values correspond closely. For example, if the stimulus series consists of weights ranging from 5 grams to 100 grams, and an anchor weighing 50 grams is provided, the psychological scale and the objective scale correspond closely and the reference scale is relatively stable (Bressler, 1933; Long, 1937). To the extent that the stimulus series lacks an explicit anchor or standard, the psychological judgment scale is less stable than when an anchor is provided. Furthermore, the placement of items located in the middle portion of the series is less accurate than those near the ends of the series (Needham, 1935; Volkmann, 1951). Therefore, it appears that the end points of a judged series of stimuli serve as anchors in the formation of judgment scales.

When the series of stimuli to be judged lacks both unambiguous graded differences and an explicit standard, the effects of internal factors and social influences on the formation of the judgment scale are increased. Evidence for this proposition comes from a number of studies in which autokinetic movement was used as the stimulus situation. When a stationary pinpoint of light is presented in a completely dark room, it appears to move. When the light is presented several times, judgments of the amount of movement become more or less stabilized within a particular range (Sherif, 1935). However, when subjects are asked to make their judgments in a group, judgments tend to converge to a common range and standard (Sherif, 1935; Bovard, 1948). This factor plays an important role in the Sherif and Hovland approach, as will be seen later.

Assimilation and Contrast Effects

It was noted in the preceding section that the judgment scale is more stable and scale values correspond more closely to objective values when an anchor is available than when it is not. It was also shown that the end points of the stimulus range serve as anchors (Volkmann, 1951). When there are no well-defined end points to the stimulus range, the first and last category labels used in the instructions serve as anchors (Eriksen & Hake, 1957).

The effects of anchors discussed thus far are those produced by an anchor within the stimulus range. But in natural situations the anchoring stimulus often lies outside the stimulus range being judged. The effects of anchors outside the stimulus range depends upon the remoteness of the anchor. An anchor placed slightly above or slightly below the ends of the series will lead to a shift in item placement *toward* the anchor, whereas an anchor considerably above or below the stimulus range will produce a judgment shift *away* from the anchor (Rogers, 1941; Postman & Miller, 1945; Heintz, 1950). Sherif and Hovland (1961) labeled the shift toward the anchor *assimilation;* presumably, the anchor is assimilated into the stimuli being judged. It is as if the stimulus range is extended to include the anchor. The shift away from the anchor in the case of remote anchors was referred to as a *contrast* effect. These effects have also been demonstrated when the anchor is internal (Hunt, 1941; Hovland & Sherif, 1952; Sherif & Hovland, 1953).

Latitudes of Acceptance, Rejection, and Noncommitment

According to Sherif and Hovland, these same judgmental processes operate when the individual is required to indicate whether he agrees or disagrees with a statement, as in the case of attitude measurement. There are, however, two features in addition to those operating in psychophysical judgment. First, if the person has an attitude toward an object or class of objects, he brings to any particular situation a set of established evaluative categories. Therefore, the question of acceptability or unacceptability of the attitude object becomes a factor in judgment. Second, social judgments vary from individual to individual, whereas in the case of psychophysical judgments there is little interindividual variability.

Individuals also differ in their acceptance or tolerance of positions other than their own and in the range of positions they regard as objectionable. Furthermore, they differ with respect to the importance of a given issue in their own psychological organization. The observation of these differences led to the concepts of latitudes of acceptance, rejection, and noncommitment. *Latitude of acceptance* refers to the range of positions that an individual is willing to accept or, at least, to tolerate. It includes not only the position that is most acceptable to the person but also other tolerable positions. *Latitude of rejection* refers to all those positions that are unacceptable or objectionable to the individual. It includes the most objectionable position and all other unacceptable positions. *Latitude of noncommitment* includes all those positions that are not included in either the latitude of acceptance or the latitude of rejection; that is, all positions that are neither acceptable nor objectionable. Thus a person's judgment of a particular statement will depend upon its relation to these latitudes. If it reflects a position that falls within the latitude of acceptance, the person will agree with it: if it falls within the latitude of rejection, he will disagree with it.

In attempting to measure latitudes of acceptance, rejection, and noncommitment, Sherif, Sherif, and Nebergall (1965) made several assumptions: (1) There are at least two positions that may be taken toward the attitude object, and these are known to the subjects. These positions need to be defined as clearly as possible. (2) The alternatives within the domain are ranked in the same order by all subjects when the dimension for ranking is degree of favorability. This applies only to unequivocal statements; no assumption was made concerning equality of intervals. (3) The individual is free to determine for himself the number of positions that he is willing to accept, reject, or remain neutral toward.

Based on several experimental studies (Hovland & Sherif, 1952; Sherif & Hovland, 1961), it was concluded that strong commitment to a position involves a lowered threshold of rejection. This led to several hypotheses about the relationship between extremity of position and size of the various latitudes: (1) With regard to controversial issues, the latitude of rejection of those taking an extreme position will be greater than those taking a moderate position. (2) For extreme subjects, the latitude of rejection will be greater than their latitude of acceptance. (3) The latitude of noncommitment will vary inversely with extremity of position. A study of the 1960 presidential campaign yielded results consistent with these hypotheses (Sherif et al., 1965).

Patterns of Acceptance and Rejection

Sherif and his associates have conducted numerous studies of the distinctive patterning of acceptance, rejection, and displacement in social judgment. Based on these studies, several propositions were formulated (Sherif et al., 1965):

1.   If an individual has an attitude toward a class of items, he will have a set of well-established categories for judging it, including ranges of acceptance and rejection. Any specific item will be judged in relation to these categories.

2.   To the extent that the person is involved with respect to the class of items, the position that he accepts as his own serves as an anchor for the placement of other items in the same class.

3.   To the extent that the individual's own position becomes the most salient anchor, his placement of an item will reflect an evaluation of it. This proposition will be true even when he is instructed to disregard his own feelings.

4.   When a person's own position serves as an anchor and when the item being judged lacks, in some degree, objective properties that cannot be ignored, items will be assimilated or contrasted in proportion to their proximity or discrepancy from the person's own position. That is, the items will be displaced toward the person's own position when they are near his position and displaced away from his own position when they are remote from it.

These propositions may be conceptualized as follows: When an individual uses his own position as an anchor, he becomes involved and hence selective about those items he is willing to accept. Only those items that are close to his own position are assimilated into the latitude of acceptance. The threshold of acceptance is high, and the range of items that will be assimilated is inversely proportional to degree of involvement. Conversely, the threshold of rejection is lowered, and the range of unacceptable items increases in proportion to degree of involvement.

These effects were said to be accentuated when subjects are permitted to use whatever number of categories seems appropriate to them. On the basis of this assumption, the following additional propositions concerning categorization were formulated:

1.   The number of categories that a person chooses to use varies inversely with his degree of involvement. If a person is strongly committed to a position, he uses fewer categories than less-involved persons.

2.   Highly involved persons place large numbers of items in the unacceptable category, put a few into the acceptable category, and tend to ignore the noncommital category. Uninvolved persons do not reveal this systematic bias in use of category widths.

3.   These variations in distribution of items are the result of assimilation-contrast effects relative to the person's own position.

4.   The degree of favorableness of the items does not affect these distributions.

Social Judgment and Attitude Change

Sherif and Hovland (1961) pointed out that studies of the effects of communications on attitude change have yielded inconclusive and sometimes contradictory results. For example, Remmers (1938) reported positive shifts in attitude scores following communications, whereas Manske (1937) and Russell and Robertson (1947) found shifts in the direction opposite to that advocated by a communication. Both positive and negative changes have been reported as a function of the subject's initial position (Wilke, 1934; Knower, 1935). Sherif and Hovland suggested that these contrasting effects were on account of the size of the discrepancy between the person's own position and that advocated by the communication. When the descrepancy is small, the communication is assimilated and hence produces positive attitude change; when it is very large, contrast effects occur and the attitude changes away from the position advocated by the communication.

This general interpretation was elaborated by Sherif et al. (1965), who suggested that placement or evaluation of a communication is relative to the individual's reference scale, which includes latitudes of acceptance, rejection, and noncommitment. Whether or not the person experiences a discrepancy between his own position and the communication (and hence whether he experiences stress) depends upon the position of the communication relative to latitudes of acceptance, rejection, and noncommitment. The degree to which these latitudes serve as this type of anchor depends upon the extent to which the individual is personally involved with the issue. The degree of involvement can be determined by comparing the number of positions in each of the three latitudes. The greater the personal involvement with the issue, the greater will be the latitude of rejection in relation to the latitude of acceptance and the more nearly will the latitude of noncommitment approach zero.

It therefore follows that when an individual is involved with an issue, his own latitude of acceptance becomes an anchoring point for the evaluation of communications concerning the issue. When the communication does not diverge greatly from the latitude of acceptance, it will be assimilated and will be judged as "fair," "unbiased," and probably "true." The person's own position is shifted in the direction of the communication. On the other hand, if the communication advocates a position that is too far removed from the person's latitude of acceptance so that it falls within his latitude of rejection, contrast effects occur and the communication is judged as "unfair," "biased," and probably "false." In such cases the attitude is likely to shift away from the position advocated by the communication (the so-called boomerang effect). Studies by Hovland, Harvey, and Sherif (1957) demonstrated that such effects do indeed occur when subjects varying in attitude toward prohibition are asked to judge a moderately "wet" communication.

Comments and Evaluation

The social judgment theory clearly reflects the transorientational approach. Sherif and his colleagues have brought together propositions and experimental findings derived from widely diverse theoretical orientations and have ingeniously interrelated these in their approach to social judgments. The result is an interesting set of propositions concerning the judgment process that fits very well the experimental data from which they were deduced. As the authors admitted, however, the propositions do not hang together as consistently as one would wish for a fully integrated theory. This comment probably reflects the fact that the theory is still being developed.

The experimental studies that have been conducted as direct tests of the theory have generally provided supporting evidence. The studies by Hovland, Harvey, and Sherif (1957) provide good support for the differential judgments of a communication as a function of the judge's own position and involvement with the issue. Similarly, the series of studies reported by Sherif, Sherif, and Nebergall (1965) are generally consistent with propositions concerning the effects of involvement and commitment on latitudes of acceptance, rejection, and noncommitment.

Perhaps the biggest difficulty is a practical one with the determination of the various latitudes and degree of involvement. According to the theory, the nature of the latitudes of acceptance, rejection, and noncommitment are so closely related to the degree of commitment that it is difficult to separate them. Progress has been made in this direction, and there is promise that this will not be a serious problem for the theory.

The theory deals with an important set of social issues that have relevance to most forms of social interaction. In fact, Sherif has applied the major concepts of the social judgment theory to such diverse social problems as norm formation, attitude change, and intergroup conflict. With additional development and empirical validation the theory may make even greater contributions to the understanding of complex social behavior.

In Chapter 3 we discussed a number of theories of behavior in groups which are basically reinforcement theories. The theory of elementary social behavior (Homans, 1950, 1961) and the theory of interaction outcomes (Thibaut & Kelley, 1959) are often referred to as exchange theories because the central concept of social interaction is one of exchange of reinforcements. The behavioral theory of authority relations (Adams & Romney, 1959) was also based on reinforcement in that authority was described in terms of control of reinforcers.

In this chapter we consider a number of theories of group process that are related to those reviewed in Chapter 3. However, the theories are not based on any particular theoretical orientation and hence are transorientational in nature. Group syntality theory (Cattell, 1948, 1951a) derives from a survey of writings about group behavior and Cattell's own factor analytic studies; a theory of group achievement (Stogdill, 1959) represents a combination of learning theory, interaction theory, and expectancy theory; a contingency model for leadership effectiveness (Fiedler, 1964, 1967) is based largely on empirical studies but elements of personality theory and structural theory are evident; and a descriptive model of social response (Willis, 1964) is related to field theory but also has similarities to other theoretical orientations. The transorientational approach should be evident in the following discussions.

GROUP SYNTALITY THEORY

The approach we have labeled group syntality theory was formulated by Cattell (1948) in an attempt to provide a foundation for the meaningful description and measurement of groups. His thesis was that exact scientific prediction requires accurate description, measurement, and classification of phenomena. Therefore, in order to discover the laws governing group behavior, there first must be some means of accurately defining the group at any given moment. In Cattell's view, this definition can be accomplished only by establishing a branch of psychology dealing with the "personality" of groups. It is not surprising, then, that his proposals are concerned more with the description of groups than with the prediction of group behavior.

Cattell's analysis was basically empirical in nature. He began by surveying the sociological and psychological literature concerning group behavior for the purpose of identifying group characteristics. These characteristics then served as data for factor analyses, although it is not clear to what extent the theory was based on the results of factor analytic studies. The resulting formulation involved two aspects of the group: dimensions of the group and dynamics of syntality. Before we consider these two aspects, a discussion of the concept of syntality will be helpful.

The Concept of Syntality

The term *syntality* was adopted by Cattell (1948) to refer to that aspect of the group which is analogous to the personality of the individual. The syntality of the group therefore refers to the "togetherness" of the group and includes the dynamic, temperamental, and ability traits of the group. In another report (Cattell, 1951b) he stated that syntality referred to the final performance of the group as a group. Cattell, Saunders, and Stice (1953) identified syntality as that which is defined by the attributes of the group as a group or that which is defined by the measured performances of the group as an integrated whole. Thus, the use of the *syntality* does not appear to be entirely consistent. In practice, it means the measured performance of the group acting as a unit.

Cattell's justification for treating the group as a single entity was based on McDougall's (1920) arguments concerning the resemblance of individuals and groups. These arguments may be stated briefly as follows:

1. A group retains its characteristic behavior and structure despite changes in membership.
2. Group experiences are remembered.
3. A group is capable of responding as a whole to stimuli directed to its parts.
4. A group possesses drives which are more or less integrated in executive functions.
5. A group reveals varying emotional states.
6. A group shows collective deliberation.

Cattell asserted that these arguments have never been refuted, and he (apparently) accepted them as demonstrating "group mentality." (Parenthetically, we might note that lack of refutation is a weak basis for assuming the truth of a conclusion.) With respect to group behavior, however, he believed that McDougall and others were guilty of confusing characteristics. He suggested that three aspects or "panels" are necessary to define a group.

Group Dimensions

The three panels needed to define a group are syntality traits, characteristics of internal structure, and population traits. The aspect of the group described as *syntality traits* concerns any effect the group has as a totality, whether it be on another group or on the physical environment. Cattell recognized that cataloging syntality traits is not an easy task, but he believed that most of these traits could be inferred from the external behavior of the group. Examples of syntality traits include decisions in committees, aggression toward other groups, energy in trading with other groups, and similar group behaviors.

Structural characteristics concern the relationships among the members of the group. These are the descriptions of the internal behavior of the group; that is, the organizational patterns within the group. Examples of structural characteristics include form of leadership, roles, cliques, status, interaction, patterns of communication, and other relationships among the behavior patterns of group members.

Population traits are the averages (mean, modal, typical) of the measured characteristics of the group members or definitions of the personality of the average member of the group. Examples include average intelligence, crime incidence, mean stature, mean attitudes toward various social issues, etc., of the group members.

The probable relationships among the three panels, according to Cattell, is one of interdependence. If we knew all the laws of social psychology, we could predict any panel from a knowledge of the other two. For example, if one knew the structure of the group and the population traits, it would be possible to predict syntality traits; that is, group behavior. Similarly, if population traits and the environment were known, group structure, and finally group behavior, could be predicted.

Cattell (1951b) noted two difficulties with the three panels. First, there is the problem of distinguishing sharply between structural and syntality characteristics. This problem can be resolved by always remembering that structural variables are statements of relations among group members or among their behaviors. Structural relations must always include all members of the group. On the other hand, observations of internal interaction that do not involve relations are in the syntality panel. The second difficulty is the problem of finding a place for cultural tradition in the three panels. Cattell's answer was that cultural tradition is found in all three panels. Personality involves cultural tradition and hence is reflected in population traits. Cultural tradition also influences group structure and therefore affects group behavior, or group snytality.

Dynamics of Syntality

In the analysis of group dimensions it was implicitly assumed that the whole existence of individual members is bound up in the group. Since this case is rare in natural situations, Cattell suggested that the dynamic relations within and between groups must be analyzed. In approaching this problem, he noted two aspects of groups that are significant. First, the existence of a group is dependent upon the needs of individuals; a group will exist only so long as it satisfies some of the psychological needs of its members. Second, groups are generally overlapping: individuals belong simultaneously to several different groups. This fact is related to what Cattell called "dynamic special-ization," which refers to the fact that a group can be made specific in func-tion. That is, a group can be formed for a specific purpose, such as collect-ing funds to fight cancer or improving city bus service.

These considerations led Cattell to formulate seven "theorems" concern-ing the psychodynamics of groups. Since these were not presented as precise statements of relationships, his ideas require more-detailed treatment than a mere restatement of single propositions.

DEFINITION OF SYNERGY   The first theorem stated that groups are formed for the purpose of satisfying individual needs and cease to exist when they no longer meet this purpose. The need satisfaction that is related to the group's existence consists of three parts, which Cattell called synergy, effec-tive synergy, and group maintenance synergy. *Synergy* refers to the total indi-vidual energy available to the group. It is the sum total of the group members' interest in the existence and work of the group. A portion of this energy must be expended in dealing with interpersonal relations in the group; that is, in dealing with friction and cohesion within the group. This part of the total energy, or synergy, was called group maintenance synergy and has priority in the group's expenditure of synergy. After the maintenance needs of the group have been met, the remaining synergy (*effective synergy*) can be used in achieving the outside goals of the group. According to Cattell, maintenance synergy is relatively great in comparison with effective synergy. For example, if there is an attempt to dissolve the group all the synergy may be devoted to maintenance.

MEASURING SYNERGY   The second theorem asserts that the total synergy of a group is the vectorial resultant of the attitudes of all members toward the group. In order to measure this vectorial resultant, account must be taken of (1) the number of persons interested in the group, (2) the strength of the satisfaction each person gains from the group, (3) the vector direction of the satisfactions, and (4) the subsidiation relations of satisfactions relative to other groups and purposes of the individuals concerned. Precise procedures for measuring these factors were not specified. However, Cattell suggested that the latter three could be measured (see Cattell, 1947) and are additive. Once these values are determined and summed, a measure of total synergy can be obtained by multiplying the sum by the number of persons interested in the group.

SYNTAL SUBSIDIATION   Effective synergy is directed to goals outside the group and hence to established patterns of reacting that are subsidiary to some ultimate goal of the group: a group gives some support to other groups (usually ancillary groups) or may form subgroups for special purposes. Cattell referred to this as a subsidiation chain and the pattern of interrelations among groups and subgroups as a *syntal dynamic lattice*. Within the syntal lattice, one group may use the other as a tool for some purposes whereas this procedure may be reversed for other purposes. For example, a nation favors the family because it is on the nation's subsidiation chain to the goal of population stability, but the family needs the nation for protection, education of children, and other purposes.

PERSONAL SUBSIDIATION   In addition to the syntal lattices, dynamic lattice patterns of individuals exist. The subsidiation chains found in the dynamic lattice of the individual often include groups as links. For example, a man may join a dinner club to meet important people or to enhance his business opportunities. Of course, not all personal subsidiation chains include groups, nor are the motivations to join a group necessarily restricted to one goal. Thus, in the calculation of dynamic energies account must be taken of redistributions of energy that may occur at any link of the subsidiation chain.

The problems of relationships between syntal lattices and personal lattices must also be considered. These problems will be different for overlapping than for nonoverlapping groups. If there is no overlap, as in the case where group members are prohibited from joining other similar groups, relational problems are not great. In most instances, however, groups have overlapping personnel, which creates complex problems with syntal subsidiation. Unfortunately, Cattell did not identify the exact nature of these problems.

LOYALTY, SUBSIDIATION, AND SUBORDINATION   Theorem 5 states that the dynamic patterns of behavior in groups are formed by trial and error or by insightful learning in which rewarded patterns of response are stabilized. Cattell's general position asserts that patterns of behavior, such as loyalty, subsidiation, and subordination, are subject to the law of effect. However, the law operates more indirectly in the case of groups than in the case of individuals. If the group fails (is punished), the effect on the individual members is indirect and may vary from member to member. For example, if a nation is defeated in war, it may mean death for some, economic loss for some, and perhaps only loss of "face" for others. Similarly, group rewards are different for different members. They also may be indirect and difficult to associate with group causes. For these reasons, learning in groups is slower than similar individual learning.

SYNERGIC CONSTANCY   The total synergy in overlapping groups is constant provided that (1) non-group investment remains constant and that (2) the group activities remain on the same level with regard to goal distance (theorem 6). There are several implications of this theorem. If some groups require less maintenance synergy than others, more of the individual's total synergy for external purposes will be released. This excess effective synergy may be redistributed among overlapping groups, in which case the total synergy for any given group may or may not remain constant. It also follows that new groups may be linked to a personal subsidiation chain without change in energy distribution only if new energy is not required. For example, a person who is interested in a golf club may join a committee to preserve the golf course without any new interest; however, if he joins a committee to improve the school, new energies may be required and a redistribution of energies would result.

ISOMORPHISM OF SYNTAL AND PERSONALITY CHANGE   Both syntal structures and personality characteristics are subject to change. Since the syntal structures of groups (group structures and functions) are ultimately shaped by conditions of reality, their form at any given moment depends upon individual characteristics. Thus theorem 7 states that there will be a close parallelism between syntality traits and personality traits of group members. The stability of group structures, for example, depends upon the stability of the corresponding sentiments of individual group members. The major parallel characteristics suggested by Cattell (1948) include syntal resistance to change and personal disposition rigidity, syntal integration and personal intelligence, syntal freedom from fashions and personal emotional maturity, and syntal political conflict and personal tolerance for mental conflict.

Implications for Group Dynamics

Cattell (1948) maintained that the seven theorems outlined above have implications for research:

1. The synergy of groups varies more in both strength and quality than the energy of individuals. For this reason it is desirable to sort groups into classes for purposes of experimentation. He suggested that the classification into *elementary groups* that satisfy a single need and *cumulative groups* that satisfy many needs (Sorokin, Zimmerman, & Galpin, 1930) is an example of this approach.

2. The dynamic content of group syntality is far narrower than the dynamic expression of individuals. Individuals can satisfy many needs by their actions, but there are some needs that can be satisfied only on a group basis (for example, sexual needs). This means that variables for factor analytic study should aim at a denser representation of needs. Cattell also believed that this fact has implications for the lawful relations between syntal and personal dynamic lattices, but he did not elaborate this point.

3. The synergy of most groups is more liable to gross fluctuation than the total dynamic traits of individuals because of the sensitive interdependence of group with respect to quantity and quality of synergy. From this fact it follows that the laws governing group interrelationships (for example, syntal subsidiation) can be discovered through the measurement of changing synergies of groups.

4. The theorems should provide a basis for relating psychology to ethics and economics. For example, morality may be reflected in the discrepancy between individual attitudes and group synergy. Similarly, the concept of synergy may be helpful in understanding economic processes. To achieve goals, groups must transmit synergy from place to place. The principal means of such transmission is money and taxation. Since group members tax them-

selves in proportion to their interest, this taxation could be used as a measure of desire. Economic and psychodynamic measures are thus united.

Evaluation of Syntality Theory

Cattell's theory is internally consistent and the implications from his theorems are amenable to empirical test. It is not inconsistent with other acceptable theories, although the translation of Cattell's theorems into the language of other theorists, or vice versa, is not always easy. The theory appears to fit known data, despite the fact that relatively little research has been conducted for the purpose of testing its predictions.

Although syntality theory has many interesting aspects, there are several criticisms that may be leveled against it. First, the terminology is unnecessarily abstruse. Expressions such as "subsidiation in the syntal lattice" are well calculated to arouse aggressive tendencies in the reader. Furthermore, not all unusual terms are unambiguously defined by Cattell. The use of *syntality* to refer to both the "personality" of the group and the behavior of the group is an example.

Second, the problem of measurement has not been adequately considered. Some progress has been made in this direction (Cattell, 1947, 1951a, b; Cattell & Wispe, 1948; Cattell, Saunders, & Stice, 1953), but much remains to be done. Perhaps this is not so much a criticism of the theory as a comment on the status of measurement in social psychology. If we knew how to measure personality traits of individuals and group behavior, the measurement of syntality and population characteristics would be easy, and the derivation of structural characteristics would be relatively simple.

The empirical support for the theory is relatively sparse. One probable reason is that the theory has not stimulated research by others. The available evidence therefore is limited to that provided by Cattell and his associates. Since their work has been directed primarily toward the identification and classification of group dimensions (for example, see Cattell, Saunders, & Stice, 1953), the degree to which their work supports the theory is difficult to assess. The fact that the theory makes few explicit predictions about group behavior is another reason support is difficult to assess, and it is perhaps one of the reasons the theory has not stimulated others to conduct related research.

A THEORY OF GROUP ACHIEVEMENT

The theory of group achievement was developed by Stogdill (1959) in an attempt to resolve deficiencies in existing theories of group organization that are based largely on the concept of interaction. He cited the works of Barnard (1948), Davis (1957), Gulick and Urwick (1937) and Simon (1947) as examples of such theories.[1] Stogdill was interested in developing a theoretical

[1] The theories cited are concerned primarily with industrial organization and hence are outside the scope of this book.

subsystem that includes the internal structure and operations of groups. He therefore excluded external factors such as the group's buildings, equipment, and the like, although he recognized that these play a role in the behavior of some groups.

The theory was based upon elements of learning theory, expectation theory, and interaction theory; hence, it was assumed that *performances*, *interactions*, and *expectations* are the necessary elements required to describe group behavior. (In our terminology, the theory draws upon reinforcement, field, and cognitive orientations.) The structure of the theory involves three sets of factors: member inputs, mediating variables, and group outputs. Member inputs include the three elements listed above: performances, interactions, and expectations. Mediating variables include two classes or sets of variables: formal structure, including *functions* and *status*, and role structure, including *responsibility* and *authority*. Group outputs represent the achievement of the group and include *productivity, morale*, and *integration*.

The input variables are the attributes of individuals, singly and in interaction. These variables lead to role structure and group operations, which are properties of groups. Role structure and group operations mediate personal and interpersonal behaviors, the end effect being group achievement; for example, productivity, morale, and integration. The general direction of effects is from input variables to mediating variables to group achievement. However, feedback effects occur such that each set of variables is influenced by the other two.

Member Inputs

The behavior input variables used to develop the theory require further elaboration before their relationship to group structure can be shown. Stogdill began by defining the group in terms of interaction. He regarded a group as an open interaction system in which the structure of the system is determined by the actions of group members, and the continuance of the system is dependent upon member interactions. *Interaction* was used to describe a situation in which the reaction of any member is a response to the reactions of some other member. *Open system* was used to refer to the situation in which individual group members are free to join or leave the group without destroying its identity. Thus interaction plays a critical role in defining the group.

INTERACTION   Social interaction is an interpersonal characteristic of behavior, since it requires the presence of at least two individuals. Stogdill referred to an interaction as a situation in which person A reacts to person B and B reacts to A in such a way that the reaction of each is a response to the other. For example, if person A threatens B and B retreats, this is an interaction. In the usual case, of course, a unit of interaction consists of several exchanges of this sort. An interaction as a unit of analysis is thus a complex element and a complete description would require a report from the participants concerning their own reactions and their perceptions of the reactions of others. Thus interaction includes actions and reactions, each of which may be regarded as a performance. These performances determine the structure of the system.

PERFORMANCE   According to Stogdill, a group derives its identity from the actions and reactions of members. When one observes a group, the behaviors of individuals are easily seen; these identify him as an individual, but they may or may not identify him as a group member. The term *performance* is used in Stogdill's theory to refer to behaviors that are relative to the group. He therefore defined performance as a response that is part of an interaction; that is, as one of the actions or reactions that are operations of an interaction system. More briefly, a performance is any response that identifies the actor as a member of the group. Examples of performances include such diverse actions as cooperative work, planning, evaluating, decision making, operating a machine, communication, and other group-related activities.

It is not always easy to apply the definition of performance. As a consequence, some members of a group may not be so identified and some non-members may be mistakenly perceived as group members. Stogdill asserted that these are errors of judgment and do not invalidate the definition of performance.

EXPECTATION   Stogdill believed that interaction and performance are bases for group structure and operations, but that they cannot account for group purpose, the differentiation of member roles, or group stability. The concept of *expectation* was introduced as a basic dimension of group organization to account for these aspects of group behavior. Although his use of expectation was based upon the views of learning theorists (for example, Tolman, 1932; MacCorquodale & Meehl, 1953; Rotter, 1954; Kelly, 1955), his definition differed from theirs in a number of ways. These differences are reflected in the assumptions adopted by Stogdill: (1) expectation is a readiness for reinforcement, (2) reinforcement differentially affects estimates of desirability and probability, and (3) drive is assumed to operate in expectation. The Stogdillian definition of expectation is contained in the first assumption; that is, expectation is defined as a readiness for reinforcement. It is a function of drive, the estimated desirability of an outcome, and the estimated probability that that outcome will occur.

Since expectation is defined in terms of reinforcement, Stogdill needed to define reinforcement. Unfortunately, his definition is circular: reinforcement is the experiencing of an outcome which satisfies or confirms an expectation. Readiness for reinforcement refers to the extent to which the individual is prepared for a given outcome. Drive is defined as the tension level and degree of reactivity exhibited by an individual. Estimates of probability of occurrence and estimates of desirability refer to the individual's judgment concerning these aspects of a given outcome. All these elements are inferred from the individual's behavior with respect to the outcome.

Stogdill made a good case for his two-dimensional concept of expectation in which estimates of probability and of desirability respond differentially to reinforcement. He pointed out that a person may estimate that the probability that a highly undesirable event will occur is equal to the probability that a very desirable event will occur. If the probability is very high that both events will occur, he may be equally willing to experience them despite their differences in estimated desirability. On the other hand, if both outcomes are equally desirable, but the estimated probabilities of occurrence are markedly different, the person's expectation will be greater for the high-probability event. Expectation is thus a result of the interaction of estimated probability and estimated desirability. These estimates may either enhance each other, or one may lower the other.

The theory also posits that positively and negatively valued desirability estimates have different effects on expectation. The general rule is that probability tends to be overestimated when expectation is positively valued and underestimated when it is negatively valued. This is not always true, however, and Stogdill suggested that experimentation is needed to determine the conditions under which the rule does and does not hold true.

Both reward and punishment were assumed to reinforce expectation. Reinforcement is accomplished through the effects of reward and punishment on both estimates of desirability and of probability of occurrence. The only differences between the effects of reward and punishment on estimates of desirability were assumed to be on polarity: reward leads to estimates of desirability and punishment to estimates of undesirability. Reinforcement generally enhances estimated probability of occurrence, regardless of the source (reward or punishment) of the reinforcement. Stogdill suggested that a single reinforcement is sufficient to confirm an estimate of desirability at or near its maximum value, whereas several reinforcements are needed to bring confirmation of a probability estimate to its maximum value. Lack of reinforcement tends to reduce or eliminate expectations; that is, they undergo extinction.

Expectation is therefore a function of estimates of desirability and estimates of probability which respond differentially to reinforcement. This conception of expectation was used by Stogdill to account for individual value systems. Since each member carries his personal values into the group, the ability of the group to reinforce members' values accounts for the development of group goals. This singleness of purpose is, of course, an important factor in determining group structure and function, and ultimately group achievement.

Group Structure and Operations

According to Stogdill's analysis, performances, interactions, and expectations are not completely independent but show varying degrees of interrelatedness. For example, performance and interaction combine to determine structure in interaction. The performances of members and continuity of interaction determine the identity of the group. Performance and expectation are interdependent in that performance provides the means for confirming expectations. The mutual reinforcement of norms and purpose is the result of the combined effects of interaction and expectation. These propositions were used by Stogdill to describe group structure and operations.

FORMAL STRUCTURE   When individuals come together in a group, they bring with them differential expectations and performances that are exhibited in the course of interaction. These differential aspects of group members are important determinants of group structure, but they are also influenced (modified) by the reactions of other members. Individuals thus tend to exhibit predictable patterns of performance which elicit predictable reactions from others in the group, which in turn lead to differentiated *positions* in the group. Once the group has been organized, the differentiated positions that compose the group structure become parts of the group rather than individual characteristics; that is, the expected behaviors derive from the group position rather than from the particular person who happens to occupy the position at any given time. The structure of an organized group thus involves a predictable pattern of action and reaction plus a system of mutually reinforced expectations.

The position in a group structure includes both *status* and *function*. Stogdill asserted that the status of a position defines the degree of freedom of the position's occupant in initiating and maintaining goal direction. Status implies a hierarchical relationship between two or more persons (positions) in the group and therefore can be defined only in relation to the status of other positions in the group structure. Such terms as *power, right,* and *privilege* refer to the kinds of freedom that are used in defining status.

The *function* of a position refers to the nature of the contribution that the occupant is expected to make to the group effort. Function, of course, varies from position to position in relation to status differences. Examples of function include decision making, planning, leadership behaviors, and similar performances that may contribute to goal achievement.

The stability of status and function is influenced by several factors. For example, initial experiences of success or failure confirm expectations that are highly resistant to extinction. The group purpose or goal also depends upon a set of mutually confirmed desirability estimates regarding the outcomes that may be experienced as a result of structure and operations. If the outcome is estimated to be highly desirable, status and function will be stable; conversely, if the outcome is estimated to be highly undesirable, the structure will be unstable.

ROLE STRUCTURE   The formal structure represents an aspect of the group and hence the occupant is largely irrelevant. Nevertheless, it is well known that the occupant does make a difference in the behavior and achievement of the group. Stogdill therefore used the term *role* to refer to the expectations that are attached to the person rather than to the position that he occupies. The role structure refers to the set of differentiated roles in the group.

Stogdill encountered a problem when he differentiated behaviors expected of a person because of the position he occupies and those expected because of personal characteristics. The pattern of performance and degree of freedom must be defined differently for the formal structure and the role structure. The concepts of *responsibility* and *authority* were invoked to solve this problem. Responsibility was defined as the set of performances that a given occupant is expected to exhibit within the formal structure and authority as the degree of freedom that the occupant of a position is expected to exercise. Responsibility and authority are related to function and status, respectively, but these relationships are not perfect. The general rules stated by Stogdill are (1) the higher the person's status the greater his authority, and (2) regardless of position, the member's responsibility is expected to be related to the functions of his position.

Group Achievement

Group achievement is the end result of the group process. Stogdill asserted that group achievement (group output) is the consequence of performances, interactions, and expectations (group inputs), mediated through group structure and operations. Although he admitted that group achievement is most commonly identified as group effectiveness in reaching its goals, he believed that this definition failed to include all aspects of group output. He therefore proposed that the essential dimensions of group achievement are *productivity, morale,* and *integration.*

PRODUCTIVITY   Productivity was defined as the degree of change in expectancy values resulting from group behavior. This definition is based upon the assumption that member performances and interaction create changes in positively or negatively valued expectations. The amount of such change reflects the group's productivity.

MORALE   Group morale was defined as degree of freedom from restraint in working toward the group goal. This refers to individual members' freedom to act, to interact, to reinforce expectations, and to perform similar goal-directed behaviors. Stogdill asserted that contrary to common belief, morale is at a minimum in a minimally structured group; the more structured the group, the greater the freedom of members, because they know the limits of acceptable behavior. He admitted, however, that there is an upper limit beyond which increased structure does not further increase freedom. The area of freedom, and hence morale, may also be increased through reinforcement of goal expectation. For example, success brings high status to a group, which leads to greater initiative and freedom of action. The successful group is likely to have high morale.

INTEGRATION   Group integration was defined as the degree to which the group can maintain its structure and operations under stressful conditions. This aspect of group achievement of course becomes more apparent in times of crises when lack of integration may lead to dissolution of the group. Group integration is reflected by member satisfactions with the group, mutual liking among members, member support for leadership, and similar positive reactions to the group. This concept refers to essentially the same aspect of the group as *cohesiveness* (Thibaut, 1950, Back, 1951).

Productivity, morale, and integration were assumed to vary together; however, when inputs remain constant, any increase in one factor occurs at a cost to at least one of the other factors. On the other hand, it is often the case that new inputs can increase one aspect of group achievement without affecting the others, or all may be increased simultaneously. This notion of a balanced system is similar to Cattell's (1948) concept of synergic constancy (see page 306).

Summary and Evaluation

Stogdill has provided a useful framework for the analysis of the process through which groups achieve their goals. He has identified the major elements in the group process, thus giving an overall picture of the many variables operating to determine the results achieved by the group. He has avoided both extremes of level of analysis; his concepts are neither so specific as to be unmanageable nor so gross as to be useless. The theory is internally consistent, testable, and in agreement with the evidence concerning group processes.

Despite these favorable aspects of his effort, however, there are some serious problems with his theory. Perhaps the most serious is the lack of precise formulations concerning the exact relations among the variables that he identified. Just how do performances and interactions combine to determine structure? In what ways does performance provide the means for confirming expectation? What is the mechanism by which group structure and operations mediate group achievement? These and many similar questions arise in connection with the theory, but answers are not readily available.

A second problem concerns the definition of terms. Stogdill defined his terms conceptually, but these definitions did not provide a basis for operational procedures. It is not always clear how the necessary measurements are to be made. Some attempts were made in this direction, but much more clarification is needed.

Although Stogdill cited a considerable amount of experimental evidence that is consistent with his theory, the theory appears not to have stimulated research by others. Therefore, evidence obtained for the purpose of directly testing Stogdill's views is still lacking. Perhaps this is a consequence of the lack of precise formulations and lack of operational definitions referred to above. Thus, while the theory has considerable descriptive appeal, its predictive value is still unestablished.

A CONTINGENCY MODEL OF LEADERSHIP EFFECTIVENESS

The contingency model (Fiedler, 1964, 1967) was the outgrowth of many years of experimentation on leadership and group effectiveness. The program of research was directed largely toward the identification of the personal characteristics that distinguish the effective leader from other leaders. The general approach adopted by Fiedler was based on the assumption that the leader's perceptions of his coworkers reflect task-relevant attitudes that influence group interaction and performance. Measures of interpersonal perception were first developed for research on psychotherapeutic relations (Fiedler, 1951) and later adapted to the study of leadership. Studies of the relationship between measures of interpersonal perception and group effectiveness yielded apparently contradictory results; the contingency model represents an attempt to reconcile these data. The general theoretical model assumes that the type of leader that will be most effective depends upon the favorability of the situation to the leader, which in turn depends upon affective leader-group relations, task structure, and the leader's position power.

Definition of Terms

The key terms used in Fiedler's (1964) analysis include *group, leader,* and *effectiveness*. Specific definitions of these key terms were presented to clarify the discussion of the theory.

GROUP   The definition of group was based upon Campbell's (1958) criteria for determining whether an aggregate constitutes an entity. Thus a group was defined as any set of individuals who are similar, who are in proximity, and who share a common fate on task-relevant events. The intent was to include those groups in which members perceive themselves as inter-dependent in achieving a common goal and to exclude those groups in which members work individually on a task (coacting groups).

LEADER   The leader was defined as the group member who directs and coordinates task-relevant group activities. Fiedler recognized that leadership functions are shared, but he was concerned only with the one person who performs the traditional leadership role. To be considered a leader, the individual must either be appointed by an agent of a larger organization of which the group is a part, or be elected by the group, or be identified as the most influential member on task-relevant questions on a sociometric questionnaire.

EFFECTIVENESS   The leader's effectiveness was defined in terms of his group's performance in achieving group goals. Implicit in this statement is the assumption that the more nearly the group achieves its goal, the more effective is the leader. It is assumed further that task-relevant abilities and skills of members of different groups are similar.

Styles of Leadership and Group Effectiveness

A considerable amount of evidence has accumulated showing that leadership style is related to group process. The early study by Lewin and his associates (Lewin, Lippitt, & White, 1939) revealed dramatic differences in behavioral and emotional aspects of group process as a consequence of autocratic, democratic, or laissez faire styles of leadership. Since that time, two major types of leadership behavior have been studied, variously labeled as autocratic versus democratic, authoritarian versus nonauthoritarian (Shaw, 1955), supervisory versus participatory (Preston & Heintz, 1949), task-oriented versus human relations–oriented (Katz & Kahn, 1952), directive versus non-directive (Shaw & Blum, 1966), initiation of structure versus consideration (Halpin, 1955), and distant, controlling, managing versus psychologically close, permissive (Fiedler, 1964). Experimental findings concerning the effects of these two styles of leadership have been inconsistent. Some investigators reported autocratic, directive, controlling leaders to be more effective, but the opposite was sometimes found, and often no statistically significant differences were observed.

Since Fiedler's assumption was that interpersonal perception reflects attitudes which influence effectiveness, his leadership styles were inferred from measures of interpersonal perception. The measure he used was the "assumed similarity of opposites" (ASo) score and, later, the "least preferred coworker" (LPC) score.

THE ASo AND LPC MEASURES   The ASo score is obtained from ratings of the most-preferred coworker and of the least-preferred coworker. The subject is asked to think of all the people with whom he has ever worked. Then he is asked to describe the one person he considers to be the most-preferred coworker (MPC) and the one he considers to be the least-preferred coworker (LPC). Ratings are made on eight-point, bipolar scales of the semantic differential type (Osgood, Suci, & Tannenbaum, 1957). The ends of the scales are anchored by bipolar adjectives, such as pleasant-unpleasant, friendly-unfriendly, rejecting-accepting, cooperative-uncooperative, distant-close, and similar adjective pairs. MPC and LPC scores may be computed by scoring each item from most to least favorable. The ASo score is computed by subtracting the LPC score from the MPC score for each item, squaring and summing these differences, and extracting the square root of the sum. This D score (Cronbach & Glesser, 1953) reflects the discrepancy between the ratings of the most-preferred and the least-preferred coworker. The ASo score and the LPC score are highly correlated (.70 to .93) and so were used interchangeably by Fiedler.

The person with a high ASo/LPC score tends to see even a poor coworker in a relatively favorable light. Thus high ASo/LPC leaders behave in a manner described as compliant, nondirective, and generally relaxed. Low ASo/LPC leaders are more demanding, controlling, and managing in their interaction with the group. Thus, high ASo/LPC leaders are similar to "democratic" and low ASo/LPC to "autocratic" leadership styles.

The ASo and LPC scores of leaders were related to measures of leadership effectiveness in numerous studies. Initially, it was predicted that the more-nondirective (high ASo) leaders would be more effective than directive (low ASo) leaders. A study of basketball teams yielded a correlation of $-.69$ between leader ASo and a measure of effectiveness, contrary to expectations. This finding was replicated by a study of twenty-two student surveying parties which yielded a correlation of $-.51$ between leader ASo and team effectiveness (Fiedler, 1954). Subsequent studies of bomber crews (Fiedler, 1955) resulted in correlations ranging from $-.33$ to $.60$. In this study, however, it was found that the direction of the relationship depended upon the leader's affective relations with key group members. Other studies (Gerard, 1957; Anderson & Fiedler, 1964) revealed that leaders in powerful positions behaved differently from those in less powerful positions. This complex set of data provided the stimulus for the development of the contingency model.

Task-situation Dimensions

The development of the contingency model involved two steps: a description of task-situation dimensions and the specification of the relation between these dimensions and leadership effectiveness. In attempting to identify the significant dimensions of the task situation, Fiedler assumed that the crucial factors would be those that determine whether the situation is favorable or unfavorable to the leader. A favorable situation was described as one in which the group environment makes it easy for the leader to influence the members of his group; an unfavorable situation makes it difficult for the leader to influence group members.

Three situational components were postulated as the critical factors determining the favorability of the situation to the leader: the leader's affective relations with group members, the power provided by his position, and the degree of structure of the group task. *Affective leader-group relations* were assumed to have the greatest effect on situation favorability. The leader who is liked and respected can obtain the compliance of the group without exercising power and can act more decisively and with more confidence than the leader who is disliked and rejected by the members of his group. This dimension was operationally defined by bipolar rating scales.

Task structure was asserted to be the second most-important determinant of favorability. The task may be highly structured in the sense that the goal is clearly specified and procedures for goal achievement are unambiguous. On the other hand, the task may be highly unstructured in that the goal is unclear and there are many paths to the goal. The theory postulates that the more structured the task, the more favorable the situation for the leader. This dimension was operationally defined by ratings of four task dimensions proposed by Shaw (1963). These are *decision verifiability* (the degree to which the correctness of the decision can be demonstrated either logically or by appeal to authority), *goal clarity* (the degree to which the requirements of the task are known to the group), *goal path multiplicity* (the degree to which the task can be accomplished by a variety of procedures), and *solution multiplicity* (the degree to which there is more than one "correct" solution).

The *power position* of the leader was the third and least important determinant of favorability. This refers to the leader's control over rewards and sanctions, his authority, over group members, and the degree to which he is supported by the organization of which the group is a part. The powerful leader may be able to influence the group even if the affective leader-group relations are poor. The more powerful the leader's position, the more favorable the situation is for the leader. This dimension was defined operationally by a checklist of items such as "leader can recommend punishments and rewards."

The Favorability Continuum

Fiedler assumed that any particular group situation could be ordered along a favorability continuum, ranging from those that are highly favorable to the leader to those that are highly unfavorable to the leader. This continuum derives from the three task-situation dimensions discussed above. The relation of the three dimensions to the favorability continuum was based on the assumption that affective leader-group relations are most important, task structure next most important, and leader power position least important as a determinant of favorability. Therefore, the most favorable situation is one in which the affective leader-member relations are good, the task is highly structured, and the leader power position is strong. The most unfavorable situation is one in which the leader-member relations are poor, the task is unstructured, and the leader power position is weak. (Fiedler suggested that an even more unfavorable situation might exist if leader-member relations are *very* poor, the task structured, and the power position strong.)

Leadership Style and Favorability

In order to determine the relationship between leadership style and effectiveness as a function of the favorability of the situation for the leader, Fiedler classified the group situations in a great many experiments that he had conducted. He then plotted the correlations between leader ASo/LPC scores and measures of group effectiveness as a function of situational favorability. The results are shown in Figure 12–1. On the basis of these data, he concluded that the style of leadership that is most effective is contingent upon the favorableness of the group-task situation. Managing, controlling, task-oriented leaders are more effective when the group-task situation is either very favorable or very unfavorable for the leader; permissive, considerate, relationship-oriented leaders are more effective when the group-task situation is of intermediate favorability.

According to Fiedler (1967), this "contingency model" generally fits our everyday experiences. When the leader has power, is on good terms with his followers, and the task is clearly structured, the group is ready to be directed and is willing to be told what to do. Similarly, when the situation is highly unfavorable, permissive leadership may lead to disintegration of the group. Only moderately favorable or moderately unfavorable situations call for considerate, relation-oriented leadership. In this case, the members must

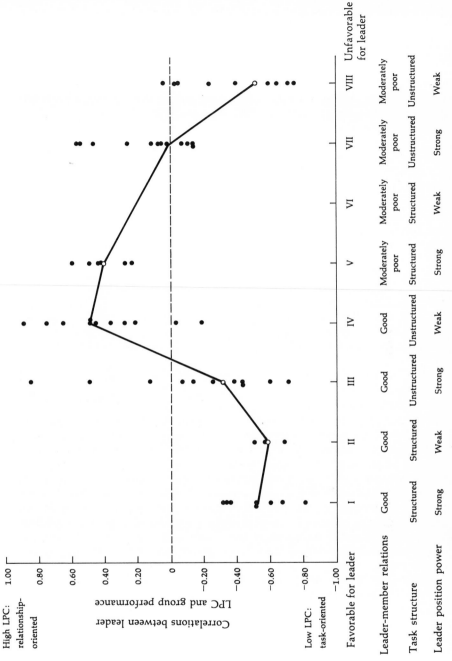

FIGURE 12–1. Correlations between leaders' LPC scores and group effectiveness plotted for each cell. The Eta^2 between the correlations LPC/ASo and performance and favorableness is .586 r^2 = .007. (Reprinted with permission from F. E. Fiedler. *A theory of leadership effectiveness.* New York: McGraw-Hill, 1967.)

be free to offer new ideas and suggestions, and the leader typically cannot force group members to comply with his wishes.

Strengths and Weaknesses of the Theory

Perhaps the major strength of the contingency model is that it specifies conditions under which different leadership behaviors may be expected to be effective. Previous theoretical analyses have suggested that leadership is a complex phenomenon that is influenced by variables such as personal attributes and situational factors, but relations among variables were not clearly indicated. The contingency theory begins to specify *how* these factors are interrelated in their influence on leadership effectiveness. The theory is logically consistent and agrees with available data concerning leadership behavior.

A second strong point is that it yields testable hypotheses. Since the theory was first conceived in 1962, Fiedler and his associates have conducted several experiments designed to test the theory; they have had generally supportive results. For example, the predicted relationship between leader LPC score and group performance as a function of favorability was found in studies of the following samples: Belgian naval personnel (Fiedler, 1966), American graduate students (Anderson, 1964), Army and Navy ROTC cadets (Meuwese & Fiedler, 1965), members of the ROTC Special Forces Company and the Arab Student Association at the University of Illinois (Chemers, Fiedler, Lekhyananda, & Stolurow, 1966), and members of industrial and business organizations (Hunt, 1967). A study by Shaw and Blum (1966) demonstrated that the theory is not limited to leader characteristics measured by the ASo/LPC scores. They found that leaders instructed to play a directive role were more effective when the task was highly structured, whereas leaders instructed to play a nondirective role were more effective when the task was less structured (presumably a moderately favorable condition for the leader).

The major weakness of the theory' is the definition of the favorability continuum. Although the experimental evidence generally supports the theory, there are wide differences between groups classified alike with regard to their favorability for the leader, suggesting that the three group-task dimensions are imperfectly measured or there are other variables which are relevant to the favorability continuum. Both of these are probably true, but the latter is of more serious consequence for the theory. (Of course, the theory itself may be incorrect, but the evidence is sufficiently strong to make this interpretation unattractive.)

Fiedler (1967) pointed to one limitation that is related to the classification of groups. He suggested that situations in which the leader-member affective relations are extremely poor are probably very unfavorable to the leader even when the task is structured and his power position is strong. The description of the favorability continuum does not provide for this possibility. Furthermore, such group situations rarely occur naturally, probably because such groups disintegrate; therefore, there is little evidence on this point.

In general, the theory is very promising, and data obtained from future research may be expected to lead to strengthening modifications. More-adequate indices of the favorability dimension are clearly needed.

A DESCRIPTIVE MODEL OF SOCIAL RESPONSE

The descriptive model of social response (also called the diamond model of conformity behavior) is concerned with responses to social influence (Willis, 1964, 1965). Willis referred to his approach as a *model* rather than as a *theory*, since he viewed a model as descriptive whereas a theory is explanatory. Nevertheless, his analysis not only described the kinds of responses that may occur but also identified the *conditions* under which the various responses occur and the relationships among them. It therefore fits our minimal definition of a theory as a set of interrelated hypotheses.

The theory (or model) consists of a set of basic definitions, a description of four modes of response to social influence, a model delineating the relationships among these response modes, a consideration of the conditions under which each type of response may be expected to occur, and a set of hypotheses regarding the consequences of the various modes of response. The explication of these aspects of the theory are drawn from several reports by Willis and his associates.

Basic Definitions

Willis (1964) believed that the usual definition of conformity in terms of agreement with a majority is inadequate for the development of a general description of social response. Instead, he proposed an approach that utilized both congruence and movement. *Congruence* referred to agreement between an individual's response and a response that is socially defined as "correct." Thus congruence refers essentially to the kind of response that has traditionally been called conformity. *Movement* was defined as a shift in response relative to the social standard. Therefore, for a social response to be called *conformity* it not only must agree with the social ideal but must represent a change (movement) of response; that is, a change from the response that was made in the absence of the social standard. (Although Willis asserted that movement usually is not considered by investigators of conformity behavior, it may be noted that the typical study includes a control group that provides an estimate of what the response would have been in the absence of the social standard. Since the response labeled *conformity* is usually different from the one made by the control subjects, it does in fact represent a change in response.) According to this analysis, then, conformity is only one *mode of social response*. Other examples of social response modes include imitation, obedience, and acceptance of persuasive communications.

The distinction between *model* and *theory* referred to above played an important role in Willis' approach. Whereas a model was considered purely descriptive, a theory was said to attempt to explain by means of causal inferences. In addition to this basic distinction, he suggested that models are often concerned with possibilities, whereas theories are concerned with probabilities. In identifying modes of social response, therefore, he was not concerned with the probability that any given type of response would occur, only whether it was possible. The model of social response was viewed as a special case of a response model and was defined as a model for specifying and interrelating possible modes of reacting to social pressure. This was contrasted with a stimulus model that deals with stimulus variables and their interrelationships and with a process model that is concerned with changes over time.

The model proposed by Willis was intended to apply to all types of social response, but he chose to present it in terms of conformity. In doing so, he distinguished between conformity in general and *psychological conformity*. The latter was defined as behavior intended to fulfill normative group expectations as perceived by the individual.

Modes of Social Response

In an earlier version of Willis' model (Hollander & Willis, 1964), three modes of response were identified: conformity, independence, and anticonformity. Later (Willis, 1964), a fourth mode was added which Willis called *variability*.

Pure *conformity* behavior was defined as a completely consistent attempt on the part of an individual to make his responses congruent with the normative expectations of a specified group; the conformer will change his responses when his perception of the normative expectations of the group changes.

Pure *independence* was defined as behavior that gives zero weight to perceived normative expectations. This response mode is of course relevant only to the situation in which normative expectations are perceived, but it does not mean that they are ignored in the decision-making process. That is, the individual may very well consider these normative expectations in deciding how he should behave, but he does not allow them to influence his response.

Pure *anticonformity* was defined as behavior in response to normative expectations but which is directly antithetical to norm prescription. When the anticonformer is faced with a choice between a response that is regarded as socially correct and one that is socially wrong, he makes the wrong response. Both conformity and anticonformity are dependent on social standards, but in opposite directions.

Pure *variability* behavior was defined as invariable change of response regardless of perceived normative expectations. Movement is thus unrelated to social pressure; absolutely no weight is given to social pressures. The variability mode was regarded as a kind of independence. Willis suggested that it might also be considered as self-anticonformity, since it represents complete and consistent disagreement with the individual's own initial response.

The Diamond Model

The diamond model is a representation of the interrelationships among the four modes of social response. This model specifies two response dimensions: independence and net conformity. The independence dimension is limited at one extreme by independent behavior and at the other by variability behavior. It reflects the degree to which changes in the individual's judgments (responses) are unrelated to social influences. Net conformity is represented at one extreme by conformity behavior and at the other by anticonformity behavior. It therefore reflects the extent to which changes in the individual's responses are influenced by social pressures, either in the direction of agreement or in the direction of disagreement with the social standard. The two dimensions are thus orthogonal, as diagrammed in Figure 12–2. Although the model is stated in terms of pure modes of social response, it should be clear that responses in natural situations are rarely pure. The response is most likely to be a mixture of the various types; the position of the individual in the diamond space represents the degree to which his responses are composites of the four modes.

Conditions Determining Response Mode

If there are four possible response modes, then it should be possible to specify the conditions under which each mode is likely to occur. Willis and Hollander (1964) hypothesized that the mode of response would be determined by the relative competencies of the individual and the social group (a partner or a group majority), the attitude adopted by the individual, and the

FIGURE 12–2. The diamond model of interrelationships among the four modes of social response. (Adapted with permission from R. H. Willis. Descriptive models of social response. Technical Report, Nonr-Contract 816(12), Washington University, 1964.)

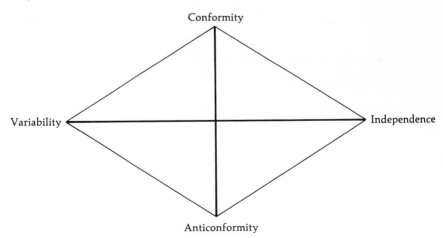

reward structure. They predicted that conformity behavior would be maximum when the competence of the group (or partner) is relatively high, the individual adopts a flexible attitude, and rewards are greater when the response agrees with the group. Independence should be maximum when the individual is relatively high in competence, he adopts an attitude of consistency, and rewards are greater when he makes a correct response. Anticonformity was predicted to occur when the group is relatively incompetent, the individual adopts a flexible attitude, and rewards are greater when the individual makes a response that is correct but which does not agree with the group's response. Variability was not considered. The results of an experimental study of these variables supported the theory.

Hollander and Willis (1967) suggested that the variability response is rare in natural settings. However, they cited a study by Aronson and Carlsmith (1962), which found that variability was associated with very low self-esteem. Hollander and Willis suggested that variability is generally associated with negative or very low self-esteem.

Consequences of Mode of Response

The individual's behavior is expected to produce measurable consequences in social interaction; therefore, Hollander and Willis (1964) predicted that conformity, independence, and anticonformity would lead to differential perceptions by group members. In general, the independent should be perceived as most attractive, the conformist as moderately attractive, and the anticonformist as least attractive. However, the competence variable was also assumed to be related to attraction, and the effects of response mode should interact with competence. For example, a competent anticonformer should be more attractive than an incompetent one; an incompetent conformer should be more attractive than a competent one; and a competent independent working with a competent group should be the most attractive individual. All these expectations were supported by the results of a study in which response mode was manipulated experimentally.

A similar study was conducted by Willis (1965) with variability behavior added. He found that conformity and variability produced perceptions which were similar but significantly different from those produced by independence and anticonformity. Conformers and variable responders were seen as being influenced more by others. This finding was interpreted in terms of the diamond model: conformity and variability are similar in that there is a tendency to change following an initial disagreement with the group, and independence and anticonformity share a tendency not to change following initial disagreement.

Comment

The descriptive model of social response is a "small" theory, at most, and perhaps Willis is correct in identifying it at a model rather than a theory. It was proposed as a description of response modes that would provide a basis for research and the formulation of a "theory." It has met the first purpose satisfactorily, as demonstrated by the significant findings of Willis and his associates. Unfortunately, the explanatory theory is only beginning to emerge. However, the hypotheses that have been formulated are internally consistent, testable, and in general agreement with other theories and known data relevant to social influence.

The descriptive model has aspects in common with several other approaches that we have not included in this book. For example, Campbell's (1961) description of compromised composites is similar to Willis' view that any given response is ordinarily a combination of more than one response mode. Kelman's (1961) analysis of social influence in terms of compliance, identification, and internalization is related to Willis' emphasis upon psychological conformity. However, Kelman was concerned with processes of conformity rather than response mode; presumably all three processes lead to what Willis called conformity behavior.

The one new form of behavior specified by Willis is variability, and it is probably the form that is most open to criticism. Originally, variability was interpreted as conformity and anticonformity in equal parts, but Willis later (1964) interpreted it as a form of independent behavior. According to this interpretation, the individual using the variable response mode is not influenced by the social pressure. Given this interpretation, it is difficult to understand why such behavior would ever occur, and, indeed, Hollander and Willis (1967) assert that it rarely occurs in natural situations. Perhaps a more logical interpretation would be in terms of conflict: the individual is torn between maintaining independence (or making the best response possible) and making a socially acceptable response.

In its present form, the model leaves much to be desired. Considerably more needs to be done in the direction of identifying the conditions under which the various forms of behavior may be expected to occur and specifying the consequences of each mode of response.

13 ‖ ROLE THEORY

Role theory is a body of knowledge and principles that at one and the same time constitutes an orientation, a group of theories, loosely linked networks of hypotheses, isolated constructs about human functioning in a social context, and a language system which pervades nearly every social scientist's vocabulary. It, more than any of the foregoing transorientational approaches, eludes the grasp of our classification system. Roles as the basic data within this "theoretical system" have been considered from many viewpoints: learning, cognitive, field-theoretical, sociocultural, and dynamic points of view. As such, role theory seems to be more of a subject matter than a theoretical framework. Indeed, it has occupied this standing in several basic social psychology texts (Sargent & Williamson, 1958; Secord & Backman, 1964; Brown, 1965; Newcomb, Turner, & Converse, 1965; McDavid & Harari, 1968).

Although specific theories of role and role processes have been proposed from various orientations and disciplines in the social and behavioral sciences, we have not chosen to exposit these specific theories. Instead, this chapter presents the language of role theory peculiar to most of these orientations. Because of the proliferation of concepts that has been classified under the role-theory rubric, we do not pretend to present every phrase, concept, or construct relevant to roles. Instead, we have drawn heavily upon the classification system proposed by Biddle and Thomas (1966) in an attempt to present the most important and relevant constructs and processes.

Before we embark on a discussion of the language of role theory, several introductory considerations about roles should be noted:

1. Historically, the concept of role has been borrowed from dramatic and theatrical circles. Beginning with the early Greek and Roman theaters, a role referred to the characterization that an actor was called upon to enact in the context of a given dramatic presentation.

2. From these roots the concept of role migrated into the language of the social sciences. In this migration, the definition of role changed very little. *It refers to the functions a person performs when occupying a particular characterization (position) within a particular social context.*

3. Just as one actor's role is partially defined by the roles that other actors take in the same performance, so one person's role is partially dependent upon the roles of related others in the social context. Neither a dramatic presentation nor a social structure could long survive if the roles of its various "actors" were not linked to one another.

4.   The evolution of the concept of role in the social sciences has been truly a transdisciplinary evolution. Most of the contributions to role theory have come from the fields of anthropology, sociology, and psychology.

5.   The early precursors of modern role-theoretical constructs uniformly alluded to the concept of role while pursuing the study of other aspects of their respective disciplines. For example, James (1890) and Baldwin (1897) were psychologists studying the "self"; Sumner (1906), Ross (1908), and Durkheim (1893) were sociologists concerned with the mores, norms, and structure of society; yet each of these contributed greatly to role theory. Some other significant works which contributed to the foundation of role theory were those of Dewey (1899), Cooley (1902), Moreno (1919), and Simmel (1920).

6.   This cross-fertilization of ideas from various social science disciplines led to the emergence of a system of linguistic and conceptual referents within role theory that defies classification as psychological, sociological, or anthropological.

THE LANGUAGE OF ROLE THEORY

Biddle and Thomas (1966) have written and edited a significant text in the area of role theory. In addressing themselves to this task, they utilized a framework or classificatory universe within which the many constructs of role theory were reduced to comparatively few basic constructs. In short, they have devised a scheme for classifying the most frequently recurrent terms from the role theory framework. In the subsequent paragraphs of this section, we use this schematic superstructure in articulating the language of role theory. It consists of four terminological classes: (1) terms for partitioning persons, (2) terms for partitioning behaviors, (3) terms for partitioning sets of persons and behaviors, and (4) terms for relating sets of persons and behaviors. Two or more descriptive terms fall within each of these general classes.

Terms for Partitioning Persons

Terms for partitioning persons break down into two basic categories. First, the *actor* is the person who is currently behaving in a given role. Secondly, the *target*, or *other*, is an individual who bears a relationship to the actor and his role. Either the actor or the other may be an individual or an aggregate of individuals. Thus, the "actor" might be the aggregate choir performing a singing-and-entertainment role in relation to the audience as the aggregate-other. In the language of role theory, the actor has been alternately referred to as the *person*, the *ego*, and the *self*; and the other has been alternately referred to as the *alter ego* (or merely *alter*), the *target*, and the *nonself* (Biddle & Thomas, 1966).

This classification of individuals or aggregates into actors or persons and others is not peculiar to role theory. The reader will recall similar classifications in Heider's theory of interpersonal relationships (Chapter 6), Heider's p-o-x theory (Chapter 8), Newcomb's A-B-X theory (Chapter 8), and Jones and Davis' theory of correspondent inferences (Chapter 11). Although these theories are not role theories in the strict sense of the term, their hypotheses and propositions concerning interpersonal relationships, interpersonal attribution, or interpersonal perception can be interpreted in a role-theoretical framework. As a matter of fact, nearly every structured two-party or multiple-party relationship in which person-other classifications are possible can be subjected to role-theoretical analysis. The basic situation within which roles can be studied is one which involves an *actor* behaving (in its broadest sense) in the presence of, toward, or in reference to an *other*, where the actor and the other have roles which are linked by factors such as similarity, complementarity, friendship, and the like.

Cooley (1902) and Mead (1934) were two of the first theorists to be concerned with the importance of person-other relationships as they predispose the person to a course of role-appropriate behavior or thought. Both these men viewed the "other" as a generalized entity which the person utilizes as a reference point for his own behavior. As such, they were not particularly concerned with the actual component interactions between a particularized person and a particularized other. Both Mead and Cooley concluded that the person, ego, or self is given its identity by the generalized other. According to Mead, the person takes the attitude of the generalized other toward himself, but Cooley maintained that the person uses the generalized other as a mirror that reflects the characteristics and effects of the person's behavior and feeling. These early views of the referential function of the other and the generalized other were later expanded by Merton and Kitt (1950), Kelley (1952), and several other theorists. Referential functions are dealt with more extensively in the subsequent section on the partitioning of behaviors.

Finally, it should be noted that Secord and Backman (1964), following the lead of Bredemeier and Stevenson (1962), have designated the *person* as the individual occupying the *focal position* in an observed relationship and the *other* as the individual occupying a *counterposition*. Thus, they viewed the other as a *role partner* to the person. This position-counterposition view of the person and his related other can be most lucidly illustrated by noting some structured role relationships, such as mother-child, boss-employee, and husband-wife. From these examples, it can be seen easily that role partners are in a reciprocal relationship with one another. Subsequent sections of this chapter will go into greater detail on the concepts of position and role partner.

Terms for Partitioning Behaviors

Biddle and Thomas (1966) cited five terms that depict role-related behaviors. They are *expectation* and *norm, performance* and *evaluation,* and *sanction.*

ROLE EXPECTATIONS AND NORMS   Role expectations are simply expectations held by particularized or generalized *others* for the appropriate behavior (again in its broadest sense) that *ought* to be exhibited by the *person* or persons holding a given role. Thus, for example, the society at large, individual patients, patients from different socioeconomic classes, and similar groups have expectations concerning how a person should function in the role of physician. Some expectations are generally held, some are held only by "pockets" of others, and some are idiosyncratic and characteristic of specific person-other relationships.

There seems to be an interchangeability of the terms "norm" and "expectation" in role-theory literature. Expectations are generally viewed as shared or individual norms of how persons occupying a given position-role should function in that role. However, Secord and Backman (1964) noted that norms are only one of two categories of expectations. They bifurcate role expectations on the basis of (1) their anticipatory nature and (2) their normative nature. McDavid and Harari (1968) made a similar distinction between *predicted role expectations* and *prescribed role expectations*. Expectations that are anticipatory or predictive in nature are generally not based on norms in the strict sense. Rather, they are used by a given individual to anticipate or predict the manner in which another will respond to him or to a particular situation. Thus, the statement, "I know my husband well, and when I tell him that I've purchased a $60 hat he will hit the ceiling," is a predictive or anticipatory expectation. It is not strictly normative because "hitting the ceiling" or losing one's temper is not a usual prescription characteristic of the role of husband (that is, it is not necessarily what a husband *ought* to do or *ought not* do in order to fulfill the husband role either in the eyes of the society at large or probably even in his wife's eyes).

Secord and Backman (1964) noted that the anticipatory quality of expectations is a guiding force in interaction. Anticipations and predictions are usually made on the basis of experiences with individual person, classes of persons, specific situations, or generalized situations. Although continuing experience in interaction may facilitate the acquisition of internal standards about the behavior of others or the reactions of others, they cannot be strictly classified as norms because these anticipations do not have obligatory qualities. That is, the fact that sound experience leads an individual to predict certain contingencies in interaction does not *obligate* another party in that interaction to live up to those predictions.

The normative or prescribed quality of role expectations represents the "oughts" and "shoulds" of a given role. Normative role expectations are the overt or covert rights and obligations that accompany the occupation of a given role position. The degree to which an individual lives up to the obligations or normative expectations of a role which he holds is a measure of his fulfillment of that role (at least insofar as social standards are concerned). The larger society and specific subgroups within it hold standards which they use to organize and evaluate the role behavior of others.

Biddle and Thomas (1966) have divided role prescriptions (the "oughts" and "shoulds" of roles) into those that are covertly held and those that are overtly expressed. They reserved the term *norm* for the former category and referred to overtly expressed prescriptions as *role demands*. Many parental prescriptions for their children are couched in the form of demands. Thus, a child may be overtly admonished to use his utensils when eating at the table, to thank others for favors, to adhere to particular authority rules, and so forth. Role demands are by no means limited to parent-child or superior-underling relationships, but they are probably most salient in these forms of relationship. Biddle and Thomas pointed out that in the course of socialization many role demands are internalized by the person and become covertly held norms. Most of the important prescriptions which govern adult role behavior and the evaluation of adult role behavior are based upon internalized norms which correspond to given roles.

ROLE PERFORMANCE   Role performance consists of the behaviors displayed by an actor which are relevant to the particular role which he is currently playing. In contrast to normative expectations, which are the "oughts" or the behavioral requirements of a given role, role performance is the actual behavior exhibited by an actor in a role. There may be considerable variation in the manner in which different actors enact the same role or in the manner in which the same actor enacts the same role on different occasions. Any number of different role behaviors may fulfill the expectations of the same role. Hence, if we assume that disciplining children is one of the expected functions of the father role, a particular father may enact this function by physical punishment, psychological deprivation, dependency manipulations, and so forth. In all cases, the father is responding to at least one of the expectations of the father role. Although any single form of role enactment may be considered to be the most adequate, the enactment of alternative acceptable modes of role behavior is not precluded. In short, role theory does account for the infinite variety of behavior that an individual may exhibit. Even though role theory tends to classify people into categories of actors (for example, father, boss), and though it tends to attribute relatively uniform expectations to a given category, it does not propose that these uniform expectations are met by all relevant actors with the same expressed behavior.

Indeed, the theater, which has been cited as the originator of the concept of role, yields the most paradigmatic examples of how different individuals playing the same role may exhibit different role behaviors. No two actors characterizing Hamlet, Macbeth, Othello, or Willie Loman enact exactly the same behaviors. The dialogue may be the same, but the gestures or vocal intonations are usually different. In the real world, the goals of the various functions associated with roles (for example, disciplining children) may be the same, but the paths to the goal may differ widely.

For these reasons, role theory tends to classify role performance not in terms of the specific behaviors performed in the enactment of a role, but rather in terms of the generic quality of the behavior and the goals or motives of that behavior (Biddle & Thomas, 1966). Thus, role behavior might be classified as "work performance," "school performance," "athletic performance," etc., or it might be classified in terms of the goals of the enacted behavior, such as "the disciplining of a child," "the earning of a living wage," "the maintenance of order," and the like. Role performance, then, is generally classified in terms of its nature and its ends rather than its means. This characteristic of role theory, however, does not preclude the fact that certain means of enacting a given role function may be sanctioned by the group. For example, a father might be fulfilling a role function in disciplining his misbehaving son by hanging him upside down by his toes. Nevertheless, this behavior would most probably be negatively sanctioned in Western culture. In general, the means of achieving a role function, or living up to a specific requirement of a given role, usually becomes important in role theory only when that means comes into conflict with other aspects of the total role. Thus, the father who disciplines his son by hanging him by his toes violates some of the expectations of the father role, such as affection toward the child, justice toward the child, and so forth. Therefore, the actor is free to vary in his expression of a role function within the limits imposed by related role functions and expectations.

Two of the more prominent role theorists concerned with role performance have been Sarbin (1966) and Goffman (1959). In defining some dimensions of role enactment, both have been concerned with the relationship between the self and the role that the self is called upon to play. Sarbin classified role enactment in terms of the intensity of the enactment. He defined intensity along a dimension of self-role differentiatedness. He proposed that there are seven levels of role enactment varying in terms of their intensity. His levels range from the lowest level of enactment, which involves a rather mechanical implementation of a role function and where self and role are clearly differentiated, to a level of enactment which involves the complete integration of self and role. In this highest level of enactment, the self and the role it is taking are undifferentiated, and hence the enactment is highly intensified. In short, Sarbin proposed that a very salient dimension of variation in role performance is represented by the individual's involvement in the role being enacted.

Goffman (1959) was concerned with the proposition that an actor performing in a role is attempting to convey, overtly or covertly, to the other that part of himself that he wishes to be known. As such, Goffman became concerned with the expressive characteristics of role performance. He termed these expressive characteristics a "front" which the actor constructs in order to impress the other with the fact that he is living up to the idealized aspects of a given role. For example, if one of the perceived expectations of a college professor is that he be scholarly in his interests and pursuits, the professor might publicly convey to the other that he is living up to this expectation by shelving scholarly periodicals in full display in his living-room bookshelves. However, he may conceal his private penchant for comic books by stacking them in a less-accessible portion of the house. Thus, Goffman implies that the public role performance of the actor in an actor-other context at least partially constitutes the construction of a role-consistent "front." The actor, then, might impress the other with his fulfillment of role expectations through the selective expression of limited facets of himself.

It should be noted that many theorists have articulated many different dimensions of role performance. That we have not covered these many views here is not intended to be an indictment of their relevance. Instead, the necessary limitation in this chapter's scope precludes their coverage. The interested reader is strongly urged to refer to Biddle and Thomas' (1966) text and readings for further discussion of and reference to the concept of role performance.

ROLE EVALUATION AND SANCTION   It is rather difficult to separate the behaviors of evaluation and sanction as they apply to role. Biddle and Thomas (1966) distinguished the two in that they defined evaluation as the expression of approval or disapproval toward the role behavior of oneself or another. They reserved the term *sanction* to apply to the behavior of oneself or another that attempts to achieve either constancy in or change of a given role behavior. Therefore, evaluation involves the making of "positive" or "negative" *judgments* about a particular role behavior, and sanctioning is a procedure engaged in either to maintain positively evaluated role behaviors or to change negatively evaluated ones.

Both evaluations and sanctions are based upon normative expectations. Thus, a role behavior will most probably be positively evaluated and sanctioned when it conforms to the normative expectations for the role in question and negatively evaluated and sanctioned when it does not. Evaluations and sanctions can be either external or internal. Secord and Backman (1964) noted that with external sanctions the source of positive or negative reward is the behavior of others. For example, a boss may negatively sanction a worker for not living up to standards of production by firing him, or he may positively sanction his adequate role performance by giving him a salary bonus. On the other hand, the source of internal sanctions is the actor himself. Thus, an individual may be dissatisfied with himself when he does not live up to the normative expectations of a role which he holds. Furthermore, Secord and Backman noted that in the socialized adult internal sanctions are usually most salient with important norms and external sanctions most salient with norms of little importance.

Biddle and Thomas (1966) made a similar distinction between the *overt* and *covert* natures of evaluations and sanctions. They referred to overt evaluations as *assessments* and covert evaluations as *values*. The former class is most frequently used by others to evaluate the role behavior of the actor, and the latter is usually used by the actor himself to evaluate his own behavior. Values might be conceptualized as the internalized assessments of others that are held by the actor. Thus, the values of the actor are based upon the communication of normative expectations by others through predominantly overt means. A mother's socialization of her child generally involves the communication of normative expectations through external assessments and sanctions to the point where the child accepts and internalizes those norms as governors of his own behavior. With the internal acceptance of other-based norms, the individual forms a system of internal values through which he self-regulates his own behaviors. Socialization is a process which occurs throughout the individual's lifetime. Each time he enters a new social situation or assumes a different role he must to some extent rely on the external assessments of others in order to derive a set of role-relevant internalized values.

Although the evaluation and sanction of the actor by others is an important aspect of role theory, the actor's evaluation of his own role behavior is even more important. We have already alluded to the proposition that the external evaluations of "others" are the source of the internalized values which the actor utilizes to evaluate his own role performance. This proposition has been repeatedly articulated by psychologists and sociologists alike. Merton and Kitt (1950) dealt extensively with the concept of *reference group* in attempting to define the source of value formation in the actor. The reference group is a group that the actor is a member of or one in which he desires membership. In either case, it serves as a *reference point* that the individual uses to derive standards that he might utilize to evaluate his own performance and to obtain or maintain membership in the group. Kelley (1952) stated two functions of reference groups. He referred to the first of these as the *normative function*. The normative function of reference groups entails the role which they play in enforcing the standards (objectively correct or not) for action and belief in the person. To perform this function, the person must have face-to-face contact with the group or its representative, and the group must have the power to sanction the person for deviation. The person is motivated to abide by normative pressure because of his desire to secure or maintain membership in the group. If the individual internalizes the standards induced by the group's normative pressure, they become his individual *values* for action. Insofar as the norms and standards enforced by the reference group deal with aspects of the actor's role behavior, the process of normative group pressure is a very important one for role-theoretical analysis.

The second function of reference groups that Kelley defined is the *comparative function*. This function involves the person's use of the group as a comparative index of the "objective correctness" of his attitudes, opinions, and behaviors. The comparative function can operate without interaction and without concerns about group membership. Here, the group usually does not exert the pressure of sanction, and the individual uses the group only for informational purposes. The comparative function of reference groups is not as relevant to self-role evaluation as the normative function.

Several other dichotomous classifications of the self-group relationships and processes involved in arriving at a self-evaluation are very similar to Kelley's descriptions. Deutsch and Gerard's (1955) concepts of normative and informational social influence, Thibaut and Strickland's (1956) group set (normative) and task set (comparative), and Jones and Gerard's (1967) reflected appraisal (normative) and comparative appraisal are some of the more-important ones. Furthermore, Festinger's social comparison theory discussed in Chapter 11 is also relevant to the self-evaluation process.

Last, it should be noted that Biddle and Thomas discussed a further term for partitioning behaviors relevant to roles. They referred to the process whereby an individual simply articulates the components of a given role as *role description.* Role description differs from role evaluation and sanction in that it does not involve affective or evaluative factors. The mere description of roles, then, is free of value judgments. A covertly held description of a role was referred to as a *role conception,* and an overtly expressed description was called a *role statement* (Biddle & Thomas, 1966). Both the individual's *cognitions* and *perceptions* of what a role consists of in terms of functions, obligations, position, and rights are involved in role description.

Terms for Partitioning Sets of Persons and Behaviors

Certain terms in the vocabulary of role theory refer to the combination of a behavioral partition with a person partition. For example, role evaluation may occur with actors or with others. The behavioral partitions and person partitions come together in the general concepts of *position* and *role.* Thus, a given role behavior is often evaluated as a function of what category the actor falls within. A position in the social structure and a role associated with that position define both the actor and the course of action he is obligated to take.

POSITION   Secord and Backman defined position as a category of persons (actors) who occupy a specified place in a social structure. Biddle and Thomas (1966) gave a similar definition to position but secondarily added that a position consists of a set of persons sharing common attributes or who are similarly perceived by others. Thus, they define position as *"a collectively recognized category of persons for whom the basis for such differentiation is their common attribute, their common behavior, or the common reactions of others toward them"* (Biddle & Thomas, 1966, p. 29. Italics ours). According to this definition, Biddle and Thomas have posited three bases for the assignment of persons into a position category. The first involves the assignment of persons on the basis of a common attribute or several common attributes. The examples they noted for this basis are classification by age, sex, or race. Thus, an individual might be classified in the category of teen-ager or female or Negro, or all three of these categories. As more attributes go into the making up of single categories, the category becomes narrower and more exclusive. Hence, only certain Negroes are females, and even fewer Negroes are both females and teen-agers.

The second basis for position categorization that Biddle and Thomas noted is common behavior. Some examples of this basis might be "criminals," "athletes," "leaders," and so forth. Individuals might be classified into such categories on the basis of the similarity in their behavior, at least on one dimension. Position categories based upon behavioral characteristics may cut across categories based on common attributes. Thus criminals, athletes, or leaders may be Caucasian or Negro, old or young, male or female and so forth. One may arrive at narrower classifications of categories by subdividing a large category into some representative components on the basis of even more precise similarity in behavior. Hence, a criminal can belong to several smaller subcategories, such as thief, murderer, kidnaper, rapist, and so forth.

More-exclusive categories of position might also be derived by combining common attributes with behavioral similarities. Thus, for example, one might speak of "teen-age criminals" (or juvenile delinquents), Negro leaders, or woman athletes.

The third basis for positional categorization is the similarity in the behavior of others toward the persons in question. A prime example of this type of categorization as noted by Biddle and Thomas is the category of "scapegoats." Scapegoats are classified together regardless of their varying attributes or behaviors because of the similarities in the manner that people treat them. As with common behavioral determinants of position, this third basis of position may be further subdivided into smaller component categories. For example, a specific category of scapegoats could be political scapegoats and this category might be distinguished from social scapegoats.

The proposition that there are at least three underlying bases for positional categorization could well be the source of various disagreements on how position should be defined. The generalized classification of bases of positional categorization proposed by Biddle and Thomas is an organizational schema that can be used to unify the several conceptualizations of the term "position." A minimally acceptable definition of position is its designation as a "unit of social structure" (Newcomb, 1950; Gross, Mason, & McEachern, 1957). Specifying the "acceptable" bases for the formation of social structure units further differentiates and articulates the concept of position.

ROLE   Biddle and Thomas noted that although role is the central concept in role theoretical analysis, it is probably the most controversial concept used by role analysts. Many definitions of role have been offered from many schools of thought. Some representative ones are presented below:

> ". . . the expectations that persons hold in common toward any person who falls in a particular category by virtue of his position in the social system" (Secord & Blackman, 1964, p. 457).
> "Behavior that is characteristic and expected of a person or persons who occupy a position in the group" (Jones & Gerard, 1967, p. 718).
> ". . . an internally consistent series of conditioned responses by one member of a social situation which represents the stimulus pattern for a similarly internally consistent series of conditioned responses of the other in that situation" (Cottrell, 1942, p. 617).
> ". . . a patterned sequence of learned actions or deeds performed by a person in an interaction situation" (Sarbin, 1954, p. 225).
> "A person's role is a pattern or type of social behavior which seems situationally appropriate to him in terms of the demands and expectations of those in his group" (Sargent, 1951).

The definitions above are merely a small sampling of the varying definitions that have been given to the concept of role. Together, Nieman and Hughes (1951) and Rommetveit (1954) reviewed 100 or more role definitions. Biddle and Thomas (1966) pointed out that a review of these many definitions indicates that the most common definition of role is that it is a set of prescriptions that define the desired behavior of a position occupant. Almost all definitions of role universally acknowledge that it pertains to the behaviors of particularized persons. Although many definitions of role confine the person-behavior relationship to behaviors associated with collective positions, Biddle and Thomas believed this to be too limiting a definition. Instead, they proposed a matrix of person-behavior relationships which they saw as giving the necessary broadness to a concept as pervasive as role.

The Biddle and Thomas person-behavior matrix consists of a set of behaviors that is ordered by both a set of subjects (persons) and a set of behavioral classes. Figure 13–1 is a prototype of the proposed matrix.

In this figure the horizontal dimension labeled P_1-P_m is the set of subjects and consists of all relevant partitions of persons. Usually, the subject set should be limited to person-units within a single larger social unit. Hence the total subject set may be the family, and P_1 the father, P_2 the mother, P_3 the son, and so forth. The vertical dimension labeled from C_1-C_n consists of all relevant classes of behavior. Each class of behavior is a category that includes specific individual behavioral partitions. Hence, C_1 might consist of a group of prescriptions, C_2 a category of evaluation, C_3 a category of actions or perhaps sanctions, and so forth. The cell entries (B_{11}, B_{12}, etc.) are the behaviors

FIGURE 13–1. The person-behavior matrix and its segments. (Reprinted with permission from E. J. Thomas and B. J. Biddle. Basic concepts for classifying the phenomena of role. In B. J. Biddle and E. J. Thomas (Eds.), *Role theory: Concepts and research.* New York: Wiley, 1966. Pp. 23–45.)

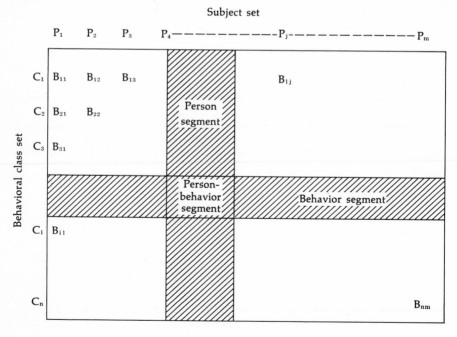

enacted by individual units of the subject set. Thus, if P_1 were father and C_1 normative expectations, then B_{11} might be a specific expectation which father holds about his own role or the role of another person in the subject set.

Essential portions of the matrix presented in Figure 13–1 are the areas that are sectioned off both horizontally and vertically. The vertical section was referred to by Biddle and Thomas as the *person segment* and is made up of all the behaviors displayed by a single person or a subset of persons, regardless of the behavioral classes from which they originate. Thus, the person segment may consist of all the prescriptions, evaluations, sanctions, actions, and descriptions taken together that are characteristic of father's behavior or both mother's and father's behavior (that is, the subset parents), or sons' and daughters' behavior (that is, the subset children), and so forth. The vertical column representing the *person segment* can vary in width with the number of persons or aggregates falling into the subject subset under investigation. Biddle and Thomas noted that the person segment of the proposed matrix can serve as a singular device to encompass the many particularized descriptions of person-roles which have been proposed in the literature. Hence, the person segment can represent:

1. *Individual roles;* that is, all the behaviors characteristic of a particular individual
2. *Aggregate roles,* or all the behaviors of an aggregate of individuals
3. *Behavior roles,* or all the behavior of the actor(s) in a role partnership or role complex
4. *Target roles,* or all the behavior of the "other(s)" in a role partnership or role complex.

Person segments can also be devised to represent the behavior of the many particularized roles that have been proliferated in role-theory literature (for example, mother role, male role, leader role).

The horizontal axis that consists of selected behavioral classes is referred to as the *behavior segment.* The behavior segment constitutes the behaviors of all persons taken together that can be placed in a single behavioral class or a set of behavioral classes. Thus, Biddle and Thomas noted that the behavior segment is made up of behaviors that are person-general and behavioral-class specific. The roles that emerge from a consideration of the behavior segment of the person-behavior matrix are the following:

1. *Overt role,* or public role
2. *Covert role,* or private role
3. *Prescriptive role,* or normative properties of roles in a selected social system
4. *Descriptive role,* or the role conceptions within a social unit
5. *Evaluative role,* or the norms for evaluating roles in a social unit
6. *Active role,* or the varying role performances of all actors in a social unit
7. *Sanctioning role,* or the sanctions which are applied to norm violation in the selected social unit.

The intersect of the person segment and the behavior segment was referred to by Biddle and Thomas as the *person-behavior* segment. In this segment of the matrix an individual's or aggregate's behaviors become classified into a specific behavioral class or into a selected set of behavioral classes. Thus, one may speak of the combination of any person segment or segments with any behavioral segment or segments. For example, person-behavior segments may consist of individual-prescriptive roles, aggregate-evaluative roles, overt-prescriptive roles, and so forth. In family systems, a classification of the father-prescriptive role would include all the prescriptions which are held by father. The examples that might be generated by a consideration of the person-behavior segment are endless, particularly if one considers the infinite variety of person roles and behavior roles that are possible within any social unit.

Biddle and Thomas' person-behavior matrix does not add any new concepts to the definition of role. Rather, it provides a descriptive schema for classifying the endless varieties of roles described in the literature into manageable categories. Furthermore, it provides a superstructure within which all roles, regardless of their description, can be classified along the same dimensions. Lastly, the person-behavior matrix provides a necessary basis for a broad definition of the role concept. It does not limit role to prescriptions of given position occupants or behaviors of role holders, but it instead envisions role as the combination of any person segment (individual or aggregate) with any behavioral segment (action, prescription, evaluation, sanction, and description).

Terms for Relating Sets of Persons and Behaviors

Although the analytical distinctions separating behaviors from other behaviors, and persons from behaviors, are necessary for an understanding of role theory, to conceptualize a *role* fully these behavioral and personal elements must be merged into an integrated picture. For example, single normative prescriptions are often *related* to other normative prescriptions, or they may be related to actions or evaluation. Similarly, behavioral partitions such as norms, actions, and evaluations are often intricately related to particular persons (for example, the specialist concept).

Biddle and Thomas (1966) proposed three criteria for inferring the existence and strength of the relationships among any set of behavioral partitions or between any person partition(s) and behavioral partition(s). (They did not consider concepts depicting the relationship between person partitions, because very few of these concepts are available in the literature of role theory.) These three criteria are (1) the degree of *similarity* or dissimilarity between or among partitions, (2) the degree of *codetermination* or interdependence for any two or more partitions, and (3) the jointly operating criteria of similarity and determination.

In the following paragraphs we give a brief resumé of Biddle and Thomas' discussion of the concepts pertaining to each of these relationship criteria.

THE CRITERION OF SIMILARITY   Any two behavioral partitions or person-behavior partitions may be related to one another on the basis of their similarity or lack of it. The role concepts for which the criterion of partition-interrelationship is similarity are *differentiation, consensus, uniformity, specialization,* and *consistency.*

Differentiation is a term reserved for the relationship between behavioral partitions. For two or more behavioral partitions to be differentiated from one another, there must be discernible differences between them. For example, the norms which a social group holds for its members may be discernibly different from the norms it holds for nonmembers. In this case, the two sets of norms are differentiated and distinguished from one another. Therefore, the relationship between them is one of dissimilarity.

Consensus is defined by Biddle and Thomas as the amount of agreement on a specific topic. As with differentiation, consensus deals with the relationship between behavioral partitions. That is, people as an undifferentiated class must agree about *something* in order to reach consensus. The objects of agreement that were cited as most relevant are prescriptions, evaluations, descriptions, and sanctions. The consensus on any one of these classes of behavioral partitions may be either overt or covert. The covert consensus among individuals on prescriptions was referred to as norm consensus while the overt prescription consensus was referred to demand consensus. Similarly, covert consensus on evaluation was referred to as value consensus and overt consensus as assessment consensus. Relationships of consensus are based upon the *similarity* between several individuals' prescriptions, evaluations, descriptions, or sanctions for specified roles. Biddle and Thomas characterized two forms of lack of consensus on these partitions. The first, *nonpolarized dissensus,* involves several disagreeing opinions on the behavioral partitions. That is, the opinions on what the appropriate prescriptions for a role are might fall into quite a few categories of opinion. The second, *polarized dissensus* or *conflict,* involves disagreements on partitions which are prone to fall into two opposing camps. This latter form of dissensus is the basis for role conflict, and this concept will be discussed in the following separate section.

Role conflict is a specific form of polarized dissensus which has been given much attention by social psychologists and sociologists alike. For this reason, we have decided to devote considerable space to a discussion of this form of dissensus. A very detailed discussion of role conflict and strain may be found in Secord and Backman's (1964) text. Here, however, we concentrate upon several basic aspects of role conflict.

Role conflict results when the expectations associated with several positions that an actor might hold are incompatible with one another (inter-role conflict) or when the expectations associated with a single position an actor holds are incompatible (intra-role conflict). Inter-role conflict occurs partly because it is highly improbable that any individual will hold only one role in the social system. Further, it is improbable that the set of roles that an individual holds (his *role set*) will consist of individual roles that do not have expectations conflicting with those of other individual roles that he holds.

Thus, a father's role in his family may consist of some expectations in direct conflict with those pertaining to his occupational role. Intra-role conflict results from a lack of clarity or consensus concerning the expectations belonging to a single role held by the actor. Thus, two expectations ascribed to the role father may conflict with one another resulting in a level of strain that hinders adequate role performance.

The source of the conflicting expectations for either inter-role or intra-role conflict may be the actor himself, his role partners, society at large, or any combination of these agencies. Regardless of the source, a general proposition about role conflict is that when it inculcates enough strain in the actor to preclude his adequate role performance, he seeks to resolve it. Several theories of and hypotheses concerning role-conflict resolution have been proposed from several theoretical orientations (Parsons, 1951; Getzels & Guba, 1954; Merton, 1957; Gross, Mason, & McEachern, 1957; Goode, 1960; Turner, 1962). The theory of conflict resolution proposed by Gross, Mason, & McEachern (1957) is presented as an example.

Gross, Mason, and McEachern's theory of role-conflict resolution is applicable to both intra-role and inter-role conflict. Essentially, they proposed that three factors that enter into the resolution of the conflict between any two expectations are (1) the relative legitimacy of the two expectations, (2) the sanctions incumbent upon the nonfulfillment of each of the expectations, and (3) the moral orientation of the actor. Expectations are classified as legitimate if the actor perceives that his role partners have the right to hold them and illegitimate if he perceives that they do not have a right to hold them. Considering this determinant of resolution independently, the actor would most probably decide to gear his role performance to the most legitimate expectations. However, additional problems arise when two conflicting expectations are equally legitimate or illegitimate or when the actor might be sanctioned for not responding to a less-legitimate or illegitimate expectation. In such cases, sanctions and/or moral orientations serve as bases of resolution.

Sanctions have already been discussed and refer to the positive or negative reinforcement which an actor might receive for not fulfilling role expectations. Gross, Mason, and McEachern defined positive sanctions as the gratification of the actor's needs by a role partner which is contingent upon his fulfillment of expectations. Negative sanctions involve the frustration of the actor's needs by his role partner. Considering this basis of resolution independently, it is reasonable that the actor would fulfill expectations that are positively sanctioned when they conflict with negatively sanctioned actions. However, when legitimacy and sanction are combined the resolution becomes much more complex than this. That is, legitimate or illegitimate expectations may be sanctioned either positively or negatively. Therefore, what does an actor do when he is experiencing a role conflict between a legitimate expectation that prescribes a negatively sanctioned behavior and an illegitimate expectation that prescribes a positively sanctioned behavior? To deal with contingencies such as these, the theorists proposed that the moral orientation of the actor will interact with both legitimacy and sanction to determine resolution strategy.

They proposed three differing moral orientations of actors: (1) the moral orientation, (2) the expedient orientation, and (3) the moral-expedient orientation. In considering all combinations of legitimate and illegitimate expectations and positive and negative sanctions that might be met in the conflict between any two expectations, they made sixteen separate predictions for *each* form of actor orientation. Their predictions may be summarized in the following statements: (1) The morally oriented actor will emphasize legitimacy over sanction. Thus, if the conflict is between any two legitimate expectations, he will take a compromise course of role behavior regardless of sanction. If role conflict is between any two illegitimate sanctions, he will choose neither and avoid acting regardless of sanction. Finally, if the choice is between an illegitimate and a legitimate sanction, he will respond to the legitimate one regardless of sanction. (2) The expediently oriented actor will emphasize sanction over legitimacy. Thus, he will compromise between any two positively sanctioned and conflicting role behaviors regardless of legitimacy. Where the choice is between a positively and negatively sanctioned role behavior, he will always respond to the positively sanctioned one regardless of legitimacy. He will respond only to legitimacy when the choice is between legitimate and illegitimate expectations that are both negatively sanctioned. He will avoid resolving the conflict when the choice is between two illegitimate expectations where the resulting behaviors are both negatively sanctioned. (3) The morally and expediently oriented actor will consider both legitimacy and sanction. He will always select the legitimate expectation over the illegitimate when the sanctions are positive or negative for both. Where both conflicting expectations are either legitimate or illegitimate, he will always select the positively sanctioned one, or he will compromise if they are both positively sanctioned. Furthermore, he will compromise in the case of an illegitimate-positive and legitimate-negative conflict. Like the other two actor orientations, he will avoid deciding between two illegitimate expectations that are both negatively sanctioned.

Gross, Mason, and McEachern (1957) present experimental findings that provide impressive support for their theory of role-conflict resolution. However, independent replications are necessary before their propositions can be accepted as substantiated.

Uniformity is the communality in the role performance of two or more individuals holding a similar role. Thus, the role performance of a given person is *related* to the role performance of another person on the basis of the similarity between their performances.

Specialization involves the distinction betwen persons that are based upon their differentiation in a given domain of behavior. For example, medical practitioners may be grouped into a large undifferentiated role category. Within the category, however, one might distinguish subcategories of roles that differentiate between the generalist and the specialist and between various types of specialists. Although there exists both uniformity and consensus with regard to the role of physician in general, there are specific prescriptions, descriptions, evaluations, sanctions, and actions characteristic of the subroles or specialties within the general category. Divisions of larger role categories into specialist categories are based upon both the absolute amount of behavior engaged in by a group of persons and the number of differentiated behaviors they engage in. Hence, a part-time occupation is not as specialized as a full-time occupation; whether part-time or full-time, a given occupation may be more specialized because a fewer number of behaviors are engaged in. Thus, a full-time teacher is more a specialist than a part-time teacher, and a music teacher is more a specialist than a teacher who instructs in several subjects.

Classifications of specialists, then, are based upon the criterion of dissimilarity of the prescriptions, evaluations, descriptions, actions, or sanctions peculiar to particularized persons. As Biddle and Thomas noted, specialization presupposes a lack of consensus or uniformity.

Consistency exists when any two or more behavioral partitions are related in such a way that one of them implies or follows from the other(s) or when any two partitions logically belong together. Thus, relationships between behavioral partitions are based upon the similarity between the implications of those partitions. Inconsistency may be of two types, *logical* or *cognitive*. Logical inconsistency involves the exhibition of two dissimilar partitions. Thus, Biddle and Thomas noted that the prescriptions of the commandment, "Thou shalt not kill," is logically inconsistent with the prescription advocating wartime killings. Cognitive inconsistency (see Chapter 8) involves the occurrence of nonfitting partitions in the same person. For example, it is cognitively inconsistent for an individual holding Christian Science norms to be at the same time a surgeon. Thus, inconsistency is one basis for the relationships of differentiation between behavioral partitions.

THE CRITERION OF DETERMINATION OR INTERDEPENDENCE   Interdependence involves a causal or determinative relationship between the behaviors or behavioral partitions of two persons. Individuals in role relationships (for example, mother-child, doctor-patient) are in certain respects dependent upon one another for norms, sanctions, behavioral goals, and so forth. The behavioral partitions of two persons may be dependent upon one another in that they facilitate or hinder one another's performance, or in that they determine the rewards and costs of one another's performance.

Facilitation and hindrance might characterize the behavioral partitions of two persons A and B. There are several types of facilitation and several types of hindrance characteristic of structured relationships. Briefly, person A's performance may facilitate or hinder person B's performance; person A's and person B's performances might be mutually facilitative or hindering; or person A's and person B's performances may be independent of one another. Thus, there may exist persons who are dependent upon other persons for the fulfillment of a role, persons who are dependent upon one another for the fulfillment of both of their roles, and persons whose roles are totally independent of one another.

Reward and cost as conceptual terms have been dealt with extensively by

Thibaut and Kelley (see Chapter 4). Biddle and Thomas' discussion of the reward-cost determinants of the relationships among role partitions is derived from their theory. In many role-interdependent relationships, facilitation and hindrance are directly related to interdependencies of rewards or costs. Simply, the behavioral partitions of any two parties may be dependent, interdependent, or independent with respect to rewards and costs. That is, one person's role behaviors may determine another's rewards or costs, both persons' role behaviors may determine one another's rewards or costs, or neither person's role behavior may be a determinant of the other's rewards or costs.

THE COMBINED CRITERIA OF SIMILARITY AND DETERMINATION   Some concepts dealing with the relationship between role partitions are jointly based on the criteria of similarity and determination; three such concepts are *conformity, adjustment,* and *accuracy:*

Conformity is the correspondence between an individual's performance and the other's performance or between his performance and the prescriptions for his performance. It is important to note that the conformity process is based upon both the similarity between the prescription or norm and the resultant behavior, and the degree to which the prescription determines the conforming performance. Conformity behavior in response to the normative prescriptions that one holds for himself or the prescriptions that another holds for him constitutes a very important functional concept in role theory. Thus, conformity or the lack of it is implied by the degree of correspondence between the role expectations for and role performance of a given role occupant.

Adjustment involves a determinative relationship between prescriptions and behavior that is the converse of that for conformity. It occurs when the role performance determines the prescriptions appropriate to the role. That is, adjustments occur whenever prescriptions are brought in line (or made similar to) the observed behavior of a role occupant. Biddle and Thomas cited the situation in which a mother of a mentally retarded child sets her prescriptions at a level commensurate with his observed performance as an example of adjustment.

Accuracy is said to characterize the relationships among role partitions when role descriptions are similar to and determined by role performance and role expectations. Role descriptions are inaccurate when they misrepresent the expectations and performance characteristic of a given role.

Comment

Our discussion of roles has concentrated upon the conceptual language of role theory as an orientation. We have dissected the concept of role into the many partitions and processes that frequently recur as foci of study among role analysts, sociologists, and social psychologists. In addressing ourselves to this task, we relied very heavily upon the conceptual superstructure and terminological discussions of Biddle and Thomas (1966). We heartily refer the interested reader to their book for more-extensive discussion and readings on the various concepts within role theory.

The relevance of roles to social psychology is pervasive. The language of roles has permeated most theoretical systems and subject areas within social psychology. Although sociologists have predominantly concerned themselves with the structural aspects of role, social psychologists have primarily been concerned with the relevance of roles to a functional analysis of interactional behavior. Topic areas such as leadership and power relations, conformity, socialization, interpersonal attraction, group and individual decision making, person perception, and social learning are all evidenced by the frequent use of role and role-related phenomena for interpretive and propositional purposes. The language of role has no theoretical boundaries. Role and role processes (role learning, role perception, prescriptions, role conflict, etc.) have been studied by social psychologists of all persuasions.

Because role concepts are so generalizable, there have been innumerable empirical investigations using roles as dependent, independent, or "interpretive" variables. Despite the ubiquity of the concept of role, it is nevertheless a rather ephemeral concept. At one and the same time, its flexibility and generalizability are assets and detriments. The most apparent detriment is that the deceptive similarity in language among the various analysts of role phenomena does not by any means reflect a similarity among them in their conceptual definitions of role phenomena. Therefore, individuals who employ role analysis in examining various sociopsychological phenomena speak similar languages but often do not communicate.

Although it would be inadvisable for social psychologists and sociologists to use a false precision in constructing a "universally acceptable" definition of role phenomena, it might be beneficial to set some conceptual limits upon role constructs. This act might serve the purpose of limiting the proliferation of terminological referents within the role-theory orientation. Perhaps Biddle and Thomas' method of defining role broadly in terms of a person-behavior matrix is a beginning step toward the goal of conceptual clarity in the language of role theory.

Finally, there is some question that role theory satisfies even our minimal definition of theory. Does it really consist of a set of interrelated hypotheses? There are some hypotheses about behavior, but role theory is largely classificatory and descriptive rather than predictive in nature

CONCLUSION

In the foregoing chapters we have considered a wide array of theories in social psychology. In this final chapter of the text we present a comparative appraisal of those theories based upon the criteria for "good theory" articulated in Chapter 1. From these appraisals, we have attempted both to describe the current status of theories in social psychology and to outline some desirable goals for the future of the field.

THEORIES OF SOCIAL PSYCHOLOGY: A COMPARATIVE APPRAISAL

In the course of our journey across the theoretical islands of thought in social psychology, it should have become quite apparent that there are many theories of social psychology. The field consists of a loosely knit collection of subareas. No single theory or system can be expected to account adequately for all those behaviors of men (or animals) that are socially mediated. The definition of social psychology as the scientific study of individual behavior as a function of social stimuli is at best a least common denominator broadly describing the general concern of all subareas in the field. Nevertheless, each specific subarea has its own problems of measurement, definition, and theory construction. Furthermore, although social psychology as a whole has witnessed a burgeoning growth in the past twenty years, the subareas within it have advanced at differential rates. For these reasons, a comparison among all the theories exposited in the foregoing chapters, without regard for subject matter, would be spurious. Thus, for comparative purposes we have grouped the theories into six subareas based upon subject matter. The theories within each given subarea have been compared to one another on the bases of (1) how well they meet the eight general criteria for theory outlined in Chapter 1, (2) the form of the theory (principle or constructive), and (3) the content of the theory (molar or molecular). In addition, consideration is given to the special problems confronted by the theorists within each given subarea. The six subareas of theory grouping are

1. Theories of attitude
2. Theories of group behavior and process
3. Theories of power relations and authority
4. Theories of interpersonal relations and interpersonal communication
5. Theories of social perception
6. Theories of social influence processes

Although these subareas are not mutually exclusive, nevertheless we have attempted to classify theories on the basis of predominant subject matter concerns. Two theories, namely Thibaut and Kelley's and Homans', have been classed in more than one subarea.

The Comparative Scheme

In order to summarize the various comparative evaluations, six separate tables are presented on the subsequent pages. Each table represents one of the above subject areas. In all of these tables, the first column lists the respective theories, the second column lists the classification on the basis of form—either principle (P), constructive (C), or mixed (P-C)—and the third column notes the classification on the basis of content—either molar (Ml) or molecular (Mc). The last eight columns contain our ratings of each of the theories on each of the necessary and desirable criteria for theory outlined in Chapter 1 and reviewed below. The ratings used were poor (P) when a theory falls well below meeting a given criterion; fair (F) when it just barely meets a criterion; good (G) when it adequately fulfills a criterion; and very good (VG) when it does an excellent job of meeting a criterion. The reader should view each rating as being preceded by the "in the opinion of the authors" caveat.

Before we move on to our tabular evaluations and discussions of the theories in the six subject matter areas, let us review the eight criteria for theory outlined in Chapter 1:

1. Logical internal consistency
2. Agreement with both known data and observations made subsequent to the proposal of the theory
3. Testability, including provability and refutability
4. Simplicity *and* clarity of terminology
5. Economy of constructs
6. Consistency with other acceptable theories (external consistency)
7. Interpretability
8. Generation of research (research productivity)

In Tables 14–1 through 14–6, the last eight columns correspond to the criteria listed above. Finally, before interpreting the tables, the reader would do well to review our definitions of molarity, molecularity, principle theory, and constructive theory that are given in Chapter 1.

Theories of Attitude

In recent years, the subarea of social psychology concerned with the formation and change of attitudes has gained much conceptual sophistication. This is due, in large measure, to the massive body of theory-related research that has emerged from the study of attitudes. The constructs, principles, and hypotheses of several of the theories of attitude have undergone constant modification and reinterpretation as a function of the impact of nonconfirmatory or questionable research findings. In fact, some of the propositions within several of these theories had their beginnings with empirical data. This state of affairs speaks well for the general flexibility of the theories of attitude and for their tendency to generate research.

In Table 14–1 we have evaluated the five theories of attitude presented in this text. The reader will note that (1) all of these theories are at least minimally acceptable according to the stated criteria; (2) they are all molecular in terms of content in that their unit of analysis is the individual attitude; and (3) the theories run the gamut in form characteristics, including principle, constructive, and mixed forms.

In taking a closer look at some of the details of Table 14–1, some relevant factors emerge. First of all, Festinger's cognitive dissonance theory has been the most exemplary on the criterion of research productivity. The proponents of this theory have been active researchers, and their studies have produced many innovations in experimental method as well as much relevant data. Although their research and that of the critics of dissonance theory have not always been clearly confirmatory, the theory has much flexibility and many research-based modifications have been made over the years. Nevertheless, dissonance theory is one of the least adequate of the attitude theories on the criterion of testability. Although research has shown that many of the propositions of dissonance theory are definitely provable and tenable, some of them are stated in such a form as to be low in refutability (for example, the problem of multiple modes of dissonance resolution). That is, in a given experiment, dissonance propositions might serve as explanations for a number of mutually exclusive outcomes. Although individual researchers have made inroads into firming up some of the looser propositions of dissonance theory, the refutability of certain propositions of the theory remains questionable (although admittedly less questionable than it was in the initial 1957 version of the theory).

Sarnoff's theory flows from an orientation traditionally cited as relatively impervious to experimental testing, internally inconsistent, uninterpretable in terms of operations, uneconomical in terms of explanation, and linguistically unclear. It is not surprising, then, that Sarnoff's attitude theory fares less well on formal criteria than the other attitude theories presented in this text. Its problems with regard to testability are probably attributable to the lack of specificity of its predictions. The mechanisms mediating the relationships among motive, tension, and attitude are never clearly articulated. Furthermore, the bases presented for the prepotency of one motive over another in the determination of attitude-motive relationships are noticeably weak. Finally, the overt behavior accompanying the same attitude in two individuals might differ as a function of the defensive process mediating that attitude. Since Sarnoff was rather vague in proposing an operational means to infer the contribution of one defense versus another, the determination of ego defense–attitude relations is vague. Thus, Sarnoff's theory has not been frequently submitted to experimental test; and when it has been, the support for the theory has been equivocal. Alternative explanations which do not postulate defensive strategies underlying attitudes are more parsimonious explanations of the research findings related to Sarnoff's theory.

TABLE 14–1. A criterion comparison of theories of attitude

Theory	Form	Content	Internal consistency	Agreement with known data	Testability	Simplicity, clarity	Economy	External consistency	Interpretability	Research productivity
Osgood & Tannenbaum	Pr-C	Mc	F-G	F-G	G	F-G	G	F-G	G	G
Festinger (dissonance)	C	Mc	F-G	F-G	F	F-G	F	F	G	VG
Sarnoff	Pr-C	Mc	F	F-G	F	F	F	F	F	F
Sherif & Hovland	Pr	Mc	F	G	VG	G	G	G-VG	G	G
Bem	Pr	Mc	G	G	VG	G-VG	VG	G	G	F-G

Key to symbols:

Pr = Principle theory
C = Constructive theory
Mc = Molecular
Ml = Molar

VG = very good
G = good
F = fair
P = poor

The theories of Sherif and Hovland and of Bem are the most adequate of the attitude theories in terms of formal criteria. This fact is not surprising since both theories are stated in terms of propositions drawn from two rather well-researched and well-established systems of thought in psychology. Although both theories are applications of more-general systems to the phenomena of attitudes, they differ in that Sherif and Hovland go beyond mere application and propose several new hypotheses and terms, whereas Bem sticks very close to Skinnerian principles and proposes no new terms and constructs to explain attitude phenomena. Both theories are adequate with regard to their simplicity and clarity of language, economy of constructs, testability, consistency with other acceptable theories, and interpretability. In its current state of development, Sherif and Hovland's theory is not as internally consistent as desirable. There are some confusing propositions concerning the constructs of latitudes of acceptance, rejection, and noncommitment that require further refinement.

Sherif and Hovland's theory has generated a considerable amount of related research, and Bem's theory promises to do so. In fact, one major contribution of Bem's analysis has been that it has led proponents of the dissonance approach to reconsider some of the principles of their theory in the light of Bem's alternative interpretation of some of their major findings. Thus, Bem's propositions have generated research designed to assess the comparative validity of his theory and the theory of cognitive dissonance. The comparative evaluation of theories within a discipline is an important aspect of theoretical advance in that discipline. In the final analysis, Bem's theory may indeed prove to be an overly simplistic interpretation of attitude phenomena, but in the meantime it promises to encourage dissonance theorists to reformulate some of their central propositions.

Table 14–1 shows that Osgood and Tannenbaum's theory fares relatively well on the stated criteria. The major asset of their theory is the precision with which it predicts the magnitude of attitude change and attitude strength. It has some limited problems with internal consistency that stem from the serendipitously arrived at "correction for incredulity"; however, these problems are of minor significance and can be effectively alleviated with a more-precise integration of the congruity principle with the correction for incredulity. Although the theory for the most part is clear and interpretable, several of its terms, such as "dissociative assertion," require more precise definition. Finally, the congruity principle is clearly testable and has generated a substantial body of related research.

Theories of Group Behavior and Process

The formal comparisons among the theories in this subarea are presented in Table 14–2. A quick overview of this table indicates that (1) the theories which this text has exposited in this subarea are on the whole the least adequate of those in any of the subareas at meeting the formal criteria, that (2) they are predominately molar in content and use group phenomena as their units of analyses (except for Schutz's theory in which group phenomena

TABLE 14-2. A criterion comparison of theories of group behavior and process

Theory	Form	Content	Internal consistency	Agreement with known data	Testability	Simplicity, clarity	Economy	External consistency	Interpretability	Research productivity
Homans	Pr-C	MI	F-G	G	F	F	G	G	G	P
Thibaut & Kelley	Pr-C	MI	G-VG	G	G	G	G	G	G	G-VG
Bennis & Shepard	Pr-C	MI	F-G	P-F	F	F	G	F	G	P-F
Bion	C	MI	P	P-F	P	P	F	P	P	P
Schutz	C	Mc	F-G	G	G	F	F	F-G	F-G	G
Cattell	Pr-C	MI	F	F	P-F	P	P-F	P-F	F	P-F
Stogdill	Pr-C	MI	F-G	G	P-F	F	G	G	F-6	P
Deutsch	C	MI	G	G	VG	P	F-G	G	G	G

Key to symbols:

Pr = Principle theory
C = Constructive theory
Mc = Molecular
MI = Molar

VG = very good
G = good
F = fair
P = poor

352

are interpreted on the basis of individual interpersonal needs), and that (3) they are all either constructive or mixed in form.

There are several sources of the seeming overall inadequacy of the theories in this subarea. First of all, much of the research in the area of group process has been based upon the working hypothesis rather than the theoretical proposition. Group phenomena are often examined quite independently of theory and with an exploratory goal. Although theories in this area are often employed to explain already accumulated data, studies are not often predesigned to test particular theories. The notable exceptions to this explanation are the theories of Deutsch, Schutz, and Thibaut and Kelley, all of which have generated a substantial body of research. It is interesting to note that their three theories are also the most testable of this group of theories. In the case of Thibaut and Kelley's theory, however, the systematic testing of its hypothesis in groups larger than the dyad has been negligible.

A second factor contributing to the rather low standing of the presented theories of group behavior and process has to do with the confusion of levels of analyses. This is particularly the case with the theories of Bennis and Shepard, Bion, and Cattell. These theories have either implicitly or explicitly used the individual system as the prototype of the group system. From this vantage point groups are seen as having many attributes (needs, emotions, "ids," motivations) that are customarily ascribed to individuals. Although it might be tenable to think of groups in these terms, the theorists who have done so have not taken care to differentiate the meanings of such concepts as they apply to the individual and the group. Therefore, there is much surplus meaning in the constructs and terms proposed in these theories. This factor at least partially accounts for the unclarity of many of their terms and for their relatively poor testability. Cattell's basic constructs not only are conceptually confusing from a definitional standpoint, but also are plagued by unnecessarily obscure terminology that renders the theory virtually uninterpretable.

A third source of difficulty with theories in this area is that several of them were derived from observations of specific types of groups, and these observations have not always been found to be applicable to groups in general. The theories of Bennis and Shepard, Bion, and Schutz have all been derived from therapy-group observations, and Stogdill's theory has been based upon studies of industrial work groups. Of these four theories only Schutz's shows overall adequacy on the formal criteria. The theories of Bennis and Shepard and Bion use terminology that is somewhat foreign to social psychologists, and thus these theories have not generated much research interest in the field. In the case of Bion's theory, this state of affairs is compounded by the relative obscurity and uninterpretability of the terminology. Stogdill's theory is neither operational nor precise enough to be adequately tested in the social psychology laboratory.

The theories least affected by the three sources of difficulty stated above emerge as the formally superior ones in the subarea of group behavior and process. However, each of these theories has its own peculiar problem or problems:

1.   Thibaut and Kelley's theory, although formally the most adequate of the group theories, has not empirically been demonstrated to extend to groups larger than the dyad.

2.   Homans' theory is somewhat difficult to test because of the vagueness of certain of its terms (particularly the *value* of a given interaction). Furthermore, it seems doubtful that Homans' theory will ever be adequately tested because it has been obscured by its ideological similarity to Thibaut and Kelley's more-extensive and more-popular propositions.

3.   Schutz's theory is sometimes plagued by unclear terminology.

4.   Deutsch's approach is overburdened by terminological excesses.

Theories of power relations and authority

A criterion comparison of the theories in this area is presented in Table 14–3. In general, this table indicates that (1) the theories in the area meet most of the criteria for theory, (2) they are all molar in content in that their unit of analysis is the social unit, and (3) they are either constructive or mixed in form.

Some specific conclusions are suggested by the table.

1.   Adams and Romney's conception of authority as a phenomenon based on reciprocal-reinforcement contingencies, although an interesting and well-stated application of operant-reinforcement principles, has not generated any direct experimental tests of its propositions. It is a most-adequate paradigm from the standpoint of testability, simplicity, and economy of constructs, but whether or not it is an oversimplification of a complex social phenomenon has not been determined. Its relatively good standing on all the stated criteria seems to be partially because of its limited scope and its reliance upon a system of thought which places a premium on operationalism.

2.   Thibaut and Kelley's theory, as it applies to power relations, is the only one of the four "power theories" presented in this text that has generated more than just a passing interest in researchers in the field. Although a more-precise specification of the conditions under which the theory applies is needed, nevertheless the research has been generally supportive of the theory. Furthermore, as noted in the previous section, Thibaut and Kelley's theory fares rather well on all of the formal criteria for theory.

3.   Although French's theory has received moderate support from research not specifically designed to test it, it has not generated a great deal of directly relevant research. The most serious problem affecting its testability is the vagueness with which it specifies a *unit* of interaction and the duration of a *unit* of interaction.

4.   Cartwright's theory has some terminological difficulties. He has been rather unclear in his definitions of *primitive* terms, and this lack of clarity has rendered the theory somewhat less testable than it might be had his terms been clearly specified.

Aside from the tabular considerations, it should be noted that the definitions of power and/or authority provided by these four theories range from

TABLE 14-3. A criterion comparison of theories of power relations and authority

Theory	Form	Content	Internal consistency	Agreement with known data	Testability	Simplicity, clarity	Economy	External consistency	Interpretability	Research productivity
Adams & Romney	Pr-C	MI	F-G	G	VG	VG	VG	G	G	P
Thibaut & Kelley	Pr-C	MI	G-VG	G	G	G	G	G	G	G-VG
French	C	MI	G	F	G	G	F-G	G	G	F
Cartwright	C	MI	F	G	F	P-F	F-G	F-G	F-G	F

Key to symbols:
Pr = Principle theory
C = Constructive theory
Mc = Molecular
MI = Molar

VG = very good
G = good
F = fair
P = poor

reinforcement-based conceptions to field conceptions. Both Thibaut and Kelley and Adams and Romney view power in terms of the asymmetrical distribution of reward and punishment capabilities between two interacting people. Cartwright, on the other hand, views power as being based upon one person's ability to control the current field of behavior within which two people are interacting. Thus, Cartwright sees power as the resultant field force that one person can muster toward another in the direction of desired influence. French's more-comprehensive and hierarchically structured theory of power takes into account both of the conceptions above. He sees power as being multiply based upon (1) reward and punishment capabilities, (2) a relationship of liking, (3) the expertness of one party over another in a given domain, and (4) "legitimacy" factors such as status, societally structured authority-underlying relationships, and so forth.

Although each of these approaches to power relations ostensibly differs in scope and range of applicability, it is apparent that each is quite relevant to the study of social power. Advances in theory-related research are sorely needed in this subarea before the conditions under which these various conceptions of power apply can be established.

Theories of Interpersonal Relations and Interpersonal Communication

The criterion ratings for the theories classed in this subarea are presented in Table 14–4. An overview of this table indicates that (1) this group of theories fares rather well on most of the formal criteria, (2) these theories are either constructive or mixed in form and, (3) three of the theories are molar and use the interaction unit as the unit of analysis. Heider's theory, although certainly concerned with the interaction unit as a unit of analysis, tends to emphasize the consequences (internal balance versus internal imbalance) of different structures of communication for the individual. Newcomb, on the other hand, tends to view balance and strain in terms of the interpersonal system.

The theories grouped in this subarea (and, admittedly, many more theories presented in this book at least indirectly deal with interaction processes) divide into two classes. The theories of Heider and Newcomb are *consistency* theories and are both concerned with the manner in which two individuals' current coorientation or noncoorientation toward an object or another person affects each of the individuals as well as their interactions and future orientation toward the object. The theories of Homans and Thibaut and Kelley are only tangentially concerned with the orientations of the two interacting parties toward an object or a third party. These latter two theories stem from the *reinforcement* orientation and are concerned with the complexities of mutual reinforcement as it operates in an interactive context. Their focus of concern is the joint behavioral unit produced when two individuals emit specific behaviors toward one another or in one another's presence.

Although these two classes of theories have ostensibly different foci, in many cases they tend to grapple with the same issues. For example, Heider

TABLE 14-4. A criterion comparison of theories of interpersonal relations and interpersonal communication

Theory	Form	Content	Internal consistency	Agreement with known data	Testability	Simplicity, clarity	Economy	External consistency	Interpretability	Research productivity
Heider (p-o-x)	C	Mc	G	F-G	F-G	F	G	G	G	G-VG
Newcomb	C	MI	F-G	F	F	F	G	G	G	F
Homans	Pr-C	MI	F-G	G	F	F	G	G	G	G-VG
Thibaut & Kelley	Pr-C	MI	G-VG	G	G	G	G	G	G	P

Key to symbols:
Pr = Principle theory
C = Constructive theory
Mc = Molecular
MI = Molar

VG = very good
G = good
F = fair
P = poor

attributes the formation of *unit relations* to factors such as similarity, proximity, complementarity, and past experience. Thibaut and Kelley also note similar bases for the formation of dyadic relationships. They refer to these bases as exogenous determinants. Furthermore, in considering the endogenous determinants of the formation and maintenance of relationships, Thibaut and Kelley often allude to concepts related to Heider's articulation of the domain of sentiment relations. Thus, although the theories in this area have concepts peculiar to the orientation from which they were drawn, they are addressed to several very similar concerns. Some of these concerns are (1) the bases for relationship formation, (2) the factors which mediate the continuance or discontinuance of a relationship, (3) the importance of the role of expectancy (either reward expectancy or the expectancy that one person has that the other will hold similar opinions) in the functioning of a relationship. As we can see from this sampling of issues, much of the concern in the subarea of interpersonal relations and communication is concentrated upon the formation and preservation of relationships. Interaction process becomes important only insofar as it facilitates the continuance and discontinuance of relationships.

It appears in Table 14–4 that, from a formal standpoint, the four theories are relatively comparable. Thibaut and Kelley's theory emerges as the most linguistically clear and the most internally consistent of these theories. The theories of Heider, Newcomb, and Homans leave something to be desired with regard to the clarity with which they state their terms and with regard to the precision of their predictive statements. Both Heider's p-o-x theory and Thibaut and Kelley's theory have generated substantial amounts of research that have been moderately confirmatory of their theoretical propositions. Homans' theory has generated much interest but no direct empirical tests of its propositions, and Newcomb's theory has generated little research beyond the classic longitudinal study of the acquaintance process.

Theories of Social Perception and Social Judgment

The evaluations of the theories exposited in this subarea are presented in Table 14–5. The table reveals that (1) all four of the theories fare quite adequately on the formal evaluation criteria; (2) they are all molecular in content since their units of analysis are the judgments, attributions, and perceptions of self and others by individuals; and (3) they are all either constructive or mixed in form.

It should be noted that three of the theories (Heider's theory of interpersonal relations, Jones and Davis' correspondent inference theory, and Kelley's theory of external attribution) very clearly belong together because they all deal with similar types of issues. However, Festinger's social comparison theory was classed with this group only because it fits the contents of this subarea better than it fits the contents of any of the other subareas.

The theories of Kelley and of Jones and Davis were derived from Heider's

TABLE 14-5. A criterion comparison of theories of social perception and social judgment

Theory	Form	Content	Internal consistency	Agreement with known data	Test-ability	Simplicity, clarity	Economy	External consistency	Interpretability	Research productivity
Heider (I. R.)	C	Mc	G	G	F-G	F	G	G	G	G-VG
Jones & Davis	Pr-C	Mc	G	G	VG	F-G	G	G-VG	G	G
Kelley	Pr-C	Mc	G	G	G	G	G	G	G	P
Festinger (comparison)	C	Mc	F-G	F	G	F	G	F	G	G-VG

Key to symbols:

Pr = Principle theory
C = Constructive theory
Mc = Molecular
Ml = Molar

VG = very good
G = good
F = fair
P = poor

theory of interpersonal relations. In this sense, Heider's theory was conceptually rich and has stimulated theoretical contributions by other social psychologists. Further, it has directly or indirectly generated many significant pieces of research. Kelley's theory is concerned with the narrower universe of attribution to the external environment, whereas Jones and Davis considered attribution to the person. Both these theories followed the Heiderian form of analysis, but they are somewhat more clearly stated and therefore more testable than Heider's more-general theory. Both theories clearly articulate the conditions under which their predictions concerning attribution should hold. Taken together, they have provided social psychologists with quite adequate frames of reference for evaluating research on social perception and attribution. Thus, the global applicability of Heider's theory of interpersonal relations reflects the richness and incisiveness of his thinking.

The correspondent inference theory of Jones and Davis is at least partially responsible for a growing body of research on personal attributions. On the other hand, despite the clarity and conciseness of Kelley's terms and propositions, his theory has not yet generated a body of research, perhaps only because of the recency of the theory. However, one might conjecture that social psychologists have consistently expressed more interest in personal perceptions, attributions, and judgments than in environmental attributions, and this factor could partially account for the relatively low level of research interest aroused by Kelley's theory as compared with that of Jones and Davis. Nevertheless, Kelley's concepts about informational dependence, judgmental confidence, distinctiveness of environmental characteristics, time consistency, modality consistency, and consensus are all quite testable and relevant to the domain of social psychology, and promise to be submitted to empirical testing in the future.

The final theory in this group, Festinger's social comparison theory, is only tangentially related to the processes of attribution and social perception. Specifically, it deals with the processes that an individual uses to evaluate the viability of his own opinions and the strength of his own abilities in relation to the opinions and abilities of others in his social environment. Although the evaluation of one's own attributes in relation to the attributes of others indeed involves the perception of the other's attributes, this is nevertheless only a secondary focus of the theory. The impact of social comparison on the individual's change of opinion is the consequence of the social comparison processes with which Festinger is most concerned. Thus, Festinger's social comparison theory is to some extent a theory of social influence as well as a theory of social judgment and perception. From a formal standpoint, social comparison theory is an adequate proposal about a rather complex process. Although there was some time lag between the initial proposal and the eventual presentation of adequate research evidence, the theory has nevertheless recently shown itself to be quite generative of empirical research. However, the research evidence for the theory has often been questionable. In its present state, the theory requires a more-precise delineation of its terms and propositions and the conditions under which they apply.

Theories of Social Influence Processes

Our grouping of theories into this subarea is probably the least justified of any of our groupings. Although the theories of Willis, Bandura, Miller and Dollard, and Fiedler all deal with processes of social influence, they address themselves to three very different components of social influence (conformity, imitation, and leadership. Each of these three processes of social influence has its own separate body of research, and each process can be thought of as a separate subarea of social psychology. Nevertheless, we have classed these theories together for evaluative purposes out of considerations of "best fit."

Table 14–6 summarizes our evaluations of each of the four theories of social influence processes. Because of the diversity of foci of the theories we have grouped into this area, we will forgo rendering an overall evaluation and look separately at the theories concerned with each of the three afore-mentioned social influence processes.

Willis' theory of conformity is constructive in form in that its predictions are based upon the "construct" of a conformity model (the diamond model) that articulates several dimensions of conformity-nonconformity. It is molecular in content in that its unit of analysis is the response mode that an individual adopts when confronted by social pressure to conform. Although the theory fares relatively well on the first seven formal criteria, it has yet to generate a substantial body of related research. The most telling drawback of the theory is not reflected in Table 14–6. That is, in its present form, the theory does not go far enough in specifying the conditions under which the several proposed modes of social response might be expected to occur in a conformity situation. In fairness to the diamond model we should note that although we classified it as a theory, it was indeed intended as a model and it does serve the exploratory goal of a model well. Furthermore, Willis' "theory" is one of the few attempts at theory building in the area of conformity. The study of conformity has characteristically proceeded without any theories or models. Thus, although conformity research has tended to proliferate, there has been no organizational schema to link the various findings. Perhaps Willis' proposal is a beginning step in the direction of theory construction about conformity behavior.

The theories of Miller and of Dollard and Bandura both deal with imitation. As Table 14–6 indicates, both are data-based in form and molecular in content. The unit of analysis in each of the theories is the imitative response of an observer which is contingent on the behavior of a model. Social imitation is clearly relevant to many separate areas of concern in social psychology. It undoubtedly plays a role in group behavior and process, social comparison, social perception, conformity, and the acquisition of "sociability." Despite its apparent relevance, however, it has until recently constituted only a minor portion of the experimental interests of social psychologists. Bandura's theory has played a substantial role in the current generation of research interest in imitation among social psychologists and developmental psychologists alike. It is an economically stated and testable theory, whose terms are appropriately simple and interpretable. In constructing the theory Bandura has paid

TABLE 14-6. A criterion comparison of theories of social influence processes

Theory	Form	Content	Internal consis-tency	Agreement with known data	Test-ability	Sim-plicity, clarity	Economy	External consis-tency	Interpret-ability	Research produc-tivity
Willis	C	Mc	F-G	F-G	G	G	G	G	G	F
Miller & Dollard	Pr	Mc	F	F-G	F	G	G	F	G	P
Bandura	Pr	Mc	VG	G	G	G	VG	G	G	VG
Fiedler	Pr	Ml	G	G	VG	G-VG	G	G	G	G

Key to symbols:

Pr = Principle theory   VG = very good
C = Constructive theory   G = good
Mc = Molecular   F = fair
Ml = Molar   P = poor

close attention to the issues raised by other theories of imitation, such as those of Miller and Dollard, Skinner, and Mowrer. All in all, Bandura's theory has fulfilled the goals of theory well and promises to continue to be a vital force in the area of socialization and social learning.

Miller and Dollard's theory, on the other hand, is of great historical interest to researchers in the area of imitation, but it does not have as much currency as Bandura's approach. As we can see in Table 14–6, it does not fare as well as Bandura's theory on most of the formal criteria. Miller and Dollard's theory of imitation is often too vaguely stated to be testable, and it has not agreed well with recent data. Furthermore, aside from the demonstrations of the imitation paradigms proposed by the theory in its initial presentation, there has been little research directly testing its propositions.

Fiedler's contingency model of leadership quite adequately fulfills all the formal criteria for theory. It is principled in nature and is based upon a large body of research in leadership. Its unit of analysis is molar in that it deals with the consequences of leadership for the group rather than with the determinants of good leadership in the individual. Fiedler's theory is well stated, internally consistent, and most definitely testable. It has generated a substantial body of research. In most cases its propositions and terms are simple and well defined (with the possible exception of the favorability continuum). Finally, Fiedler's theory of leadership promises to provide definition to a field of social psychology, which, like conformity, has been heavy on research but lacking in theory.

A LOOK AT THE FUTURE

There are many hazards involved in attempting to postulate about the future of any field of inquiry. These hazards are magnified in the case of a field such as social psychology that promises to continue to experience a burgeoning growth in the years to come. However, several outcomes of the present trends in the field are indeed plausible, and still others are both plausible and desirable. First of all, it is quite likely that the theories of social psychology will continue to play a vital role in its advance as a discipline. It is unlikely that the field will move in the direction of a strict empiricism based upon groups of working hypotheses that vary from empirical investigation to empirical investigation. It is more probable that movement away from this state of affairs will occur, particularly in subareas of study such as group behavior and conformity. It is further unlikely and undesirable that any grand theory of social behavior will be developed in the near future. Social psychology is too diverse a group of relatively young subdisciplines to be accounted for by any single network of hypotheses. It seems that theories will continue to be proposed and that research related to those theories will continue to be generated. It is inevitable that as social psychologists become confronted with some of the inadequacies of their theories through the difficulties that they experience testing them in the laboratory, theory building in the field will become more sophisticated. This sophistication will be in terms of factors such as simplicity of terminology, testability, specificity of predictions and the conditions under which predictions hold, and internal and external theoretical consistency. The laboratory, then, will most probably increasingly serve as a feedback mechanism for theories through its role as the evaluation arena of the theories in the field. Insofar as advances are made in the research methodology, this feedback function of laboratory research will be facilitated. However, will these developments be sufficient to move social psychology in the direction of formulating "laws" of social behavior which can be repeatedly demonstrated to apply when certain conditions prevail? Will the endless cycle of theory to research to theory modification to research to theory modification reach a point of diminishing returns? Will the field of social psychology eventually fall into an epistomological morass in which theories proliferate to the extent that a single postulate is needed for each possible condition in the human social environment?

Obviously, these are questions subject to endless speculation and argument. At this point in time, they are questions without answers. They are "what would happen if" types of questions, when indeed relatively little has happened in our rather infant science of social psychology. At present these questions are not real but clearly hypothetical. However, one very negative aspect of theory testing in social psychology could, if it continues to grow, render these questions as very real and immediate. That aspect has to do with the seeming nonconcern of social psychologists with the *comparative* testing of theories. Surely, theories will continue to proliferate if the research that they generate tends to be directed at proving the hypotheses *within* a given theory, for once that set of hypotheses has run its course, a new theory will be needed and proposed. The comparative testing of theories not only will lead theories to expand to encompass new conditions, but will speak to the comparative viability of one theory in relation to another. In due time, the less-viable theories will be cast aside and the more-tenable ones will survive and become guides for future research, and they will become the objects of conceptual modification. Some promising moves in this direction are currently being made (for example, the Bem-dissonance controversy), but much more comparative theory testing is needed in the field. This, in the opinion of the authors, should be one of the primary goals for the future of the discipline. The intention of this book was to exposit the theories in social psychology in a fashion clear enough to render them understandable and to stimulate the reader to make conceptual comparisons among related theories. We hope that this goal has been approached. More idealistically, we hope that this book might help in some way to stimulate theoretical advances in the field of social psychology.

REFERENCES

ABELSON, R. P., & Rosenberg, M. J. Symbolic psycho-iogic: A model of attitudinal cognition. *Behav. Sci.,* 1958, **3,** 1–13.

ADAMS, J. S., & Romney, A. K. A functional analysis of authority. *Psychol. Rev.,* 1959, **66,** 234–251.

ADAMS, J. S., & Romney, A. K. The determinants of authority interactions. In N. F. Washburne (Ed.), *Decisions, values and groups.* Vol. 2. New York: Pergamon Press, 1962. Pp. 227–256.

ADAMS, S. Status congruency as a variable in small group performance. *Soc. Forces,* 1953, **32,** 16–22.

ADORNO, T. W., Frenkel-Brunswik, E., Levinson, D. J., & Sanford, R. N. *The authoritarian personality.* New York: Harper, 1950.

ALLPORT, F. H. *Social psychology.* Cambridge, Mass.: Houghton Mifflin, 1924.

ALLPORT, G. W. *Personality: A psychological interpretation.* New York: Holt, 1937.

ALLPORT, G. W. Scientific models and human morals. *Psychol. Rev.,* 1947, **54,** 182–192.

ALLPORT, G. W., Bruner, J. S., & Jandorf, E. M. Personality under social catastrophe: Ninety life histories of the Nazi Revolution. In C. Kluckhohn & H. A. Murray (Eds.), *Personality in nature, society, and culture.* New York: Alfred A. Knopf, 1948. Pp. 347–366.

ANDERSON, L. R. Some effects of leadership training on intercultural discussion groups. Unpublished doctoral dissertation, University of Illinois, 1964.

ANDERSON, L. R., & Fiedler, F. E. The effect of participatory and supervisory leadership on group creativity. *J. appl. Psychol.,* 1964, **48,** 227–236.

ANDERSON, L. R., & Fishbein, M. Prediction of attitude from number, strength, and evaluative aspect of beliefs about the attitude object: A comparison of summation and congruity theories. *J. pers. soc. Psychol.,* 1965, **2,** 437–443.

ANREP, G. V. Pitch discrimination in the dog. *J. Physiol.,* 1920, **53,** 367–385.

ARONFREED, J. The nature, variety, and social patterning of moral responses to transgression. *J. abnorm. soc. Psychol.,* 1961, **63,** 223–241.

ARONSON, E. Dissonance theory: Progress and problems. In R. P. Abelson, E. Aronson, T. M. Newcomb, W. J. McGuire, M. J. Rosenberg, & P. H. Tannenbaum (Eds.), *Source book on cognitive consistency.* New York: Rand-McNally, 1968. Pp. 5–27.

ARONSON, E., & CARLSMITH, J. M. Performance expectancy as a determinant of actual performance. *J. abnorm. soc. Psychol.,* 1962, **65,** 178–182.

ASCH, S. E. Effects of group pressure upon the modification and distortion of judgment. In H. Guetzkow (Ed.), *Groups, leadership, and men.* Pittsburgh: Carnegie Press, 1951. Pp. 177–190.

ASCH, S. E. *Social psychology.* New York: Prentice-Hall, 1952.

AUSUBEL, D. P. In defense of verbal learning. *Educ. Theory,* 1961, **11,** 15–25.

AUSUBEL, D. P. Cognitive structure and the facilitation of meaningful verbal learning. *J. Teacher Educ.,* 1963, **14,** 217–221.

AUSUBEL, D. P. Introduction. In R. C. Anderson & D. P. Ausubel (Eds.), *Readings in the psychology of cognition.* New York: Holt, Rinehart and Winston, 1965a. Pp. 3–17.

AUSUBEL, D. P. A cognitive structure view of word and concept meaning. In R. C. Anderson & D. P. Ausubel (Eds.), *Readings in the psychology of cognition.* New York: Holt, Rinehart and Winston, 1965b. Pp. 58–86.

BACK, K. W. Influence through social communication. *J. abnorm. soc. Psychol.,* 1951, **46,** 9–23.

BALDWIN, A. L., Kallhorn, J., & Breese, F. H. Patterns of parent behavior. *Psychol. Monogr.,* 1945, **58,** No. 3 (Whole No. 268).

BALDWIN, J. M. *Le developpement mental chez l'enfant et dans la race.* London: Macmillan, 1897.

BALES, R. F. A set of categories for the analysis of small group interaction. *Amer. sociol. Rev.,* 1950, **15,** 146–159.

BALES, R. F., & Strodtbeck, F. L. Phases in group problem solving. *J. abnorm. soc. Psychol.,* 1951, **46,** 485–495.

BANDURA, A. *Relationship of family patterns to child behavior disorders.* Progress Report, Project No. M-1734, U.S.P.H.S., Stanford Univer., Stanford, California, 1960.

BANDURA, A. Social learning through imitation. In M. R. Jones (Ed.), *Nebraska symposium on motivation: 1962.* Lincoln: Univer. of Nebraska Press, 1962. Pp. 211–269.

BANDURA, A. Influence of models' reinforcement contingencies on the acquisition of imitative responses. *J. pers. soc. Psychol.,* 1965a, **1,** 589–595.

BANDURA, A. Behavioral modification through modeling procedures. In L. Krasner & L. P. Ullman (Eds.), *Research in behavior modification.* New York: Holt, 1965b. Pp. 310–340.

BANDURA, A. Vicarious processes: A case of no-trial learning. In L. Berkowitz (Ed.), *Advances in experimental social psychology.* Volume 2. New York: Academic Press, 1966. Pp. 1–55.

BANDURA, A., & Mischel, W. Modification of self-imposed delay of reward through exposure to live and symbolic models. *J. pers. soc. Psychol.,* 1965, **2,** 698–705.

BANDURA, A., & Rosenthal, T. L. Vicarious classical conditioning as a function of arousal level. *J. pers. soc. Psychol.,* 1966, **3,** 54–62.

BANDURA, A., Ross, D., & Ross, S. Transmission of aggression through imitation of aggressive models. *J. abnorm. soc. Psychol.,* 1961, **63,** 575–582.

BANDURA, A., Ross, D., & Ross, S. Imitation of film-mediated aggressive models. *J. abnorm. soc. Psychol.,* 1963, **66,** 3–11.

BANDURA, A., & Walters, R. H. *Adolescent aggression.* New York: Ronald Press, 1959.

BANDURA, A., & Walters, R. H. *Social learning and personality development.* New York: Holt, 1963.

BANDURA, A., & Whalen, C. K. The influence of antecedent reinforcement and divergent modeling cues on patterns of self-reward. *J. pers. soc. Psychol.,* 1966, **3,** 373–382.

BARNARD, C. I. *The functions of the executive.* Cambridge, Mass.: Harvard Univer. Press, 1938.

BARNARD, C. I. *Organization and management.* Cambridge: Harvard Univer. Press, 1948.

BARNETT, P. E., & Benedetti, D. T. A study in vicarious conditioning. Paper read at Rocky Mountain Psychological Association Convention, Glenwood Spring, Colorado, 1960.

BASS, M. J., & Hull, C. L. The irradiation of a tactile conditioned reflex in man. *J. Comp. Psychol.,* 1934, **17,** 47–65.

BECHTEREV, V. M. Die objective Untersuchung der neurpsychischen Tätigkeit. *Congr. Int. Psychiat. Neurol.,* Amsterdam, 1908.

BECKER, H. Some forms of sympathy: a phenomenological analysis. *J. abnorm. soc. Psychol.,* 1931, **26,** 58–68.

BECHTEREV, V. M. *General principles of human reflexology.* New York: International, 1932.

BEM, D. J. *An experimental analysis of beliefs and attitudes.* Unpublished Doctoral Dissertation, Univer. of Michigan, 1964.

BENNIS, W. G., & Shepard, H. A. A theory of group development. *Hum. Relat.,* 1956, **9,** 415–437.

BENOIT-SMULLYAN, E. Status, status types and status interrelations. *Amer. sociol. Rev.,* 1944, **9,** 155–161.

BERGER, S. M. Conditioning through vicarious instigation. *Psychol. Rev.,* 1962, **69,** 450–466.

BERLYNE, D. E. Recent developments in Piaget's work. *British J. educ. Psychol.,* 1957, **27,** 1–12.

BIDDLE, B. J., & Thomas, E. J. (Eds.) *Role theory: Concepts and research.* New York: Wiley, 1966.

BIERI, J. Cognitive complexity-simplicity and predictive behavior. *J. abnorm. soc. Psychol.,* 1955, **51,** 263–268.

BIERMAN, M. The use of modeling, reinforcement, and problem solving set in altering children's syntactic style. Unpublished manuscript, Stanford Univer., 1965.

BIERSTEDT, R. An analysis of social power. *Amer. sociol. Rev.,* 1950, **15,** 730–736.

BION, W. R. Experiences in groups: III. *Hum. Relat.,* 1949a, **2,** 13–22.

BION, W. R. Experiences in groups: IV. *Hum. Relat.,* 1949b, **2,** 295–303.

BION, W. R. *Experiences in groups, and other papers.* New York: Basic Books, 1959.

BION, W. R. *Experiences in groups.* New York: Basic Books, 1961.

BLUM, G. S. *Psychoanalytic theories of personality.* New York: McGraw-Hill, 1964.

BOVARD, E. W. Social norms and the individual. *J. abnorm. soc. Psychol.,* 1948, **43,** 62–69.

BRAMEL, D. Dissonance, expectation, and the self. In R. P. Abelson, E. Aronson, T. M. Newcomb, W. J. McGuire, M. J. Rosenberg, & P. H. Tannenbaum (Eds.), *Source book on cognitive consistency.* New York: Rand-McNally, 1968. Pp. 355–365.

BREDMEIER, H. C., & Stephenson, R. M. *The analysis of social systems.* New York: Holt, Rinehart and Winston, 1962.

BREHM, J. W., & Cohen, A. R. *Explorations in cognitive dissonance.* New York: Wiley, 1962.

BRESSLER, J. Judgments in absolute units as a psychophysical method. *Arch. Psychol.,* 1933, No. 152.

BRIDGMAN, P. W. *The logic of modern physics.* New York: Macmillan, 1927.

BRISCOE, M. E., Woodyard, H. D., & Shaw, M. E. Personality impression change as a function of the favorableness of first impressions. *J. Pers.,* 1967, **35,** 343–357.

BROWN, J. S. Factors determining conflict reactions in difficult discriminations. *J. exp. Psychol.,* 1942, **31,** 272–292.

BROWN, J. S., Bilodeau, E. A., & Baron, M. R. Bidirectional gradients in the strength of a generalized voluntary response to stimuli on a visual-spatial dimension. *J. exp. Psychol.,* 1951, **41,** 52–61.

BROWN, R. Models of attitude change. In R. Brown, E. Galanter, E. Hess, & G. Mandler (Eds.), *New directions in psychology.* New York: Holt, Rinehart and Winston, 1962. Pp. 1–85.

BROWN, R. *Social psychology.* New York: The Free Press, 1965.

BRUNER, J. S. On perceptual readiness. *Psychol. Rev.,* 1957a, **64,** 123–152.

BRUNER, J. S. On going beyond the information given. In *Contemporary approaches to cognition.* Cambridge, Mass.: Harvard Univer. Press, 1957b. Pp. 41–69.

BRUNER, J. S. Learning and thinking. *Harvard educ. Rev., 1959,* **29,** 184–192.

BRUNER, J. S., & Postman, L. Tension and tension release as organizing factors in perception. *J. Pers.,* 1947, **15,** 300–308.

BRUNER, J. S., Wallach, M. A., & Galanter, E. H. The identification of recurrent regularity. *Amer. J. Psychol.,* 1959, **72,** 200–209.

BRUNSWIK, E. Wahrnehmung und Gegenstandswelt. Leipzig and Wien: Deuticke, 1934.

BRUNSWIK, E. Discussion: Remarks on functionalism in perception. *J. Pers.,* 1949a, **18,** 56–65.

BRUNSWIK, E. *Systematic and representative design of psychological experiments.* Berkeley: Univer. of Calif. Press, 1949b.

BRUNSWIK, E. The conceptual framework of psychology. In *International Encyclopedia of Unified Science,* Vol. 1, No. 10. Chicago: Univer. of Chicago Press, 1952.

BUHLER, C. *The child and his family.* New York: Harper, 1939.

BURDICK, H. A., & Burnes, A. J. A test of "strain toward symmetry" theories. *J. abnorm. soc. Psychol.,* 1958, **57,** 367–369.

CAMPBELL, D. T. Common fate, similarity, and other indices of aggregates of persons as social entities. *Behav. Sci.,* 1958, **3,** 14–25.

CAMPBELL, D. T. Conformity in psychology's theories of acquired behavioral dispositions. In I. A. Berg and B. M. Bass (Eds.), *Conformity and deviation.* New York: Harper, 1961. Pp. 101–142.

CAMPBELL, N. R. *What is science?* London: Methuen, 1921.

CARNAP, R. The two concepts of probability. In H. Feigl and M. Brodbeck (Eds.), *Readings in the philosophy of science.* New York: Appleton-Century-Crofts, 1953.

CARTWRIGHT, D. Lewinian theory as a contemporary systematic framework. In S. Koch (Ed.), *Psychology: A study of a science.* New York: McGraw-Hill, 1959a. Pp. 7–91.

CARTWRIGHT, D. (Ed.) *Studies in social power.* Ann Arbor: Institute for Social Research, 1959b.

CARTWRIGHT, D., & Harary, F. Structural balance: A generalization of Heider's theory. *Psychol. Rev.,* 1956, **63,** 277–293.

CATTELL, R. B. The ergic theory of attitude and sentiment measurement. *Educ. psychol. Measmt.,* 1947, **7,** 221–246.

CATTELL, R. B. Concepts and methods in the measurement of group syntality. *Psychol. Rev.,* 1948, **55,** 48–63.

CATTELL, R. B. Determining syntality dimension as a basis for morale and leadership measurement. In H. Guetzkow (Ed.), *Groups, leadership and men: Research in human relations.* Pittsburgh: Carnegie Press, 1951a. Pp. 16–27.

CATTELL, R. B. New concepts for measuring leadership, in terms of group syntality. *Hum. Relat.,* 1951b, **4,** 161–184.

CATTELL, R. B., and Wispe, L. G. The dimensions of syntality in small groups. *J. soc. Psychol.,* 1948, **28,** 57–78.

CATTELL, R. B., Saunders, D. R., & Stice, G. F. The dimensions of syntality in small groups. *Hum. Relat.,* 1953, **6,** 331–356.

CHAMPNEY, H. The variables of parent behavior. *J. abnorm. soc. Psychol.,* 1941, **36,** 525–542.

CHAPANIS, N. P., & Chapanis, A. Cognitive dissonance: Five years later. *Psychol. Bull.,* 1964, **61,** 1–22.

CHAPPLE, E. D., & Arensberg, C. M. Measuring human relations: An introduction to the study of the interactions of individuals. *Genet. Psychol. Monogr.,* 1940, **22,** 3–147.

CHEMERS, M. W., Fiedler, F. E., Lekhyananda, D., & Stolurow, L. M. Some effects of cultural training on leadership in heterocultural task groups. *International J. Psychol.,* 1966, **1**, 301–314.

COCH, L., & French, J. R. P., Jr. Overcoming resistance to change. *Hum. Relat.,* 1948, **1**, 512–532.

COHEN, A. R., Stotland, E., & Wolfe, D. M. An experimental investigation of need for cognition. *J. abnorm. soc. Psychol.,* 1955, **51**, 291–294.

CONANT, J. B. *Modern science and modern man.* Garden City, N. Y.: Doubleday, 1953.

COOLEY, C. H. *Human nature and the social order.* New York: Scribner, 1902.

COTTRELL, L. S., Jr. The adjustment of the individual to his age and sex roles. *Amer. sociol. Rev.,* 1942, **7**, 617–620.

CRONBACH, L. J., & Gleser, G. C. Assessing similarity between profiles. *Psychol. Bull.,* 1953, **50**, 456–473.

DAHL, R. A. The concept of power. *Behav. Sci.,* 1957, **2**, 201–215.

DARLEY, J. M., & Aronson, E. Self-evaluation vs. direct anxiety reduction as determinants of the fear-affiliation relationship. *J. exp. soc. Psychol.,* Supplement 1, 1966, 66–79.

DARLEY, J. M., & Berscheid, E. Increased liking as a result of the anticipation of personal contact. *Hum. Relat.,* 1967, 29–40.

DAVIS, R. C. *Industrial organization and management.* New York: Harper, 1957.

DEUTSCH, M. A theory of co-operation and competition. *Hum. Relat.,* 1949a, **2**, 129–152.

DEUTSCH, M. An experimental study of the effects of co-operation and competition upon group process. *Hum. Relat.,* 1949b, **2**, 199–232.

DEUTSCH, M. Field theory in social psychology. In G. Lindzey (Ed.), *Handbook of social psychology.* Reading, Mass.: Addison-Wesley, 1954. Pp. 181–222.

DEUTSCH, M., & Gerard, H. B. A study of normative and informational social influences upon individual judgment. *J. abnorm. soc. Psychol.,* 1955, **51**, 629–636.

DEUTSCH, M., & Solomon, L. Reactions to evaluations by others as influenced by self-evaluations. *Sociometry,* 1959, **22**, 93–112.

DEWEY, J. *The school and society.* Chicago: Univer. of Chicago Press, 1899.

DEWEY, R., & Humber, W. J. *An introduction to social psychology.* New York: Macmillan, 1966.

DICKINSON, R. L., & Beam, L. *A thousand marriages.* Baltimore: Williams and Wilkins, 1931.

DOLLARD, J. C., & Miller, N. E. *Personality and psychotherapy.* New York: McGraw-Hill, 1950.

DOOB, L. W. The behavior of attitudes. *Psychol. Rev.,* 1947, **54**, 135–156.

DURKHEIM, E. *De la division du travail social.* Paris: Alcan, 1893.

EINSTEIN, A. *Essays in science.* New York: Philosophical Library, 1934.

ERIKSEN, C. W. Perceptual defense as a function of unacceptable needs. *J. abnorm. soc. Psychol.,* 1951, **46**, 557–564.

ERIKSEN, C. W., & Hake, H. W. Anchor effects in absolute judgments. *J. exp. Psychol.,* 1957, **53**, 132–138.

ERIKSON, E. H. *Childhood and society.* New York: Norton, 1963.

ESCH, J. A study of judgments of social situations. Unpublished term paper, Univer. of Kansas, 1950. Cited in F. Heider, *The psychology of interpersonal relations.* New York: Wiley, 1958.

EXLINE, R. V. Explorations in the process of person perception: Visual interaction in relation to competition, sex, and need for affiliation. *J. Pers.,* 1963, **31**, 1–20.

EXLINE, R. V., Gray, D., & Schuette, D. Visual behavior in a dyad as affected by interview content and sex of respondent. *J. pers. soc. Psychol.,* 1965, **1**, 201–209.

FENICHEL, O. *The psychoanalytic theory of neurosis*. New York: Norton, 1945.

FERNBERGER, S. W. On absolute and relative judgments in lifted weight experiments. *Amer. J. Psychol.*, 1931, **43**, 560–578.

FERSTER, C. B., & Skinner, B. F. *Schedules of reinforcement*. New York: Appleton-Century-Crofts, 1957.

FESTINGER, L. Informal social communication. *Psychol. Rev.*, 1950, **57**, 271–282.

FESTINGER, L. A theory of social comparison processes. *Hum. Relat.*, 1954, **7**, 117–140.

FESTINGER, L. *A theory of cognitive dissonance*. Stanford: Stanford Univer. Press, 1957.

FESTINGER, L. *Conflict, decision and dissonance*. Stanford: Stanford Univer. Press, 1964.

FESTINGER, L., & Carlsmith, J. M. Cognitive consequences of forced compliance. *J. abnorm. soc. Psychol.*, 1959, **58**, 203–210.

FESTINGER, L., Gerard, H. B., Hymovitch, B., Kelley, H. H., & Raven, B. The influence process in the presence of extreme deviates. *Hum. Relat.*, 1952, **5**, 327–346.

FESTINGER, L., Riecken, H., & Schachter, S. *When prophecy fails*. Minneapolis: Univer. of Minnesota Press, 1956.

FESTINGER, L., Schachter, S., & Back, K. *Social pressures in informal groups*. New York: Harper, 1950.

FESTINGER, L., & Thibaut, J. W. Interpersonal communications in small groups. *J. abnorm. soc. Psychol.*, 1951, **46**, 92–99.

FESTINGER, L., Torrey, J., & Willerman, B. Self-evaluation as a function of attraction to the group. *Hum. Relat.*, 1954, **7**, 161–174.

FIEDLER, F. E. A method of objective quantification of certain countertransference attitudes. *J. clin. Psychol.*, 1951, **7**, 101–107.

FIEDLER, F. E. Assumed similarity measures as predictors of team effectiveness. *J. abnorm. soc. Psychol.*, 1954, **49**, 381–388.

FIEDLER, F. E. The influence of leader-keyman relations on combat crew effectiveness. *J. abnorm. soc. Psychol.*, 1955, **51**, 227–235.

FIEDLER, F. E. A contingency model of leadership effectiveness. In L. Berkowitz (Ed.), *Advances in experimental social psychology*. Vol. 1. New York: Academic Press, 1964. Pp. 149–190.

FIEDLER, F. E. The effect of leadership and cultural heterogeneity on group performance: A test of the contingency model. *J. exp. soc. Psychol.*, 1966, **2**, 237–264.

FIEDLER, F. E. *A theory of leadership effectiveness*. New York: McGraw-Hill, 1967.

FIEDLER, F. E., Warrington, W. G., & Blaisdell, F. J. Unconscious attitudes as correlates of sociometric choice in a social group. *J. abnorm. soc. Psychol.*, 1952, **47**, 790–796.

FISHBEIN, M., & Hunter, R. Summation versus balance in attitude organization and change. *J. abnorm. soc. Psychol.*, 1964, **69**, 505–510.

FORD, C. S. Society, culture, and the human organism. *J. gen. Psychol.*, 1939, **20**, 135–179.

FRANK, P. *Philosophy of science*. Englewood Cliffs, N. J.: Prentice-Hall, 1957.

FREEDMAN, J. L., & Sears, D. O. Selective exposure. In L. Berkowitz (Ed.), *Advances in experimental social psychology*. Vol. 2. New York: Academic Press, 1965. Pp. 58–97.

FRENCH, J. R. P., Jr. A formal theory of social power. *Psychol. Rev.*, 1956, **63**, 181–194.

FRENCH, J. R. P., Jr., Morrison, H. W., and Levinger, G. Coercive power and forces affecting conformity. *J. abnorm. soc. Psychol.*, 1960, **61**, 93–101.

FRENCH, J. R. P., Jr., & Raven, B. The bases of social power. In D. Cartwright (Ed.), *Studies in social power*. Ann Arbor: Institute for Social Research, 1959. Pp. 150–167.

FREUD, A. *The ego and the mechanisms of defense*. New York: International Universities Press, 1946.

FREUD, S. *Group psychology and the analysis of the ego* (1921). London: Hogarth, 1945.

FREUD, S. *Civilization and its discontents* (1930). London: Hogarth, 1946.

FREUD, S. The passing of the Oedipus complex. In *Collected papers,* London: Hogarth, 1948. Vol. 1. Pp. 269–276.

FREUD, S. The future of an illusion (1928). London: Hogarth, 1949a.

FREUD, S. *An outline of psychoanalysis* (1938). New York: Norton, 1949b.

FREUD, S. Libidinal types. In *Collected papers,* London: Hogarth, 1950. Pp. 247–251.

FREUD, S. *The neuro-psychoses of defense* (1894). London: Hogarth, 1962a. Vol. 3. Pp. 45–61.

FREUD, S. *Sexuality and the aetiology of the neuroses* (1898). London: Hogarth, 1962b. Vol. 3. Pp. 263–286.

FREUD, S. *Totem and taboo* (1913). London: Hogarth, 1962c. Vol. 13. Pp. 1–162.

FREUD, S. *The ego and the id* (1923). London: Hogarth, 1962d. Vol. 19. Pp. 12–66.

FROMM, E. *Escape from freedom.* New York: Holt, Rinehart and Winston, 1941.

FROMM, E. *Man for himself.* New York: Holt, Rinehart and Winston, 1947.

GARCIA-ESTEVE, J., & Shaw, M. E. Rural and urban patterns of responsibility attribution in Puerto Rico. *J. soc. Psychol.,* 1968, **74,** 143–149.

GARDNER, J. W. Level of aspiration in response to a prearranged sequence of scores. *J. exp. Psychol.,* 1939, **25,** 601–621.

GERARD, H. The effects of different dimensions of disagreement on the communication process in small groups. *Hum. Relat.,* 1953, **6,** 249–272.

GERARD, H. B. Some effects of status, role clarity, and group goal clarity upon the individual's relations to group process. *J. Pers.,* 1957, **25,** 475–488.

GERARD, H. B. Choice difficulty, dissonance, and the decision sequence. *J. Pers.,* 1967, **35,** 91–108.

GERARD, H. B., & Fleischer, L. Recall and pleasantness of balanced and unbalanced cognitive structures. *J. pers. soc. Psychol.,* 1967, **7,** 332–337.

GETZELS, J. W., & Guba, E. G. Role, role conflict, and effectiveness: An empirical study. *Amer. sociol. Rev.,* 1954, **19,** 164–175.

GEWIRTZ, J. L., & Baer, D. M. Deprivation and satiation of social reinforcers as drive conditions. *J. abnorm. soc. Psychol.,* 1958, **57,** 165–172.

GIBSON, J. J., & Pick, A. D. Perception of another person's looking behavior. *Amer. J. Psychol.,* 1963, **76,** 86–94.

GOFFMAN, E. *The presentation of self in everyday life.* New York: Doubleday, 1959.

GOODE, W. J. A theory of role strain. *Amer. sociol. Rev.,* 1960, **25,** 483–496.

GORDON, B. F. Influence and social comparison as motives for affiliation. *J. exp. soc. Psychol.,* Supplement 1, 1966, 55–65.

GOSS, N. E., Morgan, C. H., & Golin, S. J. Paired-associates learning as a function of percentage occurrence of response members (reinforcement). *J. exp. Psychol.,* 1959, **57,** 96–104.

GOTTHEIL, E. Changes in social perceptions contingent upon competing or cooperating. *Sociometry,* 1955, **18,** 132–137.

GOULD, R. An experimental analysis of "level of aspiration." *Genet. Psychol. Monogr.,* 1939, **21,** 1–116.

GOULDNER, A. W. *Patterns of industrial bureaucracy.* Glencoe, Ill.: The Free Press, 1954.

GRANT, D. A., & Schipper, L. M. The acquisition and extinction of conditioned eyelid responses as a function of the percentage of fixed ratio random reinforcement. *J. exp. Psychol.,* 1952, **43,** 313–320.

GROSS, N., Mason, W. S., & McEachern, A. W. *Explorations in role analysis: Studies of the school superintendency role.* New York: Wiley, 1957.

GROSSACK, M. M. Some effects of cooperation and competition upon small group behavior. *J. abnorm. soc. Psychol.,* 1954, **49,** 341–348.

GULICK, L., & Urwick, L. *Papers on the science of administration.* New York: Institute of Public Administration, 1937.

GULLAHORN, J. Distance and friendship as factors in the gross interaction matrix. *Sociometry,* 1952, **15,** 123–134.

GUTHRIE, E. R. *The psychology of learning.* New York: Harper, 1935.

GUTTMAN, N., & Kalish, H. I. Discriminability and stimulus generalization. *J. exp. Psychol.,* 1956, **51,** 79–88.

HAKMILLER, K. L. Threat as a determinant of downward comparison. *J. exp. soc. Psychol.,* Supplement 1, 1966a, 32–39.

HAKMILLER, K. L. Need for self-evaluation, perceived similarity and comparison choice. *J. exp. soc. Psychol.,* Supplement 1, 1966b, 49–54.

HALL, C. S., & Lindzey, G. *Theories of personality.* New York: Wiley, 1957.

HALL, J. F. *The psychology of learning.* Philadelphia: Lippincott, 1966.

HALPIN, A. W. The leader behavior and leadership ideology of educational administrators and aircraft commanders. *Harvard educ. Rev.,* 1955, **25,** 18–32.

HAMMOND, L. K., & Goldman, M. Competition and non-competition and its relationship to individual and group productivity. *Sociometry,* 1961, **24,** 46–60.

HARDYCK, J., & Braden, M. Prophecy fails again: A report of a failure to replicate. *J. abnorm. soc. Psychol.,* 1962, **65,** 136–141.

HARTMANN, H. *Ego psychology and the problem of adaptation.* New York: International Universities Press, 1958.

HARVEY, O. J., Hunt, D. E., & Schroder, H. M. *Conceptual systems and personality organization.* New York: Wiley, 1961.

HARVEY, O. J., & Ware, R. Personality differences in dissonance resolution. *J. pers. soc. Psychol.,* 1967, **7,** 227–230.

HASTORF, A. H., Kite, W. R., Gross, A. E., & Wolfe, L. J. The perception and evaluation of behavior change. *Sociometry,* 1965, **28,** 400–410.

HEIDER, F. Social perception and phenomenal causality. *Psychol. Rev.,* 1944, **51,** 358–374.

HEIDER, F. Attitudes and cognitive organization. *J. Psychol.,* 1946, **21,** 107–112.

HEIDER, F. *The psychology of interpersonal relations.* New York: Wiley, 1958.

HEINTZ, R. K. The effect of remote anchoring points upon the judgment of lifted weights. *J. exp. Psychol.,* 1950, **40,** 584–591.

HELSON, H. Adaptation-level as a basis for a quantitative theory of frames of reference. *Psychol. Rev.,* 1948, **55,** 297–313.

HEMPEL, C. G. Fundamentals of concept formation in empirical science. *International Encycl. Unified Sci.,* vol. 2, no. 7. Chicago: Univer. of Chicago Press, 1952.

HILGARD, E. R. *Theories of learning.* 2nd ed. New York: Appleton-Century-Crofts, 1956.

HOCHBAUM, G. M. Certain personality aspects and pressures to uniformity in social group. Doctoral dissertation, Minneapolis, University of Minnesota, 1953.

HOFFMAN, P. J., Festinger, L., & Lawrence, D. H. Tendencies toward group comparability in competitive bargaining. *Hum. Relat.,* 1954, **7,** 141–159.

HOLLANDER, E. P. *Principles and methods of social psychology.* New York: Oxford Univer. Press, 1967.

HOLLANDER, E. P., & Willis, R. H. Conformity, independence, and anticonformity as determiners of perceived influence and attraction. In E. P. Hollander (Ed.), *Leaders, groups, and influence.* New York: Oxford Univer. Press, 1964. Pp. 213–224.

HOLLANDER, E. P., & Willis, R. H. Some current issues in the psychology of conformity and nonconformity. *Psychol., Bull.,* 1967, **68,** 62–76.

HOMANS, G. C. *The human group.* New York: Harcourt, Brace, 1950.

HOMANS, G. C. Status among clerical workers. *Hum. Organization,* 1953, **12,** 5–10.

HOMANS, G. C. *Social behavior: Its elementary forms.* New York: Harcourt, Brace, 1961.

HORNEY, K. *Our inner conflicts.* New York: Norton, 1945.

HOVLAND, C. I. The generalization of conditioned responses. II. The sensory generalization of conditioned responses with varying intensities of tone. *J. genet. Psychol.,* 1937, **17,** 125–148.

HOVLAND, C. I., Harvey, O. J., & Sherif, M. Assimilation and contrast effects in reaction to communication and attitude change. *J. abnorm. soc. Psychol.,* 1957, **55,** 244–252.

HOVLAND, C. I., Janis, I., & Kelley, H. *Communication and persuasion.* New Haven: Yale Univer. Press, 1953.

HOVLAND, C. I., Lumsdaine, A. A., & Sheffield, F. D. *Experiments on mass communication.* Princeton, N. J.: Princeton Univer. Press, 1949.

HOVLAND, C. I., & Sherif, M. Judgmental phenomena and scales of attitude measurement: Item displacement in Thurstone scales. *J. abnorm. soc. Psychol.,* 1952, **47,** 822–832.

HOVLAND, C. I., & Weiss, W. The influence of source credibility on communication effectiveness. *Publ. Opin. Quart.,* 1951, **15,** 635–650.

HULL, C. L. *Principles of behavior.* New York: Appleton-Century-Crofts, 1943.

HULL, C. L. *A behavior system.* New Haven: Yale Univer. Press, 1952.

HUMPHREY, G. Imitation and the conditioned reflex. *Pedagog. Sem.,* 1921, **28,** 1–21.

HUNT, E. B. *Concept learning: An information processing problem.* New York: Wiley, 1962.

HUNT, J. G. A test of the leadership contingency model in three organizations. Technical Report No. 47 (67-3), ONR Contract NR 177-472, Nonr- 1834(36), Univer. of Illinois, 1967.

HUNT, W. A. Anchoring effects in judgment. *Amer. J. Psychol.,* 1941, **54,** 395–403.

HURWITZ, J. I., Zander, A. F., & Hymovitch, B. Some effects of power on the relations among group members. In D. Cartwright & A. Zander (Eds.). *Group dynamics: Research and theory.* Evanston, Ill.: Row, Peterson, 1953. Pp. 483–492.

INSKO, C. A. *Theories of attitude change.* New York: Appleton-Century-Crofts, 1967.

JAMES, W. *The principles of psychology.* New York: Holt, 1890.

JANIS, I. L., & Feshbach, S. Effects of fear-arousing communications. *J. abnorm. soc. Psychol.,* 1953, **48,** 78–92.

JENKINS, W. D., & Stanley, J. C. Partial reinforcement: A review and critique. *Psychol. Bull.,* 1950, **47,** 193–234.

JENNINGS, H. *Leadership and isolation.* New York: Longmans Green, 1950.

JONES, E. E., & Davis, K. E. From acts to dispositions: The attribution process in person perception. In L. Berkowitz (Ed.), *Advances in experimental social psychology.* Vol. 2. New York: Academic Press, 1965. Pp. 219–266.

JONES, E. E., Davis, K. E., & Gergen, K. J. Role playing variations and their informational value for person perception. *J. abnorm. soc. Psychol.,* 1961, **63,** 302–310.

JONES, E. E., & deCharms, R. Changes in social perception as a function of the personal relevance of behavior. *Sociometry,* 1957, **20,** 75–85.

JONES, E. E., & Gerard, H. B. *Foundations of social psychology.* New York: Wiley, 1967.

JONES, E. E., Gergen, K. J., & Jones, R. G. Tactics of ingratiation among leaders and subordinates in a status hierarchy. *Psychol. Monogr.,* 1963, **77,** No. 3 (Whole No. 566).

JONES, E. E., & Kohler, R. The effects of plausibility on the learning of controversial statements. *J. abnorm. soc. Psychol.,* 1958, **57,** 315–320.

JORDON, N. Behavioral forces that are a function of attitudes and of cognitive organization. *Hum. Relat.,* 1953, **6,** 273–287.

KANAREFF, V., & Lanzetta, J. T. Effects of task definition and probability of reinforcement upon the acquisition and extinction of imitative responses. *J. exp. Psychol.,* 1960, **60,** 340–348.

KANFER, F. H. Vicarious human reinforcement: A glimpse into the back of the box. In L. Krasner and L. P. Ullman (Eds.), *Research in behavior modification.* New York: Holt, 1965. Pp. 244–267.

KANFER, F. H., & Marston, A. R. Human reinforcement: Vicarious and direct. *J. exp. Psychol.,* 1963, **65,** 292–296.

KAPLAN, A. *The conduct of inquiry: Methodology for behavioral science.* San Francisco: Chandler, 1964.

KARSTEN, A. Psychische Sättigung. *Psychol. Forsch.,* 1928, **10,** 142–154.

KATZ, D., & Kahn, R. L. Some recent findings in human relations research in industry. In G. E. Swanson, T. M. Newcomb, & E. L. Hartley (Eds.), *Readings in social psychology.* Rev. ed. New York: Holt, 1952.

KATZ, D., McClintock, C., & Sarnoff, I. The measurement of ego defense as related to attitude change. *J. Pers.,* 1957, **25,** 465–474.

KATZ, D., Sarnoff, I., & McClintock, C. Ego-defense and attitude change. *Hum. Relat.,* 1956, **9,** 27–45.

KATZ, D., & Stotland, E. A preliminary statement to a theory of attitude structure and change. In S. Koch (Ed.), *Psychology: A study of a science.* Vol. 3. New York: McGraw-Hill, 1959. Pp. 423–475.

KELLER, F. S., & Schoenfeld, W. N. *Principles of psychology.* New York: Appleton-Century-Crofts, 1950.

KELLEY, H. H. Two functions of reference groups. In G. E. Swanson, T. M. Newcomb, & E. L. Hartley (Eds.), *Readings in social psychology.* Rev. ed. New York: Holt, 1952. Pp. 410–414.

KELLEY, H. H. Attribution theory in social psychology. In D. Levine (Ed.), *Nebraska symposium on motivation, 1967.* Lincoln: Univer. of Nebraska Press, 1967. Pp. 192–238.

KELLEY, H. H., Beckman, L. L., & Fischer, C. S. Negotiating the division of reward under incomplete information. *J. exp. soc. Psychol.,* 1967, **3,** 361–398.

KELLEY, H. H., Thibaut, J. W., Radloff, R., & Mundy, D. The development of cooperation in the "minimal social situation." *Psychol. Monogr.,* 1962, **76,** No. 19 (Whole No. 538).

KELLY, G. A. *The psychology of personal constructs.* New York: Norton, 1955.

KELMAN, H. C. Three processes of social influence. *Publ. Opin. Quart.,* 1961, **25,** 57–78.

KELMAN, H. C., & Hovland, C. I. "Reinstatement" of the communicator in delayed measurements of opinion change. *J. abnorm. soc. Psychol.,* 1953, **48,** 327–335.

KERRICK, J. The effect of relevant and non-relevant sources on attitude change. *J. soc. Psychol.,* 1958, **47,** 15–20.

KERRICK, J. The effect of instructional set on the measurement of attitude change through communications. *J. soc. Psychol.,* 1961, **53,** 113–120.

KIMBLE, G. A. *Hilgard and Marquis' conditioning and learning.* New York: Appleton-Century-Crofts, 1961.

KIMBLE, G. A. *Foundations of conditioning and learning.* New York: Appleton-Century-Crofts, 1967.

KING, B. T., & Janis, I. L. Comparison of the effectiveness of improvised vs. non-improvised role-playing in producing opinion change. *Hum. Relat.,* 1956, **9,** 177–186.

KLEINER, R. J. The effects of threat reduction upon interpersonal attractiveness. *J. Pers.,* 1960, **28,** 145–156.

KNOWER, F. H. Experimental studies of change in attitudes: I. A study of the effect of oral argument on change of attitude. *J. soc. Psychol.,* 1935, **6,** 315–347.

KOHLBERG, L. The development of children's orientations toward a moral order. I. Sequence in the development of moral thought. *Vita Humana,* 1963, **6,** 11–33.

KRECH, D., & Crutchfield, R. S. *Theory and problems of social psychology.* New York: McGraw-Hill, 1948.

KRECH, D., Crutchfield, R. S., & Ballachey, E. L. *Individual in society: A textbook of social psychology.* New York: McGraw-Hill, 1962.

KRIS, E. On préconscious mental processes. *Psychoanal. Quart.,* 1950, **19,** 540–560.

LARDER, D. L. Effect of aggressive story content on nonverbal play behavior. *Psychol. Rep.,* 1962, **11,** 14–15.

LASHLEY, K. S. *Brain mechanisms and intelligence.* Chicago: Univer. of Chicago Press, 1929.

LASHLEY, K. S., & Wade, M. The Pavlovian theory of generalization. *Psychol. Rev.,* 1946, **53,** 72–87.

LASSWELL, H. D., & Kaplan, A. *Power and society.* New Haven: Yale Univer. Press, 1950.

LATANÉ, B. Studies in social comparison: Introduction and overview. *J. exp. soc. Psychol.,* Supplement 1, 1966, 1–5.

LATANÉ, B., & Wheeler, L. Emotionality and reactions to disaster. *J. exp. soc. Psychol.,* Supplement 1, 1966, 95–102.

LAZARUS, R. S., Speisman, J. C., Mordkoff, A. M., & Davison, L. A. A laboratory study of psychological stress produced by a motion picture. *Psychol. Monogr.,* 1962, **76,** No. 34 (Whole No. 553).

LEEPER, R. W. *Lewin's topological and vector psychology.* Eugene, Ore.: Univer. of Oregon Press, 1943.

LERNER, M. J., & Matthews, G. Reactions to the suffering of others under conditions of indirect responsibility. *J. pers. soc. Psychol.,* 1967, **5,** 319–325.

LERNER, M. J., & Simmons, C. H. Observer's reaction to the "innocent victim": compassion or rejection? *J. pers. soc. Psychol.,* 1966, **4,** 203–210.

LEWIN, K. *A dynamic theory of personality.* New York: McGraw-Hill, 1935.

LEWIN, K. *Principles of topological psychology.* New York: McGraw-Hill, 1936.

LEWIN, K. Formalization and progress in psychology. *Univer. of Iowa Studies in Child Welfare,* 1940, **16,** No. 3, 9–42.

LEWIN, K. Regression, retrogression, and development. In R. Barker, T. Dembo, and K. Lewin (Eds.), *Frustration and regression. Univer. of Iowa Studies in Child Welfare,* 1941, **18,** No. 1, 1–43.

LEWIN, K. Field theory and learning. *Yearbook of the National Society for the Study of Education,* 1942, **41,** part II, 215–242.

LEWIN, K. Defining the "field at a given time." *Psychol. Rev.,* 1943, **50,** 292–310.

LEWIN, K. Constructs in psychology and psychological ecology. *Univer. of Iowa Studies in Child Welfare,* 1944, **20,** 1–29.

LEWIN, K. Behavior and development as a function of the total situation. In L. Carmichael (Ed.), *Manual of child psychology.* New York: Wiley, 1946. Pp. 791–844.

LEWIN, K. Frontiers of group dynamics: I. *Hum. Relat.,* 1947a, **1,** 4–41.

LEWIN, K. Frontiers of group dynamics: II. *Hum. Relat.,* 1947b, **1,** 143–153.

LEWIN, K. *Resolving social conflicts.* New York: Harper, 1948.

LEWIN, K. *Field theory in social science.* New York: Harper, 1951.

LEWIN, K. Group decision and social change. In G. E. Swanson, T. M. Newcomb, & E. L. Hartley (Eds.), *Reading in social psychology.* (Revised edition) New York: Holt, 1952. Pp. 459–473.

LEWIN, K. Studies in group decision. In D. Cartwright & A. Zander (Eds.), *Group dynamics: research and theory*. Evanston, Ill.: Row, Peterson, 1953. Pp. 287–301.

LEWIN, K., Dembo, T., Festinger, L., & Sears, P. S. Level of aspiration. In J. McV. Hunt (Ed.), *Personality and the behavior disorders*. New York: Ronald, 1944. Pp. 333–378.

LEWIN, K., Lippitt, R., & White, R. K. Patterns of aggressive behavior in experimentally created "social climates." *J. soc. Psychol.*, 1939, **10**, 271–299.

LEWIS, H. B. An experimental study of the role of ego in work. I. The role of ego in co-operative work. *J. exp. Psychol.*, 1944, **34**, 113–127.

LIKERT, R. A technique for the measurement of attitudes. *Arch. Psychol.*, 1932, No. 140. Pp. 1–55.

LINDER, D. E., Cooper, J., & Jones, E. E. Decision freedom as a determinant of the role of incentive magnitude in attitude change. *J. pers. soc. Psychol.*, 1967, **6**, 245–254.

LINTON, R. *The cultural background of personality*. New York: Appleton-Century-Crofts, 1945.

LIPPITT, R., Polansky, N., Redl, F., & Rosen, S. The dynamics of power. *Hum. Relat.*, 1952, **5**, 37–64.

LIPPITT, R., & White, R. The "social climate" of children's groups. In R. Barker, J. Kounin, & H. Wright (Eds.), *Child behavior and development*. New York: McGraw-Hill, 1943.

LONDON, I. D. Psychologists' misuse of the auxiliary concepts of physics and mathematics. *Psychol. Rev.*, 1944, **51**, 266–291.

LONG, L. A study of the effect of preceding stimuli upon judgment of auditory intensities. *Arch. Psychol.*, 1937, No. 209.

LÖVAAS, O. I. Effect of exposure to symbolic aggression on aggressive behavior. *Child Developm.*, 1961, **32**, 37–44.

LUCE, R. D., and Raiffa, H. *Games and decisions: Introduction and critical survey.* New York: Wiley, 1957.

McALLISTER, W. R., & McAllister, D. E. Increase over time in the stimulus generalization of acquired fear. *J. exp. Psychol.*, 1963, **65**, 576–582.

McDAVID, J. W., & Harari, H. *Social psychology: Individuals, groups, societies*. New York: Harper & Row, 1968.

McDOUGALL, W. *Introduction to social psychology*. London: Methuen, 1908.

McDOUGALL, W. *The group mind*. New York: Putnam, 1920.

McGARVEY, H. R. Anchoring effects in the absolute judgment of verbal materials. *Arch. Psychol.*, 1943, No. 281.

McGINNIES, E. Emotionality and perceptual defense. *Psychol. Rev.*, 1949, **56**, 244–251.

MacCORQUODALE, K., & Meehl, P. E. Preliminary suggestions as to a formalization of expectancy theory. *Psychol. Rev.*, 1953, **60**, 55–63.

MacLEOD, R. B. The phenomenological approach to social psychology. *Psychol. Rev.*, 1947, **54**, 193–210.

MacLEOD, R. B. The place of phenomenological analysis in social psychological theory. In J. Rohrer & M. Sherif (Eds.), *Social psychology at the crossroads*. New York: Harper, 1951. Pp. 215–241.

MAHLER, V. Ersatzhandlungen verschiedenen Realitätsgrades. *Psychol. Forsch.*, 1933, **18**, 26–89.

MALLER, J. B. Co-operation and competition: An experimental study in motivation. *Teach. Coll., Contrib. to Educ.*, No. 384, 1929.

MANDLER, G., & Kessen, W. *The language of psychology*. New York: Wiley, 1959.

MANN, J. H., & Mann, C. H. The importance of a group task in producing group-member personality and behavior change. *Hum. Relat.*, 1959, **12**, 75–80.

MANN, J. H., & Mann, C. H. The relative effectiveness of role playing and task oriented group experiences in producing personality and behavior change. *J. soc. Psychol.*, 1960, *51*, 313–317.

MANSKE, A. J. The reflection of teachers' attitudes in the attitudes of their pupils. In G. Murphy, L. B. Murphy, & T. M. Newcomb, *Experimental social psychology*. New York: Harper, 1937.

MARX, M. H. The general nature of theory construction. In M. H. Marx (Ed.), *Psychological theory*. New York: Macmillan, 1951. Pp. 4–19.

MARX, M. H., & Hillix, W. A. *Systems and theories in psychology*. New York: McGraw-Hill, 1963.

MASLOW, A. H. "Higher" and "lower" needs. *J. Psychol.*, 1948, **25**, 433–436.

MAY, M. A., & Doob, L. W. Co-operation and competition. *Soc. Sci. Res. Council Bull.*, **25**, 1937.

MEAD, G. H. *Mind, self and society from the standpoint of a social behaviorist.* (Edited and with introduction by C. W. Morris). Chicago: Univer. of Chicago Press, 1934.

MEAD, M. *Co-operation and competition among primitive peoples*. New York: McGraw-Hill, 1937.

MERTON, R. K. The role set. *Brit. J. Sociol.*, 1957, **8**, 106–120.

MERTON, R. K., & Kitt, A. S. Contributions to the theory of reference group behavior. In R. K. Merton & P. F. Lazarsfeld (Eds.), *Continuities in social research: Studies in the scope and method of "The American Soldier."* Glencoe, Ill.: The Free Press, 1950. Pp. 40–105.

MEUWESE, W., & FIEDLER, F. E. Leadership and group creativity under varying conditions of stress. Technical Report No. 22, ONR Contract NR 177-472, Nonr- 1834(36), Univer. of Illinois, 1965.

MILLER, N. E. Experimental studies of conflict. In J. McV. Hunt (Ed.), *Personality and the behavior disorders*. Vol. 1. New York: Ronald, 1944. Pp. 431–465.

MILLER, N. E., & Dollard, J. *Social learning and imitation*. New Haven: Yale Univer. Press, 1941.

MORENO, J. L. *Die Gottheit als Komoediant*. Vienna: Der Neue Daimon, 1919.

MOSS, F. A. (Ed.) *Comparative psychology*. Rev. ed. New York: Prentice-Hall, 1946.

MOWRER, O. H. *Learning theory and the symbolic processes*. New York: Wiley, 1960.

MULDER, M. Power and satisfaction in task-oriented groups. *Acta Psychologica*, 1959, **16**, 178–225.

MULDER, M. The power variable in communication experiments. *Hum. Relat.*, 1960, **13**, 241–257.

MULDER, M., Van Dijk, R., Soutendijk, S., Stelwagen, T., & Verhagen, J. Non-instrumental liking tendencies toward powerful group members. *Acta Psychologica*, 1964, **22**, 367–386.

NACHSHON, I., & Wapner, S. Effect of eye contact and physiognomy on perceived location of the other person. *J. pers. soc. Psychol.*, 1967, **7**, 82–89.

NEEDHAM, J. G. Rate of presentation in the method of single stimuli. *Amer. J. Psychol.*, 1935, **47**, 275–284.

NEIMAN, L. J., & Hughes, J. W. The problem of the concept of role: A resurvey of the literature. *Soc. Forces*, 1951, **30**, 141–149.

NEISSER, U. *Cognitive psychology*. New York: Appleton-Century-Crofts, 1967.

NEWCOMB, T. M. Autistic hostility and social reality. *Hum. Relat.*, 1947, **1**, 69–86.

NEWCOMB, T. M. An approach to the study of communicative acts. *Psychol. Rev.*, 1953, **60**, 393–404.

NEWCOMB, T. M. The prediction of interpersonal attraction. *Amer. Psychologist*, 1956, **11**, 575–586.

NEWCOMB, T. M. Individual systems of orientation. In S. Koch (Ed.), *Psychology: A study of a science*. Vol. 3. New York: McGraw-Hill, 1959. Pp. 384–422.

NEWCOMB, T. M. *The acquaintance process.* New York: Holt, Rinehart and Winston, 1961.

NEWCOMB, T. M. Stabilities underlying changes in interpersonal attraction. *J. abnorm. soc. Psychol.,* 1963, **66,** 376–386.

NEWCOMB, T. M., & Svehla, G. Intra-family relationships in attitudes. *Sociometry,* 1937, **1,** 180–205.

NEWCOMB, T. M., Turner, R. H., & Converse, P. E. *Social psychology: The study of human interaction.* New York: Holt, Rinehart, and Winston, 1965.

NEWELL, A., Simon, H. A., & Shaw, J. C. Elements of a theory of human problem solving. *Psychol. Rev.,* 1958, **65,** 151–166.

ORNE, M. T. On the social psychology of the psychological experiment: With particular reference to demand characteristics and their implications. *Amer. Psychologist,* 1962, **17,** 776–783.

OSGOOD, C. E. The nature and measurement of meaning. *Psychol. Bull.,* 1952, **49,** 197–237.

OSGOOD, C. E. Cognitive dynamics in the conduct of human affairs. *Publ. Opin. Quart.,* 1960, **24,** 341–365.

OSGOOD, C. E., Suci, G. A., & Tannenbaum, P. H. *The measurement of meaning.* Urbana, Ill.: Univer. of Illinois Press, 1957.

OSGOOD, C. E., & Tannenbaum, P. H. The principle of congruity in the prediction of attitude change. *Psychol. Rev.,* 1955, **62,** 42–55.

OVSIANKINA, M. Die Wiederaufnahme von unterbrochener Handlungen. *Psychol. Forsch.,* 1928, **11,** 302–379.

PARSONS, T. *The social system.* Glencoe, Ill.: The Free Press, 1951.

PAVLOV, I. P. *The work of the digestive glands.* 2nd ed. Translated by W. H. Thompson. London: Griffin, 1910.

PAVLOV, I. P. *Conditioned reflexes.* London: Oxford Univer. Press, 1927.

PEPITONE, A. Attributions of causality, social attitudes, and cognitive matching processes. In R. Tagiuri & L. Petrullo (Eds.), *Person perception and interpersonal behavior.* Stanford: Stanford Univer. Press, 1958. Pp. 258–276.

PEPITONE, A. Some conceptual and empirical problems of consistency models. In S. Feldman (Ed.), *Cognitive consistency.* New York: Academic Press, 1966. Pp. 257–297.

PERIN, C. T. Behavior potentiality as a joint function of the amount of training and the degree of hunger at the time of extinction. *J. exp. Psychol.,* 1942, **30,** 93–113.

PERKINS, C. C., & Weyant, R. G. The interval between training and test trials as a determiner of the slope of generalization gradients. *J. comp. physiol. Psychol.,* 1958, **51,** 596–600.

PIAGET, J. *The moral judgment of the child.* New York: Harcourt, Brace, 1932.

POLANYI, M. Logic and psychology. *American Psychologist,* 1968, **23,** 27–43.

POSTMAN, L., & Miller, G. A. Anchoring of temporal judgments. *Amer. J. Psychol.,* 1945, **58,** 43–53.

POWELL, R. M. Sociometric analysis of informal groups: Their structure and function in two contrasting communities. *Sociometry,* 1952, **15,** 367–399.

PRELINGER, E. Extension and structure of the self. *J. Psychol.,* 1959, **47,** 13–23.

PRESTON, M. G., & Heintz, R. K. Effects of participatory vs. supervisory leadership on group judgment. *J. abnorm. soc. Psychol.,* 1949, **44,** 345–355.

PRICE, K. O., Harburg, E., & Newcomb, T. M. Psychological balance in situations of negative interpersonal attitudes. *J. pers. soc. Psychol.,* 1966, **3,** 265–270.

RABINOWITZ, L., Kelley, H. H., & Rosenblatt, R. M. Effects of different types of interdependence and response conditions in the minimal social situation. *J. exp. soc. Psychol.,* 1966, **2,** 169–197.

RADLOFF, R. Social comparison and ability evaluation. *J. exp. soc. Psychol.*, Supplement 1, 1966, 6–26.

RAPAPORT, D. *The structure of psychoanalytic theory.* In S. Koch (Ed.), *Psychology: A study of a science.* Vol. 3. New York: McGraw-Hill, 1959. Pp. 55–183.

RAVEN, B. H., & Eachus, H. T. Cooperation and competition in means-interdependent triads. *J. abnorm. soc. Psychol.*, 1963, **67,** 307–316.

RAVEN, B. H., & French, J. R. P., Jr. Legitimate power, coercive power, and observability in social influence. *Sociometry*, 1958a, **21,** 83–97.

RAVEN, B. H., & French, J. R. P., Jr. Group support, legitimate power, and social influence. *J. Pers.*, 1958b, **26,** 400–409.

RAZRAN, G. H. S. Stimulus generalization and conditioned responses. *Psychol. Bull.*, 1949, **46,** 337–365.

REDL, F. Group emotion and leadership. *Psychiatry*, 1942, **5,** 573–596.

REMMERS, H. H. Propaganda in the schools: Do the effects last? *Publ. Opin. Quart.*, 1938, **2,** 197–210.

RODRIGUES, A. Effects of balance, positivity, and agreement in triadic social relations. *J. pers. soc. Psychol.*, 1967, **5,** 472–476.

ROGERS, S. The anchoring of absolute judgments. *Arch. Psychol.*, 1941, No. 261.

ROMMETVEIT, R. *Social norms and roles.* Minneapolis: Univer. of Minnesota Press, 1954.

ROSENTHAL, R. *Experimenter effects in behavioral research.* New York: Appleton-Century-Crofts, 1966.

ROSS, E. A. *Social psychology: An outline and source book.* New York: Macmillan, 1908.

ROSS, N., & Abrams, S. Fundamentals of psychoanalytic theory. In B. Wolman (Ed.), *Handbook of clinical psychology.* New York: McGraw-Hill, 1965. Pp. 303–340.

ROTTER, J. B. *Social learning and clinical psychology.* New York: Prentice-Hall, 1954.

RUSSELL, D. H., & Robertson, I. V. Influencing attitudes toward minority groups in a junior high school. *School Rev.*, 1947, **55,** 205–213.

SARBIN, T. R. Role theory. In G. Lindzey (Ed.), *Handbook of social psychology.* Vol. 1. Reading, Mass.: Addison-Wesley, 1954. Pp. 223–258.

SARBIN, T. R. Role enactment. In B. J. Biddle & E. J. Thomas (Eds.), *Role theory: Concepts and research.* New York: Wiley, 1966. Pp. 195–200.

SARGENT, S. S. Conceptions of role and ego in contemporary psychology. In J. Rohrer & M. Sherif (Eds.), *Social psychology at the crossroads.* New York: Harper, 1951. Pp. 355–370.

SARGENT, S. S., & Williamson, R. C. *Social psychology.* 2nd ed. New York: Ronald, 1958.

SARNOFF, I. Psychoanalytic theory and social attitudes. *Publ. Opin. Quart.*, 1960, **24,** 251–279.

SARNOFF, I. Psychoanalytic theory and cognitive dissonance. Unpublished paper, New York Univer., 1966.

SAYLES, L. F. *Behavior of industrial work groups.* New York: Wiley, 1958.

SCHACHTER, S. Deviation, rejection and communication. *J. abnorm. soc. Psychol.*, 1951, **46,** 190–207.

SCHACHTER, S., & Singer, J. Cognitive, social, and physiological determinants of emotional state. *Psychol. Rev.*, 1962, **69,** 379–399.

SCHACHTER, S., & Wheeler, L. Epinephrine, chorpromazine, and amusement. *J. abnorm. soc. Psychol.*, 1962, **65,** 121–128.

SCHANCK, R. L. A study of a community and its groups and institutions conceived of as behaviors of individuals. *Psychol. Monogr.*, 1932, **43,** No. 2 (Whole No. 195).

SCHEERER, M. Cognitive theory. In G. Lindzey (Ed.), *Handbook of social psychology.* Vol. 1. Reading, Mass.: Addison-Wesley, 1954. Pp. 91–142.

SCHELER, M. *The nature of sympathy.* Translated by P. Heath. London: Routledge & Kegan Paul, 1954.

SCHELLING, T. C. *The strategy of conflict.* Cambridge, Mass.: Harvard Univer. Press, 1960.

SCHENITZKI, D. Bargaining, group decision making, and the attainment of maximum joint outcome. Unpublished doctoral dissertation, Univer. of Minnesota, 1962.

SCHUTZ, W. C. What makes groups productive? *Hum. Relat.,* 1955, **8,** 429–465.

SCHUTZ, W. C. *FIRO: A three dimensional theory of interpersonal behavior.* New York: Rinehart, 1958.

SCHUTZ, W. C. On group composition. *J. abnorm. soc. Psychol.,* 1961, **62,** 275–281.

SCHUTZ, W. C. *JOY: Expanding human awareness.* New York: Grove Press, 1967.

SCODEL, A., Minas, J. S., Ratoosh, P., & Lipetz, M. Some descriptive aspects of two-person non-zero-sum games. *Conflict Resolution,* 1959, **3,** 114–119.

SCOTT, W. A. Attitude change by response reinforcement: replication and extension. *Sociometry,* 1959, **22,** 328–335.

SCOTT, W. A. Cognitive structure and social structure: Some concepts and relationships. In N. F. Washburne (Ed.), *Decisions, values, and groups.* Vol. 2. New York: Pergamon Press, 1962. Pp. 86–118.

SCOTT, W. A. Conceptualizing and measuring structural properties of cognition. In O. J. Harvey (Ed.), *Motivation and social interaction.* New York: Ronald Press, 1963. Pp. 266–288.

SCOTT, W. H., Banks, J. A., Halsey, A. H., & Lupton, T. *Technical change and industrial relations.* Liverpool: Liverpool Univer. Press, 1956.

SECORD, P. F., & Backman, C. W. *Social psychology.* New York: McGraw-Hill, 1964.

SEWELL, W. H., Mussen, P. H., & Harris, C. W. Relationships among child training practices. *Amer. sociol. Rev.,* 1955, **20,** 137–148.

SHAW, M. E. A comparison of two types of leadership in various communication nets. *J. abnorm. soc. Psychol.,* 1955, **50,** 127–134.

SHAW, M. E. Some motivational factors in cooperation and competition. *J. Pers.,* 1958, *26,* 155–169.

SHAW, M. E. Some effects of individually prominent behavior upon group effectiveness and member satisfaction. *J. abnorm. soc. Psychol.,* 1959, **59,** 382–386.

SHAW, M. E. Implicit conversion of fate control of dyadic interaction. *Psychol. Repts.,* 1962, **10,** 758.

SHAW, M. E. Scaling group tasks: A method for dimensional analysis. Technical Report No. 1, ONR Contract NR 170-266, Nonr- 580(11), Univer. of Florida, 1963.

SHAW, M. E. Experimental social psychology and group processes. In J. B. Sidowski (Ed.), *Experimental methods and instrumentation in psychology.* New York: McGraw-Hill, 1966. Pp. 607–643.

SHAW, M. E., & Bensberg, G. J. Level of aspiration phenomena in mentally deficient persons. *J. Pers.,* 1955, **24,** 134–144.

SHAW, M. E., & Blum, J. M. Effects of leadership style upon group performance as a function of task structure. *J. pers. soc. Psychol.,* 1966, **3,** 238–242.

SHAW, M. E., Briscoe, M. E., & Garcia-Esteve, J. A cross-cultural study of attribution of responsibility. *International J. Psychol.,* 1968, **3,** 51–60.

SHAW, M. E., & Penrod, W. T., Jr. Group effectiveness as a function of amount of "legitimate" information. *J. soc. Psychol.,* 1964, **62,** 241–246.

SHAW, M. E., Rothschild, G. H., & Strickland, J. F. Decision processes in communication nets. *J. abnorm. soc. Psychol.,* 1957, **54,** 323–330.

SHAW, M. E., & Schneider, F. W. Negro-white differences in attribution of responsibility as a function of age. Research Rept. No. 8, (NSF GS-647), Univer. of Florida, November, 1967.

SHAW, M. E., & Sulzer, J. L. An empirical test of Heider's levels in attribution of responsibility. *J. abnorm. soc. Psychol.*, 1964, **69,** 39–46.

SHAW, M. E., & Wright, J. M. *Scales for the measurement of attitudes.* New York: McGraw-Hill, 1967.

SHEPARD, H. A., & Bennis, W. G. A theory of training by group methods. *Hum. Relat.*, 1956, **9,** 403–414.

SHERIF, M. A study of some social factors in perception. *Arch. Psychol.*, 1935, **27,** No. 187.

SHERIF, M. *The psychology of social norms.* New York: Harper, 1936.

SHERIF, M. *Social interaction.* Chicago: Aldine, 1967.

SHERIF, M., & Hovland, C. I. Judgmental phenomena and scales of attitude measurement: Placement of items with individual choice of number of categories. *J. abnorm. soc. Psychol.*, 1953, **48,** 135–141.

SHERIF, M., & Hovland, C. I. *Social judgment: Assimilation and contrast effects in communication and attitude change.* New Haven: Yale Univer. Press, 1961.

SHERIF, M., & Sherif, C. W. *An outline of social psychology.* Rev. ed. New York: Harper, 1956.

SHERIF, C. W., Sherif, M., & Nebergall, R. E. *Attitude and attitude change: The social judgment-involvement approach.* Philadelphia: W. B. Saunders, 1956.

SIEGEL, A. E. Film mediated fantasy aggression and strength of aggressive drive. *Child Develpm.*, 1956, **27,** 365–378.

SIEGEL, S., & Fouraker, L. E. *Bargaining and group decision making.* New York: McGraw-Hill, 1960.

SIDOWSKI, J. B. Reward and punishment in a minimal social situation. *J. exp. Psychol.*, 1957, **54,** 318–326.

SIDOWSKI, J. B., Wycoff, L. B., & Tabory, L. The influence of reinforcement and punishment in a minimal social situation. *J. abnorm. soc. Psychol.*, 1956, **52,** 115–119.

SIMMEL, G. Zur Philosophie des Schauspielers. *Logos,* 1920, **1,** 339–362.

SIMON, H. A. *Administrative behavior: A study of decision-making processes in administrative organization.* New York: Macmillan, 1947.

SIMON, H. A. *Administrative behavior.* New York: Macmillan, 1956.

SIMON, H. A., & Newell, A. Models: Their uses and limitations. In L. D. White (Ed.), *The state of the social sciences.* Chicago: Univer. of Chicago Press, 1956. Pp. 67–83.

SKINNER, B. F. On the rate of formation of a conditioned reflex. *J. gen. Psychol.*, 1932, **7,** 274–285.

SKINNER, B. F. *Science and human behavior.* New York: Macmillan, 1953.

SKINNER, B. F. *Verbal Behavior.* New York: Appleton-Century-Crofts, 1957.

SOROKIN, R. A., Zimmerman, C. C., & Galpin, C. J. *A systematic source book in rural sociology.* Minneapolis: Univer. of Minnesota Press, 1930.

STOGDILL, R. M. *Individual behavior and group achievement.* New York: Oxford Univer. Press, 1959.

STOTLAND, E., Katz, D., & Patchen, M. The reduction of prejudice through the arousal of self-insight. *J. Pers.*, 1959, **27,** 507–531.

STRICKLAND, L. H., Jones, E. E., & Smith, W. P. Effects of group support on the evaluation of an antagonist. *J. abnorm. soc. Psychol.*, 1960, **61,** 73–81.

SULLIVAN, H. S. *Conceptions of modern psychiatry.* New York: Norton, 1953a.

SULLIVAN, H. S. *The interpersonal theory of psychiatry.* New York: Norton, 1953b.

SULZER, J. L. Attribution of responsibility as a function of the structure, quality, and the intensity of the event. Unpublished doctoral dissertation, Univer. of Florida, Gainesville, Florida, 1964.

SUMNER, W. G. *Folkways.* New York: Ginn, 1906.

SUMNER, W. G., & Keller, A. G. *The science of society.* New Haven: Yale Univer. Press, 1927.

TANNENBAUM, P. H., & Gengel, R. W. Generalization of attitude change through congruity principle relationships. *J. pers. soc. Psychol.,* 1966, **3,** 299–304.

TANNER, W. P., Jr., & Swets, J. A. A decision-making theory of human detection. *Psychol. Rev.,* 1954, **61,** 401–409.

TARDE, G. *The laws of imitation.* New York: Holt, 1903.

THIBAUT, J. W. An experimental study of the cohesiveness of underprivileged groups. *Hum. Relat.,* 1950, **3,** 251–278.

THIBAUT, J. W., & Kelley, H. H. *The social psychology of groups.* New York: Wiley, 1959.

THIBAUT, J. W., & Riecken, H. W. Some determinants and consequences of the perception of social causality. *J. Pers.,* 1955, **24,** 113–133.

THIBAUT, J. W., & Riecken, H. W. Some determinants and consequences of the perception of social causality. In H. Proshansky & B. Seidenberg (Eds.), *Basic studies in social psychology.* New York: Holt, Rinehart and Winston, 1965. Pp. 81–94.

THIBAUT, J. W., & Strickland, L. H. Psychological set and social conformity. *J. Pers.,* 1956, **25,** 115–129.

THOMAS, D. R., & Lopez, L. J. The effects of delayed testing on generalization slope. *J. comp. physiol. Psychol.,* 1962, **55,** 541–544.

THOMAS, E. J., & Biddle, B. J. Basic concepts of classifying the phenomena of role. In B. J. Biddle & E. J. Thomas (Eds.), *Role theory: Concepts and research.* New York: Wiley, 1966. Pp. 23–45.

THORNDIKE, E. L. *Animal intelligence.* New York: Macmillan, 1898.

THORNDIKE, E. L. *The psychology of learning.* New York: Teachers College, Columbia Univer., 1913.

THORNDIKE, E. L. *Educational psychology.* New York: Teachers College, Columbia Univer., 1932.

THORNDIKE, E. L. *The psychology of wants, interests, and attitudes.* New York: Appleton-Century-Crofts, 1935.

THORNDIKE, E. L. *Selected writings from a connectionist's psychoolgy.* New York: Appleton-Century-Crofts, 1949.

THORNTON, D. A., & Arrowood, A. J. Self-evaluation, self-enhancement, and the locus of social comparison. *J. exp. soc. Psychol.,* Supplement 1, 1966, 40–48.

THURSTONE, L. L., & Chave, E. J. *The measurement of attitude.* Chicago: Univer. of Chicago Press, 1929.

TOLMAN, E. C. Principles of purposive behavior. In S. Koch (Ed.), *Psychology: A study of a science.* Vol. 2. New York: McGraw-Hill, 1959. Pp. 92–157.

TOLMAN, E. C. *Purposive behavior in animals and men.* New York: Appleton-Century, 1932.

TOLMAN, E. C. The determiners of behavior at a choice point. *Psychol. Rev.,* 1938, **45,** 1–41.

TOLMAN, E. C., & Honzik, C. H. Introduction and removal of reward, and maze performance in rats. *Univer. Calif. Publ. Psychol.,* 1930, **4,** 257–275.

TRIANDIS, H., & Fishbein, M. Cognitive interaction in person perception. *J. abnorm. soc. Psychol.,* 1963, **67,** 446–453.

TROTTER, W. *Instincts of the herd in peace and war.* New York: Macmillan, 1917.

TURNER, R. H. Role taking: Process versus conformity. In A. M. Rose (Ed.), *Human behavior and social processes: An interactionist approach.* Boston: Houghton-Mifflin, 1962. Pp. 20–40.

VOLKMANN, J. Scales of judgment and their implications for social psychology. In J. H. Rohrer & M. Sherif (Eds.), *Social psychology at the crossroads.* New York: Harper, 1951.

WALSTER, B. Who's afraid of dissonant information? Unpublished manuscript, Univer. of Minnesota, 1965.

WALSTER, E., Berscheid, E., & Barclay, A. M. A determinant of preference among modes of dissonance reduction. *J. pers. soc. Psychol.,* 1967, **7,** 211–216.

WALTERS, R. H., Leat, M., & Mezei, L. Inhibition and disinhibition of response through empathetic learning. *Canad. J. Psychol.,* 1963, **17,** 235–243.

WALTERS, R. H., & Parke, R. D. Influence of response consequences to a social model on resistance to deviation. *J. exp. child Psychol.,* 1964, **1,** 269–280.

WALY, P., & Cook, S. W. Attitude as a determinant of learning and memory: A failure to confirm. *J. pers. soc. Psychol.,* 1966, **4,** 280–288.

WATSON, G. *Social psychology: Issues and insights.* Philadelphia: Lippincott, 1966.

WATSON, J. B. Psychology as the behaviorist views it. *Psychol. Rev.,* 1913, **20,** 158–177.

WATSON, J. B. *Behavior: An introduction to comparative psychology.* New York: Holt, 1914.

WATSON, J. B. *Psychology from the standpoint of a behaviorist.* Philadelphia: Lippincott, 1919.

WATSON, J. B., & Rayner, R. Conditioned emotional reactions. *J. exp. Psychol.,* 1920, **3,** 1–14.

WERTHEIMER, M. Experimentelle Studien uber das Sehen von Bewegunen. *Zool. Psychol.,* 1912, **61,** 121–165.

WERTHEIMER, M. Some problems in the theory of ethics. *Social Research,* 1935, **2,** 353–367.

WESTERMARCK, E. *Ethical relativity.* New York: Harcourt, Brace, 1932.

WEVER, E. G., & Zener, K. E. Method of absolute judgment in psychophysics. *Psychol. Rev.,* 1928, **35,** 466–493.

WHEELER, L. Motivation as a determinant of upward comparison. *J. exp. soc. Psychol.,* Supplement 1, 1966, 27–31.

WHEELER, R. H. *The science of psychology.* 2nd ed. New York: Crowell, 1940.

WHITTEMORE, I. C. The influence of competition on performance. *J. abnorm. soc. Psychol.,* 1925, **20,** 17–33.

WILKE, W. H. An experimental comparison of the speech, the radio, and the printed page as propaganda devices. *Arch. Psychol.,* 1934, No. 169.

WILLIAMS, R. M., et al. *Friendship and social values in a suburban community.* Eugene, Oregon: Univer. of Oregon Press, 1956.

WILLIS, R. H. Descriptive models of social response. Technical Report, Nonr- Contract 816(12), Washington Univer., 1964.

WILLIS, R. H. The phenomenology of shifting agreement and disagreement in dyads. *J. Pers.,* 1965, **33,** 188–199.

WILLIS, R. H., & Hollander, E. P. An experimental study of three response modes in social influence situations. *J. abnorm. soc. Psychol.,* 1964, **69,** 150–156.

WILLIS, R. H., & Joseph, M. L. Bargaining behavior. I. "Prominence" as a predictor of the outcome of games of agreement. *Conflict Resolution,* 1959, **3,** 102–113.

WILSON, K. V., & Bixenstine, V. E. Forms of social control in two person, two-choice games. *Behav. Sci.,* 1962, **7,** 92–102.

WILSON, R. S. Personality patterns, source attractiveness, and conformity. *J. Pers.,* 1960, **28,** 186–199.

WINCH, R. F. *The modern family.* New York: Holt, 1952.

WINCH, R. F. The theory of complementarity of needs in mate-selection: A test of one kind of complementariness. *Amer. sociol. Rev.,* 1955, **20,** 52–56.

YALOM, I. D., & Rand, K. Compatibility and cohesiveness in therapy groups. *Arch. gen. Psychiat.,* 1966, **15,** 267–275.

ZAJONC, R. B. The process of cognitive tuning in communication. *J. abnorm. soc. Psychol.,* 1960, **61,** 159–167.

ZAJONC, R. B., & Burnstein, E. The learning of balanced and unbalanced social structures. *J. Pers.,* 1965, **33,** 153–163.

ZALEZNIK, A. *Worker satisfaction and development: A case study of work and social behavior in a factory group.* Boston: Harvard Graduate School of Business Administration, 1956.

ZALEZNIK, A., Christensen, C. R., & Roethlisberger, F. J. *The motivation, productivity and satisfaction of workers.* Boston: Harvard Graduate School of Business Administration, 1958.

ZEIGARNIK, B. Uber das Behalten von erledigten und unerledigten Handlungen. *Psychol. Forsch.,* 1927, **9,** 1–85.

ZIPF, S. G. Resistance and conformity under reward and punishment. *J. abnorm. soc. Psychol.,* 1960, **61,** 102–109.

GLOSSARY

ACTIVITY. In Homans' theory, an alternative term for Skinner's operant; any voluntary behavior emitted by an organism.

AFFECTION NEED. In Schutz's theory, the need to establish and maintain a feeling of mutual affection with others.

ANTICONFORMITY. Behavior in response to normative expectations of the group, but directly opposite to norm prescription.

ASSIMILATION. A process in which a new stimulus is integrated into a set of previously experienced stimuli, thus shifting the internal standard toward the new stimulus.

ASSUMED SIMILARITY OF OPPOSITES (ASo). The degree to which an individual perceives his most- and least-preferred coworkers as similar.

ATTRIBUTION. The process of perceiving the dispositional properties of objects (including other persons) in the environment.

AUTHORITY. In Stogdill's theory, the degree of freedom that the occupant of a position in the group is expected to exercise. In Adams and Romney's theory, the control of reinforcers.

AUTHORITY PHASE OF GROUP DEVELOPMENT. According to Bennis and Shepard, the initial phase in the development of a group, during which the group members are preoccupied with problems of dependency and rebellion against the perceived source of authority in the group.

AUTHORITY SEQUENCE. In Adams and Romney's theory, the sequence of reciprocal stimuli, responses, and rewards emitted by the parties in an authority relationship which serve to sustain that relationship.

BALANCED STATE. According to Heider, a state in which unit and sentiment (liking) relations can coexist without stress.

BARRIER. In Lewin's system, a boundary between regions of the life space which offers resistance to locomotion.

BASIC ASSUMPTION GROUP. In Bion's theory, the variable, emotionally based structure of the group which the members superimpose upon the underlying work group structure; the group's instinct-laden definition of its reason for being.

BEHAVIOR. In Lewin's system, any change in the life space; that is, any locomotion of the person in his life space.

BEHAVIOR CONTROL. In Thibaut and Kelley's theory, a form of power dependence in which person A can control the behavior of person B by enacting behaviors rewarding to B only when B enacts behaviors desired by A.

BEHAVIOR SEQUENCE.   Thibaut and Kelley's unit of analysis, defined as a number of verbal and motor acts which are sequentially organized and directed toward a goal.

CAUSAL DESCRIPTION.   Analysis of the underlying conditions that give rise to perceptual experience.

COGNITION.   That which is known; knowledge acquired through personal experience.

COGNITIVE DISSONANCE.   An unpleasant psychological state arising from the existence of "nonfitting" or inconsistent relations among cognitions.

COGNITIVE STRUCTURE.   An organized subset of the attributes an individual uses to identify and discriminate a specific object or event; a set of ideas maintained by a person and relatively available to conscious awareness.

COGNITIVE THEORY.   A general orientation that emphasizes central processes in the explanation of behavior.

COMMONALITY OF EFFECTS.   Consequences that are produced by each of two or more possible actions.

COMMUNICATIVE ACT.   In Newcomb's theory, a transmission of information from a source to a recipient.

COMPARISON LEVEL (CL).   In Thibaut and Kelley's theory, the standard against which group members evaluate the attractiveness of the relationship.

COMPARISON LEVEL FOR ALTERNATIVES (CLalt).   In Thibaut and Kelley's theory, the standard which the individual uses to determine whether or not he will remain in a relationship.

COMPATIBILITY.   In Schutz's theory, a property of a relation between a person and another person, role, or task situation that leads to mutual satisfaction of interpersonal needs. Types of compatibility include the following:

1. *Interchange compatibility.* Compatibility based upon the mutual expression of affection, control, and/or inclusion between two or more individuals.

2. *Originator compatibility.* Compatibility based upon complementarity of needs between the initiator and the receiver of an interaction.

3. *Reciprocal compatibility.* Compatibility based upon the expression of affection, control, and/or inclusion by each group member which meets the needs of others in the group for affection, control, and/or inclusion.

COMPETITION.   A social process in which goal achievement by one group member to some extent impedes goal achievement by other group members.

CONFLICT.   In Lewin's system, a situation in which forces in the life space are opposite in direction and about equal in strength.

CONGRUITY PRINCIPLE.   A proposition advanced by Osgood and Tannenbaum which holds that changes in evaluation always occur in the direction of increased congruence with the person's frame of reference.

CONTRAST EFFECT.   A process in which a new stimulus is perceived as not belonging to the set of stimuli previously experienced, thus shifting the internal standard away from the new stimulus.

CONTROL NEED.   In Schutz's theory, the need to establish and maintain a satisfactory relation with people with respect to power and control of others.

CONSTRUCT.   An explanatory concept; a hypothetical process invoked to account for observed relationships between antecedent and consequent conditions.

COOPERATION.   A social process in which achievement of a goal by each group member facilitates goal achievement by all other group members.

COORIENTATION.   In Newcomb's theory, simultaneous orientation toward another person and an object.

CORRESPONDENT INFERENCE.   In Jones and Davis' theory, an inference about an underlying attribute based on an action which is assumed to be similar to the attribute.

COST.   In Thibaut and Kelley's theory, those factors which inhibit the adequate performance of a sequence of behavior or factors which restrict the individual's consummation of the rewards of enacting a sequence of behavior. In Homans' theory, rewards foregone by an individual because he enacts one activity rather than an alternative activity or activities.

COVERT REHEARSAL.   In Bandura's theory, the internal or "mental" rehearsal of the performance of an observed response.

DECISION VERIFIABILITY.   The degree to which the correctness of a decision or task solution can be demonstrated by logic or by appeal to authority.

DIFFERENTIATION.   In Lewin's system, a process by which the life space becomes separated into functional regions.

DISPOSITIONAL PROPERTIES.   Those properties that cause objects and events to manifest themselves in certain ways under certain conditions; the unchanging aspects of the phenomenal world.

DISTAL STIMULUS.   The starting point of perception; the object that is experienced as being "out there" in the environment.

DISTRIBUTIVE JUSTICE.   The fair exchange of rewards and costs in a social interaction; a rule of human exchange stating that each participant of an interaction should expect and receive rewards that are proportional to the costs he incurs for participating in that interaction.

EGO DEFENSES.   In Freud's system, a group of strategies which the ego utilizes to defend itself and the entire personality against intolerable increments of tension.

EGO SYSTEM.   From Freud's point of view, the executive arm of personality; the conglomerate of those perceptual and cognitive processes which mediate the individual's contact with and organization of the environment.

ELEMENTARY SOCIAL BEHAVIOR.   In Homans' theory, a two-party interaction in which there is a direct and immediate exchange of rewards and punishments between the two parties.

ENDOGENEOUS DETERMINANTS.   Term used by Thibaut and Kelley to refer to those determinants of the outcomes of an interaction which arise during the course of the interaction.

EXISTENCE.   In Lewin's system, the state of having demonstrable effects.

EXOGENEOUS DETERMINANTS.   A term used by Thibaut and Kelley to refer to those determinants of the outcomes of an interaction which are external to the actual process of interaction; the boundary conditions which define the maximum and minimum outcomes which are possible within an interaction.

EXPECTATION.   A term used by Stogdill to designate a readiness for reinforcement.

EXPEDIENT ORIENTATION.   In Gross, Mason, and McEachern's view, an orientation that characterizes the person whose fulfillment or nonfulfillment of role expectations is based upon the sanctions that might subsequently be administered to him rather than upon the legitimacy of the expectations.

EXTINCTION.   The progressive decrement in the frequency of performance of a response under conditions of nonreinforcement.

FATE CONTROL.   In Thibaut and Kelley's theory, a form of power dependence in which person A can control the outcomes of person B regardless of the behavior that person B enacts.

FAVORABILITY CONTINUUM.   In Fiedler's theory, the range of group situations with respect to leader advantages.

FORCE.   In Lewin's system, that which causes change.

FRAME OF REFERENCE.   An internal standard against which an individual judges any specific stimulus.

GOAL CLARITY.   The degree to which the requirements of a task are known to the members of the group.

GOAL PATH MULTIPLICITY.   The degree to which a task may be completed by alternative procedures.

GROUP INTEGRATION.   In Stogdill's theory, the degree to which the group can maintain its structure and operations under stressful conditions.

GROUP STRUCTURE.   The pattern of relations among the differentiated parts of a group.

HEDONIC RELEVANCE.   The significance of an action to a perceiver based upon the degree to which the action is gratifying or disappointing to the perceiver.

HUMAN EXCHANGE.   In Homans' theory, the exchange of human social activities during interaction.

ID SYSTEM.   In Freud's formulation, the original subsystem of personality; the reservoir and source of all psychic energy, based upon the individual's intrusive needs for instinctual gratification.

IMPERSONAL CAUSALITY.   According to Heider, a situation in which the production of a given outcome does not involve intentionality.

INCLUSION NEED.   In Schutz's theory, the need to establish and maintain a satisfactory relation with people with respect to association and interaction.

INDEPENDENCE.   Behavior that disregards the normative expectations of the group.

INTERACTION.   In Stogdill's theory, a situation in which the reaction of any member is a response to the reactions of some other group members.

LATITUDE OF ACCEPTANCE.   The range of attitudinal positions an individual finds acceptable or tolerable.

LATITUDE OF NONCOMMITMENT.   All attitudinal positions that are neither acceptable nor objectionable to an individual.

LATITUDE OF REJECTION.   The range of attitudinal positions that are unacceptable or objectionable to an individual.

LIFE SPACE.   In Lewin's system, the totality of all psychological factors that influence the individual at any given moment; the person and the psychological environment as it exists for him.

LOCAL STIMULUS.   That part of the stimulus pattern that is of particular relevance to the percept.

LOCOMOTION.   In Lewin's system, movement in the life space.

MAND.   A stimulus (usually verbal) which specifies or demands the organism's performance of a particular response; in social interaction, a response by a given person which indicates the singular response of another person which will be reinforcing.

MATCHED-DEPENDENT BEHAVIOR.   In Miller and Dollard's theory, a form of imitation in which the leader is able to "read" relevant environmental cues but the follower is not; hence the follower is dependent upon the leader for information (cues, signals) regarding appropriate behavior.

MEDIATION.   In Heider's analysis of person perception, the manifestations of the other person's personality which determine the proximal stimulus pattern. Mediation may be (1) *synonymous* (each specific manifestation coordinated to a specific environmental content) or (2) *ambiguous* (each specific manifestation coordinated to more than one specific content).

METHOD OF CONSTRUCTION.   A term used by Lewin to refer to an approach to science which considers general laws as statements of empirical relations between psychological constructs or certain properties of them.

MODELING EFFECTS.   In Bandura's theory, the acquisition of novel responses by an observer which occurs through his observation of the responses of another person.

MORAL-EXPEDIENT ORIENTATION.   According to Gross, Mason, and McEachern, an orientation characterizing a person whose fulfillment of role expectations is jointly based upon the legitimacy of those expectations and the sanctions contingent upon his fulfillment or nonfulfillment of them.

MORAL ORIENTATION.   A term used by Gross, Mason, and McEachern to characterize the orientation of a person whose fulfillment or nonfulfillment of role expectations is based upon the legitimacy of those expectations.

OBJECTIVE REALITY.   A situation in which evaluations can be tested by direct examination of the "real world."

OPEN SYSTEM.   A situation in which individual group members are free to join or leave the group without destroying its identity.

OPERANT.   A response that operates upon the environment to satisfy the basic needs of the organism, and thus leads to reinforcement.

ORIENTATION.   In Newcomb's theory, an individual's cognitive and affective mode of relating to others and to objects around him.

OUTCOME.   The result of enacting a given activity (sequence of behavior) jointly with another's enactment of an activity. In Homans' theory, positive outcomes are referred to as profits (rewards are greater than costs); negative outcomes are referred to as losses (rewards are less than costs).

OUTCOME MATRIX.   Thibaut and Kelley's major technique for the analysis of interaction outcomes; a matrix showing the outcomes for each member of a relationship as a function of their joint enactment of behavior sequences.

PERFORMANCE.   In Stogdill's theory, behaviors that are relevant to the group.

PERSON-BEHAVIOR MATRIX.   A descriptive tool in Biddle and Thomas' analysis of role; a matrix which consists of a set of behaviors ordered by both a set of subjects and a set of behavioral classes.

PERSONAL CAUSALITY.   In Heider's theory, a situation in which a person intentionally produces a given outcome or event.

PERSONAL PHASE OF GROUP DEVELOPMENT.   According to Bennis and Shepard, that phase in the development of the group which follows the authority phase, during which group members are concerned with inter-member relationships and interdependence.

PERSONALISM.   In Heider's analysis of person perception, a situation in which the perceiver believes that he is the target of an action by another.

PHENOMENAL DESCRIPTION.   A delineation of the nature of the contact between a person and his environment as he experiences it.

POPULATION TRAITS.   Cattell's term for the averages of the measured characteristics of group members; definitions of the personality of the average group member.

POSITION.   According to Biddle and Thomas, a generally recognized category of persons who are classed together because of common attributes, common behaviors, or the common reactions of others toward them.

PRIMARY PROCESS.   A term used by Freud to refer to a process of thinking characteristic of the unconscious which consists of the nonlogical, symbolic, and fantasy-laden components of thought.

PROXIMAL STIMULUS.   The perceptual pattern that impinges directly upon the sense organs.

PSYCHOLOGICAL CONFORMITY.   Behavior intended to fulfill normative group expectations as perceived by the individual.

PSYCHOSEXUAL STAGES.   In Freud's analysis, a series of sequentially dependent phases in human development which are characterized by different sources of psychic energy based upon the sexual relevance of particular bodily zones and certain correspondent intrapsychic and interpersonal conflicts.

RESPONSIBILITY. In Stogdill's theory, the set of performances that a given occupant is expected to exhibit within the formal group structure.

ROLE CONFLICT. Conflict which results when the expectations associated with two or more positions which a person occupies are incompatible with one another (inter-role conflict) or when the various expectations associated with a single position which a person occupies are mutually incompatible (intra-role conflict).

SAME BEHAVIOR. A process described by Miller and Dollard whereby two individuals emit the same response as a function of independent stimulation by the same cue.

SECONDARY PROCESS. Freud's term for the customary, reality-oriented process of thought characteristic of the conscious state of the mind.

SENTIMENTS. A term used by Homans to denote activities which are signs of an individual's feelings and attitudes toward another or others. The same term was used by Heider to denote a liking relation between two persons.

SOCIAL COMPARISON. The act of evaluating one's opinions and abilities by relating them to the opinions and abilities of others.

SOCIAL POWER. A term variously defined as (1) the quotient of the maximum force which one person can induce on another and the maximum resistance the other person can mobilize in the opposite direction (Lewin), (2) the maximum resultant force that one person can exert on another at a specific time and in a specific direction (Cartwright), and (3) the strength of the force fields which one person can induce on another (French).

SOCIAL REALITY. A situation in which the person must rely upon the opinions of others for evaluation of his own opinions and abilities.

SOCIAL ROLE. The set of behaviors expected of an individual by virtue of his position in the group; a term also used to refer to the behavioral expectations attached to the person rather than to the group position.

STIMULUS. An internal or external event which occasions an alteration in the behavior of the organism. Kimble identified the following kinds of stimuli:

1. *Eliciting stimulus.* A part or a change in a part of the environment which calls forth a specific and almost reflexive response.

2. *Discriminative stimulus.* A stimulus which does not directly elicit a response, but rather sets the occasion or context for the occurrence of a particular response.

3. *Reinforcing stimulus.* A positive (for example, food) or negative (for example, shock) stimulus which is contingent upon the occurrence of a response.

STIMULUS GENERALIZATION. A process whereby a novel stimulus elicits a response which has been previously learned in the presence of another but similar stimulus.

SUPEREGO SYSTEM. From Freud's point of view, that mostly unconscious subsystem of personality which contains the rules, norms, and strictures internalized from the external sanctions of parental and social agents; a social conscience which guides and censors behavior.

SYNERGY.   Cattell's term for the total individual energy available to the group.

SYNTALITY.   In Cattell's theory, that aspect of the group which is analogous to the personality of the individual; the measured performance of the group acting as a unit.

SYSTEM STRAIN; STRAIN TOWARD SYMMETRY.   In Newcomb's theory, a state of psychological tension resulting from the perceived discrepancy of self-other orientations or from uncertainity as to the other person's orientation.

TACT.   A discriminative stimulus (usually verbal) which sets the occasion for the emission of a response which is not under specified reinforcement control.

TENSION.   In Lewin's system, a psychological state produced by opposing forces in the life space.

THEORY.   A set of interrelated hypotheses or propositions concerning a phenomenon or set of phenomena. Types of theories include the following:

1. *Concatenated theory*. A theory whose component propositions form a network of relations which constitute an identifiable pattern.

2. *Constructive theory*. A theory that attempts to map complex phenomena from materials of a relatively simple scheme.

3. *Field theory*. A theory that explains phenomena in terms of relations among specified elements.

4. *Hierarchical theory*. A theory whose component propositions are deduced from a set of basic principles.

5. *Monadic theory*. A theory that explains phenomena by reference to the elements or attributes of elements which are related by propositions.

6. *Principle theory*. A theory derived by the analytic method, starting with a set of empirical data.

7. *Reductive theory*. A theory that attempts to explain phenomena by appealing to lower levels of analysis.

THEORETICAL ORIENTATION.   A general approach to the analysis and interpretation of behavior; a system of psychology.

TRANSORIENTATIONAL APPROACH.   A theory that utilizes elements from two or more general orientations in the explanation of behavior, or a theory that adopts an orientation which is independent of popular general orientations.

UNIT FORMATION.   A term used by Heider to refer to the quality of belongingness.

VALENCE.   In Lewin's system, a field of forces in the life space which may be either positive or negative in direction.

VICARIOUS REINFORCEMENT.   A process by which any observer experiences the rewards and punishments of another; a hypothetical construct inferred from an observer's "no-trial" learning of a response after observing another person make the response.

WORK GROUP. In Bion's theory, the underlying structure of a group which focuses the members upon the goals of the group; an indispensable aspect of the group which serves to orient the group toward external reality as well as toward the rules (implicit and explicit) of procedure necessary for the maintenance of the group.

SUBJECT INDEX

Abilities, social comparison and, 278–283

A-B-X system, 188, 193–199, 328
  basic definition of, 193–194
  evaluation of, 197–199, 356, 358
  systems of orientation in, 194–195

Accessibility in formative relationships, 91–92

Accuracy in relationship between role description and role performance, 343

Action, naive analysis of, 142–143

Activity, 71–81
  quantity of, 75

Actor in role theory, 327–328

Acts, as defined by Jones and Davis, 286–287

Adjustment in relationship between role description and role performance, 343

Affection behavior, 259–261

Affection need, 258
  (See also FIRO)

Alter ego, 327

Anthropology, definition of, 5–6

Anticonformity, 322–323
  (See also Diamond model of conformity)

Approach-approach conflict, 118–119

Assertions, 200, 204
  correction for direction of, 204–205
  types of, 201–203

Assessments of roles, 332

Assimilation:
  and anchor effects, 297
  social judgment and, 297, 299–300

Assumed desirability, factors determining, 287–288

Assumed similarity of opposites (ASo), 316–317

Asymmetry, consequences of, 196–197

Attitudes:
  beliefs and, 41–49
  as cognitive elements, 208
  comparison of theories of, 348–351
  as congruent with motives, 268–269
  and consciously acceptable motives, 269–270
  and consciously unacceptable motives, 270
  definition of, 268
  mediational approach to, 45–49
  motive congruency and, 268–272
  as object orientations, 194
  and social judgment theory, 294–301
  as tension reducing response, 268
  theory of, 265–274
    basic concepts in, 265–267
    evaluation of, 273–274
  which facilitate denial, 270
  which facilitate identification with aggressor, 270
  which facilitate projection, 270
  which facilitate reaction formation, 270–271

DATE DUE